GRIFFITH TAYLOR

visionary environmentalist explorer

Carolyn Strange   Alison Bashford

UNIVERSITY OF TORONTO PRESS
Toronto   Buffalo

First published in North America in 2009
by University of Toronto Press, Incorporated
Toronto and Buffalo

Library and Archives Canada Cataloguing in Publication

A catalogue record for this title is available
from Library and Archives Canada.

ISBN 978-0-8020-9663-0 (paper)

Project Management: Susan Hall

Editors: Paul Cliff and Joanna Karmel

Picture Research: Lee Ellwood

Design: Andrew Rankine Design Associates

Print: Everbest

Contents

Introduction

Griffith Taylor was the sort of person who never stood still, and never stopped talking about it. As one of the twentieth century's leading geographers, his scientific travels took him to every continent, the greatest journey of all being his 1910 voyage to Antarctica on Captain Robert Scott's final expedition. Taylor's intellectual travels as a geologist, meteorologist and anthropologist were no less spectacular. Beginning with his microscopic study of fossils, Taylor moved backwards to geological deep time and outwards to the solar system before settling, modestly, on the planet. Everything he saw and reckoned along the way he poured into his diaries, field notes, letters, sketches, maps and lantern slides, which he repackaged into public talks, lectures, scholarly articles, books, newspaper columns and magazine features. Taylor's itch to write and draw was as powerful as his yearn to travel, and Scott's 1911 assessment of the man proved to be prescient: a 'fertile brain and a prolific pen'.[1]

Taylor could never have roamed so far, nor published so much, without causing a stir, and those who knew him best knew to give him space. When his University of Toronto colleagues gathered at his retirement in 1951 to acknowledge him as the founding

Sketch of Taylor, 1938. One of the leading cartographers in the US, Harvard's Erwin Raisz, lampooned Taylor's staggering productivity, depicting a torrent of essays, books and diagrams. He drew this image on Taylor's dinner card, set at the head table for the Association of American Geographers annual dinner in 1938, when Taylor was vice-president.

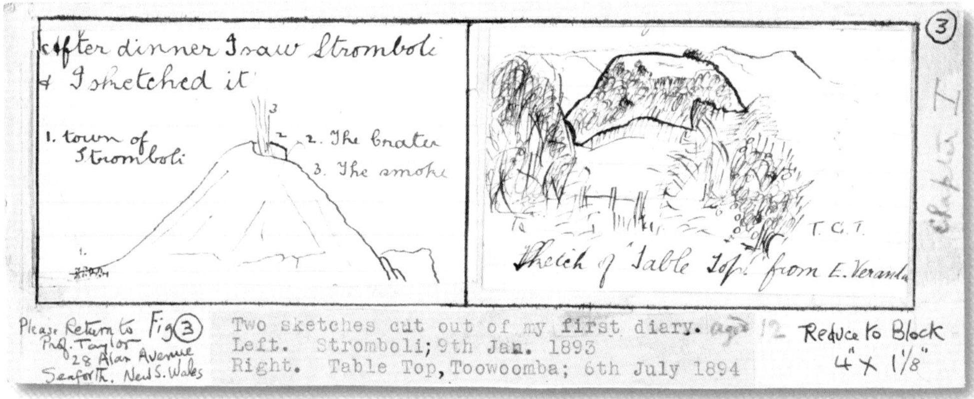

Taylor drew these images as a boy in 1893 and 1894, showing the young sketcher and future mapper at work. Mt Stromboli was drawn en route from England to Australia, the family migrating after James Taylor became an employee of the New South Wales Government.

father of geography in Canada, they roasted him about his most memorable qualities—his self-aggrandisement, his pugnacious defence of his ideas, his peculiar blend of abstemiousness and exuberance. One colleague, who knew his meteorology as well as he knew 'Griff', compared Taylor to a cyclone,[2] an apt description for an academic who studied the relationship of humans to climate and environment, and the perfect metaphor to capture a person constantly on the move, leaving most others in his wake.

Of the many topics Taylor studied, his favourite subject was himself. Encouraged by his parents, he kept a diary from the age of 12, and one of its first entries was his account of the trip his family took in 1893 from Sheffield, England, to Sydney, Australia. Already a keen observer and skilled mapper, he sketched the landscapes that drifted past as the family of six steamed from the Northern to the Southern Hemisphere. Throughout his life, Taylor was rarely without a pencil, prepared at every moment to describe the environment as he saw it. From boyhood to 1963, the year he died, he constructed a record of his life and observations, supplemented by the letters he kept, including those he received and copies of those he sent. When he turned to writing an autobiography in his retirement years, he drew on this massive archive of papers as well as his large opus of published work, never doubting that his was a life worth recording, sufficiently significant that the world should know about him.[3]

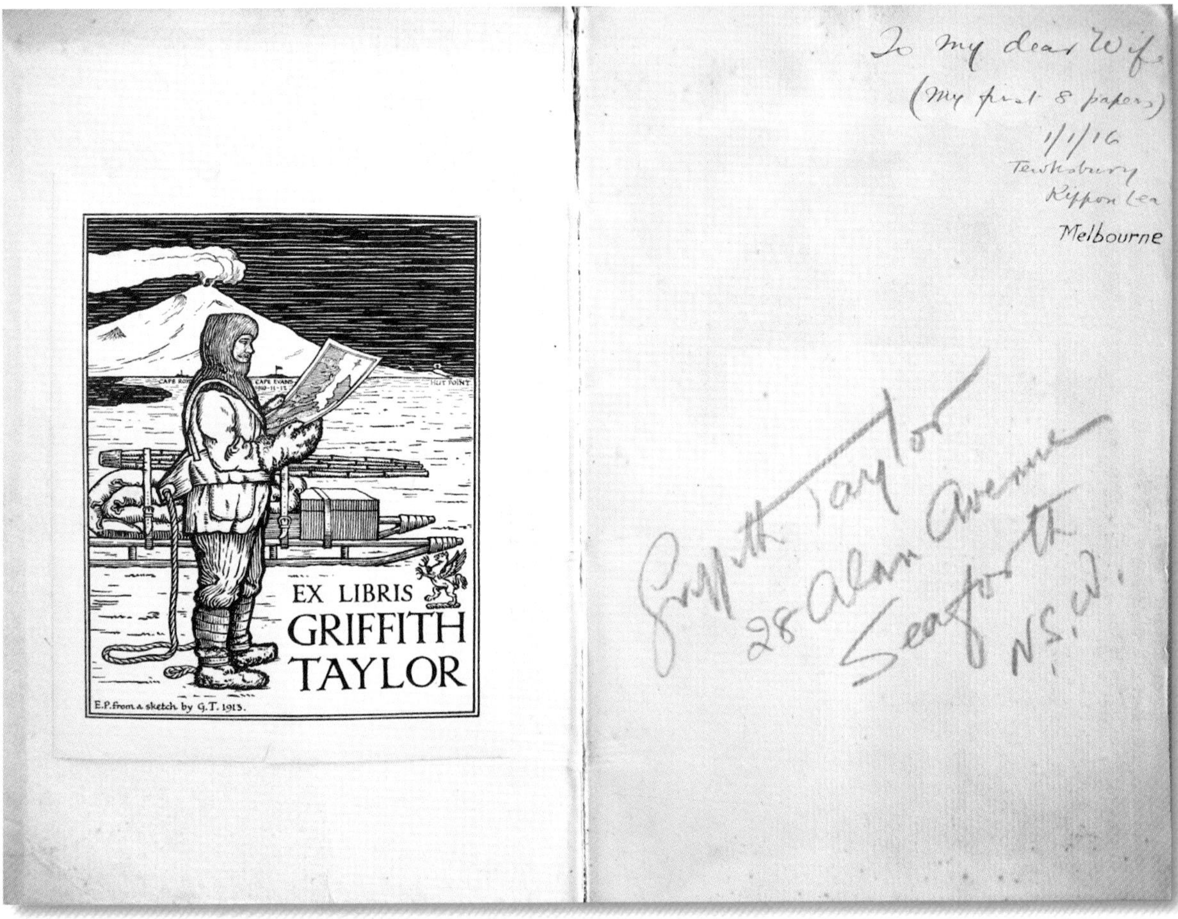

Taylor's bookplate, 1916. This image of Taylor appeared in *With Scott: The Silver Lining* (1916), his long account of the British Antarctic Expedition (1910–1913). With Mt Erebus steaming in the background Taylor, dressed in his polar gear, reads a map that included the glacier he named after himself (with Captain Scott's approval).

Likewise, many of Taylor's contemporaries considered him noteworthy, though not always for reasons he considered valid. On the Australian domestic landscape, Taylor became a public figure by the late 1910s, thanks to his own promotional efforts and the often derisive commentary his work inspired. Appointed to the University of Sydney in 1920, he became Australia's first academic geographer, and one of its most controversial public intellectuals. Taylor felt duty-bound to oppose those who believed Australia's capacity for economic growth and population expansion was unlimited, a position he reached through his training in geology and his work on climate and environment with the Commonwealth Meteorological Service. But condemning development schemes as

foolish and wasteful was risky business in this period of fanatical nationalism, and he quickly became something of a public pariah. When he went on record to oppose the White Australia policy—one of only a handful of scholars to do so—Taylor managed to marginalise himself even further. The geographer's ready resort to the popular press and its vernacular, trading insult for insult, fulfilled his mission to spread his message while it compromised his ability to rise in academic standing within Australia. In contrast, influential overseas scholars working on issues of climate and settlement from a global perspective became admirers of his work. Only after Taylor moved to the University of Chicago in 1929, followed by the University of Toronto in 1935, did the heat subside. In North America, Taylor's profile lowered publicly but rose academically as he established himself as a pioneer of modern geography, respected and honoured internationally. By the time he retired to Australia from Canada in the 1950s, the tempestuous 1920s were only a memory. As an elderly man he reappeared on the public stage, his image now in magazines and on television, where journalists portrayed him as a polar veteran—one of the last living relics of Scott's famous expedition.

Although he was confident that he would intrigue scholars and captivate the public well after his death, Taylor underestimated the scope of interest and range of interpretations his life and career would generate. In Australia and Canada, his name now adorns buildings, lecture series, and student prizes, all of which commemorate his contribution to the establishment of geography as a discipline. In philosophical histories of geographic thought, however, his name arises in definitions of environmental determinism, a school of thought that the twentieth century's leading geographers came to dismiss as old-fashioned. Ironically, concerns over global warming, drought, salinity, and unsustainable resource exploitation have prompted environmental scientists, such as Tim Flannery, to restore respect for Taylor's early 'deterministic' predictions. Indeed, some recent commentators on Taylor declare that the one-time pariah ought to be hailed as a prophet.[4] Similarly his disapproval of anti-Asian racial exclusion laws, which critics panned as outlandish in the 1920s, is increasingly compatible with immigration policies and patterns in today's multicultural Australia; in addition, he rightly anticipated recent geopolitical shifts towards Asia. Although Taylor's research focus changed over his career, his earliest scholarly contributions to geology and his extraordinarily accurate sketching skills continue to command scientific respect and inspire imagination. Never a 'lyric geologist' himself, Taylor appears as a key character in Anne Michaels's *Fugitive Pieces* (1996).[5] In the 2007 feature film as well as the novel, Taylor's geological expertise stands for the persistent play of the past in the present, unfolding in cycles of slow change and sudden rupture. An apt metaphor for the man as well as his life's work.

Taylor claimed authority over many realms of knowledge, including self-appraisal. He published one autobiography, *Journeyman Taylor*, in 1958 and followed it, in 1960, with 'Journeyman at Cambridge', so massive and rambling that publishers rejected it. Taylor's carefully chosen subtitles for these life accounts reveal as much as the torrent of words within them. *The Education of a Scientist* was the subtitle of

Journeyman Taylor, and 'The Lighter Side of Science' subtitled 'Journeyman at Cambridge'. These phrases expressed his greatest wish: that he be recognised as a man of science. Had he stuck to his undergraduate specialties of geology, chemistry, physics and palaeontology, this might have come true, but then no-one would likely have written about him, then or now. As his life played out, Taylor turned into a most idiosyncratic scientist, at once an Enlightenment-style polymath, oddly misplaced in the twentieth century, and a visionary interdisciplinarian, who found history and human difference as engrossing as glaciers and fossils. Taylor simply could not resist the temptation to push and pull science over the widest possible range of historical, cultural, political, environmental and philosophical questions, even if that meant stretching his science just this side of credibility. Educated at the turn of the twentieth century, he inherited a Victorian natural history tradition, which applied the conceptual wonder of classifying and correlating all life and all time under the mysterious mechanism of evolution. He linked the 'antiquity of man' to climate, languages to ecology, the evolution of races to the Ice Ages: Taylor thought big, unlimited by scale, by discipline, and sometimes by evidence. This breadth of scope and imagination impressed some colleagues and perplexed many more.

It wasn't that stricter science was beyond Taylor intellectually; rather, his character and the scientific method made an awkward fit. Oscar Spate, a friend and colleague, understood that Taylor's impatience was the issue: 'he was all thesis and couldn't accept there ever *was*

Caricature of Taylor, 1919. Taylor's lean physique, high forehead and prominent jaw made him an easy target for caricature, as this sketch shows.

an antithesis, and then work to a synthesis'.[6] Yet Spate knew Taylor only in the final phase of his career, when he was busy working out the relations between the study of geography and world peace (what he called 'geopacifics'). Spate never met the young Taylor, whose meticulous work in the fields of palaeontology, meteorology and geology won him significant awards, starting with a post-graduate scholarship for British Empire scientists, followed by the American Geographical Society's Livingstone Medal. His Antarctic geological research earned him a Doctor of Science degree from the University of Sydney in 1916, and the British Museum published a revised version of his thesis soon after, confirming Taylor's international standing in the field.

Even then, Taylor was well on his way to 'desert[ing] underground earth-science for earth-surface science'.[7] There was no lack of rocks and glaciers in Antarctica to intrigue a geologist but the continent offered no human beings to study, so its intellectual attraction for Taylor was limited. Analysing the relation between humans and the environment proved far more compelling for him, and becoming a geographer provided a way to fold his training in natural sciences into his emerging interest in social sciences, particularly anthropology, through which he developed, over the 1920s and 1930s, his theories of race and race-mixing. In an approach that would now be termed interdisciplinary, he saw and promoted geography as the 'liaison' discipline, an intellectual bridge between the physical and social sciences. Taylor's reorientation to the study of 'man' unleashed an excited rush of scholarship that made imaginative use of data. Refreshing to some and outrageous to others, the work Taylor published touched on topics that ranged from racial classification and the evolution of languages, to geopolitics and the causes of war.

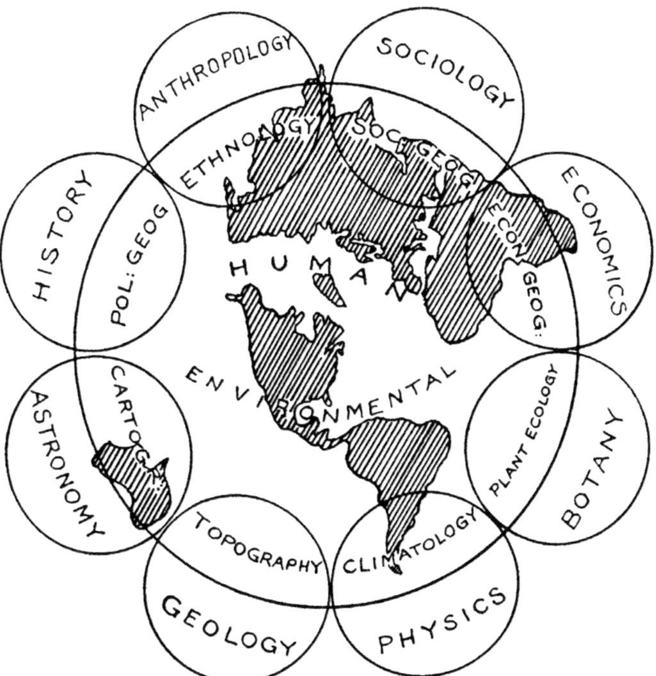

Diagram from *Geography in the Twentieth Century*, which Taylor edited in 1951. Taylor always considered geography as the 'liaison' discipline, which incorporated 'environmental' and 'human' sciences but never the arts.

Doris Taylor, 1914. Before he met Doris Priestley, the younger sister of geologist and fellow Antarcticker Raymond Priestley, Taylor showed little interest in romance. In 1913 that changed as soon as Taylor met Doris during his visit to England. After a short courtship Doris joined him in Australia. The couple married on 8 July 1914 at the University of Melbourne's Queen's College chapel.

What drove and sustained such a man? Taylor attributed his 'buccaneering character' to his forebears on his mother's side,[8] while he judged that he owed his intellect and drive to his father, James, who made a meteoric rise from industrial midlands poverty to life as an international mining engineer and consultant. James credited his own spectacular success to simple living, ceaseless toil and formidable intelligence, and Taylor felt certain that he had inherited his father's extraordinary qualities and habits. There was pride and egotism in that belief, but there was a strong measure of anxiety in the mix: was it possible, ever, to live up to his father's example? And would he honour his father and enhance his own standing by transmitting these characteristics to his own children, spurring them to reach even greater heights?

One of the secrets to success, Taylor learned, was to surround himself with supporters—mentors, colleagues, friends, students and family members—able and willing to offer affirmation. No matter how many letters he tagged onto his name, how many books he added to his list of publications, or how many medals and honorary titles he was awarded, there was always something more to achieve, something more for which he needed to be recognised. As a child he was eager to please; as an adult he was anxious to be noticed. This over-riding desire produced contradictory impulses: on the one hand Taylor craved customary credentials and titles, and maintained and imposed strict hierarchical relationships; on the other he took political stances and intellectual positions that pushed him to the margins of professional respectability. If he couldn't always stand above the crowd, he often managed to find a way, even in group photos, to stand slightly outside the circle of convention.

Taylor's parents encouraged this independence of thought, as did his academic father, geology professor T.W. Edgeworth David, who created the post that established Taylor as Australia's pioneer geographer. When Taylor left the University of Sydney for Chicago in 1928, David wished him well and hoped that his controversial acolyte would go on to 'bring more light to dark places'.[9] International colleagues, notably Isaiah Bowman and Ellsworth Huntington, were senior friends who paved the way for Taylor's appointment at the University of Chicago. Both men advised him to taper his torch of geographical enlightenment but they always appreciated Taylor's energy and purpose, that 'outer fringe of lunacy' his admirers considered part of his charm.[10] Chief among them were his oldest associates and sometime rivals—Douglas Mawson, Frank Debenham and Raymond Priestley, faithful friends and Antarctickers all.

Taylor's friendship with Priestley, which developed over the course of the Scott expedition, led to the most vital and sustaining relationship of Taylor's life—his marriage in 1914 to Doris Priestley, Raymond's younger sister. As husband-to-be, Taylor made Doris many promises: to treat her as an equal, to face adversity together, to tutor her in German, Greek history and botany, and to teach her how to read geological formations. He also gave his Methodist-raised fiancé fair warning: he was a secular rationalist. 'And I'll tell you a deep and deadly secret,' he wrote to her between appearances on his Antarctic lecture tour in South Africa, 'Ye Griffon really <u>does</u> work hard, when he's really <u>interested</u> in a piece of work.'[11] If this was news to Doris in 1914, he would provide her with daily reminders over the next 49 years.

Doris was worth waiting for. For one thing she had grown up in an academic household. Though Doris subsequently showed little inclination to take up her husband's tutorial offerings, she fully supported his endeavours and his hungry pursuit of accolades, even though this meant spending frequent and long periods apart as Taylor traversed the world. With his wife's Priestley blood in the union, Taylor confidently assumed that their children, the clutch of scientists he hoped to raise, would have a noble inheritance: marrying Doris linked Taylor to a line of scientists longer and more stellar than his own. His forecasts in this sector of his life proved less reliable than his predictions of future population and settlement, however. He came eventually to accept that none of their three children would follow him, like the sons of other colleagues, into geography. His eldest son pursued an academic career in engineering while his second son experienced physical and emotional difficulties in childhood and grew too ill in adulthood to support himself. His daughter died suddenly at the age of two in 1923, a loss so painful that Taylor never mentioned it publicly. Matters of this nature were kept within the family circle and recorded sketchily in a handful of personal letters and diary entries.

As self-referential as Taylor was in his publications and public talks, there was much that he kept to himself. No dark secrets, just a complex personality. While his diaries and personal letters chart his emotional landscape, clues to his character also appear in his professional correspondence. The favoured son, the admired and loved brother, the lifelong mate, the adored teacher, the demanding father and proud grandfather, emerge vividly. He appreciated his family and took pride in his pedigree but he saw himself as a heroic modern actor, striding about in a world of ideas and action, not feelings. In thousands of letters to family members and friends, even his most intimate missives slip quickly from domestic matters to accounts of his every observation and idea, illustrated with diagrams and landscape sketches, and accompanied by helpful scales, explanatory notes and codes. In page after page he recounts his battles with uncooperative editors and dismissive reviewers as well as his latest accolades and academic coups. His keenness to impress, and his readiness to vanquish opponents, real and imagined, was deeply personal, although he never considered it so. Yet Taylor never quite measured up to the men he most admired, despite the academic standing and international recognition he attained. The 2001 Australian postage stamp in honour of Antarctic explorers depicts Taylor in the background of the more famous Sir Douglas Mawson. Taylor was lauded as an explorer and honoured as a father of modern geography; he dined at the table of knighted men, but he never hosted as one. Only those closest to him—his wife Doris, his sister Dorothy, his sons, and a handful of lifelong friends—knew the vulnerabilities hidden under his carapace of confidence.

But *what* confidence. Raymond Priestley's obituary of Taylor conveyed the insight of a university colleague and brother-in-law:

> He was very sure of himself and his opinions and had reason so to be. He was one of those rather infuriating people who are quite certain their own particular view of a problem is the right one and are the more annoying because they are often correct in so thinking.[12]

This obituary appeared in a festschrift published by a former student of Taylor. Its title, *Frontiers and Men* (1966), summarised the content of Taylor's opus and conveyed his persistent drive to push against and to cross intellectual boundaries.

The controversies he helped to instigate left Taylor scowling and grumbling, but throughout it all his winning boyishness and curious naivety rescued him from being over-earnest. His certainty of opinion stimulated students and his imaginative theories earned him grudging respect even from those who questioned the content of his arguments. Taylor's all-encompassing vision propelled him around the world and across variegated fields of research, hurrying him to reach the next horizon. As a liaison geographer he moved conceptually and literally from rocks to race, from climatology to geopolitics, from the South Pole to the North Pole, over the course of a life that reached from the Boer War to the Cold War. Journeyman Taylor, indeed.

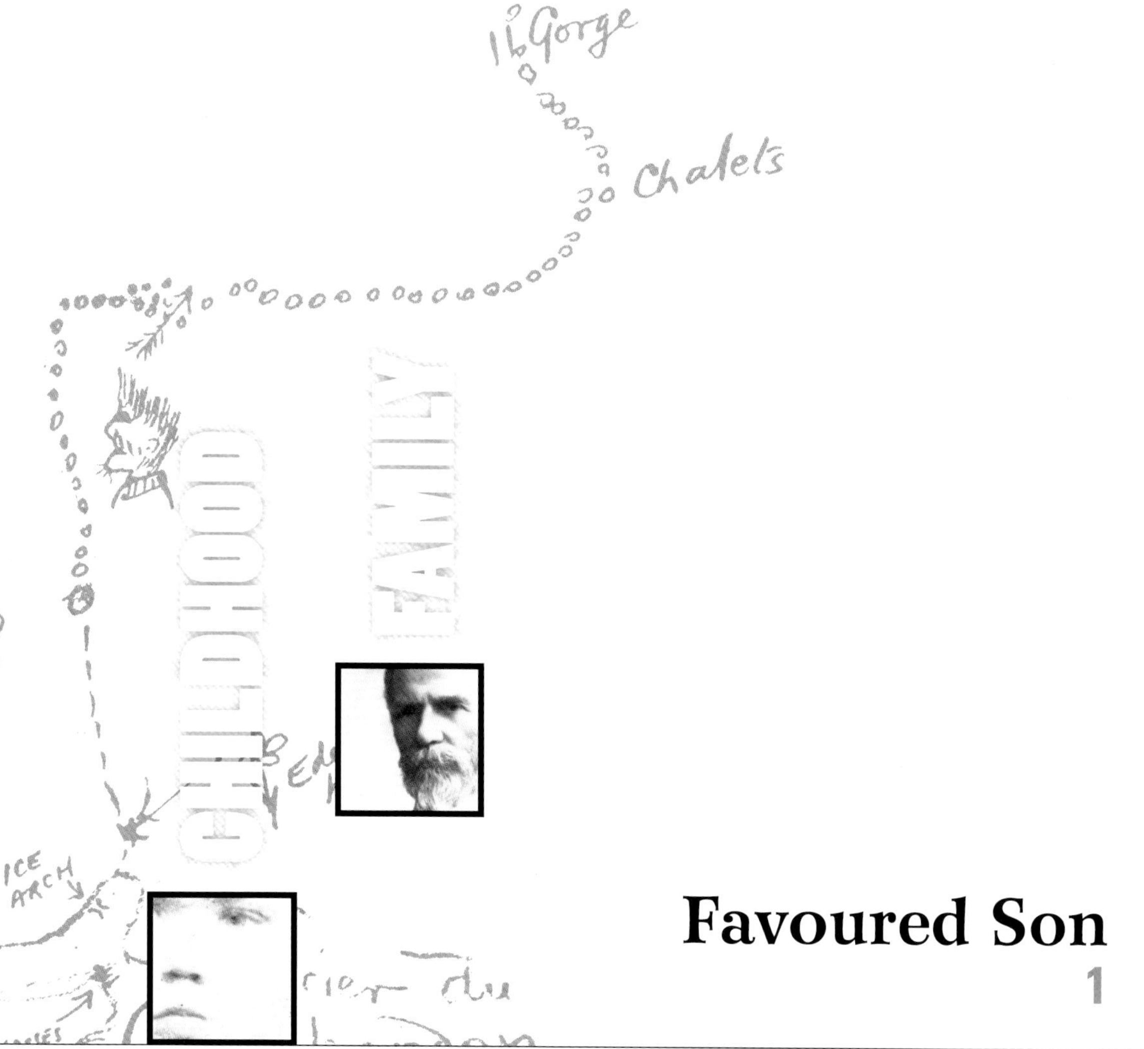

Favoured Son

1

Taylor never entirely grew up. A colleague, who met Taylor when he was 71, felt 'there was always a rather school boyish perversity in Griff's fun—sometimes irritating, more often engaging'.[1] By no means was this an atypical description of his character. No-one who met Taylor, even in his old age, failed to notice how he sparked with youthful enthusiasm, while remaining anxious to impress. Not that this wish always produced the desired results. His 'curious boyishness' backfired in Antarctica, for instance, when he harnessed himself and his sled to a seal, which nearly dragged him to his death.[2] In this context, it was the formidable Captain Scott whom he displeased; an unusual event, since Taylor had an inborn talent for impressing his elders and gaining their favour. He was the typical eldest son in this respect, burdened and inspired by his parents' high expectations. He seems to have borne them lightly in his youth, when he was their golden boy, or as his sister put it, 'a flaxen-haired fairy child, light-footed and extraordinarily merry'.[3] While his hairline receded into baldness as he reached adulthood, Taylor's need for affirmation never disappeared, no matter how many laurels he earned.

Elizabeth Griffiths, James Taylor's mother-in-law, c.1860. A critical step in James Taylor's class elevation was his marriage to Lily Agnes Griffiths in 1879. A year after James and Lily married they had their first child, Thomas Griffith Taylor.

There was no greater publicist for Taylor than Taylor himself, who drew attention in every talk and publication to his remarkable achievements. While he generally gave the impression that talent and industry produced his impressive results, his autobiography reveals the degree to which he saw those traits as inherited. Both of Taylor's parents inspired him to greatness, through their personalities and their ancestry. He admired his mother, Lily Agnes, for her intelligence and spirit but he openly idolised his father, James. Lily (who he called 'Mater') came from comfortable circumstances, the daughter of a deeply religious accountant in the industrial heartland of England; his father, in contrast, was brought up in desperate poverty by a mother who toiled in cotton mills and a drunkard father who barely worked at all. Though in material terms James had nothing (his mother could barely feed and clothe her family), measured by character and intelligence he was fabulously wealthy. Although he never rose to great heights in industry or in the academy, as his eldest son would, James's shift from labourer in Manchester's mills, to medal-winning scholar in London, to internationally recognised mining engineer, was astonishing. This was the towering figure against whom Taylor measured and modelled himself—outwardly exceeding James's accomplishments, inwardly conscious of the long shadow his father cast.

James Taylor: 'His Own Arduous Boyhood'

James Taylor (1849–1927) grew up in a crowded back-lane cottage in Oldham, a cotton mill town north-east of Manchester. This was the epicentre of the industrial revolution, where a few made fortunes and most made do. While thousands of working-class Englishmen opted for emigration, colonial adventure or the old standbys of army and navy service, others proceeded along more parochial paths that local philanthropists began to establish. Beginning in the early nineteenth century, a few capitalists of conscience invested in projects designed to improve the workers' lot by enabling the working class to attend free lectures and read improving literature. James Taylor selected this course; by day he laboured in the deafening cotton mills for pennies and at night he studied by candlelight with no stops at the pub along the way. He was the model subject for the era's emphasis on improvement: a hard-working teetotaller, intent on overcoming the obstacles that blocked a poor boy's road to success.

James Taylor (undated). Extraordinary self-discipline, ambition and intelligence took Taylor's father from a life of poverty in England's industrial midlands to international work as a mining engineer and consultant. Taylor gave this picture of James to Doris as a courtship gift: 'but you can't marry him!'.

Science was James Taylor's chosen path, made smoother through the efforts of Sir Joseph Whitworth, one of Manchester's wealthiest scientific manufacturers and a supporter of the city's Mechanics Institute. In 1868, Whitworth set up a scholarship scheme for young men of 'intelligence and proficiency in the theory and practice of mechanics and its cognate Sciences'. James won the scholarship in the first round of competition, holding a junior position of 'exhibitioner'; then in 1870, at the age of 21, he won a scholarship of £100 for further study at Owens College. As a non-sectarian college for men, the college had been founded to support 'learning and science'. Its ethos challenged Victorian convention: 'The institution shall be open to all applicants for admission without respect to place of birth, and without distinction of rank or condition in society.'[4] Thanks to these radical initiatives on the local educational front, James Taylor was the right candidate at the right time and place.[5]

In mid century Manchester, religious non-conformity was close to conformity, and some sects, particularly Congregationalism and Unitarianism, attracted both the humble and the wealthy. While Congregationalists upheld the right of individual congregations to self-govern, Unitarians went further and maintained the right of individuals to develop their own religious convictions. Unitarianism flourished in Manchester, in part due to the stature and influence of Elizabeth and William Gaskell: she wrote popular novels that exposed the suffering of industrial mill workers, like the Taylors of Oldham, while he preached rational reform as a Unitarian Minister and night lecturer at Owens College. This brand of Protestantism appealed to those who believed that human effort, rather than faith or dogmatism, was the means to individual improvement and social betterment, and many self-made men were drawn to it. Whether James Taylor came to Unitarianism after attending Reverend Gaskell's inspiring night classes is unclear, but an aspiring scientist like James could comfortably embrace a gospel that rewarded reason and application. This was the creed he would pass on to his first son, whose agnostic inclinations made Unitarianism one of the few forms of faith Thomas Griffith could abide. This never stopped him from considering himself a prophet; it just meant that he dressed his prophecies as appeals for rationality. When he entered the pulpit for the first time, at Toronto's First Unitarian Church in 1943, the title of his talk was 'Race Problems in the Post-war World'. 'My first sermon,' he wrote ironically on the flyer.[6]

While Christian non-conformity provided a formula for respectability, James believed strongly that man governed his fate. An ambitious lad could not rely solely on scholastic success but needed earthly assistance in the form of a personal mentor, a scientific patron. James was fortunate that his aptitude in chemistry and metallurgy attracted the attention of Sir Henry Roscoe, his Owens College chemistry professor, who began to cultivate the young scholarship student. To work closely under the direction of the scientist who established Britain's first practical chemistry laboratory and to help him explore the chemical properties of vanadium (a recently discovered metal) provided far more than intellectual stimulation. Sir Henry's professional stature and his willingness to sponsor his protégé allowed James to dream of a future in which he would join the professional classes. This form of scientific apprenticeship was career development nineteenth-century style—an era when a man of influence need only have a quiet word with a colleague or jot a personal note to secure his student a position. Armed with Roscoe's professional benediction, James Taylor launched his career as a mining consultant.

James was on the move geographically, as well as in class terms, by the late 1870s. His first posting took him to a Chilean mining operation, hardly glamorous work but a life of adventure and opportunity and a million miles from Lancashire's gloomy mills. Appointed as a chemical consultant James's work so impressed his employers that he received, on top of his wages, a bonus of £1000, a sizeable amount of money for a young man previously unable to afford pencil or paper. While others might have squandered the sum, James returned to England to enhance his employment prospects and to court Lily Agnes Griffiths.

Studying at Owens College allowed students like James Taylor to mix with the families of like-minded men. For James, the critical social contact was fellow mining student and Whitworth scholarship holder Alfred Griffiths, an older brother of Lily's. The Griffiths were also non-conformists and the father, Thomas, was an occasional preacher in the Congregational church. Their non-conformity extended to a positive assessment of James as a potential son-in-law—bright, determined, abstemious, clean-living and a man with promise. For her part, Lily had already shown that she was game for adventure. While James worked in Chilean mines, she had travelled even further to Australia, where one of her brothers, George, had established a foundry in Toowoomba, Queensland. Although barely five feet tall and plump, her solid jaw and high broad forehead (the prominent facial traits she passed on to her son) gave the impression of a woman who knew her own mind. The couple married in 1879 and James enrolled at the prestigious Royal London School of Mines, hoping to raise his qualifications and his financial prospects. In the meantime, the newlyweds made their home in a modest row house in Walthamstow, about three miles from Hackney, north-east of London. It was a 10-mile walk to the school in Kensington but for James educational opportunities like this were worth every step.

The Taylors and Lily's sister, Harriot, dressed for a special occasion at Adderton, the name the family gave their 10-acre property on Sydney's outskirts. After moving there from Sydney in 1895, Taylor began to study at The King's School in Parramatta. Taylor, aged 14, appears front, left.

Taylor, 1885. In 1882, James Taylor was hired to manage a copper mining operation in Serbia. On the family's return to England in 1885, they stopped in Stuttgart for a studio portrait of their son, considerably chubbier at the age of four than later in his life.

James Taylor with his three eldest children in 1889: Griffith, Dorothy and Rhys. In 1892, the family moved to Sheffield, England, after James's appointment as an analytical chemist at Firth's, a major steel manufacturer. 'As a boy I occasionally visited his laboratory there, since it was situated not far from the public library, where I was a constant reader of books' (Taylor, *Journeyman Taylor*, 1958).

Thomas Griffith Taylor, named after his maternal grandfather, was the couple's first child, born on 1 December 1880 in Walthamstow. The family grew quickly: his sister Dorothy arrived in 1881 and three brothers—Rhys, Evan and Jeff—followed over the next few years. Shortly before Dorothy was born, the Taylors moved to Maidanpek, Serbia, where James became the manager of a German copper mine. Fatherhood failed to dampen James Taylor's preparedness to accept contracts, wherever they might lead him, and his wife followed faithfully with the children in the early years of their marriage. The posting to Maidanpek came with perquisites that neither husband nor wife had experienced previously, including two household servants and a nursemaid. However, an opportunity for an attractive research position at Firth's steelworks in Sheffield prompted the family's return to England in 1884. It now fell to James—married man, father and head of the company's analytical chemistry department—to support a family and to train smart young men.

At Firth's, Taylor tutored an inquisitive lab assistant, Harry Brearley, setting rigorous personal as well as professional standards for the boy. Brearley's background in poverty resembled his sponsor's and he understood what had made James Taylor 'an apostle of the simple life'.[7] As a mentor, James demanded hard work and top results, yet he also offered scientific fellowship. Brearley ended up being his prize pupil (whose discovery in 1913 of the processes necessary to produce stainless steel stimulated Sheffield's industrial economy), and he spoke with fondness and respect about Taylor in his autobiography. This custom—a senior man's cultivation of a junior man's intellect and career—was the model that James would apply in training his son, and a convention that Griffith Taylor would later follow in his own career.

Although James had reached an impressive plateau of middle-class respectability by the 1890s as a company scientist at the heart of England's industrial power, his £250 salary seemed a poor reflection of his worth. Family fortunes changed when an offer of £1000 arrived in 1892 from New South Wales, where the state government was seeking a chief metallurgist. This offer allowed James to take his family to Australia in style on the *Orient Line*. Almost 60 years later, the voyage remained vivid in Dorothy Taylor's memory: 'We were bloated plutocrats on first class tickets in a new and up-to-date luxury liner. It was dazzling and like a fairy tale.' James's eldest son found the changing landscape more interesting than the comforts (a sign of things to come). When he wasn't sketching he was dipping into the ship's collection of Parliamentary papers and statistical registers, which enabled him to gain a respectable knowledge of Australian geography by the time the family arrived.[8]

Grooming for Greatness

Unlike his father, Griffith Taylor (he never favoured his first name) faced no pressure as a youth to support his family, nor did he need to study at night. Instead, his parents planned that he would spend his youth in school, thanks to his father's reliable earnings and his mother's tight management of the family's finances. Although Lily had received far less formal education than her husband, she believed that formal institutional learning was the surest path to financial security and professional status. In Sheffield, they had enrolled Taylor, at the age of four, in a small private school, and he had demonstrated a precocious talent for drawing and writing, which both parents encouraged and promoted. His first appearance in print occurred in 1888, a few months after his seventh birthday, in the *Manchester Weekly Times*, which published letters from children to a columnist, 'Uncle Oldham'. James Taylor cut out the Uncle Oldham newspaper column and preserved it among his personal papers. His son provided descriptions of the family garden and stories of neighbourhood exploration and holiday adventures in five issues of the *Times* between 1888 and 1891, helping to establish his self-awareness as an author. More than that, these miniature surveys and travelogues, saturated with detail, foreshadowed Taylor's later career in travel and exploration writing. When 'Uncle Oldham' published his first submission ('I hope Griffith Taylor will write and tell us what adventures he meets'), he could hardly have imagined the seven-decade torrent of letters, diaries, sketches, articles and books that would follow.[9]

On the family's voyage to Australia, Taylor began a lifelong habit of diary writing—a self-conscious record of observations and ideas rather than an outlet for intimacies. The ship functioned as a floating school where he constantly tested himself: how accurately could he describe a port of call? Could he map a coastline to scale? These were not the diaries of an unconfident 12-year-old and they certainly betray no hint of childish pranks or crushes; they were written in full anticipation that they would be read by others, particularly his parents. 'After dinner I saw [Mount] Stromboli and I sketched it,' he penned on 9 January 1893, as the family steamed past Italy. Under this statement appears a sketch, complete with helpful key: '1. town of Stromboli, 2. The Crater, 3. The Smoke.'[10]

James Taylor was proud of his son but he also expected a great deal of him. By taking the New South Wales job, he ensured that his children would enjoy the educational advantages that he had missed, though neither he nor Lily would allow them to take those opportunities for granted. 'Home interests were as formative as were my school interests,' Taylor later wrote. James impressed his son with his humble-boy-to-professional-man story, emphasising toil and teetotalism as the essential ingredients for success. Along with stern advice to avoid alcohol and tobacco (which Taylor took to heart), at some point James undoubtedly gave his son a valuable tip for a budding scientist: find yourself a great man and you'll get ahead.

Taylor craved approval from his mother as ardently as he sought it from his father. He respected Lily's 'sharp mind' but his respect was coupled with an assumption (which he never lost) that anything he found fascinating must fascinate her as well. From the age of five, he informed his mother of his latest achievements ('Dear Mama, I have learnt to play Chinese Dominoes, and have won it twice') and he continued to do so even after he held professorial posts. From his first independent trip (from Sydney to Adelaide), he wrote to his parents letter after letter, accounting for everything he saw, and many more of those were addressed to Mater than to Pater. He maintained this habit until Mater's death in 1943, whether he was revealing his interpretation of palaeontological specimens, recounting university curriculum squabbles, or sketching out his theories about the evolution of races. At no point did Mater intimate that she was anything but intensely interested; consistently offering Taylor advice and encouragement, she adopted his passions as her own and even provided a newspaper-clippings service when he was away on expeditions or based overseas. James, the scientist who directly inspired Taylor's intellectual inclinations, spent far less time than his wife did with their son. Once the family settled in Australia, James's state-wide mining consultations made him a satellite figure, powerful enough to continue steering his son's career but not his emotional centre of gravity.

Starting with 'the four Misses Smith' back in Sheffield and proceeding to Miss Macaulay's School in inner Sydney, where he studied for three years after his arrival, Taylor's first teachers were women. After that point, however, his teachers and mentors were exclusively male—for a short time at the prestigious Sydney Grammar School, and later at the small but equally respectable The King's School in Parramatta, 11 kilometres west of Sydney. The shift was prompted by the family's purchase of Adderton in 1896, a homestead six kilometres from King's. Although the Taylors could afford to send their eldest to a school dominated by the sons of wealthy farmers, Taylor regarded himself their inferior in class terms but their superior in intelligence. They were the sons of colonial masters who stood to inherit land, whereas his inheritance was a hunger for learning. As a slim, studious teen he became a target of other boys' abuse. His distaste for rugby and cricket made him a marked man:

> There was a great deal of bullying of the weaker boys, especially if, like myself, they exhibited no liking for sport ... [I] regard my days at King's as the unhappiest in my recollection'.[11]

His pleasure in masculine comradeship beyond the family flowered only after he entered university.

As a youth Taylor's imagination was fed by the pages of boys' adventure novels by G.A. Henty, Baynes Reid and Manville Fenn. He consumed these books by the shelf-full, inspired by their locales (ancient Rome, frontier America) and their tales of heroic struggle and triumph. At the same time, he extended his curiosity in the Australian environment by turning himself into a walker, thinking nothing of tramping across inhospitable landscapes in search of little treasures—a plant here, a fossil there. James's own habits made Taylor's preference for field study over playing fields perfectly normal; indeed a father who valued stamina and solo pursuits must have provided solace for the bullied boy as well as inspiration. At the same time, James set one record that was unbeatable: at the age of 70 he cycled from Sydney to Melbourne (a trip of 970 kilometres) in three days. While Taylor would never match this feat, his early adoption of long-distance traversing would help him meet a far more famous physical and mental challenge in the Antarctic on Scott's final expedition.

Taylor did set one significant record in his youth by becoming the first in the family to attend university. He accomplished this after a brief period in the public service. Finally through with The King's School (graduating second in mathematics, first in French, first in Latin, first in Greek and first in his form), he took a break from study and sat the public service exam at the age of 17. In March 1898, he entered the workforce as a junior clerk in the New South Wales Treasury. For a young man without a university education this was a promising position, particularly on the eve of Federation. If the anticipated Commonwealth Government were to form, ambitious junior clerks might rise quickly through the public service, and there was always the possibility of joining the colonial service elsewhere in the British Empire. The small income was welcome, and he acquired the useful new skill of typing, a talent he continued to practise and even boasted about. More significantly, and in keeping with his father's earlier experience, his clerkship in the colonial bureaucracy allowed him to rub elbows with prominent men, including the New South Wales Treasurer—sometime premier and later prime minister, Sir George Reid. The Treasurer came to know Taylor by name and he seems to have noted his capacity for 'systematising facts'.[12] Reid certainly remembered Taylor well enough to invite him a decade later (when Reid was Australian High Commissioner to Britain) to help write the Australian chapters for *The Oxford Survey of the British Empire*, published in 1914. Reid was an early influential figure in Taylor's career, but a more significant and enduring mentorship was to develop once he left the public service in 1899 to explore what university had to offer.

The Grand Old Man of Australian Science

A few months after his eighteenth birthday, Griffith Taylor strode confidently through the University of Sydney's neo-gothic sandstone buildings, ready to learn. Australasia's oldest university was an architectural imitation of the medieval colleges in the 'home' country, staffed largely by men who had graduated from English and Scottish institutions in the mid to late nineteenth century. It clung to some British academic traditions, such as the wearing of regalia, while dropping others, in particular the preservation of higher education as a male privilege. The University of Sydney admitted women students to degrees in 1881 (66 years before Cambridge relented). One of those would be Taylor's sister, Dorothy—'Pal', as she was always called by the family—who studied at Abbotsleigh Girls' School, tutored for several years, then registered for a bachelor's degree in science four years after her elder brother enrolled. Taylor formed friendships with other bright and ambitious students and consumed courses voraciously, sampling from several disciplines. Although both of his parents encouraged him to study broadly, believing in the merits of liberal education, Taylor's interest in the physical world (combined with his distaste of Latin, Greek and classical studies) convinced him that 'Science was to be my métier'. The science he referred to consisted of chemistry, physics and physiography, in each of which he scored top marks. After earning a Bachelor of Science degree in Geology and Physics in 1904, he briefly pursued work as a schoolteacher at a boys' school but quickly gravitated back to university to study mining engineering. He resumed his studies with a focus on applied mechanics, mechanical drawing and plane geometry, leading to a second bachelor's degree in mining engineering in 1905. In this change of course, he was pushed less by his father than pulled by geology professor, T.W. Edgeworth David.

The man whom he came quickly to regard as the father of his academic career, Edgeworth David (after 1920, Sir Edgeworth), was one of the university's most popular professors. As James Taylor spent increasing periods away from the family home, travelling interstate to undertake mining consultancies, his son gravitated towards the lecturer with legendary oratory skills. David inspired his students and lavished attention on the most eager and the most talented of them. Taylor fitted easily into both categories but was only one of several students whose careers were launched by Professor David. He also fostered the academic fortunes of Douglas Mawson (who became Taylor's lifelong friend and rival); Raymond Priestley (Taylor's future brother-in-law); Frank Debenham (his future Antarctic mate); and Leo Cotton (colleague, friend of Taylor and Dorothy, and later Professor David's successor as the university's chair of geology). 'If any young scientist were to ask my advice as to the best way to advance in his chosen field,' Taylor later commented, they should 'try to obtain a position, however junior, on the staff of a well-known leader in [their] subject.'[13]

Taylor's chosen leader was born in Wales in 1858, the son of an Anglican rector.[14] Edgeworth David studied geology at Oxford as part of a Bachelor of Arts degree. In 1882, David arrived in Sydney as assistant geological surveyor for the New South Wales Government. He remained in that post (possibly meeting James Taylor through his travels) for almost 10 years before being appointed professor of geology at the University of Sydney. Although he came with a reputation for having discovered a coal seam in the Hunter Valley, which became a major site of coal production, his interests ranged far wider. David's research spanned the broad rubric of natural history—geology, glaciology, physiography and palaeontology. Most significantly, David was a resolute Darwinist—like many who studied geology after 1859, when *On the Origin of Species* appeared and sparked major scientific debate (led in part by Thomas Henry Huxley, sometime professor of natural history at the Royal School of Mines). Seeking empirical proof for the theory of evolution through natural selection, David led an expedition to the Funafuti Atoll (Tuvalu) in 1897 to drill coral samples. His analysis of the organisms was accepted subsequently as evidence that life forms evolved in stages. The Royal Society in London, the most prestigious science body in the English-speaking world, recognised the significance of David's contribution by admitting him as a fellow in 1900, just as Taylor was embarking on his studies. The brand of geology David taught, like Thomas Huxley's version of natural history, was as much about evolutionary science and anthropology as it was about rocks; when David lectured on the formation of the earth's crust, he covered the evolution of the human race over 'deep time' in the same breath.

The content of David's teaching and his captivating personal style electrified Taylor and numerous other Sydney students, who attended his lectures just to hear him speak. 'He had a magnetic personality and a clarion voice,' Taylor eulogised in the obituary he published on David, recalling him as 'The Grand Old Man of Australian Science'.[15] David's lectures in geology and palaeontology gave 'a vivid picture of "living" science', which he conveyed by laying out specimens on the demonstration table and by preparing models designed 'to illustrate physical phenomena'. These sorts of lectures required two teachers: the Orator (the senior man) and his Demonstrator (the junior man) who set up materials and ran experiments (and cleaned the chalk brushes afterwards). David was always on the lookout for an able junior, and in 1905 asked Taylor, his prize-winning pupil in physiography, if he'd care to be that man. Mindful of his father's experience, Taylor knew that David was offering far more than a salary; indeed, he absorbed a significant pay cut when he gave up his teaching position to accept David's offer. It was a personal commitment for both men—to science and to each other in their complementary roles. Apprenticing with Professor David—as Harry Brearley had apprenticed with James Taylor and as James had earlier apprenticed with Sir Henry Roscoe—allowed Taylor to serve under a master, learning not only from his scientific expertise but also from his oratorical skills, his enthusiasm for teaching, and his commitment to fieldwork.

By the time Taylor began to study with David, the university-based discipline of geology had turned the centuries-old practice of natural history into a field-based science, and that transition was paralleled in miniature by Taylor's move from his sample collecting on childhood walks with his father to field excursions with his professor. These studies began for Taylor in 1901, while he was still a student of David, who was an early advocate of on-site research as an educational tool. In 1903, the professor persuaded the university to make field trips a compulsory component of the geology course.[16] These 'tramps' were training grounds in data collection and also in the formation of friendships, both hierarchical relations between the professor and his juniors, and lateral bonds with fellow students. With the energetic David at the head, excursions were literally exercises in follow-the-leader:

> About six the bugler would waken us; and after a rapid breakfast we would set off, laden with hammers, collecting bags, and maps, David leading at his rapid

> Chinaman's trot. We had to keep going to arrive in time at some promising outcrop.

Field study involved locating and assessing specimens, but talk drifted at mealtimes to life beyond science and fostered fellowship in the bush:

> We made porridge in kerosene tins. Chops we grilled over logs in a trench. Our meals always concluded with billy tea, sipped leisurely round the camp-fire in good weather.[17]

Of Taylor's fellow students, the stand-out was Douglas Mawson, who became one of Australia's first geochemical specialists. Between 1902 and 1903, David sent the pair to the Mittagong region, 130 kilometres south-west of Sydney, and assigned them the task of preparing more detailed topographical studies of the area than the official Geological Survey then provided. Offering an entrée to the pantheon of science, David read his assistants' paper before the Royal Society of New South Wales, the state's leading scientific society. The resulting co-publication, 'The Geology of Mittagong', which appeared in October 1903, was Taylor's first illustrated academic article.[18] In 1931, in an address before the British Association for the Advancement of Science, Taylor referred to that paper as 'the beginning of my love for "three-dimension" representation'. Two decades later, he bound it with seven other articles in a volume inscribed 'My first 8' and dedicated 'to my dear wife' (Doris). When the paper first appeared, however, he presented the off-print proudly to Pater and Mater.

The 1903 breakthrough article led to a small stream of publications concerning Australian geology, palaeontology and physiography, all of them closely related to David's work or to assignments set by David. In 1905, after Mawson was appointed lecturer in mineralogy and petrology at Adelaide University, and Taylor became David's demonstrator, Taylor could stand before the professor more squarely on his own. His early publications under David's supervision all conformed to standard scientific method: questions derived from field data were pitched against prevailing theory, assessed through recognised forms of analysis, and brought to tentative conclusions based on evaluations of the newly discovered against the known. The seven-year-old boy who had explored plant and animal life in his back garden, reporting his observations to Uncle Oldham, had developed by his twenties into the professionally trained scientist—still just as thrilled at the discovery process and just as eager to share it. In 'The First Recorded Occurrence of *Blastoeidea* in New South Wales' (a paper Taylor introduced to the state Linnean Society in 1906), he recorded how he had uncovered the world's largest blastoid (the fossil of a marine invertebrate that died out in the Palaeozoic period) while on a field trip near Newcastle, on the central coast of New South Wales.[19] Alongside his hand-drawn pen-and-ink diagrams of the specimen, he laid out his rationale for categorising the organism's phylum and genus according to its shape, radials, age and habitat. Professor David did not co-author this piece but his precise standards are apparent in his student's care and caution, qualities that Taylor would later relax and even abandon when theorising on a grand scale. Sole authorship of a scientific publication at this stage in his career gave Taylor a puff of pride. 'To Dad ... with the author's kind regards,' he hand-wrote on the article's title page, adding 'my third!' on the inside cover.

Although Taylor laboured over specimens in laboratory settings, both he and his mentor were happier in the field, and happiest when communicating their research to a wider audience. In tandem with the establishment of public museums and libraries was a commitment, widely shared among scientists of the time, to educate the public in terms which they could understand about scientific discoveries and insights. Professor David's lecturing talents made him a popular public speaker and, in post-Federation Australia, everyone, it seemed, was eager to learn about the newly formed nation's natural resources and its potential for economic and population growth. It was heady times for scientists knowledgeable on the structure and mineral content of the land—exactly the expertise that nation-planners needed. In Taylor's opinion:

> David's elementary lectures on 'Physiography' determined the career of many a young scientist in Australia ... none forgot the intimate connection between human affairs, climate, and geology demonstrated in those admirable lectures.[20]

A geologist of David's stature could present himself to his peers as a pure scientist while claiming, simultaneously, that his work directly interested the public and the state, and could be applied in the national interest. Well before the Australian colonies had federated in 1901, David had reported his Hunter Valley coal seam discovery to the colonial government, so that it could secure a Crown reservation over the site.[21] After Federation, David expanded his public service role by impressing upon his students their duty to serve the new nation through the special training and knowledge they acquired in their studies. Taylor readily accepted David's mission as his own, although he would never develop his master's capacity to charm the unconverted.

As a geology student, and later as the professor's right-hand man in the lecture hall and the field, Taylor had the opportunity to participate in nation-planning, literally from the ground up. While federal politicians were bickering over the prospective location of Australia's new capital (in an effort to balance rivalries between the former colonies of New South Wales and Victoria and their capitals, Sydney and Melbourne), physiographers were studying the meteorological and physiographical qualities of the various sites under consideration. From 1902, David and his students had produced some of the earliest physiographical surveys in New South Wales, including the Yass–Canberra region which ended up on the shortlist of possible capital locations. Consequently, Taylor and Mawson were particularly well suited to assist in any future surveys of the capital, once it was selected. With Mawson conveniently away in Adelaide in 1905, Taylor stepped up and produced a contour map of New South Wales, the most detailed and accurate produced to that date, and one that later provided crucial information for the capital's site selection. Taylor presented this work independently in a talk to the Linnean Society but identified himself as 'assistant demonstrator in palaeontology and geology, University of Sydney'. The respectful junior made sure to credit his professor:

> To lectures by him I owe my knowledge of the fundamental principles involved in this paper, and I desire to acknowledge the continued help and advice I have received from that gentleman.[22]

David taught Taylor science and, more significantly, inspired him to see himself as a scientist in the service of humanity; for his part, Taylor regarded David as the apotheosis of science, a man whose good opinion meant the world.

Pulling against Taylor's filial loyalty was his ambition and, as David's junior, he grew restless, intellectually and geographically. Would he ever attain his mentor's status if he remained in his shadow, working in a land far removed from Britain's, Europe's and North America's seats of learning? David, like Taylor's father and most Sydney University professors, had gained his credentials in Britain. As a fellow Britisher, Taylor's advanced scientific studies and academic job prospects oriented him towards England too. Lacking the funds to study abroad, however, he remained reliant on his professor's backing. Although he completed the qualifications necessary to receive a second bachelor degree in mining engineering in 1905, the career Taylor eyed for himself at this point was not that of his father, who had turned around his humble fortunes with practical and applied training, but rather that of his professor, nurtured in the intellectual climate of Oxbridge.

While Taylor was beginning to publish his own papers, he also gained a sense of a possible professorial future after David embarked in 1906 on a five-month tour, leaving his demonstrator to act in his place. Although Taylor assumed the responsibility without complaint, David did have a reputation for dumping his duties in his juniors' laps. One of them, Bristol geologist Raymond Priestley, whom David later hired to write up his Antarctic field notes, would privately complain that David was:

> a damned slacker, with all due deference to his many good qualities. He trots about interviewing dead-beats and distinguished visitors ... absolutely full up with outside—work, he calls it (Lectures to dog's homes etc.).[23]

In other respects, however, David worked in his assistants' best interest, even when trotting about overseas. On this 1906 trip, David attended the Geological Congress in Mexico City and the British Association for the Advancement of Science meeting in York, England. Although an Oxford man, David also dropped by the University of Cambridge, calling in at the impressive new Sedgwick Museum of Earth Sciences, which had opened in 1904. A man of David's reputation could expect to receive a guided tour, and such professional visits typically included informal discussions in which a professor could drop his students' credentials and ambitions into conversation. Perhaps a spot might be found at Cambridge for a talented young Australian geologist?

Perhaps, but first the challenge of financing overseas study had to be overcome somehow. Demonstrators were paid an insignificant salary and Taylor's parents, with three children at university and two still in school, could not afford to send their eldest to England, no matter how keenly they wished him success.[24] Fortuitously, another opportunity emerged. In order to facilitate his university studies, Taylor had moved from the family's semi-rural homestead to board in a more convenient Sydney home, run by a widow, Jane Laby. Taylor had met her son, Thomas, when both were working in the Treasury Department before they began their studies at Sydney University (Thomas opting for chemistry). Mrs Laby, 'a stout old lady', was as interested in Taylor's career as she was in her son's. She operated both as a housekeeper and well-informed career advisor. According to Taylor, it was she, not Professor David, who first informed him about a British scholarship for science graduates, and she encouraged him to apply after her son was awarded one in 1905.[25] Called the '1851 Science Research Scholarship', it commemorated the Great Exhibition of 1851—Prince Albert's highly successful enterprise in public science education. One outcome of the Exhibition's profits was the establishment of the Royal School of Mines, James Taylor's alma mater; another was the launch in 1891 of a scholarship scheme for science and engineering graduates in Britain and throughout the Empire, to undertake research degrees in British universities. Like his father, Taylor also had to compete for and win intellectual contests to establish his career, rather than rely on family fortunes.

To win an 1851 Scholarship required high academic standing in suitable subjects, as well as a proposed research project whose study might arguably benefit an applicant's home country. Taylor had earned top marks (his method of composing poems to help memorise facts for exams had paid off) and his two undergraduate degrees were in science and engineering, so he matched the 1851 profile perfectly. Devising a worthy research project was trickier, however. Professor David, back from his tour by late 1906, recommended that Taylor elect to study at Cambridge, basing himself at the Sedgwick Museum, which housed many of Charles Darwin's specimens. Yet neither could conjure up a suitable geological project. 'I experienced some difficulty in finding geological material that could be better worked out in Cambridge than in Australia itself,' Taylor reflected. Because Taylor had already begun to study a class of Cambrian fossils (*archaeo-cyathinae*), which he had collected with Mawson on a field trip to the geologically rich Flinders Ranges of South Australia, David suggested that he might extend this preliminary analysis. Until that point *archaeo-cyathinae* (light green, marble-like fossils with white circular markings) had been classed as corals; however, Mawson speculated that they were more likely to be sponges. Taylor tested Mawson's hypothesis and presented his preliminary assessment of the fossils at the 1906 meeting of the Australasian Association for the Advancement of Science (AAAS). This palaeontological work closely resembled the research which David had conducted from his samples of the Funafuti Atoll in the late 1890s, and Taylor's research could possibly make a similar contribution to evolutionary science. In his AAAS talk, Taylor predicted that further study of *archaeo-cyathinae* might throw light 'on the evolution of two out of the eight subdivisions of the Animal Kingdom. Hence the investigation is of fundamental importance in the great scheme of biogenesis.'[26] Thus an ideal project emerged for the scholarship aspirant. To the Scholarship committee, Taylor offered a study that would explore possible connections between Cambrian limestone reefs and the live coral reefs along Australia's east coast. In May 1907, his landlady's cajoling paid off: Taylor won the scholarship and was on his way to Cambridge.

Taylor, 1907. Looking every inch the young Edwardian gentleman, Taylor had this photograph taken in Sydney before he left for Cambridge. Like his father, he relied on a scholarship to fund his studies, which introduced him to an international world of science.

Journeyman at Cambridge

An Englishman by birth and a self-declared 'Britisher', Taylor took up his scholarship as a son of the Empire. Aside from the first 12 years of his life, he had lived in Australia. His Sydney undergraduate degrees and his accent (a mixture of his parents' Midlands and educated Australian) further identified him as a colonial. Attending Cambridge allowed Taylor to connect with England in ways that his father never could: through one of its oldest and most elite institutions, whose students were the sons of gentlemen and aristocrats. In contrast to Oxford, Cambridge was known as the science university, based on its mathematics standing and for the fact that Darwin had studied there, just prior to setting off on HMS *Beagle* in 1831. Cambridge was an undergraduate university that catered to men barely past their teens, for whom university life involved the transition from boyhood to manhood. While the 1851 Scholarship was a respectable and impressive way for a bachelor to move towards independent adulthood, Taylor's transition, at the age of 26, was more a cultural one; it entailed moving from an elite colonial institution to the very definition of academic elitism at the heart of the Empire, overlaid with class privilege. He performed the Oxbridge social rituals clumsily but fell in comfortably and enthusiastically with Cambridge's intellectual culture, based at Emmanuel College. Accepting the scholarship meant leaving the support and counsel of his parents and his professor. Now Taylor would explore the fairest horizon of academic life on his own.

In preparation for his studies, Taylor had sent his fossil specimens—six large cases of rocks—on ahead of his scheduled arrival in July 1907. Rather than take the standard route back to the old country, travelling westward through the Suez Canal, Taylor made an eastward trip for education and adventure—beginning with stops in New Zealand and smaller South Pacific islands. His mate Mawson couldn't resist teasing him that the strait-laced scientist might turn into a Gauguin:

> The gentle maidens you will also no doubt find enticing … beware lest a budding career be cut short by women's charms; and a calm, serene island life be chosen, instead of an arduous uphill climb with extremes of climate, rocks and prehistoric animals.[27]

Taylor appreciated the irony, since both men knew he was far more comfortable with rocks and fossils than with women and romance. ('[I]n my undergraduate days I blush to state that I only remember speaking to one "co-ed",' he later confessed.)[28] Nevertheless, he revealed his ethnological inclinations in an amused and superior account of the 'antics' of indigenous women and men from Tonga, Samoa and Fiji, and was equally captivated by geological features, which he described to his family in considerably greater detail. The Pacific region to Australia's north-east offered an Australian-based geologist an intriguing contrast to the physiography of a stable continent, and this was the first time that Taylor had seen evidence of recent volcanic action and earthquakes.

The letters he wrote to 'dear family' formed the basis for articles he rewrote for Australian dailies, a habit that was to continue for much of his life. Well-read in popular travel and adventure writing, Taylor bent to the genre, conflating exotic physiographic features with unfamiliar physiques and customs:

> In place of the servile, lanky, or diminutive [Ceylonese] 'native' is the Tongan, one of the finest physical types in existence. Aware at the time of my visit that his was the only independent island in the Pacific, he felt himself the equal of the white man.[29]

At this early point in his career Taylor identified and categorised people on an evolutionary scale. Anticipating his later intellectual project, he casually applied taxonomical analysis drawn from his palaeontological project to humans.

As Taylor sailed for England, Edgeworth David was preparing for a rather different voyage to Antarctica, on Shackleton's *Nimrod* expedition. David had earlier established his expertise in glaciology by his analyses of the effects of glaciation in the Snowy Mountains region between New South Wales and Victoria, and Taylor had talked with David before his departure about the exciting opportunity to study the 'ice age in being'. While David prepared for Antarctic glacial study, Taylor pursued his own interest in glaciation through self-designed field studies in New Zealand and California while on route to Cambridge. Over the northern summer of 1907, he travelled across North America from south-west to north-east, travelling by coach and on trains, sleeping in his seat to save money. He economised further by living on biscuits, peanuts and chocolate, washed down with glasses of water or milk, treating himself with an occasional glass of ginger ale. (As he later joked to his sister Pal, '"meillieur un vie d'eau qu'eau-de-vie". How's that for "hot stuff" French?')[30] At Niagara Falls, another geological feature that fascinated him, he spent a few precious pennies on a postcard, printed with his

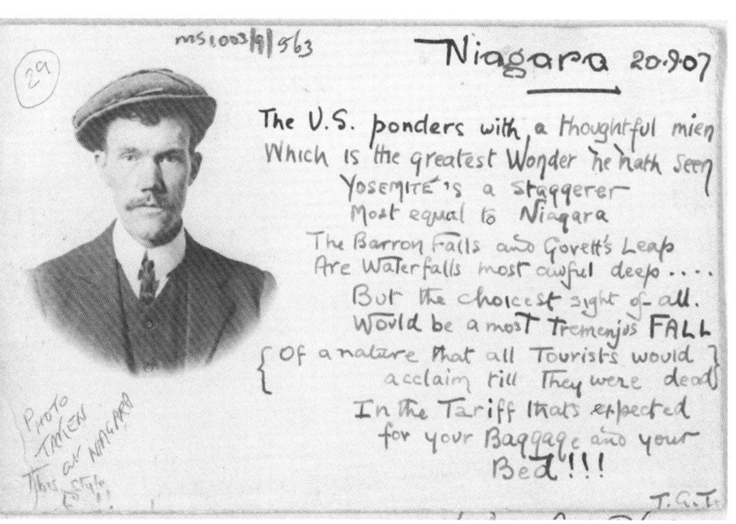

Postcard from Niagara Falls, 1907. Taylor played the tourist at Niagara Falls while undertaking the North American leg of his journey to England. On the back of the postcard he sent his family, he wrote a rhyme that referred to the geological features he had travelled to see.

image which a Falls-side photographer had produced. The card, sent to Mater on 20 September 1907, shows a moustachioed young man in jacket and tie with a cloth cap, peering straight at the camera and vainly attempting to look dangerous. He added an original verse, written to amuse and impress:

The U.S. ponders with a thoughtful mien
Which is the greatest Wonder he hath seen
Yosemite's a staggerer
Most equal to Niagara
The Barron Falls and Govett's Leap
Are waterfalls most awful deep ...
But the choicest sight of all
Would be a most tremenjos FALL
Of a nature that all Tourists would
acclaim till they were dead
In the Tariff that's expected
for your Baggage and your
Bed!!![31]

Family members knew that 'U.S.' in the poem referred to Taylor himself, not the United States: it stood for 'unassuming scientist', in contrast to A1 ('autocratic one'), the nickname he gave to Douglas Mawson, who at that point was about to join David on Shackleton's expedition.[32]

Taylor shared jokes about his travels and the characters he found amusing most readily with his sister Dorothy and his youngest brother, Jeff. Mater and his two other brothers received their share of 'hot stuff' (his favourite slang term) as well but he tended to write to his father about more serious matters. Nevertheless, every family member ('dear people') received letters stroked with exclamation marks, sketches and 'yarns' about life's blunders and absurdities. He wrote home several times a day and sent scores of letters each week, many of them needling the family for failing to respond at the same pace. The fact was that nobody could keep up with him. Aside from relentlessly penning letters home, he proceeded with one of the projects he had begun in Sydney—his textbook, *Australia in Its Physiographic and Economic Aspects* (which Clarendon would publish in 1911). He wrote faithfully for the same reason that he kept a daily diary from the time he entered university: to preserve a full and accurate record of his intellectual life, for future reference and chronicling.

Cambridge was a world unto itself, almost as odd as Tonga, though considerably more pretentious. Although the cream of British society—sons of the wealthy, whose lessons in status began at Rugby and Eton—no longer maintained an exclusive hold, the Cambridge man was offered every encouragement to consider himself superior to all others, on the basis of his Britishness, his class and his gender. Most signs of its modernisation were evident by the time Taylor arrived. Anglican religious conformity requirements were removed, and non-Christians and men of colour from the colonies began to enrol (Jawaharlal Nehru became a King's College undergraduate in 1907, the same year Taylor enrolled at Emmanuel). After Girton College was founded in 1869 and Newnham in 1872, women had their own colleges, although the senate barred them from receiving degrees. In 1869, Fitzwilliam Hall was established for students who could not afford to live in a college. This drift towards meritocratic principles in England's universities was aided by competitive funding schemes, such as the 1851 Scholarship, and, by 1902, the Rhodes Scholarship to Oxford, which offered promising colonials the opportunity to study in England, no matter how small their families' bank accounts. While James Taylor had earned a similar scholarship, based on merit rather than rank, Owens College was no Cambridge. In spite of its creeping democratisation, Cambridge remained a centre and symbol of power, which served and reproduced the Anglo world's elite.[33]

In the autumn of 1907, when Taylor arrived, the university was alive as always with intellectual projects, many of them inspired by creative individuals. Several Cambridge men and women became members of the Bloomsbury group of writers and critics, including Lytton Strachey (who wrote to John Maynard Keynes about 'a new kind of love') and Rupert Brooke, who enjoyed reciting poetry at pagan garden parties. Such goings on might have taken place on another planet as far as Taylor was concerned. He was a scientist, there to study with Cambridge professors. And he was a scholarship holder, under pressure to produce results. Fortunately, he arrived just as preparations to mark the 1909 centenary of Darwin's birth and the fiftieth anniversary of *On the Origin of Species* were under way. Although Darwinists had split into numerous camps by 1909, delegates agreed that his work represented a scientific watershed.[34] Exhibitions and lectures drew scientists and dignitaries from 167 countries, climaxing with a banquet held on 23 June 1909. Although Taylor was away in Europe at the time, studying geology and glaciation, he would likely have read the banquet speeches, which were published and widely distributed. Former prime minister and then Leader of the Opposition, Arthur J. Balfour, vividly painted Darwin's impact on modern scientific thought:

> He is the fount, he is the origin, and he will stand to all time as the man who made this great—as I think—beneficent revolution in the mode in which educated mankind conceive the history, not merely of their own institutions, not merely of their own race, but of everything which has that unexplained attribute of life, everything which lives on the surface of the globe, or even the depths of its oceans.[35]

Studying geology in Sydney with Professor David had already given Taylor a taste for such expansive thinking but at Cambridge, encouraged by its heady scientific atmosphere, he sensed the possibility that his own genius might emerge.

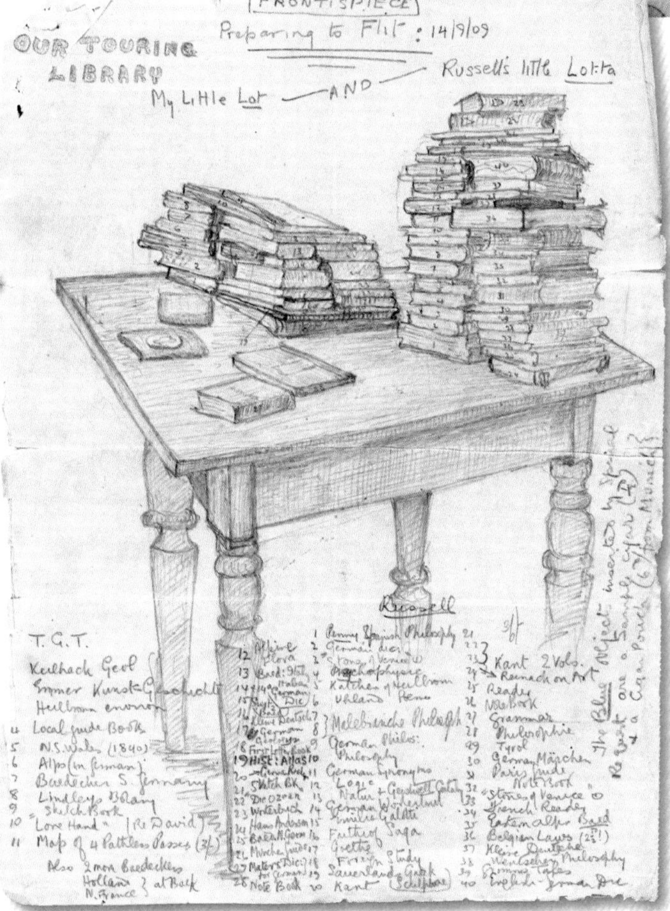

above

Taylor often included humorous self-portraits in his correspondence. In this 1909 letter to his sister, Pal, he charts his progress from infancy to manhood through his numerous trips to Paris.

left

On his study breaks Taylor continued to read voraciously. This sketch of his academic reading material appeared in a letter home, written in September 1909 while he was hiking through Europe.

Since he was enrolled in a 'research' degree (Cambridge didn't confer doctoral degrees until 1920), Taylor had no formal course of study to follow. Nor was he provided with close supervision, since none of the university's geologists was an expert in the analysis of coral or sponges. His fortunes improved when his Sydney friend, Thomas Laby, moved to Cambridge from Birmingham University in 1907, allowing Taylor to consult a mate for guidance on settling in, both socially and intellectually. 'He soon put me wise on matters of behaviour and etiquette at Cambridge,' Taylor recalled in his autobiography. 'He grounded me well in sartorial requirements relating to stiff collars, bowler hats, dark trousers, and the carrying of umbrellas.' Even a laboratory-based scientist had to *look* a Cambridge man before he could be taken seriously.[36]

Emmanuel College suited Taylor because it offered students work as exhibitors and, with that, the prospect of working closely with professors. As a non-smoker and non-drinker, and teased for his lack of sexual adventurism, he conformed with the College's Puritan origins but bristled against its infantilising rules which regulated students' comings and goings. He was readier to accept the social norms that defined one as a college man (such as how and when to shake hands). He kept rooms, like other students with limited funds, on Clarendon Street, and his upstairs neighbour was a fellow 1851 Scholarship holder, James C. Simpson, a Canadian from Montreal's McGill University. Having begun his career in art, Simpson helped Taylor prepare 50 pen drawings of fossil samples, and his own project, an analysis of evolution based on the study of sea cucumbers, made them science mates and colonial comrades, who travelled together on European tours during vacation breaks.

During term the College's strict regime helped foster a diurnal culture, which meant, where Taylor was concerned, concentrating on fossil study by day, followed by nightly discussions with Simpson and other scientists eager to discuss their research:

> How well I remember the tolling of the College bell at 5 p.m., when work ceased in the labs! It was then we visited our friends' rooms, while each student donned his gown before strolling leisurely to Hall, that beautiful room of polished panels where, once in the day, one felt so truly a member of one's College. The meal over, we dispersed to our apartments, and, after pleasant talk or heated argument, settled down to a few hours' quiet reading. And so to bed![37]

Taylor found talk, pleasant and heated, as enjoyable as his writing. In his letters home, he referred frequently to these discussions, more stimulating than any he had enjoyed at Sydney University and a world away from the intellectual and social alienation he had experienced at The King's School. Convinced that he could hold his own against any intellectual competitor, he adapted to Cambridge club culture as if born to it. The Research Club, the Advanced Students Club and the Sedgwick Club were the groups where Taylor did most of his formal debating. The last of these was one of the few Cambridge clubs open equally to men and women. Over his time at Cambridge (1907–1910), several women joined the Sedgwick Club, and one was elected president. Taylor (whose sister Dorothy had also studied under Professor David at Sydney) consistently supported co-education and, unlike many of his colleagues, also supported women's suffrage—a lively topic at Cambridge and beyond, as 'Votes for Women' became one of the most divisive issues of the period.

Working on fossils did not prevent Taylor from taking long walks and participating in a variety of sports that he preferred over cricket and rugby, the banes of his youth. He picked up the public school game of fives (a local variety of handball), and played regularly as a member of the Cavendish Tennis Club (named after Cambridge's physics laboratory). 'Our club was "long on brains" and "short on brawn",' he later admitted in his unpublished autobiography, 'Journeyman at Cambridge'.[38] Without knowing it, his debates with physicists, geologists and biologists, and the games he played with them over his three years at Cambridge, laid the groundwork for his invitation to join Robert Scott's expedition. While his physical recreation did little to prepare him for the rigours of work in Antarctica, the lively friendships he developed through his verbal sparring with Cambridge researchers helped to make the Australian a candidate who might meet Antarctic science's intellectual and mental challenges.

Amidst his constant round of peer-based social activities, Taylor never neglected to seek out academic superiors. Geological work at Cambridge was conducted in a laboratory at the Sedgwick Museum, where he had the palaeontology floor more or less to himself. While he could easily have hidden away, he made it his mission to seek out senior men within and beyond the Museum. One was 60-year-old geologist, Professor John (Johnnie) Marr, a glaciation specialist, who invited Taylor to Sunday seminars in his home and led him on local geological field trips. Although Thomas Hughes, the chair of

geology and the Sedgwick Museum's director, had introduced Taylor to the department, another man, Professor Thomas Bonney, proved to be more affable and solicitous of Taylor's career.[39] Taylor could discuss his *archaeo-cyathinae* findings with Bonney and could also count on the old professor for dinner invitations and introductions to other eminent geologists such as Sir Archibald Geikie and Sir William Ramsay. While none of these men ever replaced Edgeworth David as Taylor's chief intellectual inspiration and career counsellor, they widened and internationalised his network of advisors and advocates. And their endorsement certainly helped later to elect him a fellow of the Royal Geological Society (gaining him a few more initials after his name).[40]

Earning a place in the scientific fraternity also required a young scientist to test prevailing theories, proffering his own, and defending his work against critics. In a fortuitous chain of events, this process led to Taylor's meeting and working with William Morris Davis of Harvard University. Davis's and Johnnie Marr's explanations for the origin of hanging valleys and the drainage patterns of lakes differed, with Davis emphasising glacial erosion and Marr favouring aqueous erosion. Glaciers were very much on Taylor's mind when he arrived at Cambridge. Aside from the imminent departure of Shackleton's *Nimrod* expedition, which reached Antarctica not long after Taylor began at Cambridge, there was the geological survey he and Mawson had earlier conducted at Professor David's request on Mount Kosciuszko. Their work confirmed David's claim that he had discovered moraines on an earlier visit, and further supported David's theory that glacial action had occurred as recently as the Pleistocene Era.[41]

Taylor had begun corresponding with Professor Davis in 1907, after the Harvard man had read his article on the Canberra–Yass region and pointed out 'some wrong premises' Taylor had made regarding the relationship between contours and river flow in the

The Sedgwick Club, Cambridge, 1908. Taylor revelled in Cambridge club life. He posed for this picture with fellow members of the Sedgwick Club, which was for students interested in geology (Taylor is in the last row at the far right). Taylor lobbied successfully for the admission of women students to the club. Unlike many other club members, he also supported women's suffrage.

western slopes of New South Wales. Despite Davis's criticism, Taylor felt flattered that 'the eminent American' had taken his work seriously. They proceeded to correspond on geology, glaciology and the fieldwork and the mapping techniques best suited to test geomorphological theories, and they remained in touch after Taylor arrived in Cambridge. Early in 1908, Davis offered an exciting invitation: would Taylor like to join Davis's Alpine expedition the following summer? If Mawson was at David's side in Antarctica, studying with a world authority on glaciation in the European Alps was the next best thing.

As usual, the only impediment was financial. Because Taylor scrimped during term time and ate modestly (unless invited to a professorial dinner) he had saved enough money to fund a trip to Europe on a miserly budget. He joined Davis's party of geologists at Lake Como late in June 1908, after his own stretch of mountain hiking. For the next month, they conducted surveys of glaciated topography in the Swiss, Italian and French Alps. 'We were, indeed, a polyglot company of fourteen—American, French, Swiss, Italian, German, and Polish. I was the sole Britisher.'[42] Most considered him Australian, on account of his accent (which made it difficult for some to understand him) and his being an 1851 Scholarship holder.[43] Taylor brushed off taunts about his colonial status: he was walking on top of the world with one of the world's leading geologists, and no sense of parochialism restrained him from projecting his own career towards similar heights. Although he remained unconvinced of Davis's erosion thesis, he expressed his

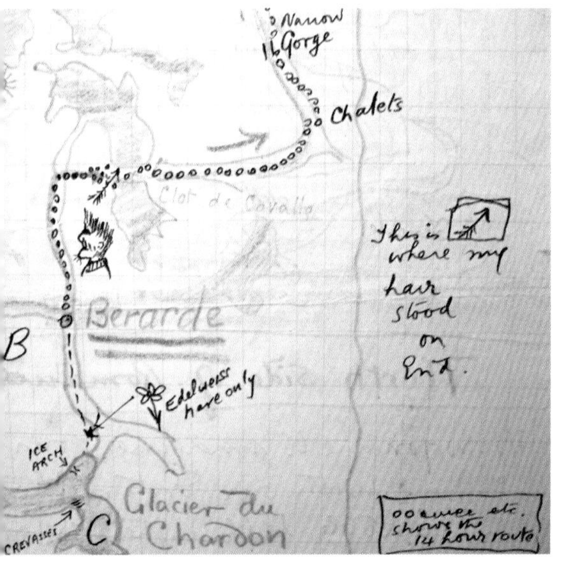

left

Taylor's sketch of his route through the French Alps, 10 July 1908. Taylor was an inveterate walker long before he travelled to Antarctica. During Cambridge University's summer breaks he tramped over much of Europe. This drawing of his walk through the French Alps includes one stretch where his steep and slippery walk became hair-raising.

right

Diagram by Taylor from *Preliminary Note on Archaeocyathinae from the Cambrian 'Coral Reefs' of South Australia*, January 1907. Taylor's Cambridge research project, which earned him a BA research degree in 1909, involved analysing *archaeo-cyathinae* (Cambrian sponges), traces of which he found in fossils in the Flinders Ranges of South Australia. After completing his microscopic studies in 1909, Taylor moved towards topics that he analysed on a global scale.

doubts dispassionately and respectfully. And he remained conscious that he had much to learn from Davis, not the least of which was his expertise in the block diagram, a technique well-suited to representing topographical features in three-dimensional isometric projection before the days of stereoscopic aerial photography.

After tramping though the Alps, microscopic *archaeo-cyathinae* samples must have looked even smaller to Taylor when he returned to his palaeontology lab in the autumn of 1908. Even before his departure from Australia, his interests had grown more geographical than palaeontological. In particular, he found the work of Melbourne geologist J.W. Gregory intriguing, and credited him with modernising geography from its fixation on exploration and discoveries towards its nobler purpose of explaining and predicting the relationship of land to settlement. Gregory's 1903 text *The Geography of Victoria* was, in Taylor's opinion, 'the first modern geography written in Australia', and he was eager to add his own contributions to this virgin field. 'I remember vividly the flood of new ideas dealing with what was to be my own life-work which burst upon me on reading this volume,' he would recall in 1932. This early inspiration had prompted him to deliver, in 1906, what he claimed to be the first university course of geography instruction (extension lectures delivered through the economics department at Sydney). At the same time, Professor David had recommended Taylor to Gregory as a suitable contributor to the New South Wales edition of Gregory's *Australian Geography* series. Then there was Taylor's textbook on the economic geography of Australia,

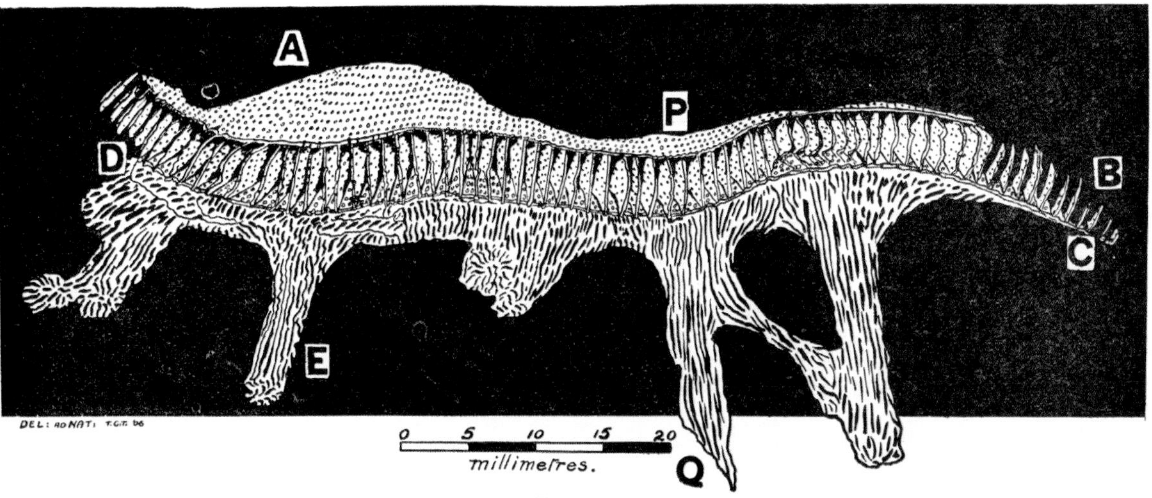

FIG. 7.

Strongly etched section of a Flabellate Archæocyathenoid, showing Upper Surface (A) *with fine pores, the Vertical "Septa"* (B) *remotely perforate, the coarsely perforate Lower Surface* (C), *the Proximal Rhizoid Zone* (D), *and the Cylindrical Rhizoids* (E). *Outer black portion is the Dark Matrix.*

commissioned by Oxford professor of geography, A.J. Herbertson, whom Taylor had met on a motorbike trip to the university. In a reference letter that Professor Bonney wrote for Taylor as his scholarship was coming to an end, with no firm academic posts appearing on the horizon, he painted Taylor as a polymath. In addition to predicting that the scholarship holder would secure 'a high place among Palaeontologists', Bonney described Taylor as:

> so far from being a narrow specialist, that he has now in the press a treatise on the economics of Australian Physiography, and from what I have already seen of this, I am sure it will be found not only very valuable to those who live in that continent but also suggestive to geologists in all parts of the world.[44]

Taylor's project on Cambrian fossils had won him a prestigious scholarship and his studies at the Sedgwick Museum had earned him a BA (research) at Cambridge in 1909, but neither would ensure an academic appointment in any of these specialties.

Taylor's father and Professor David (now safely back from Antarctica) resolved to combine their contacts in government and academia in an effort to find Taylor a landing place once he returned to Australia. Taylor had already earned a year's reprieve after the Scholarship committee found his preliminary fossil work (later published by the Royal Society of South Australia) impressive.[45] With his allowance petering out and no guarantee that remaining in England would net him a university position, Taylor found his last months at Cambridge frustrating. He looked on jealously as Thomas Laby was appointed professor of physics in 1909 at the Victorian University College in Wellington, New Zealand, with a salary of £600 per annum. Laby had earlier been one of Taylor's opponents in a Research Club debate, the resolution of which was that professors ought to be chosen for their teaching rather than research skills (the position Taylor supported). Petulantly, he broke the news to Mater: 'It is rather funny that Laby is my chief opponent! He never <u>taught</u> Physics and has done good <u>research</u> in it so he's a living awful example!'[46] When in October 1909 the news arrived from Professor David that the Australian Government would consider hiring Taylor as a physiographer in the Commonwealth Bureau of Meteorology—salary £310—he wasn't overly impressed. Yet how could he reject the offer without disappointing his father, or offending the mentor he most admired and respected?

A Cambridge Philosophical Society dinner provided an unexpected solution. The society had formed in 1819 'for the purpose of promoting scientific inquiry', and a tutor at Pembroke College, Arthur Hutchinson, invited his young Australian friend to dine with the society at St John's College. On the menu was a nine-course meal of classic English and French dishes, served by suited waiters, and on the agenda was naval Captain Robert Scott's leadership of the British Antarctic Expedition (BAE) and his search for scientists to man the 1910 mission. Somewhere between the saddle of mutton and the *faisans rôtis*, Professor Johnnie Marr turned to Taylor and asked, 'How would you like to go with Scott to Antarctica as English geologist? With your stamina and your knowledge of glaciology, you're just the man.' By the time the *beignets de pêches* were served, the other professors had piped in with their endorsements: 'Don't you think Taylor should go to Antarctica?' Taylor saved the dinner menu and wrote on the back: 'The day I was pushed into the Antarctic! GT.'[47]

Scott's scientific leader, Dr Edward Wilson, contacted Taylor the next day with a formal invitation. Under ideal circumstances, Taylor's choice would have been simple: seize the opportunity to test Davis's and Marr's competing glaciological and geological theories in a little-explored field, and catch up with Mawson, who had just returned from a part of the world only a handful of men had ever visited. Science and heroic adventure beckoned. Taylor's problem was the security of the Commonwealth Bureau of Meteorology offer and his sense of duty and obligation. Taylor wasn't the same man who had left Sydney in 1907, however. The Philosophical Society dinner took place a week after his twenty-ninth birthday and he had lived away from home for more than two-and-a-half years, over which time he had travelled on his own and with men he met through his research. Although he dreaded disappointing his Sydney seniors, he was ready to plot his own course, even if it diverged from the plans they had made for his future. Tension and irritation suddenly appeared in his correspondence with his parents and with David, who joined forces in an effort to sway him from the Antarctic option.

Taylor attempted to avoid confrontation by stalling, but his protracted negotiations began to try the expedition leader's patience as well. On 23 January, Dr Wilson asked Taylor to confirm whether or not he intended to accept the Bureau of Meteorology job. The next day, Captain Scott himself wrote, pressing for Taylor's answer. Still Taylor prevaricated and the matter dragged on for another two weeks. From London, he wrote to Mater in an effort to explain his preference for the BAE opportunity. He told her that he planned to join the expedition, return to Cambridge, and write up his results for a Doctor of Science degree. Speaking to her on financial terms that he hoped his thrifty mother would appreciate, he further explained that a man with his qualifications and experience was worth at least £510 per annum, not the paltry amount the Bureau of Meteorology had offered. Worried that Taylor might find himself jobless after returning from the expedition, Professor David managed to convince the Commonwealth to come up with a compromise. On 15 February, the Australian Government cabled Taylor an offer that would allow him to join both the Bureau and participate in the BAE as well. After waiting 10 days, Taylor turned down the Commonwealth's offer, 'on the grounds that salary and meteorological duties do not attract', and he let Captain Scott know that he would serve as a geologist on his expedition.

The Bureau of Meteorology was determined to have him, however, and Taylor received a counter-proposal in August 1910. The Commonwealth Meteorologist, H.A. Hunt, and Atlee Hunt, the Secretary of the Department of External Affairs, devised an arrangement (cleared by the *Public Service Act*, section 79) that would permit Taylor to receive his Australian Government salary while simultaneously drawing his expedition salary;

furthermore, he would move to a higher rate of pay at the Bureau after he returned. Their only condition was that he conduct meteorological research for the Commonwealth while based in Antarctica.[48]

Brinkmanship of this ilk might easily have left Taylor with angry parents, an insulted mentor, and no job. His financially conservative parents certainly thought the ploy unwise,[49] especially after his father had had to scramble from contract to contract after leaving his government mineralogist position back in 1900.[50] For the self-confident son, though, the gamble had paid off—in financial terms, in career terms and, perhaps most importantly, as a means to demonstrate that he had come of age as a professional scientist in his own right. The favoured son, eyeing his thirtieth birthday, was finally about to become his own man.

Taylor, 1909. Among his many titles, Taylor greatly valued his BA (research) degree from Cambridge University. In 1909, when he graduated, he had high hopes that his degree would win him a position as a geology professor; instead, it earned him an invitation to join the British Antarctic Expedition.

CAMBRIDGE.

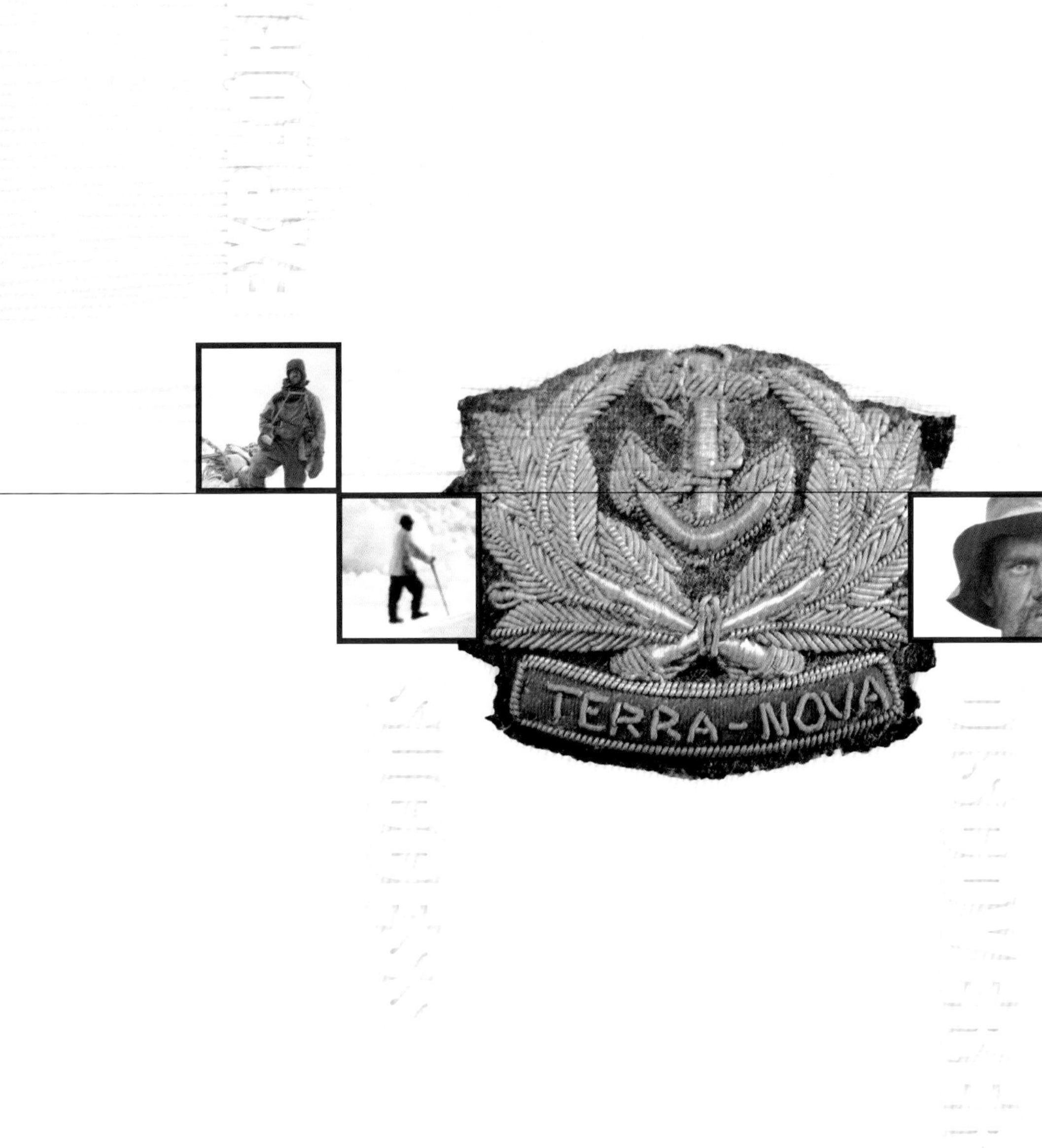
TERRA-NOVA

The Furthest Frontier

2

Like the sinking of the *Titanic* in 1912, the death of Robert Falcon Scott and his party in 1913, shortly after Norwegian Roald Amundsen beat them to the Pole, symbolised both the grandeur and folly of modern ambition. Taylor saw the expedition differently, however. Thanks to his own and his fellow scientists' efforts it was a roaring success. The geological work undertaken in Antarctica advanced scientific knowledge while his own contribution brought Taylor significant academic rewards. In 1916, after an examination of his glaciological research, passed by Professor David and Melbourne geology professor Edward Skeats, the University of Sydney awarded him a doctoral degree in science. Later published by the British Museum as *The Physiography of the MacMurdo Sound and Granite Harbour Region* (1922), the work was Taylor at his most dispassionate and scientific best.[1] Taylor consistently argued that the BAE's contribution to science should be celebrated as a success story in a tale otherwise characterised as tragedy and failure, owing to the deaths of Captain Scott and his polar party. Scientific discovery was 'the silver lining', he insisted, and it shone to the day he died.

When Taylor disembarked from the *Terra Nova* to set foot on the shore of Cape Evans in January 1911, the scientist travelled back 500 million years in the earth's history, while the 30-year-old bachelor took a significant step forward into his professional and personal future. Despite his official research brief, Taylor's Antarctic journey was never purely scientific, for it drew him into a new circle of colleagues and friends, and it led him to form a new family. Once the expedition ended and the men separated to resume their previous lives, Raymond Priestley hosted Taylor at his family home in Tewkesbury, England. There they wrote up their scientific accounts with fellow expedition member Canadian physicist Charles 'Silas' Wright, and also worked on their personal memoirs of their Antarctic experiences. Priestley called his account 'Antarctic Adventure', while Taylor, with trademark optimism, titled his 'With Scott, the Silver Lining'. During his post-expedition sojourn his high spirits and 'long, lean, lanky body' caught the eye of Priestley's younger sister, Doris. Over the summer of 1913, the polar scientist's and the 18-year-old 'Honorary Antarcticker's' courtship began with sessions bent over the dining room table, editing Taylor's manuscript. Once Silas Wright proposed to another Priestley sister, Edith, the connections between the Antarcticker's science and family grew even richer. Taylor knew that Scott and Wilson had carefully considered the need to find men for the BAE who would get along well, but no-one had imagined that his Antarctic invitation would lead to an unmatchable experience of scholarship, fellowship and family.

The Journey South

Interest in polar exploration had first been spurred by its commercial prospects in the mid eighteenth century, with the search for efficient shipping routes and the harvesting of whales and seals the foremost objectives. Over the nineteenth century, scientific and political ambitions surfaced as well, and learned societies established polar research committees to lobby national governments and private financiers to fund expeditions, and to collect data on terrestrial magnetism, meteorology and geology. While the first International Polar Year (1882–1883) put science on the polar expedition map, it took a series of well-publicised expeditions, starting with Sir John Franklin's fatal Arctic expedition of 1845 and protracted efforts to find the party's remains, to rouse public enthusiasm and political support. While northern polar research advanced quickly in the late nineteenth century, due to superior mapping and less severe weather and seas, Australians cast their eyes on Antarctica across the Great Southern Ocean. The more that Arctic discoveries filled scientific journals and newspapers, and the further that explorers advanced towards the North Pole itself, the more Antarctica loomed as the 'final frontier', inspiring a feverish race for knowledge and glory in an era of mounting international tension.

Taylor penned 'Sledgemates at Cambridge, 1913' on this studio portrait of Frank Debenham (standing, left), Raymond Priestley (standing, centre) and Charles Wright (seated, right). All four served on the British Antarctic Expedition and two of them—Priestley and Wright—became his brothers-in-law. The book in Taylor's lap is likely open to his chapter in *Scott's Last Expedition* (1913).

Australian scientists played a prominent part in this drama from its commencement at the beginning of the twentieth century.[2] As Taylor embarked on his university studies, Tasmanian scientist Louis Charles Bernacchi became the first to land on Antarctica and to conduct research over winter, a feat many had imagined impossible. Setting a publicity pattern for Taylor to follow, the Melbourne *Age* covered Bernacchi's part in the expedition extensively between 1899 and 1900, and he published his own book on the trip a year later (*To the South Polar Regions: The Expedition 1898–1900*). The next trip to capture Australian interest, the British National Antarctic Expedition (1901–1904), was headed by Royal Navy captain, Robert Falcon Scott, commander of the *Discovery*, with Ernest Shackleton his third lieutenant. As a geology student, Taylor closely followed this expedition—sponsored by the Royal Geographical Society—particularly because Antarctic scientific research had the potential to shed light on the effects of glaciation and the history of climate change elsewhere on the planet. Edgeworth David was fascinated by Antarctic geology and inspired his students to share his enthusiasm. As *Discovery* was about to begin its journey, David and his geology students wrote to the captain to convey their best wishes.[3] Although David developed a cordial relationship with Scott, his passion for Antarctic research knew no specific loyalties. So when Ernest Shackleton, now Scott's rival, looked for geologists to serve on the British Imperial Antarctic Expedition (1907–1909), David put his name forward for the post of chief geologist, and suggested his team comprise his top pupils, Douglas Mawson, Leo Cotton and W.L. Hammond. A recent geology graduate from Bristol University, Raymond Priestley, also joined the *Nimrod* before it set south from England with the greatest complement of scientists ever assembled for such an expedition.

While his Sydney mates and mentor charted unknown territory and searched for the South Magnetic Pole, Taylor stood at his Sedgwick Museum bench slicing fossils. And so when he received his invitation to join Scott's second expedition in December 1909, it wasn't just good news for a geologist in search of further funded research—it was an opportunity to catch up to his fellow Sydney students, who had returned from Antarctica with masses of original and potentially ground-breaking research findings. Taylor might well do the same, while serving under a captain known for his respect for scientists, as opposed to Shackleton, dismissed by Royal Geographical Society stalwarts and men loyal to Scott as a mere 'pole-bagger'.[4] One of the most loyal was zoologist Edward Wilson; as the expedition's chief science officer he offered prestige that helped compensate for Taylor's later start. Patriots across Britain were roused by Scott's inspiring speeches, their appetite for discovery and possession whetted with his every appearance. Scott's claim of disinterested scientific exploration was compromised by the imperialistic ambition that drove early twentieth-century polar exploration, as competing packs of explorers planted flags and triumphantly posed for pictures. Scott was no different. From the outset he declared his intention to reach the South Pole, not in the self-glorifying manner of Robert Peary, recognised for discovering the North Pole in 1909, but in the name and honour of the British Empire.[5]

Although the *Terra Nova* carried an international contingent of explorers, it was in all respects British. The Royal Society was one of Scott's chief sources of funding, and he was able to court its august membership on the basis of the findings of his earlier *Discovery* expedition. Its scientific team, he credibly claimed, had significantly advanced geographical, geological and meteorological knowledge of the continent's western sector, but that was just the beginning. The British Government contributed funds to his new expedition in 1910—£20 000—but only after Parliamentarians saw the value of polar exploration as an assertion of British might. Still short of supplies, Scott had to scramble for British purveyors to provide free provisions, on the condition that Scott and his men appear in publicity photos posed beside and atop crates of cocoa, golden syrup and sherry.

Only six months away from travelling to Antarctica in May 1910, Taylor attended a ceremony at London's Royal Albert Hall, held to honour Commander Robert E. Peary for his discovery of the North Pole.[6] As a geologist, dreaming of similar acclaim, Taylor nearly missed his chance to conduct Antarctic research, since he had been Captain Scott's second choice as geologist. The first, and the man whom David had recommended, was Douglas Mawson.[7] After returning from the *Nimrod* expedition in March 1909, David and Mawson had received a heroes' welcome.[8] On this expedition Mawson had been more than David's right-hand man; on several occasions he had saved his life. No-one, least of all David, could have questioned Mawson's expertise, his courage or his strength, all of which had held up admirably under impossibly challenging conditions. In 1910, Mawson was clearly the better choice as a seasoned scientist, and he briefly considered taking up Scott's offer to serve as his chief geologist. He decided, instead, to turn the captain down, thinking (correctly) that a veteran with his reputation could mount and lead his own expedition.[9] Mawson's rebuff of Scott became Taylor's break.

Scott was an experienced commander who selected men prepared to respect naval discipline and a clear hierarchy in which he sat at the top. He also needed suitable subcommanders, men prepared to follow his orders and to impose their own. On an expedition where parties of men were separated by vast distances for months at a time, he needed to appoint leaders he could trust to make their own well-reasoned judgments. Taylor came well recommended by David (who endorsed his geological credentials); however, unlike Mawson, Taylor had no leadership experience. Scott wisely chose to appoint him as a member of the geological party, not as chief geologist. There was another reason for Scott to be cautious: Taylor's physical make-up. When Taylor showed up for his appointment at Scott's offices in Westminster ('a district peculiarly devoted to the empire's interests'), Scott's secretary was still sifting through some 8000 applications for the various positions on the BAE.[10] Scott had honoured him with a personal invitation but that also allowed for a personal inspection: could the gaunt Australian stand up to Antarctic conditions? Every member of the party had to be extraordinarily fit and strong, as Scott knew from experience. Thus, when he hired the wiry Cambridge man as one of his science officers, the captain took a calculated risk.

Meanwhile, over the early part of 1910, Mawson was touring England in an effort to raise funds for his own Australian Antarctic Expedition. Before he left Cambridge, however, Mawson offered his old mate a few polar exploration tips.[11] First was the question of Taylor's physical limitations. Back home in Sydney, as a scrawny older brother, Taylor had mercilessly teased his sister Dorothy by comparing his physique to her stockier build.[12] When he sized himself up against Mawson, however, the shoe was on the other foot. Observing that Taylor's 5-foot 11-inch frame—at 155 pounds—carried more bones than flesh, Mawson, a far taller and brawnier man, prescribed a program of boxing and weight-lifting.[13] Taylor took his advice, and started up a boxing club for scientists, but was far happier extending his capacity to walk great distances, a physical forté that would not go amiss on polar treks, he reassured himself, if not his trainer.

Taylor warmed up for the expedition with a long winter's walk from Cambridge to London with another Canadian holder of the 1851 Scholarship, Torontonian Charles Wright. He and Taylor had become friends at Cambridge through overlapping interests (Wright was an expert on the physics of ice) and their membership in the Peripatetic Club for walking enthusiasts. The pair had discussed their shared dream of one day joining a polar expedition, so when Taylor received his offer, he promptly asked if Wright might be added to the science team, a request that met Dr Wilson's approval. The physical test the men set themselves was to walk the 80-kilometre distance to London within 12 hours, without stopping to rest. The real object, however, was to demonstrate their ability to match 'the naval men in every branch of athletics' and prove 'the scientists had *some* muscle'.[14] On a frosty February morning in 1910, Wright and Taylor set out with boiled eggs and chocolate, and they reached their destination within the time limit. Taylor later commented: 'Tales Mawson had told us of the prowess of explorers encouraged Wright and myself to demonstrate that we were no weaklings!' (the exclamation mark Taylor's version of a counterpunch).[15]

Concerned that Taylor reach an optimal level of fitness and enhance his scientific preparedness, Captain Scott placed him on the BAE's payroll in March 1910, well ahead of November when he was scheduled to join the expedition in New Zealand. Scott advised him to train his body and mind in the European Alps, where he had already travelled with Professor Davis in 1908, and with a group of Sydney mates who visited him in the autumn of 1909. Combining his expedition salary with the last pennies of his 1851 Scholarship, Taylor covered thousands of kilometres over two months—travelling by train (third class), and walking from Belgium to Berlin and down the Rhine Valley towards Switzerland. On these 'strenuous tramps' he examined glaciological and aqueous erosion and continued testing his capacity to plough on with minimal rations. Nuts, chocolate, biscuits, plus the odd egg and slice of bread, comprised his daily diet, while water, milk and tea slaked his thirst. Even on a side-trip to Italy, he never indulged in wine—just Italian art and architecture. In contrast to his father James's ability to survive on porridge and water, Taylor's tramping fare was extravagant, yet far simpler than the sumptuous meals and intoxicants the more refined expeditioners would later crave on polar treks.

Taylor returned from Europe in April 1910 with stronger limbs and further knowledge of glacial topography and postglacial geology. He tidied up his affairs in Cambridge and began his voyage south—not to Antarctica yet, but to Melbourne and the head office of the Commonwealth Bureau of Meteorology. From June to November 1910, he experienced an interminable lull before the spectacular Antarctic adventure lying ahead. Life as a public servant was decidedly less glamorous than exploring glaciers, yet his Bureau work entailed more than wearing a pressed shirt and sitting at a desk, as he had done a decade earlier in the Treasury office. His paperwork consisted largely of editing Professor David's meteorological field notes from the Shackleton expedition. He also had the opportunity to conduct a follow-up survey of the Canberra district, now that Commonwealth politicians had finally agreed on a site for the proposed capital.[16] Taylor travelled 1450 square kilometres of the territory by foot, bicycle and cart, and he constructed a relief map which district planners and the capital's official city designer, Walter Burley Griffin, consulted extensively. Taylor also added to his list of publications with an official Bureau of Meteorology Bulletin, *The Physiography of the Proposed Federal Territory at Canberra, Australia* (1910). This was Taylor's opportunity to apply the lessons he had learned from Professor David, on the physiographer's role in nation-planning, from the ground up. It was also a chance to live in a tent with a group of surveyors, and to wonder what it would be like, in a few months, to share similar quarters with fellow scientists in conditions unimaginably harsher than a chilly Canberra winter.

The *Terra Nova*, meanwhile, was making its way from England towards the Southern Ocean, with landings planned in Australia and New Zealand. The Australian stopover was critical: even after Scott's deals with commercial suppliers, the funds he raised for the expedition prior to his planned June departure fell short of his goal. When the ship docked in Melbourne and Sydney in October, Scott stepped ashore in navy finery, endeavouring to inspire public enthusiasm among British subjects and to attract assistance from the Commonwealth Government or private backers—anyone willing to chip in. Professor David, who had set up an Antarctic Room in the University of Sydney's geology department, welcomed the party in Sydney and arranged a grand reception.

In between his speeches, receptions and interviews with journalists, Scott met with Taylor and instructed him to spend several weeks in the New Zealand Alps to enhance his physical conditioning and conduct geological fieldwork. This was a far more palatable program of training for Taylor than boxing or weight-lifting, so he eagerly obliged. Two of the expedition's scientists agreed to join him: Wright and geologist Frank Debenham, the younger brother of one of Taylor's King's School friends and another member of David's stable of graduates.[17] In addition, Scott allowed Dorothy Taylor (like her

brother, recipient of Sydney University's physiography prize) to join the men. The husband of the imposing Kathleen Scott—artist, member of the Fabian Society and suffragist—the captain was well acquainted with women's strengths.

None of the New Zealand Alps party proved him or herself a weakling. Their ascent of the Hochstetter Dome was especially arduous, though from Taylor's perspective it didn't make him a mountain climber. Normally given to boasting, he was diffident about his climbing skills, later commenting that: 'Even in New Zealand and in Antarctica I have done little climbing more strenuous than the easy ascent of the Clot des Cavalles.'[18] Nevertheless, Hochstetter's summit was a respectable 2800 metres and the quartet accomplished their one-day climb, trudging through snow and ice. Dorothy (a 'valiant walker') kept up and led the men at many points, while knowing that each step took her closer to a return trip to Sydney rather than to Antarctica. Indeed it would be another 49 years before women scientists participated in Antarctic research. When four women (two zoologists, a botanist and a biologist) broke the male monopoly in November 1959, the Sydney *Sun Herald* interviewed Taylor for his opinion. Unlike most polar scientists, he greeted the news warmly, even claiming that he'd urged his sister to join the Scott expedition.[19] In 1910, however, no-one, including Dorothy, took seriously the prospect that polar exploration was anything but men's work.

Taylor, Wright and Debenham boarded the *Terra Nova* on 30 November at Lyttelton, New Zealand. When J. Allan Thompson, a palaeontologist attached to the New Zealand Geological Survey, fell ill, Professor David offered the services of Raymond Priestley. As David's geology research scholar, Priestley was a former member of the *Nimrod* expedition and he and Taylor had met earlier through their work on the professor's field notes.[20] Like the other bachelors aboard the *Terra Nova*, their thoughts on leaving for Antarctica and its perils lay with their parents and siblings, as yet unburdened by the worries of the married men.

opposite

Diary sketch of Frank Debenham, 1911. As Captain Scott's chief geologist, Taylor led the Western Geological Party. Frank Debenham was one of his party—a fellow geologist who later became the first director of the Scott Polar Research Institute. They worked closely together, writing up their notes after their sledging expeditions. Taylor drew 'something like Deb' in the winter quarters at Cape Evans. The pair and their families remained close for the remainder of Taylor's life.

above

'A Very "Ordinary Seaman"', from Taylor, *With Scott: The Silver Lining*, 1916. When a violent storm in the Southern Ocean threw the *Terra Nova* into peril shortly after setting out from Lyttelton, New Zealand, in November 1910, Taylor and his fellow scientists had to pitch in to save the ship. He enjoyed the camaraderie of ship life, though he never fancied himself a sailor.

Taylor was a realist when it came to considering the risks that lay ahead. Like a soldier readying for battle, he prepared for the worst while hoping for the best. He drew up an informal will a month before leaving and mailed it to his father. In it he indicated that his expedition salary was £250, in addition to his £310 per annum from the Commonwealth Bureau. Scott had also agreed that Taylor could supplement his salary with royalties for 12 syndicated articles on the expedition, contracted for the Melbourne *Argus*. Mindful of his father's irregular earnings and dangerous work in the mining industry, Taylor provided that Mater and Pal should share his assets equally.[21] Out of necessity he took very few of his valuables with him. Aside from practical items, like sledge repair tools and an ice axe, he tucked away a compass (engraved with his name and given to him by his father for his twenty-first birthday), a pack of playing cards with the royal blue crest of Emmanuel College, a copy of *Martin Chuzzlewit* (his favourite Dickens novel), the sheet music for a nonsense song, *Alcala*, and a pair of thick worsted wool socks knitted by Pal.

From Lyttelton southward, Taylor became an assiduous diarist, fully intending to turn his daily observations into articles and a book. His Cambridge years had given him plenty of practice: almost daily accounts of his experiences sent home in letters to his family. Taylor would record his Antarctic experiences and findings in words and images as a matter of professional responsibility, by force of personal and professional habit, and in keeping with prevailing exploration practices. His earlier fieldwork under

Professor David had also trained him in constant observation and record-keeping: 'Take notes of what ever you see. In earth-sciences sketch everything.'[22] Taylor consciously followed the long tradition of weighty scientific exploration narratives, written by 'men-who-were-there'. Scott himself was a gifted writer and a master at the craft. His account of his earlier expedition, *The Voyage of the Discovery* (1905), had added to his fame, while Shackleton's story of the *Nimrod* expedition, *The Heart of the Antarctic* (1909), had likewise made him an instant celebrity. Every member of Scott's expedition who fancied himself a writer intended to capitalise on this market. Taylor and aristocrat Apsley Cherry-Garrard were well ahead of the others, since the former had already published textbooks, papers and a handful of popular pieces for journals, while the latter had studied literature at Oxford. Cherry-Garrard would edit a revived edition of *The South Polar Times*, an illustrated in-house publication started by the *Discovery* expedition. When the editor put out the call for 'prose, poetry, or drawings', Taylor would reliably respond, supplying more material (mainly satirical sketches and poems) than any other member of the expedition.[23]

The voyage south was to provide material for Taylor's *Argus* dispatches, which the paper promoted with the misleading series title, 'The Race for the Pole'. Before the first month had passed, Taylor had filled over 100 journal pages, while writing a parallel daily diary for his family (intended for his future expedition account). All on-board diarists recorded one especially dramatic moment at the outset of the voyage, when a violent storm nearly scuttled the ship, laden with its top-heavy cargo of fuel, food, dogs, horses, sledges, tools, instruments and men. With heavy seas heaving over the decks, crates were sent crashing, flinging ponies and dogs to their deaths. All hands were needed to man the pumps and form bucket brigades to keep the *Terra Nova* from being swamped. Of the worst night, Frank Debenham wrote: 'I never wish to see a greater abomination of desolation'.[24] Taylor agreed that 'it was about as miserable a time as I've had'—even the captain admitted that 'it was touch and go'.[25] Though many of his books and his camera were damaged and clothes soiled, Taylor managed to lift the party's spirits with his improvised costume. Having only one pair of trousers (now soaked) his makeshift outfit 'caused some amusement' when he appeared on deck 'in Tudor rig, i.e. a sort of sweater and a pair of very long warm bright blue stockings!'.[26] Other men, like 'Birdie' Bowers, also gained reputations for their capacity to lighten the darkest moments with humour but Taylor's flair for the ridiculous won him mates from the outset.

Monotony followed the unnerving storm, as the *Terra Nova* now carefully nudged its way through thickening pack ice. 'Teetotally stuck', Taylor recorded in his diary.[27] While the ship waited for an opportunity to land, Taylor and his fellow expedition members began to find their places among the men, aided by formal ranks and roles but also cued by the ways in which their personalities emerged. The navy men had the easiest time: there were seamen and there were officers of various ranks. But Scott granted the scientists, along with the expedition's photographer, Herbert Ponting, officer status as well. The scientific leader, Dr Wilson, quickly earned his men's respect, while the scientists beneath him had yet to determine the hierarchy below the chief, Captain Scott.

Shipboard social conditions levelled some differences but only among men of officer status. Describing the wardroom's dining table, Taylor depicted its cramped seating arrangements:

> geologist next to pony expert, chemist, and motorman, taxidermist, navigator, lord of the dogs, doctors etc. etc., each with his elbows lovingly exploring his neighbour's anatomy.

Roast mutton, potatoes and vegetables was the standard ship fare, always followed by desserts, including some of Taylor's favourites: 'plum-duff, roly-poly, apple pie, or stewed fruits and blancmange'.[28] He dived into postprandial musical entertainment with equal gusto, without need of spirits to rouse him to sing or to 'strum' the piano, a limited talent he had inflicted on friends in his Cambridge days. Camp renditions of romantic ballads and rousing sea shanties brought the men together in chorus and horseplay, which the dour Scott tolerated in the interest of esprit de corps. Nevertheless, Taylor, along with his fellow scientists and officers, took for granted the status distinctions between themselves and the sailors and stewards who served the officers and sailed the ship. Only in emergencies were officers' hands required for the dirty work. Their sleeping quarters were separate from the crew's and so were their more cerebral amusements—bridge, self-referential poetry and debates on socialism, suffrage and the merits of Latin education. There was no question where Taylor would place himself. With his science degrees and his Cambridge club experience behind him, he was one of a group of men who transplanted Oxbridge culture to Antarctica; along with sherry glasses and photos of the new royal family, it travelled to the Southern Ocean perfectly intact.

The *Terra Nova* epaulet (1910). Taylor never served in the military but he was proud of his connection to the British Navy as a scientist aboard the *Terra Nova*, the ship Captain Scott selected for the British Antarctic Expedition.

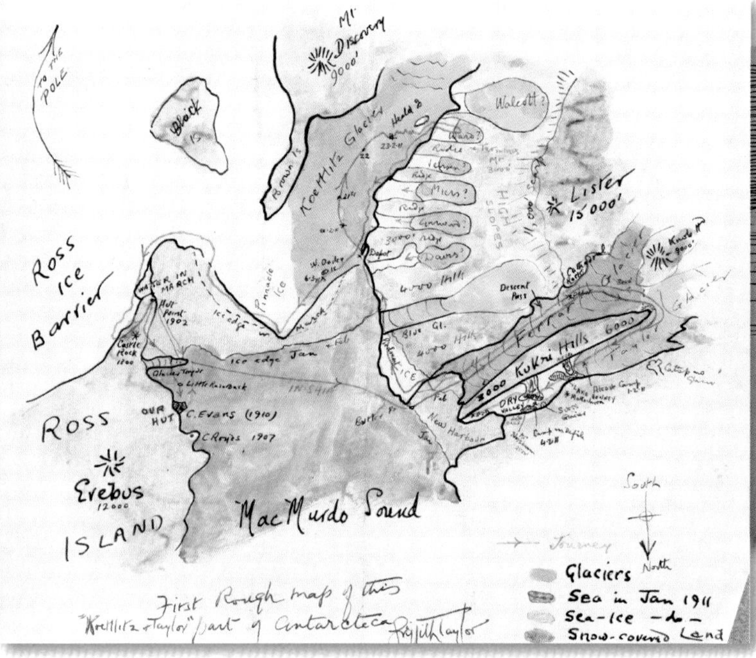
To the Pole
Mt Discovery 9000'
Koettlitz Glacier
Lister 15000'
Ross Ice Barrier
Kukri Hills 6000
Ferrar
Our Hut
C. Evans (1910)
C Royds 1907
Ross
Erebus 12000
Island
MacMurdo Sound
South
North
Journey
Glaciers
Sea in Jan 1911
Sea-Ice -do-
Snow-covered Land
First Rough map of this "Koettlitz & Taylor" part of Antarctica
Griffith Taylor

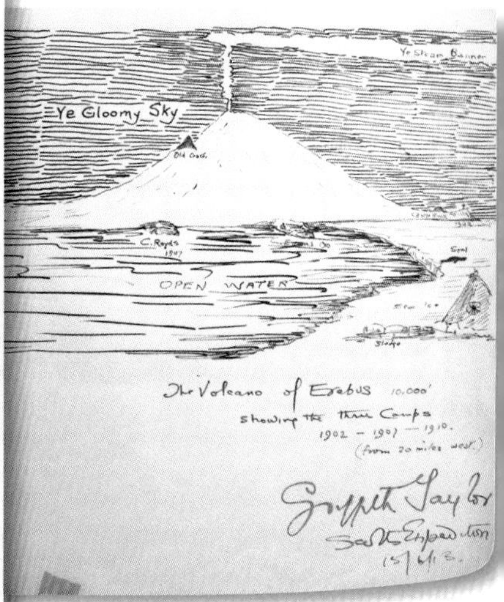
Ye Steam Banner
Ye Gloomy Sky
C. Royds 1907
Open Water
The Volcano of Erebus 10,000'
showing the three Camps
1902 – 1907 – 1910.
(from 20 miles west.)
Griffith Taylor
South Expedition
15/6/13.

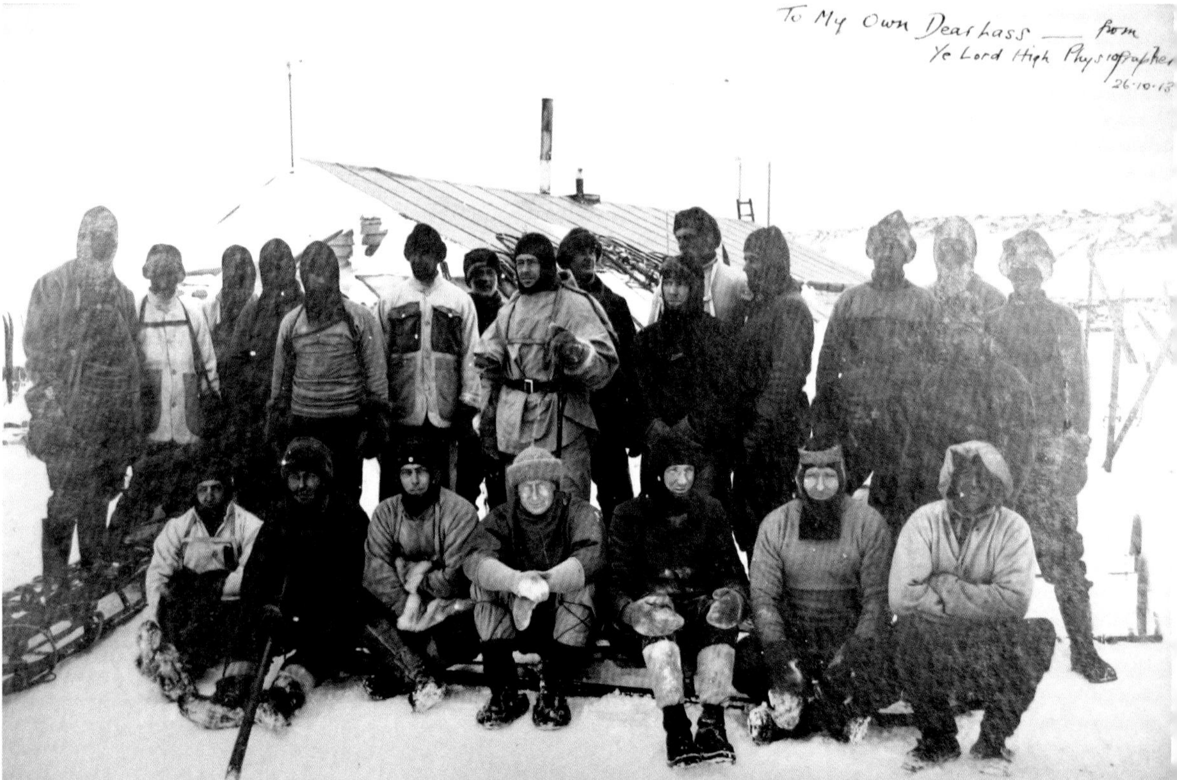
To My Own Dear Lass — from
Ye Lord High Physiographer
26·10·13

On Science Grounds

Ship life was about to transform into shore life, where new hierarchies would be shaped. The first task was to land the *Terra Nova* at a site suitable for building a hut to serve as the base from which the various parties would set out, and to which they would return after completing their separate exploratory missions. Cape Crozier, the optimal site for zoological study, was tried, as was Cape Royds, where two of the men, Priestley and Day, had conducted research on Shackleton's expedition. Faced with treacherous icebergs and the solid walls of sea ice blocking these landings, the ship moved towards a more accessible site at Cape Evans (named after Scott's second-in-command, Lieutenant Edward 'Teddy' Evans). Scott, Evans and Wilson ('Uncle Bill') chose a site on a small bay scattered with kenyte gravel, the dark volcanic rock spewed out from Mt Erebus, a 4000-metre volcano exhaling smoke and steam in the distance. Unloading tonnes of supplies and building a hut that would protect men, animals and food stores until the *Terra Nova's* scheduled return a year later, required all hands. None of the scientists received concessions, which meant that Taylor found it difficult to keep up his writing. 'Still miles behind in diary work,' he wrote on 6 January, 'up at 5 a.m. and hauling 200lbs a day from ship to hut. However it is not too tiring now.'[29]

A change in Taylor's status soon put a spring in his step. Initially Scott had placed Ponting in charge of the Western Geological Party (WGP). Ten years Taylor's senior, Ponting had impressed the captain with his experience in numerous earlier expeditions as 'photographer of the world'. Taylor protested that he knew far more about geology than a 'camera artist' and he convinced Scott to place him in charge of the WGP (adding that he had turned 30 while the *Terra Nova* was pitching at sea). Taylor's men included Frank Debenham ('Deb'), Charles 'Silas' Wright and Petty Officer Edgar 'Taff' Evans, a polar veteran who was to take charge of their sledging. Navy Lieutenant Victor Campbell was

opposite top left

This map records the expedition taken by the Western Geological Party in 1911 as well as key sites, including 'Our Hut' at Cape Evans. The trip netted Taylor a glacier and a dry valley named after him (with Captain Scott's approval).

opposite top right

Taylor drew this sketch in 1913 for his expedition memoir. He indicates the sites of earlier expedition huts—Cape Royds (1907), Cape Evans (1910) and Castle Rock (1902)—under Mt Erebus's 'gloomy sky'.

opposite bottom

Taylor (far left) gave this group portrait of British Antarctic Expedition members, taken in 1911, to Doris Priestley as a courtship gift in 1913. He addressed it 'To My Own Dear Lass' and signed it, 'Ye Lord High Physiographer'.

appointed to head the other party of geologists (the Eastern Geological Party), which included 'Ray' Priestley and biologist Dr Murray Levick. Taylor turned his unloading duties into a test of his own physical strength and a chance to demonstrate the WGP's superiority. At first, they slipped behind 'the famous Eastern Party' in the crew's round-the-clock efforts; it didn't help that Campbell taunted Taylor over his team's failure to pull its weight. However, the tables turned on 15 January. 'At last,' Taylor wrote in his diary, 'we have broken the record and the western glaciologists have teetotally wiped the eye of the eastern party!'[30] Taylor proved to himself and, more importantly, to his fellow explorers that he was no effete scholar but a man among equals.[31]

Once the base was established, Scott instructed the WGP to explore the physiography and geology of South Victoria Land, the British sector of Antarctica recognised since the 1899 International Geographical Conference. Taylor was assigned to lead his men to the Western Mountain region between the Dry Valley and the Koetlitz Glacier, approximately 50 kilometres to the north of Cape Evans. Provisions were allotted for an eight-week trip, with further supplies to be picked up at Hut Point, where Scott's *Discovery* expedition hut, built in 1902, still stood. Equipped with two 'man-hauling' sledges to carry food, fuel, tools, instruments and personal gear (weighing more than half a tonne), Taylor and his party set out on 25 January 1911. 'Wishing you the best of luck,' Scott ended his letter of instruction.[32]

Every successful Antarctic venture requires good luck, as well as survival skills; Taylor succeeded more through the former than the latter. His compatriots on other parties endured fouler weather, more serious illnesses and life-threatening accidents, and overcame challenges far greater than the WGP faced. For Taylor, the challenge was to command respect as a leader, something he had just begun to do as a teacher in Sydney. It helped that he was the eldest of the WGP scientists (Taff Evans was slightly older but was only a petty officer). More significantly, his close association with David and Mawson, combined with his training in geology and glaciation, added to his leadership credentials. Taylor could never outhaul his team members but nor did he have to lean on them for support, as 50-year-old David had earlier relied on Mawson.

Taylor launched into the WGP's first expedition in a bright mood, with a prediction that came true: 'we'll have a ripping time I expect with no more risk than is good for us'.[33] Each scientist in the WGP had his special duties: Wright was to examine and photograph ice crystals; Debenham to survey and collect rock and fossil samples; and Taylor to concentrate on evidence of geomorphological and glaciological processes. 'How has the land surface been affected by the flow of glaciers, by the action of wind, frost, water, and ice?' was the question that drove his research.[34] By applying his knowledge of European and New Zealand Alps he could compare well-documented topographical features in those now-temperate regions to those he was about to sketch and photograph, many for the first time in history. 'Taylor and his merry men were in high spirits with the weather, the scenery and their prospects as they started for the

Ferrar Glacier,' wrote Ponting, perhaps with a tinge of jealousy.[35] But if the photographer was envious of missing the stunning mountain views the WGP would encounter, the scenery mattered little to its leader, who kept his eye on the ground. Taylor oriented himself to Antarctica's physiography in surveyor's terms: '[T]he Antarctic continent is possibly the only mass of land on the Earth's surface which would impress an extra-terrestrial visitor as worthy of notice.'[36] He appreciated that other expedition members had more artistic ways to express emotional responses. Wilson, the zoologist, had the field naturalist's talent for artistry, and his Antarctic watercolours had a mystical quality that evoked his Christian spirituality. Ponting knew how to combine his artistic vision with the technical expertise necessary to create marketable images. Before the WGP set out, Ponting used Taylor and Silas Wright as subjects in what turned out to be his most spectacular image. While the two scientists were out on Cape Evans, exploring tidal action on sea ice, Ponting directed them to climb inside a huge teardrop hole in an iceberg that had suddenly tipped upwards. Positioning the pair in the tunnel, Ponting used the ice walls to frame their silhouettes, with the *Terra Nova* visible a mile in the distance. While Taylor admired the image, he predicted that 'the cinema set' would view the photo as he did: as a study of the 'Glaciologist at work in the Antarctic'.[37]

'I Became a Cartographic Entity!'

Taylor's enthusiasm came out most clearly in his scientific observations. After a five-day, 900-metre ascent of Ferrar Glacier, which afforded views of adjoining glaciers and mountains reaching as high as 4000 metres, the party approached the valley that Professor David had recently visited on the *Nimrod* expedition, and which they were now assigned to analyse in further detail: 'To our surprise ... we found no snow in the adjoining valley!'[38] This meant a treasure trove of geological and biological specimens awaited them. The slopes of the valley were strewn with igneous rocks (primarily granite, felspar and dolerite), showing signs of wind erosion, while evidence of primitive flora and micro-organisms appeared in fossils that Evans helped Debenham to collect. 'No better opportunity for studying the way in which a great glacier has eroded earth's crust can be imagined,' Taylor wrote later in *Antarctic Adventure and Research* (1930). To have 'marched ... mile after mile down this great valley which had never before been traversed by man' was thrilling; no less thrilling was the likelihood that this research would make his name as a man of science.[39]

Applying names to newly discovered features was a recognised right of discovery in this era of desperately competitive exploration. In the Antarctic, explorers encountered an unpeopled space where names had only begun to appear on eighteenth-century coastal maps. By the turn of the twentieth century, as expeditions started to move inland, the naming derby heated up. As party leader, Taylor exercised his right to name the features

they mapped, subject to Scott's final approval. Some names were visually descriptive, such as the 'catspaw' and 'stockings' glaciers; others related to familiar European features, such as 'Luzern Lake'. Then there were the name choices that honoured the men Taylor admired: Davis Valley (for William Davis), and Bonney Lake and Bonney Riegel (for his Cambridge geology mentor, T.G. Bonney). While Professor David's name already adorned a valley and glacier, the name of Taylor had yet to appear, so he determined that the dry valley he had mapped, along with the glacier that lay at its head, would be suitable recipients. Taylor Glacier and Taylor Dry Valley were merely provisional names at this stage but Taylor made no attempt to conceal his delight when the 'Owner' (as they called Scott) later granted his permission: 'I became a cartographic entity!'[40] No matter how scientifically oriented the expedition, Scott's, like others of the era of exploration, was driven by this naming and claiming urge—for King and country, but for heroic individuals as well.

In mid March, the WGP, having completed its exploration of the coast and hinterland between the Koetlitz Glacier to the region just south of Cape Bernacchi, made its way back without serious mishap to Discovery Hut, the temporary winter quarters. They brought sacks full of geological and fossil samples, plus, in Taylor's case, a new theory concerning the evolution of glacier valleys. Aware that geologists studying the Swiss Alps had failed to provide a convincing theory to account for the origins of steps and basins, Taylor believed that his findings in Antarctic glacial valleys provided a plausible explanation. He called it the 'palimpsest theory', and elaborated it with a multistage model to explain how initial cirque erosion is later swamped by expanding outlet glaciers, forming basins. When these glaciers subsequently retreat, in a process of freezing and thawing, they leave valleys whose topography retains the imprint of each episode, rather than fully obliterating earlier ones. This concept led Taylor to an intriguing hypothesis: if 'some such cycle of evolution' was apparent in the south, perhaps the same cycle had occurred in more temperate regions? The palimpsest theory marked a significant imaginative step in Taylor's thinking—less in the substance of his idea than in its underlying conceptualisation, which involved theorisation through metaphor and the application of empirical findings from one region of the world to another, closely related in environmental terms.[41]

Taylor (left, with ice axe) and Charles Wright, 1911. 'Though we scarcely had standing room on the slippery ice, [Herbert] Ponting adjured us to assume the mien of intrepid explorers. When, in London, a year or two later, I eventually saw the result of Ponting's efforts, Wright and I were as the merest specks on the huge berg. You would never have known that our knees were shaking while we occupied this precarious position to satisfy our enthusiastic photographer!' (Taylor, *Journeyman Taylor*, 1958).

Having led his party on a journey of discovery, Taylor now stepped back down to being an assistant. When all of the parties reunited for the winter at Cape Evans in April 1911, daily life involved constant activity. For Taylor, this included filling in as meteorologist when 'Sunny Jim' Simpson, the chief meteorologist, was away on sledging trips, and he found maintaining 'a first-class weather station' arduous work:

> 1. When I hear the automatic signal I have to fly around and mark all the recording instruments to show exactly eight o'clock on their charts.
>
> 2. I read the standard barometer and its attached thermometer.
>
> 3. Change the chronometer papers and put ink into the pens, for the blizzometer, thermograph, barograph and wind velocity charts ...
>
> 4. Wind up the various clocks (once a week, on Monday ...
>
> 5. I stagger up to the top of Wind Vane Hill ... [and] read the anemometer figures alongside the anemometer cups.
>
> 6. Then I press four times on a button alongside, and this is electronically transmitted to the record in the hut, and so gives a datum each day on that record.
>
> 7. I walk across to the screen and read the three thermometers—present, maximum, and minimum ...
>
> 8. By this time three minutes have elapsed, and I return a few paces to the anemometer and read the latter figures again ...
>
> 9. Read the wind direction from the arrow on the hill and note the steam-cloud direction on Erebus.
>
> 10. Change the blue paper in the sunshine recorder and clean the glass sphere ... A slow and painful job at –40°![42]

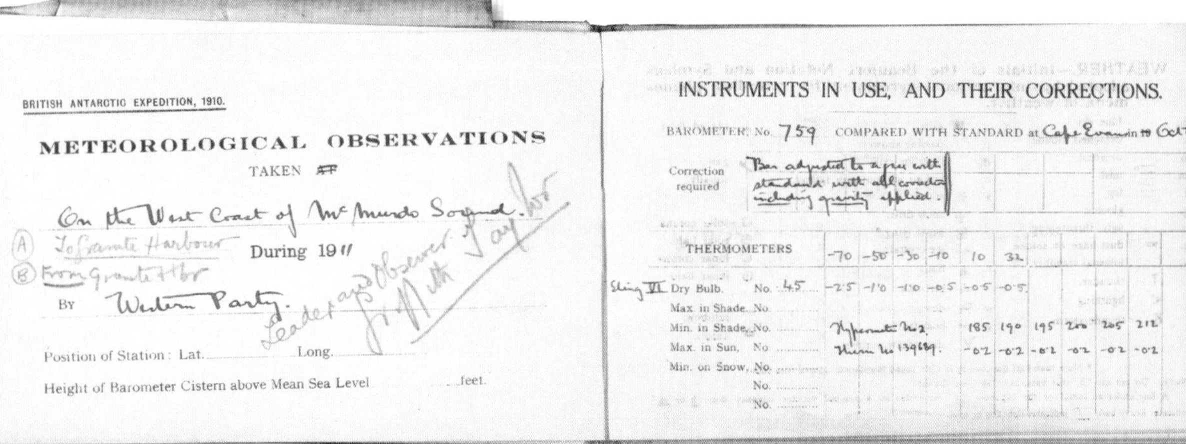

BRITISH ANTARCTIC EXPEDITION, 1910.

METEOROLOGICAL OBSERVATIONS

TAKEN ~~AT~~

On the West Coast of McMurdo Sound.

(A) To Granite Harbour During 1911

(B) From Granite Hbr

BY Western Party.

Leader and Observer Griffith Taylor

Position of Station: Lat. ……… Long. ………

Height of Barometer Cistern above Mean Sea Level ……… feet.

INSTRUMENTS IN USE, AND THEIR CORRECTIONS.

BAROMETER, No. 759 COMPARED WITH STANDARD at Cape Evans in 19 Oct

Correction required: Bar adjusted to agree with standard with all corrections including gravity applied.

THERMOMETERS		-70	-50	-30	-10	10	32
Sling VI Dry Bulb.	No. 45	-2.5	-1.0	-1.0	-0.5	-0.5	-0.5
Max. in Shade.	No.						
Min. in Shade.	No.	185	190	195	200	205	212
Max. in Sun.	No.	-0.2	-0.2	-0.2	-0.2	-0.2	-0.2
Min. on Snow.	No.						
	No.						
	No.						

Our Beauteous Curtains
Secluding the Experts Den

no connection with the bunk — too much gas is there usually

acetylene

N.B.
This table is never so tidy

Very little doing this morning. Not so stiff as on previous "post-footie" days. Watched Dr Bell drawing Suess Glacier for Deb. Sunny Jim translating from diary, latter writes Teilos and Teilos for Silas & so it's diff. to distinguish them. (Deb is writing diary) Notice curtains. The red draws across doorway. My box forms a good seat. Deb is under table. Latter has shelves under head of (wooden) bed, with books & a Microscope. His mattress is too long & reaches into bookshelves at foot. Above is stained venesta with photos. Below Rucksac & a medley of other objects I feared to attempt.

opposite

Meteorology Logbook, 1911. Taylor was employed by the Commonwealth Bureau of Meteorology as well as the British Antarctic Expedition while based in Antarctica. This arrangement required him to record and analyse meteorological as well as geographical data during his posting.

above

'Our Beauteous Curtains Secluding the Experts Den' (diary page from 6 May 1911). After Taylor returned from Antarctica his sister, Dorothy, embroidered a map of MacMurdo Sound on a piece of the curtain fabric he brought back as a souvenir.

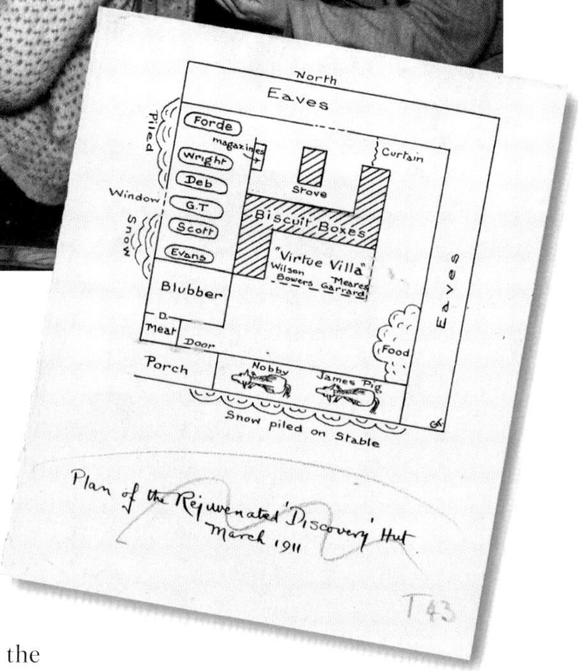

Taylor's data collection helped to establish how trade winds and Antarctic anticyclones (high pressure cells) produced aridity in central Australia, as well as arid northern winters and southern summers.[43] The work fulfilled his Bureau of Meteorology obligations, but he was far keener to get back to his geological studies and the headship of his party.

It was not all serious science for Taylor and the other researchers, however, even if Ponting did photograph him almost invariably bending over a book either reading or writing—more often the latter. The men spent months over the winter packed tightly in confined quarters through the endless darkness and bitter cold. Writing up their field notes and analysing data occupied a great deal of their time when they weren't out hunting seals and penguins or hauling in snow for drinking water. Captain Scott knew that his men needed structured duties and pleasant diversions if they were to remain sane and civil. Taylor pitched in uncomplainingly, helping to maintain the blubber stove and keeping night watch. Although he had a fondness for Cambridge tea and cakes,[44] he

above

Plan of Discovery Hut, 1911. On Scott's earlier expedition to Antarctica in 1902 his men built a hut which Taylor and other members of Captain Scott's second expedition 'rejuvenated' in 1911. The names indicate where expedition members—and two horses—slept in the hut. Taylor was honoured to bunk beside Scott (the Owner).

top

The science wing of Discovery Hut, c.1911. Frank Debenham (left), Raymond Priestley (centre) and Taylor (right) pose for expedition photographer Herbert Ponting.

quickly adapted to polar fare, including fried seal liver and 'hoosh' (a thick stew made from meat, fresh or dried, plus fat, a thickener—usually biscuits or oatmeal—and water). Even when served without a little onion powder or Bovril (added by the expedition's more creative cooks), Taylor's unrefined tastes made him an uncomplaining diner.[45]

Taylor thrived on the intellectual community. 'At lunch we had a discussion on Browning and Tennyson,' he wrote, recalling a day in the Discovery Hut. This discussion was followed several days later by an argument over competing theories of urban design, in which Taylor praised Burley Griffin's radically modern plan for Canberra. By the time the parties reassembled at Cape Evans, Captain Scott decided to build on this culture with a more systematic approach to mental stimulation: three one-hour lectures per week, followed by general discussion on topics that included mineralogy (Debenham), meteorological instruments (Simpson), and tips on sketching (Dr Wilson). Taylor volunteered three talks on physiography, based on his initial research in the Australian Capital Territory conducted just prior to the expedition. 'Taylor, I dreamt of your lecture last night,' the Owner reportedly exclaimed after one of his chief geologist's physiography talks. 'How could I live so long in the world and not know something of so fascinating a subject!'[46] Apparently the remark was delivered without irony, or at least Taylor registered it as genuine. Only he and the other scientists attended every lecture, prompting them to confer the title 'Universitas Antarctica' on their educational series.[47] The crewmen opted for six-handed euchre games instead, and everyone, even Taylor, indulged in the occasional football match on ice. Scott, meanwhile, remained the stern captain. In a letter Taylor sent home to his 'people', marked 'private', he gave his frank opinion of the man. Relations among the men were 'wonderfully harmonious', he thought, with:

> the only disturbing element being—my opinion—our esteemed leader! However he's O.K. if you 'watch his moods' as Sunny Jim says. I don't and one or two of us have been under a cloud in consekens. Still he has all the worry on his shoulders and doesn't mean as much as he says.[48]

This sketch, by John Murray, shows a 'bold explorer' chasing penguins. On the edge of a crevice he is about to play his part in the cycle of life, from diatom to killer whale.

The final stanza of Taylor's poem reads:
'So the protoplasm passes
on its never-ceasing round,
Like a huge recurring decimal;
to which no end is found.'

Taylor's ice axe, British Antarctic Expedition, 1910–1913. For geologists working in Antarctica an ice axe was an essential tool. Taylor customised his by carving his initials and the expedition's title into the wooden handle.

Taylor never expressed such misgivings publicly. Even after Scott's death he would continue to respect the captain's rank.

The ability to get along peaceably with others—up to 23 men, with their stores and laboratories, in a hut measuring 380 square metres—was never more critical than over the Antarctic winter. Taylor spent the entire winter of 1911 with most of the men at the base, while three members (Wilson, Cherry-Garrard and seaman 'Birdie' Bowers) undertook a nightmarish mid-winter trip to an Emperor penguin colony at Cape Crozier, in order to obtain eggs, then understood to provide critical evidence for the study of evolution. Battling monstrous blizzards and the lowest temperatures ever endured by Antarctic explorers, the party returned (with the eggs unbroken) to the warmth and conviviality of hut life. As Cherry-Garrard recovered, he wrote character sketches of the men around him, including Taylor: a 'greedy scientist' who 'also wielded a fluent pen'. What struck him most clearly was that the man never stopped: 'When his pen was still, his tongue wagged, and the arguments he led were legion.' Though irritating at times, Taylor's nervous energy ultimately endeared him to his colleagues: 'The hut was a merrier place for his presence.' To the officers and scientists he was a likeable, even lovable, eccentric: 'His gaunt, untamed appearance was atoned for by a halo of good-fellowship which hovered about his head.'[49]

Taylor's merriness slipped into dangerous foolishness, however, when he set out in October 1911 on a bicycle that the expedition's motor sledge engineer, Bernard Day, had brought from New Zealand. Scott knew of Taylor's earlier bicycle trip in the French Alps in the autumn of 1909, when he and three mates rode almost to the icy summit of the Puy de Dôme, so he permitted his chief geologist to attempt a solo 40-kilometre round trip to examine curious erosion patterns. Before Taylor even reached his destination of Glacial Tongue, though, the bicycle became 'an exhausting encumbrance', and he had to walk it.[50] He clambered over the ice tongue to examine promontories and bays and cliff outcrops but once he turned back, exhaustion struck hard. He knew that stopping in the intense cold meant certain death but he couldn't move. Fortuitously, his mate Silas was conducting research nearby and, despite his short-sightedness, he managed to spot the stranded cyclist. Confronted by a stern captain after Wright helped him back to the hut, Taylor vowed that 'the first bicycle ride in the Antarctic should be [his] last'.[51] Still, it was he who had been 'the first', and the venture left him with an entertaining story for his post-expedition career (rejuvenated in 1961, when a New Zealand team involved in the refurbishment of the huts near Mt Erebus would discover the mangled remains of a bicycle frame).[52]

This brush with disaster in 1911 was the first of two incidents that might easily have led Taylor to his death. In both instances he had luck on his side. The second near-disaster occurred at the end of the second WGP expedition, in which Taylor, along with Debenham, Tryggve ('Trigger') Gran and petty officer Forde journeyed to Granite Harbour, approximately 80 kilometres north of the Taylor Dry Valley at 77 degrees latitude. This party left base on 5 November 1911, five days after Scott and his polar party had departed, never to return. As the WGP made its way past Taylor Dry Valley up the coast of MacMurdo Sound, Taylor used a theodolite to fix distant mountain peaks accurately while Debenham used a plane table to plot the outline of the land and its principal physiographic features. On this trip Debenham earned himself a glacier. Of their accomplishments on this expedition, Taylor would boast: 'I think we brought back from our sledging trip an Antarctic survey unique for its completeness in the field.'[53] By 30 November, they had established a base camp at the southern end of Granite Harbour, just in time to celebrate Taylor's thirty-first birthday. From that position, they conducted extensive geological and topographic surveys of the harbour, then sledged

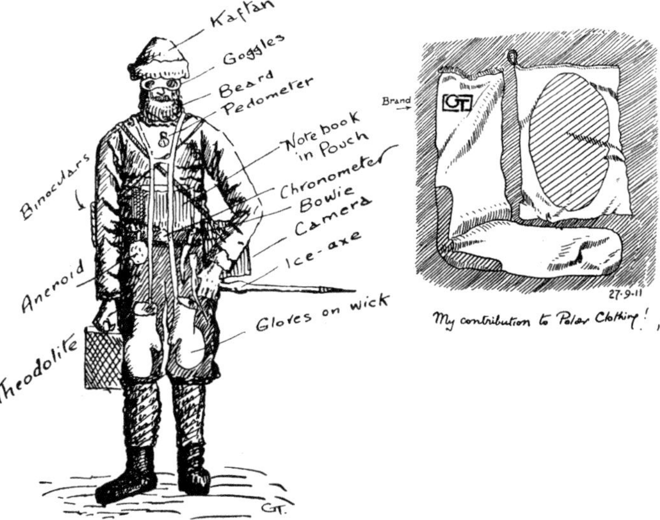

right

Taylor often mocked (and never followed) fashion conventions. For his memoir, *With Scott: The Silver Lining* (1916), he itemised the scientific and sartorial accoutrements of 'The Compleat Explorer'.

far right

This sketch appeared in Taylor's *With Scott: The Silver Lining* (1916). GT, Taylor's logo, marked all of his polar gear, including his socks.

up the Mackay Glacier and ascended 1200-metre Mount Suess, where he and Deb discovered a large deposit of coal as well as fossil-bearing sandstone. Before leaving, Trigger and Taylor climbed Discovery Bluff, 150 metres above their base, in order to secure a signal flag to a pole along with a note for Captain Pennell of the *Terra Nova*: Scott's instructions for Taylor were that his party explore the inland region of Granite Harbour until 8 January; Pennell was instructed to pick the men up on the 15th.

Taylor made sure to arrive at the pick-up point on time, but the party saw no sign of the ship in the harbour. This left him with a leader's dilemma: whether to stay put where the ship had been instructed to meet them, or lead his men back to a point where the ship might more easily see them, and gamble that they would neither starve nor succumb to the cold as the summer sun sank lower in the sky. Taylor resolved to move his party almost 15 kilometres east to Cape Roberts, where they did spot the *Terra Nova* offshore. However, hope slipped to desperation once they realised that the ship was too far away for the crew to spot the signal flag. Twenty-five kilometres of ice separated them, he wrote in his diary on 20 January, but it wasn't yet solid: 'We could not get out to the ship even with a light sledge.' The *Terra Nova* shunted back and forth along the coast, slipping

in and out of view in the ice fog while the men gainlessly waved the flag and marched it along the glacier. With their rations dwindling and the temperature dropping, Taylor held 'a council of war' on 1 February. With his men's consent, he developed a plan to attempt the entire return journey by sledge, via the Piedmont Glacier. Keeping watch for the *Terra Nova* along the way, the party sledged back down towards the coast at Cape Bernacchi, then circled New Harbour and the tongue of the Ferrar Glacier. Under such anxious circumstances gloom could easily have settled in, but not with this group: Trigger remained light-hearted, his talent for reciting adventure stories earning him the title 'Society Entertainer'; Deb and Taylor continued to play chess with cardboard pieces; and, over those anxious weeks, Taylor read his copy of *Martin Chuzzlewit*—'for the ninth time and found it, as always, very interesting'.[54] Relief finally came on 15 February, at the edge of the sea ice north of Cape Chocolate, where the ship spotted them and managed to get them on board, weather-worn but in good health and spirits. Taylor was fortunate that he hadn't had to meet the harrowing challenges his fellow party leaders faced—Wilson at Cape Crozier, Campbell at Cape Adare, and Scott at the South Pole. Under such circumstances his good spirits might have flagged; instead, his halo still hovered.

opposite

The Second Geological Party, 1912 (from left: Gran, Debenham, Taylor and seaman Forde). Although the *Terra Nova* was scheduled to pick up the Second Geological Party on 15 January 1912, it took another month before Taylor and his men could sight and board the ship. Over that anxious month he kept up his spirits by playing chess with Frank Debenham and by reading his copy of *Martin Chuzzlewit* 'for the ninth time'.

right

Taylor posed in his polar gear for the expedition's photographer, Herbert Ponting, c.1911. He is standing in front of one of the sledges that expedition members 'man-hauled' across the Antarctic.

New Horizons

While rescue offered relief it also signalled the beginning of the end for Taylor and several other expedition members who had now completed their missions. 'What does it feel like to be in touch with civilization after a year's absence?', he wondered on his return journey to Lyttelton, New Zealand. His reorientation to Australia began in his cabin, where a pillowcase full of letters and parcels from home awaited him. Cakes, sweets and nuts made a welcome change after half-rations of seal meat and ship biscuits. A belated birthday present from Professor David—the 1911 satirical novel *Queed*—offered Taylor an alternative to attacking *Martin Chuzzlewit* a tenth time. But he also got straight to work, by transcribing Sunny Jim's meteorological data and comparing those readings to the barometric and temperature data he had charted throughout his journeys in the Western Mountains: just the task an employee of the Bureau of Meteorology might do.

With each degree of latitude crossed moving further north, Taylor approached the explorer's greatest challenge: after this, after *all* of this, what next? Life as a public servant was the less than appealing answer. Formally, Taylor's new base would be Melbourne, the provisional seat of the Commonwealth Government and the Bureau's headquarters. Fortunately, however, his services as a physiographer were still in demand in the federal territory, so he had barely arrived before he left again to conduct further fieldwork. Never comfortable with the thought of remaining with the Bureau of Meteorology, he pursued other leads, driven by restlessness and ambition. The most promising was the prospect

The Taylor family, 1912 (back row from left: Evan, Lily and Taylor; front row from left: Jeff, James, Dorothy [Pal] and Rhys). After Taylor returned from Antarctica, his family reunited and spent a short holiday midway through 1912 at Thirroul, on the coast of New South Wales.

of a two-year contract as director of the Geological Survey of the Federal Capital, for which he would have been the obvious choice. There was also the possibility that the newly established University of Western Australia might appoint a foundation professor of geology. On 24 November 1912, he wrote from Canberra to Captain Scott about his plans, confessing that his work duties, plus pre-existing publishing contracts, made it difficult to devote much time to writing up his Antarctic research. He looked forward to his scheduled trip to England in 1913, when he could work with some of the other expedition scientists under Scott's direction. 'I would like very much to get a month in England when all the fellows meet again, and it might be managed,' he pledged to his leader. Indeed, the very obliging Bureau had agreed in advance to grant him a year's leave once all members returned from the expedition. In February 1913, however, he learned that his plans would have to change: the polar party had perished after reaching the South Pole weeks after Amundsen had been first to arrive. 'Undelivered owing to the sad death of Captain Scott' was the official notice Taylor received from Scott's secretary, along with his unopened letter.

The effects of Scott's fatal journey were far wider in reach than the impact on the surviving British Antarctic Expedition (BAE) members and the widows and families of the five fallen men. All England, it seemed, mourned its martyrs and exalted the stoic manliness and self-sacrifice they embodied. Clements Markham, president of the Royal Geographical Society, and Scott's widow, Lady Kathleen, nurtured that image and worked hard to keep the dead hero's memory alive and venerated. Taylor felt the loss as well but looked on the bright side of the tragedy: science. He did so with the official expedition histories and scientific papers he prepared under the supervision of British Museum authorities, in addition to the papers in geographical and geological journals published under his own name. There were also his *Argus* articles, written 'by the Australian scientific member of the Scott expedition', which appeared in April and May 1911. The papers sold out instantly and won him acclaim as well as an impressive £100 fee. He contributed to the official account, *Scott's Last Expedition* (1913), on the physiography and geology of South Victoria Land.[55] Although the volume was dry in title, his submission was written in the style that Scott's and Shackleton's earlier volumes had perfected—the popular genre of scientific observation narrative. The *Times Literary Supplement* pointed to Taylor's contribution as the best at providing a lively verbal picture of the BAE.[56] Taylor planned to take this one step further by focusing on the more pleasurable aspects of the expedition. Concerned, though, that his lighter touch might offend Lady Scott, he wrote to explain his approach:

> my account will be colloquial and, I fear, will differ greatly from Captain Scott's in literary style. However he himself paid me the finest compliment about my writing ... You will gather the type of book from my a/c of the ship-life in the *Argus*—which I propose to incorporate. I am sure you will find the book interesting and I trust not unworthy of the great enterprise in which I am more and more proud to have had a part.[57]

While Taylor started to work on his popular account, Raymond Priestley began a book of his own (later published as *Antarctic Research*, 1914). The authors had much to discuss aboard the *Mongolia*, the ship they took to England in May 1913, for a reunion of surviving expeditioners.

All but a few of the survivors gathered for the occasion—the presentation of the King's Polar Medal, held at Buckingham Palace, on 26 July 1913. Griffith Taylor, the son of a former mill worker, was about to meet King George V. But what to wear? The Navy men wore their dress uniforms but the scientists had to find their own wardrobe. The Priestley men came to Taylor's rescue, with Raymond's uncle providing spats, and his father lending Taylor a top hat. Every member, including the *Terra Nova*'s crew, was rewarded, and those who had landed received a medal with a special bar, marked '1910 to 1913'. Relatives of those who had died were also invited to the ceremony, which added a sombre note to the august occasion. There was nothing, though, that could dampen Taylor's spirits. In spite of the fact that his left-leaning positions in Antarctic debates had prompted the more conservative Antarctickers to nickname him 'Keir Hardie' (after the socialist founder of the Labour Party and advocate of women's suffrage), the self-described 'Liberal Socialist' proudly puffed out his 36½-inch chest to receive his medal from the King.[58]

'Geologists jolly, we three, Debenham, Raymond & me!', 1913. Taylor gave Doris Priestley, his fiancée, this image of the Polar Medal recipients, taken after they received their honours from King George V. Taylor had to ask his future brother-in-law, Raymond Priestley, to supply him with clothing suitable for an appearance at Buckingham Palace.

Geologists jolly, we three
Debenham, Raymond & me!
from Griff
26.7.13.

Prior to his palace appearance, Taylor had visited Priestley's family home, where he finished editing his diary entries on the Granite Harbour expedition into a narrative. Earlier in June and July, he had stayed at Cherry-Garrard's home (Lamer), while working on his account of the Western Geological Party's first expedition. The surroundings were grander than the Priestley household but the latter included Doris, Raymond's younger sister, who found her elder brother's quirky Australian Antarctic mate attractive. The men had had plenty of opportunity to discuss their sisters. When Dorothy Taylor had seen the men off at Lyttelton in 1910, the two women were a study in contrast: Pal was a 28-year-old geologist, heavy-set and 5 foot 6 inches tall, Doris was a diminutive 15-year-old. Taylor barely noticed her at first, as he admitted in *Journeyman Taylor*:

> After the royal presentation, Priestley, Debenham, and I, to the clicking of cameras and the joy of innumerable onlookers, walked together to the Caxton Hall, where the surviving members of our Expedition met for the last time, and our organisation was formally disbanded. Among the onlookers, although I did not happen to see her, was Doris Priestley.[59]

Spending two months with the family made all the difference, and he later captioned a photo of the Polar Medallists for her, 'Geologists jolly, we three, Debenham, Raymond & me!'. At 32 years old, Taylor, for the first time, contemplated the prospect of marriage. Doris's father worried about his young daughter's naivety and inexperience; however, he granted them permission to marry. In October, the couple announced their engagement and their plans to settle in Australia the following year.

My Dearest Lassie

Once Taylor found his life partner, he became an ardent and impatient suitor. At the same time, he recognised that setting up a household with a woman who had grown up in a comfortable home would be an expensive business. Writing a popular book on the Scott expedition was one way to generate money, but a quicker one was to give illustrated lectures. In late 1913, he gave 10 public talks in England to promote his book, which was still in manuscript. Because these talks, featuring 100 lantern slides produced from Ponting's images, had 'aroused enthusiasm',[60] he explored their commercial potential further afield. Interest in polar exploration remained intense around the world, due largely to the publicity surrounding Scott's death and Amundsen's coup. He was helped in his endeavours by a positive reference from the highest-ranking survivor of the expedition, Lieutenant Evans. He and a manager arranged for Taylor to deliver a series of talks in South Africa. Evans's endorsement highlighted Taylor's part in an expedition rich in imperial meaning:

> Mr Griffith Taylor commanded two of the most important independent sledging parties that left our winter quarters ... It will be a splendid opportunity for those who have assisted our expedition in the Overseas dominions to hear from one of its prominent members the story of Captain Scott's undying heroism. Griffith Taylor has a natural aptitude for expressing himself well as a lecturer and I feel sure that the lectures he delivers will do much to tighten the bonds of Empire.[61]

The only problem with the tour, which began at the end of January 1914, was that it strained the bond between the betrothed couple. Taylor and Doris had wished to marry prior to his departure, but her father refused. It was one thing to resist his own parents' career plans; it was quite another for Taylor to anger his future in-laws with an impetuous elopement.

The Priestleys were a rather formidable clan, both in size and status. The father was headmaster at Tewkesbury Grammar School, and he and his wife, Henrietta, ran the household of eight children along strict Methodist principles. By the standards of Cherry-Garrard's grand home, they lived modestly on the banks of the Avon; measured by scientific standards, however, they stood tall. Apart from Raymond, whom Taylor had first met as a junior geologist but quickly came to respect as an equal, there was Bert, the botanist, on his way to a professorship. There was also their forebear, Sir Joseph Priestley, a proponent of civil and religious liberty, who had been knighted for discovering oxygen gas in 1774. Despite his scholarship and the royal recognition received for his work as an Antarctic scientist, Taylor was anxious to assure Doris that

Taylor and Doris, 1913. Doris Priestley was acting as an academic secretary for her older brother, Bert, a botanist, when she met Taylor. As the couple began to court in 1913, they spent many hours together, editing his Antarctic memoirs for his book, eventually published in 1916 as *With Scott: The Silver Lining.*

he came with his own science pedigree. He followed the courtship custom of providing a photograph of himself but also gave her one of his father, James. On the back he wrote a brief resumé:

> My Father James Taylor
>
> BSc. Wh.S. A.R.S.M. FCS
>
> Demonstrator for Sir Henry Roscoe Manchester 1878
> all sorts of gold medallists in Physics, Maths Chem and Engin g
> Head Chemist Firths' Lab
> Shet Works Sheffield, 1881–93
> Government Metallurgist 93–1900
> etc. etc.
>
> And the merriest simple liver alive
> He's not half so terrible as I but you can't marry him!
>
> T[62]

If Doris could overlook the fact that the Taylor men were comparative newcomers in the pantheon of science, he hoped to reassure her, and himself, that he approached the Priestleys as an intellectual equal.

When Taylor left for South Africa on 28 January 1914, the couple faced a six-month separation before their planned reunion and marriage in Melbourne. This was less a hiatus in their relationship, however, than the continuance of a connection made through words, which had started at the Priestley dining room table, where they'd sat close together, bent over an early draft of 'With Scott, the Silver Lining'. When Doris had turned 14, her father had determined that her older brother Bert (later professor of botany at the University of Leeds) would profit from her assistance as an academic secretary, so she was well trained in editing and correcting manuscripts by the time Taylor arrived. The letters he wrote to her as he travelled down the west coast of Africa (delivering 12 lectures in Cape Town, Port Elizabeth, Durban, Johannesburg and Pietermarizburg) revealed a different Taylor—warm, loving and entranced by his bride-to be:

> My dear little lady if you know anyone so staunch and true and industrious and honest and pretty and varsity and active and clerical and Priestleyish and explorery and housewifey and matey as Doris—why—I'll marry her.

Although she was blessed with so many admirable qualities, they were both aware that her formal education had ended once she'd begun to assist her brother. Not to worry: 'What's the good of being a tutor husband if I don't tute?' In this role he offered her 'indefinite time, and a love for his pupil and I believe some ability to teach'. Any feelings of inferiority she might harbour at this point would soon fade, he predicted: 'She shall learn all I can teach her.'[63]

One of the things Doris had to learn was that she was marrying a religious sceptic. She wrote to him about her religious beliefs; he wrote back with his rationalist critique of religion: 'Philosophy is religion for a Scientist ... I meant that the dreamy irrational side of religion attracts no trained scientist.' He would not ask her to abandon her beliefs as long as she respected his. 'We are here to assist evolution; not to earn a crown of glory and sing hymns to eternity.'[64] Taylor's creed was simple and it offered a prescription for the next generation as well: 'the true aim of life is to leave the world happier than you found it—with (necessarily) well trained descendents to carry out the work'.[65] In their

opposite left

Drawing of Doris Priestley's engagement ring (Taylor, *With Scott: The Silver Lining*, 1916). Designed by Captain Scott's widow, sculptor Lady Kathleen Scott, the ring was set with a piece of green marble, which Professor Edgeworth David had given Taylor, after taking it from Beardmore Glacier while serving with Shackleton's *Nimrod* expedition to Antarctica. She 'advised a border of Saxon design round a central D, a device executed by an artistic jeweller, without in the least spoiling the smooth surface produced by the blizzards of the Plateau' (Taylor, *Journeyman Taylor*, 1958).

opposite right

Taylor the suitor, dressed in his best clothes. This photo, taken in 1913, is stamped Tewkesbury, the Gloucestershire town where the Priestleys lived.

shared future, each would fulfil a complementary role: he would strive and she would guide—both him and their children:

> There be two words that guide the strong man's life
> and one is STRIFE ...
> The other word is WIFE.
> She is the living guide that e'er doth bide
> To modulate the movements of a man
> and if God wills it so—then may their children grow
> To carry on their work another span.[66]

Until that time, he looked forward to their union as a combination of 'the two things I've loved best—cags and yarns at Cambridge and the presence of my dear girl interested in "things that matter"'. Few women would share his eagerness to spend evenings together discussing German, Greek, history and botany, but his 'Dearest Lass' was special 'coz she's a Priestley, with fighting blood'.[67]

Science, exploration and marriage also linked another member of Scott's Antarctic team to the Priestleys, when 'Silas' Wright married another Priestley sister, Edith, in 1914. This union created what Taylor called a 'triple alliance' between the three polar scientists, soon to be brothers-in-law. The men called the Priestley sisters 'honorary Antarctickers', both through their families of origin as well as their marriages. Taylor bestowed the honour on Doris symbolically, with an engagement ring designed by Lady Scott. Rather than a diamond, its stone was taken from a watch-chain pendant that Professor David had given Taylor—a fossil-bearing green marble which the professor had collected on the *Nimrod* expedition from the top of Beardmore Glacier. Like the male Adelie penguins depositing pebbles before females in their mating rituals, Taylor courted Doris Antarctic-style, and she responded, sharing his fascination with the Antarctic throughout their marriage.

The Silver Lining

When Taylor's South African tour ended in March 1914, he sailed to Melbourne, where he awaited Doris's scheduled arrival in June. Happily, his lectures had earned him enough to buy her a grand piano,[68] and he looked forward to earning further royalties after Smith Elder, a prestigious English publisher, said it would publish his Antarctic manuscript. Because Leonard Huxley, who had edited the official Scott volume (*Scott's Last Expedition*) had enjoyed Taylor's contribution to it he agreed to edit his manuscript, with the allowance that he be given leave to trim 'the pages where your pen has run away with you in sheer exuberance of spirit'.[69] Taylor agreed, well aware of his 'vice' for what 'the Greeks called *kako èthès scribendí* = the itch for writing'.[70] Captain Scott had earlier noted the same in a letter to Edgeworth David writing that Taylor's 'fertile brain and prolific pen would yield a maximum result'.[71] Scott was right to think in terms of volume: Taylor's manuscript was 200 000 words in length, and included dozens of photographs and over 100 maps and pen-and-ink sketches.[72] This left Huxley with a taxing editorial job, and also allowed Mawson to scoop Taylor again with his Antarctic memoir, *Home of the Blizzard*, which was published to great acclaim in 1915. It took another year for Smith Elder to produce *With Scott*, a delay due as much to the war as to Taylor's 'prolific pen'.

After war engulfed the world, interest in Scott's polar journey began to wane. What did the deaths of one band of brave men amount to, next to the sacrifice of tens of thousands? All of the men who served on Scott's expedition asked themselves this question, and most responded by serving as soldiers. Doris's brother Bert signed up and served in France from 1914 to 1918; Raymond served as well, and his work with the signal corps in France earned him a Military Cross. Charles Wright, now Taylor's brother-in-law, joined the Royal Engineers, the first step in what became a military career; he too was awarded the Military Cross and an OBE by the war's end. Only a year after he returned from the Australasian Antarctic Expedition, Mawson joined the British Munitions Ministry and quickly rose through the ranks as a chemical expert. Even Professor David traded his academic gown for a uniform. In 1916, at the age of 58, he volunteered with the Australian Imperial Force, serving on the Western Front with the mining corps and applying his expertise in military geological mapping for trenches and the laying of mines. When he returned to Australia, he was hailed a hero, having been awarded a Distinguished Service Order and a promotion to the rank of Lieutenant Colonel.

Taylor was the odd man out of this group—a perfectly fit 33-year-old who served only as a public servant. In his work with the Bureau he may have been considered an essential worker, especially after his services were seconded by the Commonwealth flight school shortly after war was declared. Other more personal factors likely played a greater role. When Britain declared war on Germany, he and Doris were not even a month into their marriage. Doris had left England for Australia in May 1914, accompanied by Edgeworth David's wife, Cara, acting as chaperone. Shortly after Doris landed in Australia, the couple were married on 8 July at the University of Melbourne's Queen's College Chapel, with Mrs David filling in for the bride's mother and the professor giving Doris away. With his young bride far from home and without a network of family or friends, the prospect of leaving for a war would have been particularly painful. Yet Taylor left no evidence to suggest he had found it difficult not to join the service; instead he was content to contribute to the war effort without fighting. He served by putting his map reading and meteorological expertise to use as a flying school instructor for Australia's first military pilots, and the closest he came to active service was to toss war bond posters from a plane buzzing above Melbourne.[73] Patriotism from a distance was the Taylor family approach to war: the Taylor men were not keen on soldiering and the

Taylor women seem not to have minded. In Dorothy Taylor's biography of their father, James, she described him proudly as a 'non-military minded Britisher'.[74]

After marrying, the Taylors settled in a small house in the semi-rural suburb of Heidelberg, north-east of Melbourne's centre. 'Doris is taking to housekeeping like a duck,' the groom reported happily to his sister. 'But there's rather a lot of it and charwomen are scarce. I do boots and fires and cut wood.'[75] Domestic life and Taylor's career aspirations improved through the connections he cultivated with members of the University of Melbourne's professorial staff and their families, just as he had done in Sydney and Cambridge. Prominent professors and their wives took the couple's welfare to heart, especially after Doris discovered, early in 1916, that she was to have a child. Among their friends and advisors were David Orme Masson, professor of chemistry, and his wife Mary (both awarded CBEs in 1918). Sir Baldwin Spencer (foundation chair of biology at Melbourne and one of the leading anthropologists of central Australian Aboriginal peoples) and his wife, Lady Lillie, also became close friends of the family. Spencer, a Lancashire man, had graduated, like Taylor's father, from Owens College, and took a fatherly interest in the couple.

On 28 August 1916, five months after Taylor received his doctoral degree for his Antarctic research, and shortly after *With Scott* appeared, the Taylors' first child was born—a healthy 8½-pound boy. Doris was exhausted by her ordeal but Taylor was elated: together they had now established the much anticipated Taylor–Priestley line. While he gave the new mother a book to relax (volume 1 of Viscount Bryce's *A History of All Nations from Earliest Times to the Present*), he wrote Mater excitedly with an assessment of her first grandson: 'Nurse says he's one her best babies and comments on his firm flesh and big hands and feet—!' He tucked a lock of the baby's hair into the envelope along with a further endorsement: 'He has the Taylor big toe—though Dr Davenport declares this is no sign of advanced evolution. But he's wrong!'[76] Officially, the parents named their baby Griffith Priestley Taylor, to honour both families; unofficially, they called him 'Bill' after 'Uncle Bill' Wilson, the kindly senior scientist who had perished along with Scott on the polar journey.

Taylor, *With Scott: The Silver Lining*, 1916. Leonard Huxley commissioned Taylor to write his memoir of the Scott expedition but he warned the loquacious author: 'Give me leave to use my editorial judgement in ... trimming the pages where your pen has run away with you in sheer exuberance of spirit'.

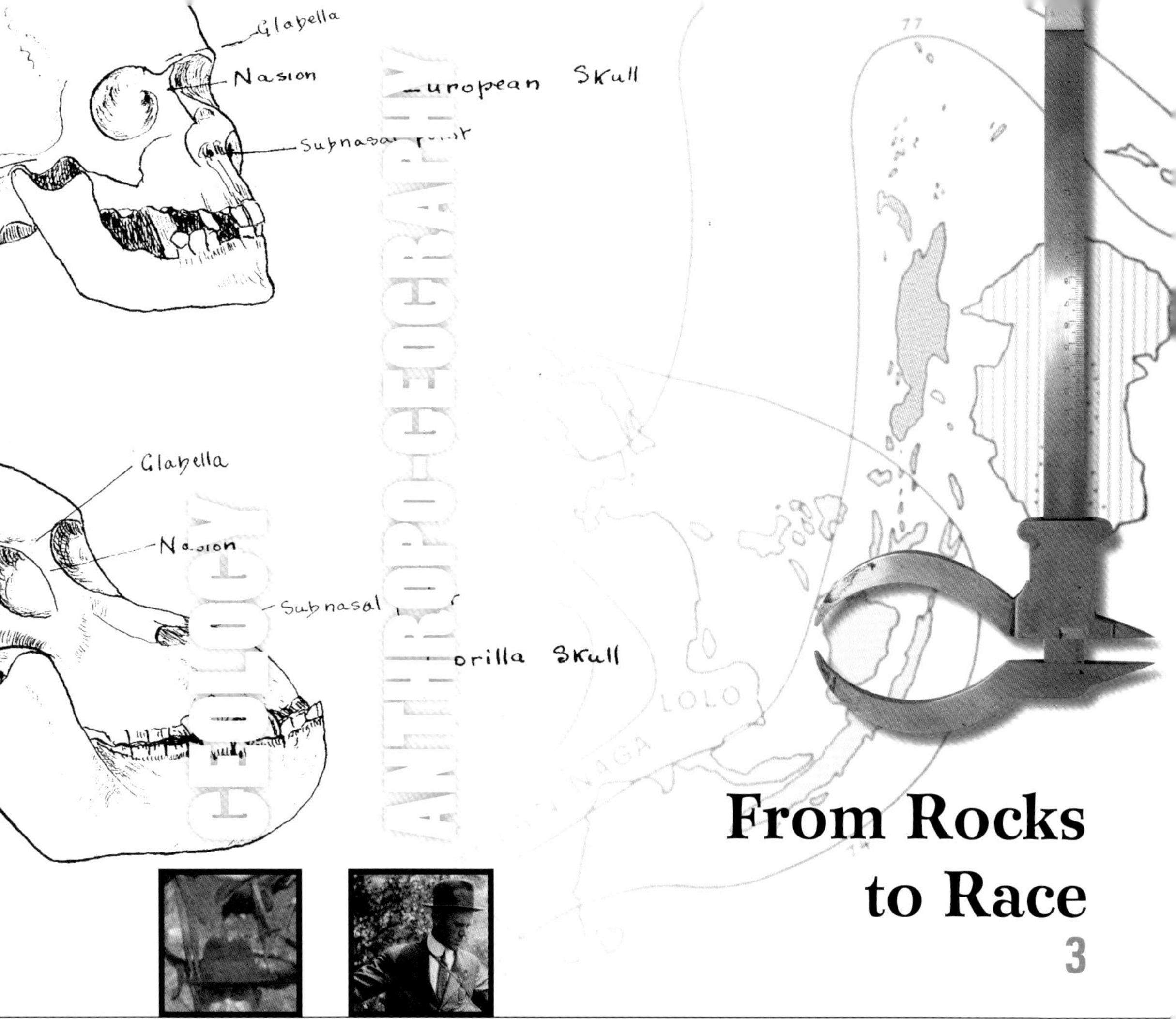

From Rocks to Race

3

Despite Taylor's contribution to 'the silver lining' of Antarctic science, his work was never recognised with a knighthood or membership of the prestigious Royal Society in London, as was the case with several of his polar associates. He certainly chased these goals, though. In 1949, on the cusp of retirement, he wrote to distinguished geographer and anthropologist Herbert John Fleure FRS, with whom he had developed a friendly professional relationship. Once again, he was inquiring about the prospect of his appointment to the Royal Society. His old friend Sir Douglas Mawson would support him; indeed, Taylor assured Fleure that Mawson would 'press hard for my election'. So would Sir George ('Sunny Jim') Simpson. When he turned to define his contribution to science, however, Taylor downplayed his Antarctic research and highlighted his subsequent and more voluminous writings on race:

> I feel that these studies are more worthy of recognition than my earlier work on geology in the Antarctic, or of Paleontology for Australia—though these won me a number of medals and prizes some 30 years ago.[1]

In many respects he was right.

Over the 1910s and 1920s, Taylor moved from studying the planet's coldest environment to analysing some of its hottest—the tropics and the deserts of Australia. The shift involved an intellectual reorientation as well. In 1910, when he was on the payroll of both the British Antarctic Expedition and the Bureau of Meteorology, Taylor defined himself as a natural scientist trained in geology and palaeontology; over the following decade he became, in addition, a human scientist, a geographer and ethnographer deeply interested in race. Had Taylor followed in his mentor Edgeworth David's footsteps as a geology professor, he might have trodden a narrower, more predictable scholarly path. But the Bureau job, which he accepted grudgingly, ended up catapulting him into unforeseen places, professionally and intellectually, and in ways he did not foresee.

Taylor was enlisted in the Bureau to study Australia's climate and assess the prospect of white settlement, a question then dramatically alive in Australian policy and national culture.[2] Considering contemporary race and settlement issues turned Taylor's mind back to his earlier student interest in the 'Antiquity of Man', which evolved into elaborate theories concerning climate, the origin of humans and the evolution of races. Taylor was not content simply to *theorise* race, however. Once he traded his Melbourne Bureau job for his post as professor of geography at the University of Sydney in 1920, Taylor began to connect his work on the 'Antiquity of Man' to the anthropological study of present-day humans: Australian Aboriginal people, whom he considered primitive. No longer a geologist focused on fossil remains, Taylor replaced his rock hammers with cephalic callipers in the 1920s, setting off for rural New South Wales and Queensland to gauge the physical and cultural characteristics of Indigenous people. These studies culminated in his magnum opus, *Environment and Race*, published in 1927, just before he moved from the University of Sydney to the University of Chicago.

Energised by curiosity and driven by ambition, Taylor strode into fields that could not be more expansive—encompassing the globe and the evolution of man, from deep time to the present. This was his very large canvas by the 1920s. If Taylor's route from rock study to racial scrutiny could hardly match the Scott expedition for drama in the eyes of others, for Taylor, claiming intellectual ground by addressing old questions in novel ways was a journey every bit as thrilling.

Climate and White Australia: Taylor the Physiographer

Although Taylor always referred to himself as the Scott expedition's 'senior geologist', he dutifully fulfilled his contracted Bureau of Meteorology obligations while stationed in Antarctica in 1911 and 1912. The data he collected, primarily at Cape Evans, supplemented evidence gathered by Bernacchi and others on earlier expeditions, which had allowed scientists to begin to determine the influence of Antarctica on weather systems in the Southern Hemisphere, particularly in Australia. Geologists, including Professor David and Melbourne geology professor John Walter Gregory (author of *The Climate of Australasia: In Reference to Its Control by the Southern Ocean*, 1904), were at the forefront of this research, and both became leading experts through their participation in Antarctic expeditions.[3]

Had Taylor considered meteorology to be as intriguing as geology he would have been well-positioned to develop a career in this field, but his meteorological research in Antarctica bored him. In a frank letter (marked 'private') written from the hut at Cape Evans, he had updated his People:

> For the government I have copied out the meteor:log and have done all I could at meteorol.; I can now send up [weather] Balloons for high level work and have run a first-class station ... I don't think they'll get £450 worth thro' my presence, but if they didn't know that they should have!

As a returning employee of the Bureau of Meteorology in 1914, he was off to an unpromising start. Working at Bureau headquarters made him even more anxious about his new identity as a public servant. In May 1914, Taylor received a stern letter from the usually gracious Professor David, advising him, 'as your old teacher', to settle down to his duties. 'I am taking the privilege of telling you frankly' that the Bureau chief, Henry Ambrose Hunt, was 'very disappointed that you seem, particularly since your return from your last trip to England, to have lost interest in Meteorology as a distinct subject'.[4] David and Hunt were right: Taylor had no use for 'pondering the vagaries of weather',[5] even if he noted daily Melbourne temperatures and wind directions in his diary alongside his and Doris's tennis and card-playing dates with public service and university couples. Hunt and his wife were frequent bridge partners with the Taylors in their early years in Melbourne but the two men's relationship showed signs of strain at a professional level. Taylor was unwilling to surrender the independence to which he had become accustomed as a Cambridge researcher and as leader of the Western Geological Party. Although Hunt and Taylor shared a similar background (born in England, fathers engineers, boyhoods spent overseas), Hunt was a career public servant, a reserved man and a careful administrator, who expected his staff to follow orders as diligently as he did.[6] Supervising an ambitious employee with a long list of publications and academic degrees (adding Doctor of Science in 1916) was a trial for both, especially since the junior man loved the limelight and courted it by writing newspaper articles alongside his Bureau publications.

Throughout his tenure at the Bureau, Taylor outproduced and outshone his boss. At the time of his hiring in 1910, he was already contributing chapters to the *Oxford Survey of the British Empire*. His *Australia in Its Physiographic and Economic Aspects* came out in 1911, while *A Geography of Australasia* (commissioned by A.J. Herbertson, Oxford geography professor and expert on the seasonal distribution of rainfall) was

'The Distribution of Future White Settlement', Taylor, *Environment and Race*, 1927. Taylor engaged in the longstanding scientific debate about where, and whether, 'white races' could settle across the tropical regions of the globe.

published in 1914, the year Taylor moved to Melbourne and took on the responsibilities of married life. Over 1915 and 1916, he spent much of his spare time writing up his Antarctic work. This scholarly moonlighting allowed Taylor to pad his salary of £620 per annum with royalties while keeping him in contention for an academic job—a more palatable prospect than waiting to rise through the ranks in the Commonwealth Bureau of Meteorology.[7] Not only did he have a wife to support and impress but he now headed his own household, complete with Mary the maid and, by 1916, his son Bill.

Taylor's assigned Bureau work primarily involved producing monthly weather reports and periodic publications known as 'bulletins'.[8] These substantial, bound volumes, distributed to government offices and libraries within Australia and around the world, provided up-to-the-minute environmental data as well as analysis and commentary. His first bulletin, *The Physiography of the Proposed Federal Territory at Canberra*,[9] summarised the topographical, geological and meteorological research he had conducted in the district before he'd left for Antarctica. After that point, most of his bulletins synthesised data collected by other weather watchers at observation stations around the country. On some assignments Taylor and his office mate, assistant meteorologist E.T. Quayle, worked together with their boss on publications—the foremost being the pioneering textbook *The Climate and Weather of Australia* (1913). Taylor presented a specially bound copy to Doris as a Christmas present in 1914, seven months after their marriage, helpfully pencilling in the contributions each man had made: Hunt, half a chapter; Quale, one-and-a-half chapters; her 'loving Griff'—ten.[10]

The Bureau of Meteorology had been established in 1908, one of the earliest national agencies following the federation of the Australian colonies in 1901.[11] Administered for most of its early years by the Department of Home Affairs in the nation's temporary capital, Melbourne, it was called upon to inform a national strategy for settlement and economic development. The prime question of the day was whether or not 'white man' could possibly settle and prosper in tropical environments. Australian politicians

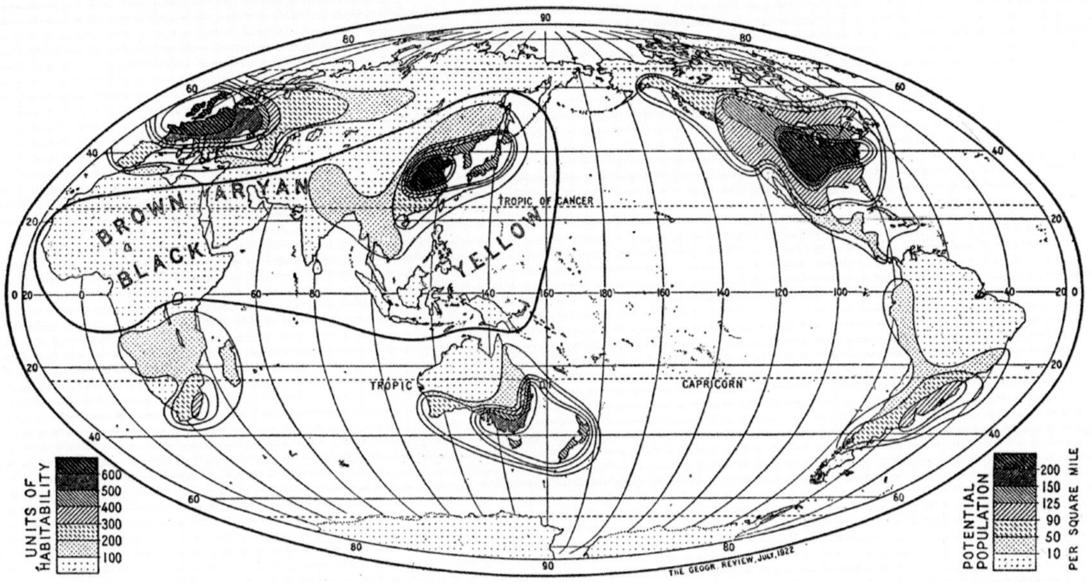

Fig. 90. The distribution of future white settlement according to the economic value of the world regions. The area within the heavy black line is not available for white settlement, but has been treated uniformly here. The facts of the distribution shown in this figure may be expressed by degrees of habitability, shown by 'isoiketes' (see legend to left) where the optimum of habitability is 1,000, or by the corresponding potential population density (see legend to right.) The 'yellow' race will certainly expand beyond Asia, but this aspect is not here discussed.

and bureaucrats considered it critical to evaluate the nation's climate in relation to its racial policy, which the Commonwealth's *Immigration Restriction Act* of 1901 had set in place. Because this law effectively cut off the immigration of Indians, Chinese and Japanese to Australia, it became known as the White Australia policy. A related Act of 1901 determined that most South Pacific Islanders, whose labour had helped build Queensland's sugar cane industry, would be deported to clear the way for white workers. But there was serious doubt that the settlers favoured by Australia's racially restrictive laws were fit to survive in the country's tropical north. This was the great irony of the country's racial policy. In the early twentieth century, many Australians, influenced by a long tradition of natural history and natural philosophy, considered tropical climates a physical mismatch with white constitutions; thus individual and racial decline would result, men could not labour adequately, and women could not bear and raise healthy children. These assumptions underwrote the argument that the tropics should be a place of temporary or, at best, rotating residence for white people, rather than permanent settlement. Thus, a haunting doubt loomed: was White Australia possible?[12]

In such a political climate, 'weather' was no mundane matter. Anxiously searching for answers to the settlement question, the Commonwealth turned to experts, not just physiographer Taylor but physiologists, pathologists and public health experts, mostly in the government's employ and some commissioned from overseas. Doctors at the Australian Institute of Tropical Medicine in Townsville (Queensland) tested the responses of white men (wharf labourers, in one study) to extreme heat and humidity by examining their respiration, melanin skin content, blood pressure and rectal temperatures. Such experiments supported a growing school of thought that White Australia *was* in fact possible after all. In 1920, members of the Australasian Medical Congress announced that it was 'unable to find anything pointing to the inherent or insuperable obstacles in the way of the permanent occupation of Tropical Australia by a healthy indigenous white race'.[13]

Although Taylor largely agreed with these medical 'possibilists' on the capacity of whites to acclimatise, his contribution to the debate, based on his interpretation of meteorological data, set him apart. If medical experts asked whether white people *could* settle in hot and humid climates, Taylor's research question was whether they would or *should*, given the discomfort which 'British stock' typically experienced in tropical environments. Speaking as a weather expert, his answer was a resounding 'no'—primarily because the country still offered plenty of land to settle in more comfortable and temperate regions south of the Tropic of Capricorn. When Taylor first assessed the question through his discussion of 'Future Close Settlement in Australia', he predicted that settlement would flourish only in climatic regions 'resembling those of

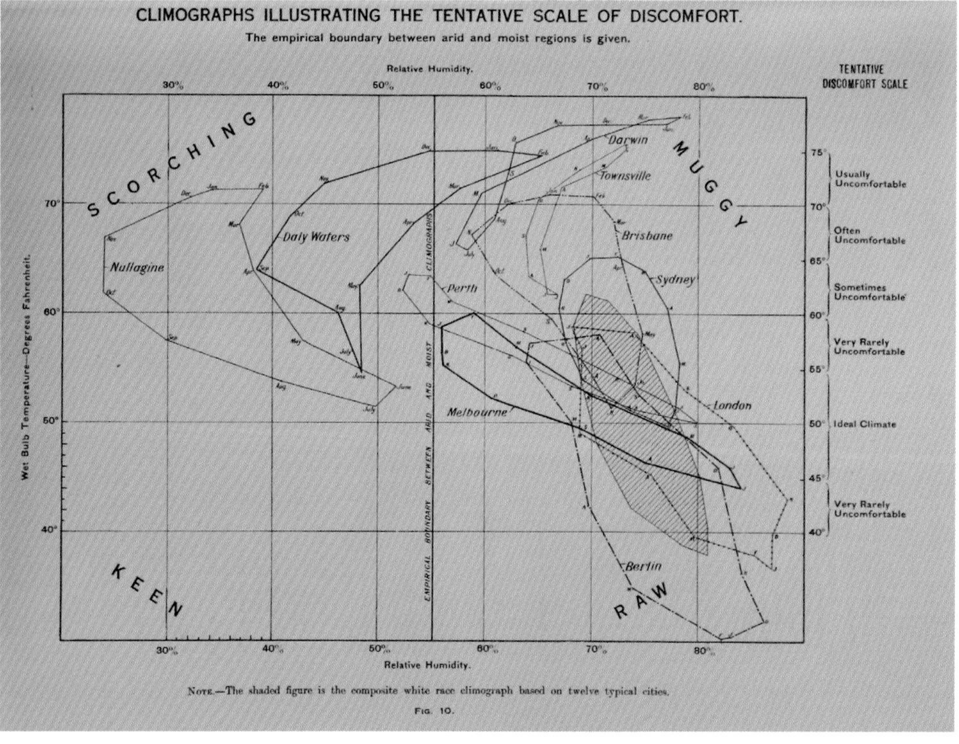

older countries where our white kindred have built towns and founded flourishing and well-established communities'.[14] While they bucked the dominant trend in Australian national debates on race and climate, Taylor's findings attracted greater interest and more positive responses among international scholars, unswayed by nationalist ambitions. By the mid 1910s, as Taylor's Bureau bulletins appeared in government offices and university libraries in North America, Europe and across the British Empire, scholars based outside Australia began to rank Taylor as one of the world's leading authorities on climate, race and settlement.

Bureau of Meteorology Bulletin 14, published in 1916, was the first of Taylor's reports to generate keen interest internationally. In 'The Control of Settlement by Humidity and Temperature (with Special Reference to Australia and the Empire)', Taylor introduced a new tool, his 'tentative scale of discomfort', which related seasonal wet-bulb temperatures—based on measuring the rate of cooling of thermometers wrapped in wet linen jackets—to relative humidity readings in various climatic zones. Taylor was only the latest in a line of researchers studying the human sense of 'comfort', which scientists attempted to quantify with physiological and meteorological data. Some, such as Melbourne physiologist William Osborne and Institute of Tropical Medicine biochemist William Young, disagreed with Taylor's conclusion that white settlers experienced discomfort beyond a relatively narrow temperature and humidity range, yet even his critics admired the novel techniques Taylor devised to present data. This was to become a common response to his published work: odd conclusions but engaging visuals. This bulletin's subtitle, 'An Introduction to Comparative Climatology; Illustrated by 70 Climographs',[15] signalled Taylor's new technique for characterising climatic regions as: 'raw', 'muggy', 'scorching' or 'keen'. In order to plot the relative comfort of the climate in various Australian towns and regions, Taylor first established an ideal standard of comfort, which he based on the temperature and humidity readings for 12 cities—five in the Southern Hemisphere and seven in the Northern—where whites had settled successfully. Combining these data, he designed a composite climograph, 'the white race climograph', which indicated the most comfortable conditions for white settlement. As two commentators, A. Breinl and W.J. Young, declared, this was 'an ingenious and striking method of comparing in a general way the climate of any given locality with a type'.[16] Taylor himself boasted in a subsequent bulletin that his climograph technique

Taylor's 'climographs' from *Bureau of Meteorology Bulletin 14*, 1916. These climographs show Taylor's 'scale of discomfort' for white settlement. Taylor's early graphs and diagrams brought him international scholarly attention. 'I do not believe that either mental or physical work of a high order is possible for the average Britisher when the wet bulb registers much above 75°.'

was favourably reviewed in the US *Geographical Journal*, bringing his work to a wide international readership.

More personally gratifying was the enthusiastic response of Yale-based geographer and climate specialist Ellsworth Huntington (1876–1947).[17] Immediately after reading Taylor's 'The Control of Settlement', he admitted that he had 'stayed up till one o'clock studying it'. Huntington, who had published for several years on climate as a factor in settlement in various regions, including Australia, seized upon Taylor's climograph as a useful new explanatory device: 'The diagrams are most illuminating.'[18] Huntington paid Taylor the highest form of flattery by using climographs in his 1919 book *World Power and Evolution*.

In Australia, Taylor's work began to attract the attention of government departments outside his own, thanks largely to the social network he had established in Melbourne. The circle he and Doris moved in was small but highly influential, not the high-end Melbourne Club but senior public servants and scientific advisors for the new Commonwealth Government, and a range of professors from the university. He was, in fact, surrounded by key scholars with whom he lunched, played bridge and picnicked; Commonwealth statistician Sir George Knibbs and professor of chemistry David Orme Masson (a leading player in the formation of the Council for Scientific and Industrial Research) were close associates, as was Ernest Skeats, professor of geology and mineralogy. Taylor also sought out Baldwin Spencer, the foundation chair of biology at the university, who exchanged his insights on race and ethnography with the eager public servant. As each of his bulletins appeared, Taylor sent copies to these men (as well as to Mater and to coteries of US figures).[19]

Working his way into this Melbourne network was Taylor's means of ensuring that his name might come up whenever government departments sought experts from its tiny pool of bureaucrats. Senior figures in the Department of External Affairs were among those who regarded Taylor's work very highly, and they asked him, rather than Hunt, to evaluate 'the probabilities of Tropical settlement'.[20] Climate was not only an economic issue but a matter of national security, if it turned out that 'a contented weaker race'[21] was better suited than whites to settle comfortably in the tropics. Abutting Australia's sparsely settled north, densely populated South-East Asia was filled with non-white people evidently acclimatised to life and work in muggy and scorching environments. As a result, Australians were concerned that the country's tropics might be vulnerable to invasion by its suspected land-hungry neighbours, if white settlers were fit only for Australia's temperate south-east. Taylor had placed himself perfectly to profit from this range of national anxieties. One senior public servant commented that his work constituted 'the most valuable contributions to the climatology of Australia generally—and especially of the North—that have been made'.[22] As War World I entered its final months, the Department of External Affairs determined that the issue of Australia's vulnerability to foreign occupation be investigated by a continent-wide study of climate, to be conducted by Taylor.

Hunt, the Commonwealth Meteorologist, took Taylor's invitation as a personal slight. He, not Taylor, was the country's foremost meteorological expert, with years of fieldwork to his credit. The disgruntled senior man complained that since he had 'been over most of the country' he could provide his views on health, climate and future settlement for the department—if they 'are of any value', he added petulantly.[23] Hunt protested that it was *his* research on temperatures, not Taylor's, which had produced data vital for the assessment of climate and health, as the work of physiologist Professor Osborne and other medical researchers had shown.[24] And it was Hunt who had published the first wet-bulb isothermal charts of Australia; consequently, he was 'keenly alive to the importance of wet bulb temperature on health'. At the very least, he thought that an expert, such as Osborne, ought to accompany Taylor on the prospective trip. Only then, he advised, would his assistant's work be of real value to the Commonwealth.[25] If those arguments failed to persuade Hunt's bureaucratic masters, he had a final card to play: since 1914, Taylor had lectured on meteorology at the Commonwealth's aviation school and, as late as August 1918, two months before the expedition was set to leave, he was still training military pilots. Surely this was vital war work?[26]

The patriotic ploy may have done the trick for the Commonwealth Meteorologist: the trip planned by the Department of External Affairs never transpired and Taylor remained stuck in the Melbourne office. Yet, from that post, his publications and reputation had already spread far wider than government-funded travels could ever have taken him. The whole world was concerned about settlement problems, as military conflict in Europe and in colonial theatres persisted and as world population grew, bringing the so-called 'empty places' of the globe under international scrutiny. When influential Canadian-born geographer Isaiah Bowman (1878–1950) got hold of *Bulletin 11*, Taylor's study of 'The Climatic Control of Australian Production' (1915), Taylor's international career took off.[27] A colleague of Huntington's, Bowman was president of the American Geographical Society and, in 1916, became editor of the *Geographical Review*, which he successfully moulded into the journal of record in the field. Bowman was the man who had alerted Huntington to Taylor's work: 'I feel quite sure that the methods suggested [by Taylor] are going to play a most important part in the future development of geography,' he wrote excitedly.[28] Bowman agreed with Huntington that Taylor ought to develop his theories of climate, race and settlement along more academic lines and should publish in more scholarly journals, such as the *Review*. While Hunt was a government officer 'who blocked my publications (with great zeal!)',[29] Bowman and Huntington positively encouraged him to pursue an academic career. Towards the end of the 1910s, Taylor no longer needed Hunt or the Bureau. Thanks to his new mentors and the ever-supportive Professor David, he had his own card to play.

The Antiquity of Man: The Evolution of a Racial Theorist

In spite of the publishing and self-advancement opportunities he wrested from the public service, Taylor was always eager to be elsewhere. In 1916, he had written in desperation to Professor Osborne:

> End my condition as senile desk researcher. I feel like the lunatic who wanders gaily around in his youth & then puts his nose to the grindstone & it sticks there for the rest of his life.[30]

Scanning the horizon for academic positions that would allow him to set his own research agenda, he applied unsuccessfully for a chair of geography at Oxford and a foundation chair of geology at the University of Otago in New Zealand.[31] While others might have read such rejections as a cue to settle into a future as a senior bureaucrat, Taylor remained fixed on his academic aspirations. Sitting in his Melbourne office shared with his junior colleague Quayle, he began supplementing his work on white settlement in Australia with after-hours reading in evolutionary biology and natural history, as well as geologically inspired inquiry into the emergence and dispersal of primitive humans, then called the study of the 'Antiquity of Man'.

Taylor had become interested in this field as early as 1906. While still a student at the University of Sydney, he gave a lecture to the University Science Society (which he co-founded) on 'The Antiquity of Man'. His chosen topic synthesised massive fields, he told his fellow students, bringing together the 'four great divisions of science, namely anthropology, archaeology, geology and biology'.[32] What he later referred to as 'the first public lecture I gave on Ethnology' was an expansive and scattered talk, yet it provides a clear sense of Taylor's easy move from his base in earth sciences towards the study of human sciences.[33] Picking up this interest again a decade later, Taylor re-entered a long tradition, a large intellectual family, of natural historians and natural philosophers whose inquiries into the 'age of the Earth' and the 'origins of man' were twinned scholarly endeavours. Data from one substantiated theories about the other. As Taylor put it: 'It is from the ethnological fossil record (i.e. in archeological strata etc.) that we shall learn the evolution of the races of man.'[34] Taylor read and absorbed foundational nineteenth-century work by scientists such as taxonomist Georges Cuvier, who wrote *Essay on the Theory of the Earth* (1813), and geologist Charles Lyell, author of *The Geological Evidence of the Antiquity of Man* (1863). Thomas Huxley played a major role by connecting Darwin's evolutionary theories directly to humans, in such sweeping texts as *Evidence as to Man's Place in Nature* (1863) and *Discourses: Biological and Geological Essays* (1897). Big books by big thinkers on big subjects—this was the grand model to which Taylor aspired and to which he later made his own contribution: *Environment and Race*.[35]

Edgeworth David, Taylor's mentor, never wrote a book of such scope himself but he was a direct inheritor and teacher of what was essentially a geological tradition, in which the study of rocks and fossils and the study of early humans were allied. In 1914, for example, David presented a paper to the anthropology section of the British Association for the Advancement of Science on the 'Talgai Skull', skeletal remains found in Queensland. Applying his geological expertise, David caused a stir among the British world's most prominent scientists by arguing that the skull was that of Pleistocene man—the first such evidence found in Australia. David proclaimed: 'Now if we are asked, "Is man a geological antiquity in Australia" ... we can reply, "Yes, he is".'[36] The proof was momentarily endangered, however, when David's colleague, Oxford geologist and anthropologist William Sollas, almost dropped the skull in his excitement and enthusiasm. Sollas was engaged far more deeply than David in the Antiquity of Man project, which moved constantly between the evolutionary study of rocks, corals and early humans. When Taylor was a student at Cambridge, Sollas was busy comparing Neanderthal skulls with various Aboriginal Australian remains, which European explorers and scientists had removed, without consent, for museum collections. As a standard practice for geologists of their era, geologists like David and Sollas drew on these collections to provide corroborative evidence for their estimates of the age of the earth. Indeed, David's teaching lantern slides, now lying in dusty boxes in a cupboard at the University of Sydney, include an Antiquity of Man series. Several images, comparing chimpanzee and Cro-Magnon skulls, were penned by an avid young demonstrator, who even then couldn't resist leaving his trademark, 'TGT', on the corner of each slide.

In Melbourne, bored with the weather and looking for ways to make it all add up to something, Taylor frequented the State Library, where he copied pictures of skull types and read up on the latest findings on evolution and the Antiquity of Man.[37] Doing this he came across the work of W.D. Matthew, vertebrate curator at the American Museum of Natural History in New York, who fired Taylor's imagination. Canadian-born Matthew had also begun his academic career by studying geology, after which he branched out to biology and zoology. He made his name in 1915 with his work 'Climate and Evolution', which concerned the distribution of mammals.[38] In a lengthy thesis, illustrated with 30 maps, Matthew argued that vertebrates had originated in the more climatically challenging northern zones of the globe, after which they dispersed in waves to fill habitable regions further from their centre of origin. Reading Matthew in April 1916, Taylor compressed the thesis in his diary: 'Poor animals flee from bad land: Stronger stay and adapt.'[39] The two men soon corresponded, and Matthew sent Taylor a copy of his paper in June that year, suggesting that Taylor and his 'Australian confrères' test his mammalian migration theory in light of geological evidence from the Southern Hemisphere: 'I believe that climatic change is fundamental to understanding the past history of Evolution.' Taylor interpreted Matthew's remark as a tantalising suggestion that his theory might explain human evolution as well. With time on his hands (despite his bulletin writing, his teaching at the aviation school and his outside publishing activities, not to mention the impending arrival of his first child), Taylor right

Taylor's mother Lily—'Mater', c.1916.

below

Taylor often first reported his scientific breakthroughs to his mother. This 1916 letter is the earliest recorded rendition of what was to become Taylor's famous zones-and-strata theory of racial migration.

1003 19/1185

Re Start of my Race theories

25 July 191[illegible]
1:30 pm
Office

Dear Mater,
I am to try & write you an ~~interesting~~ and cheerful le[illegible]
I have just finished lunch - from my Vanity case. It consisted of
sandwiches of potted meat & cheese (I don't like either much, bu[illegible]
we have such a willing servant in Mary that I haven't said so, ye[illegible]
and milk out a bottle has cheered me for the remaining hours o[illegible]
Just now the bureau is in a turmoil because the sun [illegible]
as to take a rest on Sunday. We are meteorologists here but if I ca[illegible]
spend hours on Antarctic physiography (by permission), cannot [illegible]
Griffith & Barkley spend days preparing to watch eclipses on the 3[illegible]
So we see opera glasses mounted on camera stands cruising around [illegible]
and we test glasses on the sun's warts (he has lots about now)
Generally don't attend to rain & weather as we ought to.
The two specified are making a pilgrimage to Camperdown to see it [illegible]
the fall in temperature & how the cows and goats [illegible] the funereal gloo[illegible]

applied Matthew's theory to the question of human origins and dispersal. Towards the end of July 1916, he began to fill up his diaries with hurriedly sketched charts and diagrams of world climates, races and migrations. Writing to his mother from his Bureau office, after lunching on potted meat and cheese sandwiches prepared by the maid, he reported that he had discovered a new theory that explained the origin and migration of human races:

> I have spent an hour or two in [the] Library this morning reading up the connection between climate and evolution ... Matthew says all mammals spread out from S. Siberia. So did man and gradually colonised the world. Hence the primitive types are furthest from the centre of origin, where the latest types continue to be produced. Thus we get zones of culture around the centre.

Along with this excited intellectual update, Taylor provided his mother with an explanatory map of the world, which he sketched in coloured pencil to denote the lands to which 'negritos', 'negroes', 'Indo Aryans' and 'Americans' had migrated from central Asia, leaving 'the Chinese, who still occupy the birthplace of all!'.[40] This was the inception of an idea he later called his 'migration zone theory', which he refined and republished for the rest of his life, never failing to credit Matthew, the mammal specialist, as the man responsible for 'the start of my racial theories'.[41] What began as lunchtime letters to Mater and hurried maps and diagrams on the back of Bureau stationery, evolved into extensively illustrated scholarly articles, the first in 1919.

The year 1919 was Taylor's *annis mirabilis*. Coincident with his suddenly renewed interest in evolutionary theory, a fresh request for his expertise on race and settlement arrived from another government unit. In February, the Chief of General Staff Major General James Legge asked the Secretary of the Home and Territories Department to assess the prospect of 'Asiatic settlement in the Tropics' through climatological analysis. Specifically, he sought information on the conditions 'that may be expected to control the settlement of the Chinese and Japanese races, not only in the tropical areas of Australia but in the islands of the Dutch East Indies and the Pacific'. Taylor saved this memo and, decades later, when sorting his papers for his autobiography, he wrote on it: 'This letter started my anthropological research.'[42] Referred to in his diary as his 'Yellow Races' research, this work was overseen by Atlee Hunt, then an appointee to a postwar committee considering enemy aliens.[43] Taylor boasted to Edgeworth David that his study on 'Mongolian settlement for the Intelligence Staff' had produced 'surprising results'. In fact, he had come up with new explanations for racial differentiation and similarities. After only a few months of research, he saw that 'the Polynesians are blood brothers to the Celt. The [Australian] aborigines and Dravidians are indisputably kin. The Jap is akin to the Britisher'.[44]

On the last day of July 1919, Taylor's research on 'Mongolian controls' conducted for the Asiatic settlement inquiry and his understanding of climatic cycles derived from his

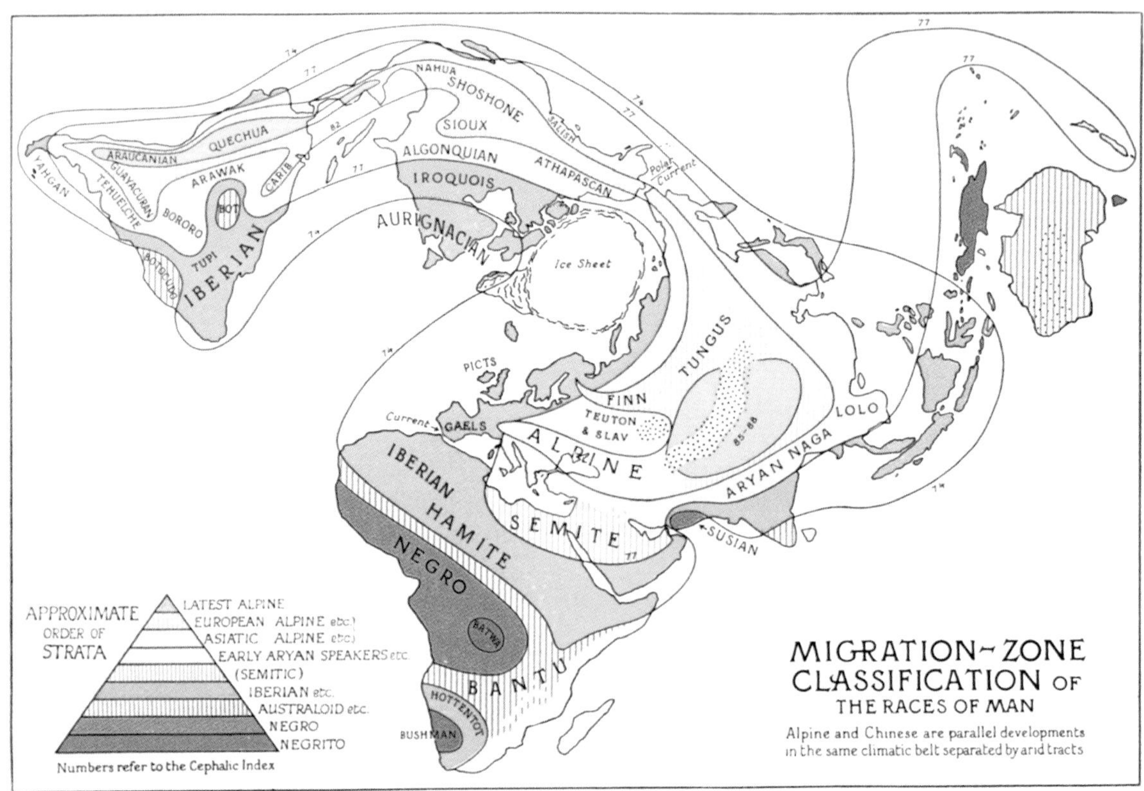

The Zones are generalized, and based on the primitive races in the regions
'Semitic' is a later variety of the Iberian zone
(The map is slightly modified from that given in the author's paper in the American 'Geographical Review' of 1919)

meteorological and physiographic work on whites, collided in his head like two tectonic plates. Feverishly, he recorded the moment in his diary:

> At 5 am I discovered the cause of the Ice Age … Believe found key past climates and Continents. Theory correlates Archaen complex, Ice Ages, Gondwana, ages of plantation, rapid evolution, mountain building and races of man.[45]

With a steadier pen, the following morning he confidently wrote to his father: 'I really think I can explain the cause of the Ice Ages, and of the origins of the human race, the stages of evolution of life, and the periods when life evolved so rapidly.' Out sprang an article on his new theory, published in Bowman's *Geographical Review* in December 1919 as 'Climatic Cycles and Evolution'. Reflecting on his landmark publication, he later penned on an off-print, 'My first article on Racial Evolution'.

From his interest in the causes of the Ice Ages, Taylor moved quickly to the impact of glacial and interglacial cycles on human migration by applying Matthew's ideas on mammalian evolution. Climatic cycles, he contended, were the causative factors or mechanisms that led to the origins and distribution of the primitive 'races of man'. He

'Migration-Zone Classification of the Races of Man' was the frontispiece to Taylor's *Environment and Race* (1927). The lines connect equal cephalic index readings which, according to Taylor, provided definitive evidence of the zones and strata of early migration. Those with the highest cephalic index—the 'Latest Alpines'—remained in Central Asia. 'World history might be summarised in five words: *Centrifugal migrations of Asiatic broad-heads.*'

began to gather corroborative evidence from the fossil record, the geological record and the anthropological record, all of which convinced him he was right. Elaborating his theory and illustrating it with maps, metaphors and diagrams, he now began to attract a wider audience than he had previously commanded though his Bureau publications. Gloating to Professor David, he predicted that his ideas would incite scholarly controversy: '[T]he wigs will be on the green among Conservative climatologists, Erudite ethnologists and Gingerly geologists!'[46]

Taylor's argument was that four races of man had migrated in 'thrusts' in response to cycles of climatic change, approximately 200 000 years each in duration, during the Pleistocene Era. The four great ice ages (in Proterozoic, Devonian, Permian and late Tertiary time) produced 'striking breaks in the biological succession', including the human migrations.[47] This was a controversial argument, since his thesis countered the prevailing idea that humankind had originated where the 'oldest' of these races currently dwells (Africa considered the cradle-land of humanity) and that the more evolved races had subsequently moved outwards from there. Taylor provocatively argued the opposite: the most 'primitive' races today (by which he meant 'negritos' and 'negros') are found at the outer edges of inhabited land, *furthest away* from the central origin point, which he plotted (after Matthew), in central Asia, not Africa. The most 'highly evolved' races ('the yellow man') had adapted most fully and recently in the oldest zone of human habitation and remained there. All races were related but some were, in evolutionary terms, less mature than others:

> The childlike behaviour of the negro has often been referred to as a primitive characteristic. The white races are versatile, gay, and inventive—all attributes of youth. The yellow peoples are grave, meditative, and melancholic—which possibly indicates their more mature position in the evolution of races.[48]

In this respect, Taylor's thesis owed much to Darwinian thinking and extended the *monogenism*, or single-origin, hypothesis of human origin. Primitive humans were subject to the same laws of evolution that governed mammals, and the strongest evolved over time. But for Taylor, who always thought in terms of space as well as time, evolution was fundamentally a geographic question: the weakest did not *die* out, they were *pushed* out. And the strongest did not just *survive*, they remained in the most environmentally

left

This rendition of the zones-and-strata theory from Taylor's article in *Human Biology* (vol. 8, 1936) is a typical example of his use of block diagrams. Always interested in visualising both time and space, the block diagram gave Taylor the dimensions he needed.

bottom

Recently returned from the Dutch East Indies, Taylor chose this volcanic analogy to visualise his theory of race migration. This diagram from Taylor's article in the *Geographical Review* (vol. 11, 1919) flagged his emerging interest in the evolution and distribution of language.

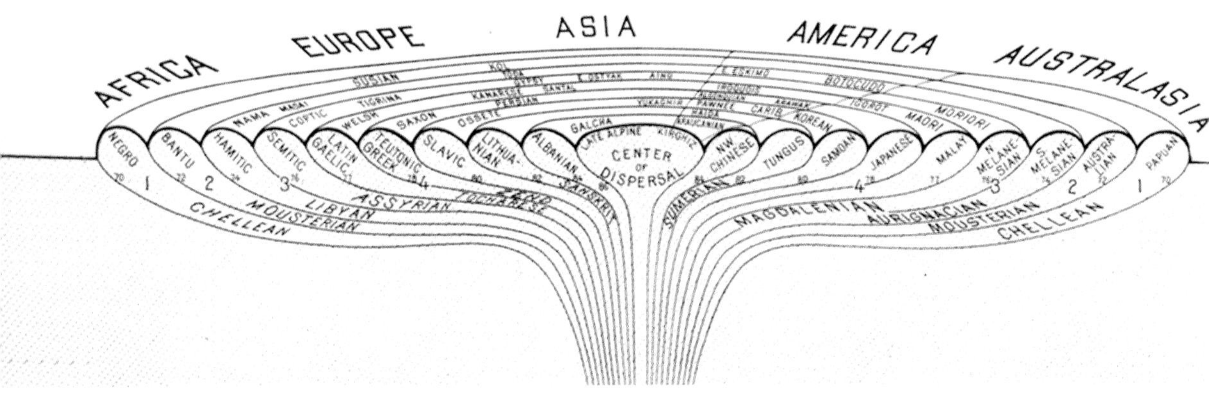

'stimulating' regions, where they adapted to climatic challenge. In Taylor's view, the Darwinian concept of the survival of the fittest had to be rethought spatially with respect to humans, and rephrased, even more ruthlessly, as 'the weakest goes to the wall'. 'The paper is somewhat revolutionary,' he immodestly alerted the editor of *Nature* magazine, anticipating that his advance on Darwin would provoke a major response.[49]

Taylor's facility at translating his ideas into innovative imagery helped establish his reputation as a popular lecturer, journalist and aspiring academic. This impulse towards colourful language and arresting diagrams was reinforced by the positive responses his climographs had elicited. Now he sought equally effective ways to convey his rethinking of racial evolution. 'Going to the wall' was a verbal metaphor that captured the sense of forced dispersal, but he also tried out alternative analogies to explain where and why racial contests over territory occurred over time. He began with a homespun comparison that likened racial migration over millennia to spectator arrival patterns at football matches (the youngest and poorest arriving first, only to find themselves pushed to the cheap seats by the higher status latecomers).[50] More in keeping with his interests, since Taylor hated team sports, were his geological analogies: not only did the geological record and fossil evidence support evolutionary theory, it also provided ways to imagine the processes and stages through which human migration had occurred. After he returned from a trip to the Dutch East Indies with its active volcanoes, he came up with a 'lava flow' metaphor. This image, which his sister Dorothy copied for display and explication at local meetings of the Sydney Eugenics Society,[51] dramatically represented the displacement of primitive peoples, in Taylor's reckoning, by those more advanced:

> We may picture the centre of dispersal in Central Asia as a sort of 'fissure eruption' sending forth streams of lava in all directions. Each new eruption arises from the center and, while covering some portion of the previous flow, pushes most of the previous lavas out to the periphery. If we postulate that the early lavas still retain some mobility and occasionally flow across later lavas, we get a very close analogy to what has happened in the migrations of man.[52]

The lava flow analogy had significant advantages over the playing field metaphor, not least of which was its expressibility in a simple, arresting image. Taylor's illustration depicted a series of 'eruptions' in which High Alpines vaulted into existence at the dynamic centre, while those who evolved first—humans still reified in the 'stone age'—languished on the periphery.

The zones-and-strata explanation of human migration supplemented and enhanced Taylor's geological analogies. This more elaborate metaphor, floated in a lengthy presidential address he gave at the Australian and New Zealand Association for the Advancement of Science meetings in Wellington in 1923, interpreted racial evolution in its temporal and geographic dimensions, and found visual form in a crude block diagram. Taylor had picked up this drawing technique from William Davis, who was an early master and exponent. Like many other physiographers, Taylor appreciated how block diagrams lent a three-dimensional perspective to surface features that would normally be represented only in two dimensions, width and length. By depicting depth, Taylor's zones-and-strata block diagrams provided an impression of underlying structures (strata) and allowed him to illustrate his theory that more recently evolved races overtook more primitive races over time and across space. Retreating 'primitive' races did not disappear: they left traces of their existence (in fossil records, graves, artefacts, folklore), which more advanced, later evolved races buried. 'The result,' Taylor explained, 'is a series of *strata*, of which the upper represents the dominant race.'[53] There were some exceptions to this pattern (such as the Basque, supposedly more primitive than their immediate Iberian neighbours) but Taylor conveniently explained them away by resorting to further geological metaphors: they were 'inliers'—older racial types surrounded by new. Taylor was convinced that his zones-and-strata model offered a significant advance over the older, biologically inspired 'tree of man' image (which he sometimes reproduced) and ought entirely to replace it, since it could explain how racial hybridity developed through contact along the edges of racial zones. Theorists of the races of man would do far better, Taylor judged, to think like geologists rather than biologists.

Anthropo-geography

Taylor's reasoning was consistent with the nineteenth-century tradition of natural history, where the study of environment, climate and man blurred.[54] But his was a twentieth-century career, lived through a period when disciplines were being defined and refined, one against the other. Turning from rocks to race meant that Taylor had evolved into a human geographer. In this respect, he followed biologist-turned-geographer Friedrich Ratzel (1844–1904), whose two-volume opus, *Anthropogeographie*, Taylor read in the original German. Through this work and his teaching at the University of Leipzig, Ratzel gained a reputation as human geography's originator. Taylor never gave Ratzel the credit he bestowed on biologist Matthew and geologist David, yet he frequently referred to his own work as 'anthropogeography' and adhered to the Ratzelian notion that the physical environment controls 'the distribution of humankind'. Indeed, he referred to Australia as 'an experiment in anthropogeography'. Others were equally drawn to Ratzel, including Ellsworth Huntington and Ratzel's American pupil, Ellen Churchill Semple (1863–1932), who lectured in geography at the University of Chicago from 1906 to 1924. Although historians of geography typically trace the lineage of environmental determinism from Ratzel to Semple and thence to Huntington and Taylor, Taylor never acknowledged an intellectual debt to Semple's work, nor did he ever publicly recognise that she was his immediate institutional predecessor at Chicago. Despite their shared attraction to Ratzelian ideas, their study of climate and their conviction that 'Man is a

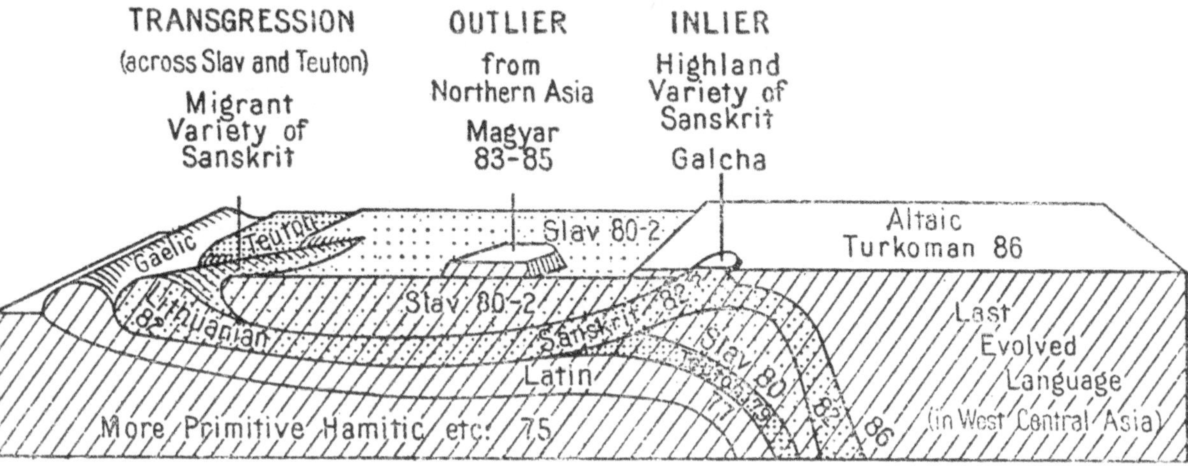

above

Taylor applied geological terms to almost any criteria as a way to clarify his ideas. In this diagram from *Environment and Race* (1927), 'outlier' and 'inlier' explained irregularities in what he understood to be correlations between languages and head indices.

below

The geography family tree, from Taylor (ed.), *Geography in the Twentieth Century* (1951). Typically preferring geological to biological or horticultural metaphors, Taylor made an exception here to represent his own intellectual family tree, linking explorers, natural historians and ethnographers.

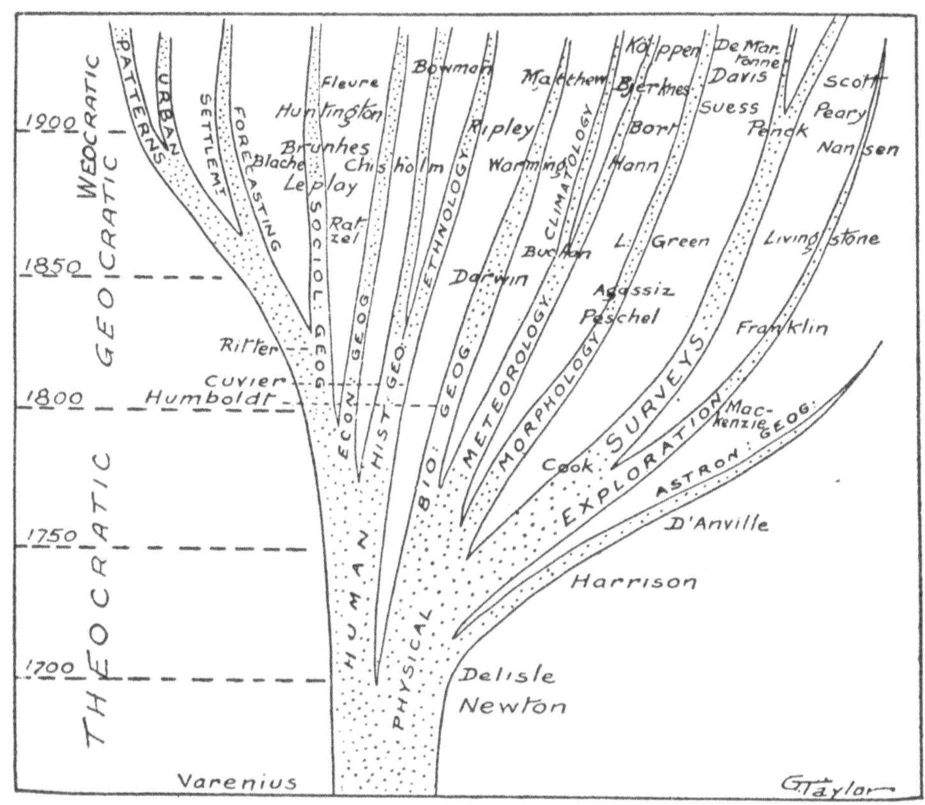

product of the earth's surface' (the sentence that starts Semple's *Influences of Geographic Environment*)[55] and, notwithstanding Semple's position as president of the Association of American Geographers in 1921, Taylor essentially ignored her. For Taylor, intellectual pedigree was traced and formed through the male line—a patrilineal stance that his own training of female geographers, including his sister, never shook.

In contrast to his rebuff of Semple, Taylor positively courted Ellsworth Huntington, who he may first have heard about on one of the European glacier valley walks he took in 1908 with Professor Davis, who had taught Huntington as well as Bowman at Harvard. Huntington taught geography at Yale University, where he specialised in the study of climate and man on a scale that appealed to Taylor. Like Taylor, he began publishing on environment and race in the 1910s, with *Civilization and Climate* (1915) his major compendium on the subject.[56] Taylor and Huntington could easily have become rivals, since they shared a belief in 'the geographic basis of history' (which was the subtitle of Huntington's 1907 book). Taylor privately compared his output to Huntington's ('H has done 14 books')[57] but his competitiveness never undermined their lifelong mutual admiration. By the time that Taylor's 'Climatic Cycles and Evolution' appeared late in 1919, the pair had been corresponding for two years. Huntington admired this article primarily for its intellectual breadth, rather than its empirical offerings: 'A real inspiration ... a great sweep of vision.'[58] Taylor was deeply flattered that a man who had established an academic reputation directly in this field admired his work. Only four years older than Taylor, Huntington was the more established scholar. While Taylor had been Professor David's demonstrator at the University of Sydney, Huntington was journeying through Central Asia, gathering data which resulted in *The Pulse of Asia*; when Huntington published *Civilization and Climate*, Taylor was teaching pilots how to read weather maps. So Taylor responded gratefully to Huntington's praise:

> [T]here are some letters which one always treasures as marks of one's progress in science ... I know of noone whose good opinion I would rather have, on these world problems.

In 1920, on the eve of his move to Sydney and finally released from his Melbourne public service role under Hunt, Taylor pledged to follow Huntington's advice by planning a big book on 'Environment, Evolution and Ethnography'.[59] It became his major publishing preoccupation during his Sydney years.

Although Taylor's initial physical impression of the American was, in a crisply noted diary entry—'5 foot, shrewd look'—the two men were drawn to each other, not just intellectually but personally. Huntington wrote:

> I see in your work so many resemblances to my own that I somehow feel as if I understood how you react scientifically. I have not felt quite sure, however, how you react emotionally ... Let me begin by saying that your ideas have set me to thinking as have those of few other geographers.[60]

Theirs was a fraternal bond (similar to that he shared with his Antarctic hut mates) that Taylor could never have formed with a woman intellectual like Ellen Semple. The men exchanged portrait photographs and, during his Australian trip in 1923, Huntington spent one month with the Taylors, their son Bill and daughter Natalie (born in Sydney in October 1921). This trip brought the men and their families still closer: 'You and I are unusually near together ... the resemblance between your children and mine increased that feeling.' Huntington reflected that Natalie reminded him of his own daughter, Anna.[61] Yet Taylor was not so close as to inform Huntington that Natalie died suddenly, shortly after his visit. Taylor never wrote about this family tragedy outside a few pages of his diary.

By the year's close Taylor resumed his frenetic pace of writing, teaching and travelling. In some respects, Huntington admired Taylor's irrepressibility, both personal and intellectual: 'One of the greatest things that a scientist can do is to generalise without letting himself be confused by minor details.'[62] Coming to know Taylor better over the 1920s, he more fully realised that details never restrained Taylor from expounding grand theories, even when they appeared to undermine his arguments. Huntington shared Taylor's intellectual impatience, expecting that the *Character of Races* would receive 'enough criticism as well as praise ... I feel quite sure that it amounts to something'.[63] Yet Huntington had a word of warning for Taylor: solicit the advice of experts before publishing. He informed Taylor that he had tested the Australian's theory of the cosmic causes of climatic changes with his astronomer friends, who were dubious. And when Huntington put Taylor's race work under the nose of his anthropologist colleagues, he reported that they 'questioned some of your assertions even more than I did'.[64] The problem, thought Huntington, was that Taylor readily declared as fact that which was merely speculative. Huntington believed that he had mended his own ways in this regard, always testing out his insights with experts in climate, geology, astronomy, physics and mathematics.

Ironically, when Isaiah Bowman offered Taylor the same general advice, he warned that Huntington's work was the worst possible model to follow. Bowman found Taylor's work admirable in many respects, reassuring him: 'The [Geographical] Review has been proud to offer you a stage from which to speak. We have recognized your achievements with a gold medal.' Then came the qualification:

> But it is with some amazement that I see you accepting in what seems to be an uncritical way the loose generalities of my friend Ellsworth Huntington [who] ... has an almost fine disdain for facts ... I regard a large part of Huntington's writing as a waste of time to read. Anyone with a facile pen can express himself on a wide variety of topics in a sufficiently interesting way to arouse the interest of several thousand readers. But what do scholars say of them?[65]

If Huntington was Taylor's intellectual soul mate, Bowman was his senior advisor—an institutional powerbroker securely lodged in the highest echelons of academia and

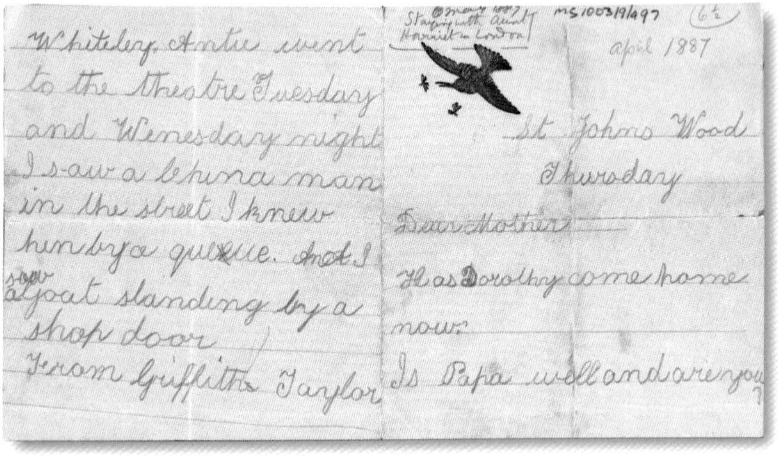
Whiteley. Antie went
to the theatre Tuesday
and Wenesday night
I saw a China man
in the street I knew
him by a queue. And I
saw a goat standing by a
shop door
From Griffith Taylor

MS1003/9/497
april 1887
St Johns Wood
Thursday
Dear Mother
Has Dorothy come home
now?
Is Papa well and are you
?

Letter from Taylor to Mater, April 1887. From childhood Taylor displayed an interest in 'the exotic'. James and Lily Taylor kept much of their son's precocious correspondence.

politics. Nevertheless, no-one, including Bowman, could persuade Taylor that his constant rush to publish undermined his scholarly credibility. In what was to become a pattern, Taylor responded to Bowman's advice by affecting the persona of the hard-done-by scholar, consigned to break new ground in a sparse Australian intellectual landscape. Apart from anthropologist Baldwin Spencer, his closest associate from his Melbourne years, Taylor claimed there was no-one in Australia with whom he could discuss his theories of race, climate and evolution. These complaints, along with Taylor's public persecution over his criticism of Australian land settlement plans and its immigration policy, prompted both Bowman and Huntington to suggest that Taylor move to the United States, where a wider pool of experts would provide the stimulation he sought.[66] Between the two men, Taylor would eventually gain the loft he needed to spread his wings and migrate to North America in 1929—but not before he managed to establish his idiosyncratic version of anthropo-geography at Sydney University.

'I Saw a China Man': Taylor the Anthropologist

As a six-year-old visiting his aunt in London, Taylor wrote home: 'Dear Mother, Wenesday night I saw a China man in the street. I knew him by a qu~~e~~eue.'[67] Taylor's early tendency to ethnographic observation persisted through his life, and he never lost his childhood sense of curiosity for racial and cultural difference. In his twenties, he expressed this inclination through stories written and published in the scientist-chronicler tradition of imperial travel. For example, when he participated in a study of coral formations in the Great Barrier Reef in 1906, he provided his family with detailed accounts of the appearance, speech and actions of the non-Europeans encountered along the coast and aboard the ship. In what was to become a lifelong pattern, he subsequently turned those letters into chatty articles that rehashed standard native 'types', more in the style of

'½ Caste Driver & GT, Ooldea', c.1919. 'The following morning, we found at our service a team of four camels in charge of a half-caste driver' (Taylor, *Journeyman Taylor*, 1958). On a trip to South Australia in 1919, when Taylor passed through Ooldea, he gathered all kinds of 'data' which would soon appear in scholarly articles as lantern slides for lectures and in columns for the popular press.

colonial travelogues than the conventions of ethnological observation. When he returned from that trip, he published 'Humorous Stories of the Savage Character and Cannibal Propensities of the North Queensland Blacks' under the slightly inflated title 'Science Rambles'—perfect light material for the Sydney University's undergraduate journal *Hermes*. He continued this pattern on the journey he took through the South Pacific on his way to Cambridge in 1907. The 1851 Scholar, bound to conduct palaeontological research, travelled with imperial eyes, taking in the unfamiliar costumes and customs in New Zealand, Fiji, Samoa and Hawaii, and penning exotic accounts for an appreciative audience of fellow Britishers.

As he immersed himself in anthropological theory, Taylor's descriptions of other cultures gradually assumed a more ethnographic air. While continuing to publish travel accounts for the popular press, he began to include observations cued by his reading. Shortly before leaving the Bureau of Meteorology, he travelled to South Australia in May 1919 on behalf of the Commonwealth, which faced a lawsuit over its alleged diversion of well water from pastoral land during construction of the transcontinental rail line across the Nullarbor Plain. Taylor's official physiographic brief was to study the artesian water supply of the larger zone under dispute. He established a base of operations in remote Ooldea for several weeks, during which he moonlighted as a journalist for the *Sydney Mail*. In a series of articles published under the title 'The Fringe of the Australian Desert', Taylor's narratives on the landscape were interlaced with accounts of Aboriginal life in the district, including descriptions of their dwellings, games, child-rearing practices, cooking techniques and weaponry. Taylor knew he was travelling in the footsteps of Ernest Giles, who had encountered the people and land at this traditional Aboriginal meeting place and vital watering point in 1875. In his own articles, he quoted Giles's sexually explicit account of meeting and embracing 'very pretty' and 'bashful' naked young women (calling the encounter 'amusing'). Then he followed with his own aesthetic evaluation, with a hint of Giles's style: 'The children

'Child-study in the Buitenzorg Gardens!', 1920. On a trip to the Dutch East Indies in 1920, Taylor extended his ethnographic tendencies, becoming increasingly interested in both cultural and physical human difference. 'I applied myself to Malay, each day testing my progress with this language on such members of the crew as hailed from Amboyna, Celebes, and Java' (Taylor, *Journeyman Taylor*, 1958).

were quite attractive in appearance; the little girls had long eyelashes, large dark velvety eyes, and their features, if unformed, were very like those of white children.'[68]

Taylor followed up his earlier arrangements for popular journalism with the *Argus* by contracting with the Melbourne *Sun* to publish a series of articles describing his tour of the Dutch East Indies (now Indonesia) in 1920. On this trip, funded by the bonus he'd received for defending the Commonwealth in the suit over well water, his orientalist-tourist persona came out in full in photos he snapped with friends Betty and Theo Ruthven-Smith, who dressed up in 'native' costume. The style was equally apparent in the articles he published in the *Sun*, in October 1920, under the banner of 'By Orient Ways'. In 'The Peoples of the Pacific' and 'Stumblings of a New Tongue', along with several other similar submissions, he described the local topography, the 'exotic' local people and the 'barbaric' customs he encountered in Java, Sumatra, Singapore and Borneo. Doris and four-year-old Bill were away in England visiting relatives at the time the articles appeared so he cut them out and pasted them to pages he bow-tied with string, inscribing the sheaf 'Wanderings in the East Indies: Written and illustrated by

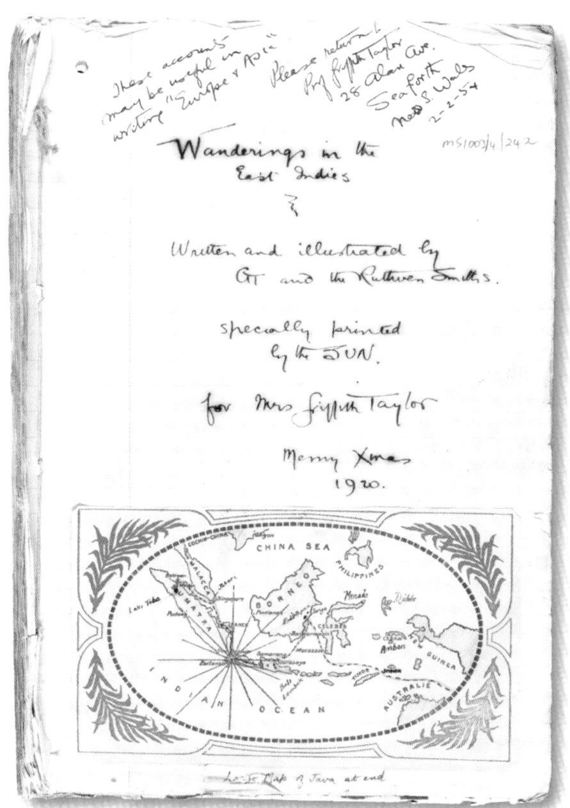

Taylor's Christmas gift to Doris, 1920. Taylor bound his diaries, sketches and articles for his wife, labelling them, 'Wanderings in the East Indies'.

GT and the Ruthven Smiths specially printed by the *Sun*, for Mrs. Griffith Taylor, Merry Xmas 1920'.[69] These stories marked the last time that he wrote purely in the orientalist tradition. From that point on, Taylor gave his observations of Indigenous peoples a more scientific and professional twist.

When he returned home from this Dutch East Indies trip, it was no longer to Melbourne and the public service, but to Sydney and the foundation chair of geography. From his position at the University, Taylor began to turn his pleasure in travel, his interest in race and his colonial-ethnographic tendencies, to concerted anthropological study, research and teaching. His geological, anthropological and geographic reading made him especially eager to enter the world of Indigenous people, not just on paper, but in the field. He began with a series of field trips to Aboriginal carvings made in Sydney sandstone and in 1924 embarked on a program of community fieldwork to scientifically study a people who he, like many other European authorities in the period, considered both a primitive and vanishing race. In this move to ethnographic fieldwork, Taylor took a disciplinary and methodological leap well beyond the 'Antiquity of Man', beyond the fossil and remains-inspired work of geologists like Edgeworth David and William Sollas, and beyond anthropo-geographers like Ellen Semple. Taylor's new 'study of contemporary man'[70] involved travelling to make direct contact with his research subjects. Aside from rock and fossil evidence, he now sought out Aboriginal women, men and children, as the 'data' to substantiate his racial migration theory: Aboriginal people, according to Taylor, were '[i]n effect primitive man ... preserved right down to modern times'.[71] Armed with the latest anthropometric instruction manual, Louis Sullivan's *Essentials of Anthropology: A Handbook for Explorers and Museum Collectors*,[72] and authorised by the Aborigines Protection Board, he put that theory to the test in reserves and towns in New South Wales.

During the summer teaching recess of 1924, two months after his daughter Natalie's death, Taylor set off with one of his top students, war veteran Fitzroy Jardine, for northern and western New South Wales, supported by the University of Sydney Research Fund. After arriving at the Pilliga reserve on 5 February, he wrote home to Doris: 'There were only 4–5 Full-bloods ... about 25 children & 12 half-caste adults ... I don't believe such a complete photo and anthropometric survey has been done in Australia.' Cephalic callipers, cameras and hair clippers at the ready, Taylor measured, photographed, and lopped hair samples. 'We were not popular at first,' he admitted; however, he and Jardine managed eventually to gain their subjects' cooperation: '[W]e had little trouble later & measured almost all the adults and many children.' One family that interested him thought the researchers' object was: '1/ Pictures for Bulletin or 2/ To sift out ½ castes & chuck them out of reserve!'[73] Taylor's exclamation mark anticipated Doris's amusement at the thought of her slight bookish husband's capacity to intimidate; in the same stroke, it exposed his self-serving inattention to these people's justifiable reluctance to participate in the research of white 'experts'. On a trip later that year to the New South Wales north coast, he wrote again to Doris about the resistance he had had to overcome: 'I have to explain that I'm not from the Police, not doing it for the Board, or for the *Sydney Mail*. But they're always suspicious; poor Beggars!'[74] In fact, these unwilling subjects were right to be suspicious.

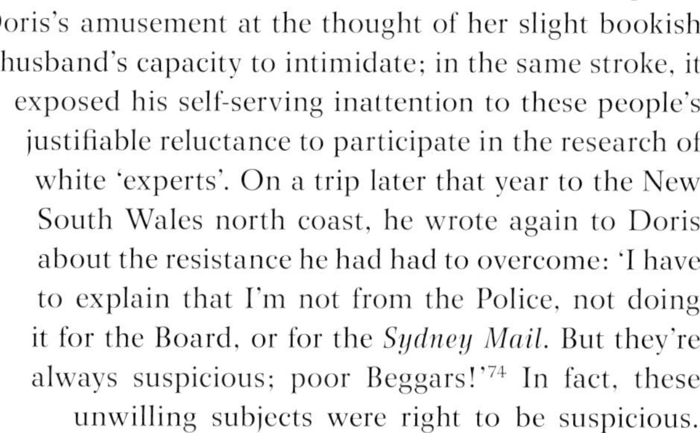

The inquiries he made about individuals' kinship groups, physical features and levels of intelligence leapt, within months of his visit, from chatty letters home to columns published in *The Sydney Morning Herald*, thence to a series of scholarly articles on race-mixing.[75]

Taylor's declarations about the comprehensiveness of this research notwithstanding, he conducted it rather hastily, no doubt to these people's relief. He rarely spent more than a day in a single community, sometimes staying overnight with schoolteachers and station masters. His whirlwind approach was consistent with the tradition of exploratory travel he had always followed in his perennial attempt to see as much as possible on a minimal budget; yet in so doing he upheld neither the amateur tradition of living with Indigenous people before writing about them, nor the emerging standards of research conducted by cultural anthropologists, whose fieldwork lasted months and even years. Taylor's temperament was unsuited to prolonged engagement with people, unless they were fellow scientists. From North Lismore, he described his interviewing style to Doris:

> in a sort of fodder-shed I found two or 3 families of fullbloods, halfbloods and quadroons. One boy of 14 was quite white looking. A girl of 17 was a rather good looking quadroon, there were 3 old full bloods. I palavered as usual & got them to be photoed ... I didn't bother to try and measure them.

His flying visits and patchy results not only failed to impress most anthropologists who reviewed his work; they also contrasted with the meticulous thoroughness of his geological research, which not even the frigid conditions of Antarctica had been able to compromise.

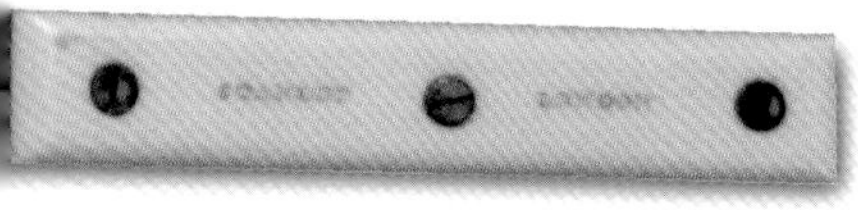

Taylor's cephalic callipers, which he used most extensively for his 'half-caste' research in New South Wales during his time at the University of Sydney (1921–1928).

	Negrito	Sudan Negro	Iberian	Nordic	Alpine-Mongol
HAIR Section	40	50	60	70	80
HAIR Color	Black	Black	Black	Brown to Black	Brown to Black
HAIR Wave					
Skull		73	76	79	85
Jaw					
Eye	83 100 Bushman	85 100 Negro	87 100 Fuegian	88 100 English	90 100 Tatar
Nose	100 100	100 100	Kol 82	Paris 69	Galcha 66
Height	Akka 1400 m.m.	Wolof 1725	Corsican 1630	English 1700	Kirghiz 1640
Skin Color	Usually Black	Black to Chocolate	Dark brown to Olive	Light brown to white	Light brown White+yellow

Fig. 12. Scheme illustrating variation in Ethnological Criteria.

Taylor's table of 'Ethnological Criteria' from *Environment and Race* (1927) represented his multifaceted method of race classification. This, he considered, placed him as a more sophisticated racial theorist than many of his contemporaries.

The anthropological research Taylor conducted in the 1920s relied on the technique of anthropometry—the science of quantifying human physical characteristics. In several articles that led up to the publication of *Environment and Race*, he advocated distinguishing between races on the basis of three measurable physical features: cephalic index (head form), hair texture classifications, and nasal index. In so doing, Taylor took up a position in the longer history of modern ethnological taxonomy.[76] Dismissing the classic work of Cuvier and Blumenbach, he traced the greatest advances in modern taxonomy back to 1860 with Saint Hilaire's and, subsequently, Thomas Huxley's work on skin colour. An advance was made, he thought in the 1870s, with French anthropologist Paul Topinard's classification based on hair types, followed by Joseph Deniker's *Races of Man and Privileging of Hair as a Criteria of Classification* (1900), to which he often referred. Although he greatly admired William Ripley's *The Races of Europe* (1899), his own 'Migration-Zones and Strata' theory represented, in his mind, the most advanced application of modern racial classification methods, precisely because he classified race according to multiple physical criteria.

Taylor felt most certain about the merit of the cephalic index, which featured almost as a fetish in his theories and his fieldwork. 'Of all the coefficients which have been used to classify man,' he wrote in 1921, 'the measurement of the shape of the cranium is still in my opinion the best single standard.'[77] He argued that the first migrations from Central Asia were of peoples with narrow heads. By contrast: 'In Central Asia and along the main corridor to Europe are the broadest-headed races which I call "late-Alpine".'[78] His provocative intervention was to counter the claims that the races of Europe were the most evolved. Taylor disagreed and offered the cephalic evidence to prove it: the average Aryan skull index was 79; that of the people he termed 'Alpine-Mongol' was 85.

The 1920s was a period when race was constantly under discussion, at both popular and expert levels. The utopian novelist H.G. Wells wrote a laconic note to Taylor, puncturing his serious commitment to the science of anthropometry: 'If ever I knew why I don't believe in cephalic indices, as indicating racial difference, I have forgotten, but I don't believe. I believe heads have "gone square" lots of times all over the world.'[79] Most commentators, who took the issue every bit as seriously as Taylor did, disagreed with him, since he directly confronted such emerging manifestos of 'Nordic' superiority as Lothrop Stoddard's *Rising Tide of Color* (1920) with counterclaims of 'Alpine' (or Asian) superiority.[80] Aware that he courted controversy, Taylor boldly declared: 'I have come to the conclusion that the so-called Nordic races do not stand out as the most advanced type of man. This will not please a powerful section in American circles.'[81] Not only were Aryans not the master race, but 'the yellow type of man had developed from the Aryan type'.[82] As was the case with most other racial taxonomists, Taylor's categories and terminology slipped and changed over time, and from one draft of his work to the next. Using 'Aryan' in his first full draft of *Environment and Race* in 1924, he was even then unsure, scratching out Aryan for Caucasian, and leaving inconsistent usages in his final proofs. But his main intervention, following Ripley and others, was that Europeans should not consider themselves one race, distinct from Asians, but as variously 'Mediterranean', 'Nordic' and 'Alpine', with the last 'as Asiatic as the Chinese'.[83]

At the crux of Taylor's racial evolution theory was the deep-rootedness and future inevitability of racial hybridity. No matter how civilised or advanced, no race was 'pure', save the most primitive, who had been isolated from contact with other peoples. This belief drove Taylor to conduct research among 'half-caste' people in Australia's south-east, not the 'full-bloods' who dominated in the north and interior and attracted the lion's share of anthropologists' interest. Like many experts of his time, Taylor thought that the Aboriginal race was on the road to extinction: 'At the first approach of a more progressive race they have almost vanished from the face of the earth.' But unlike other researchers, he collected anthropometric data in an effort to plot the pace and precise nature of this inexorable process. He saw nothing regrettable about the decline of 'full-blooded' Aboriginals, for:

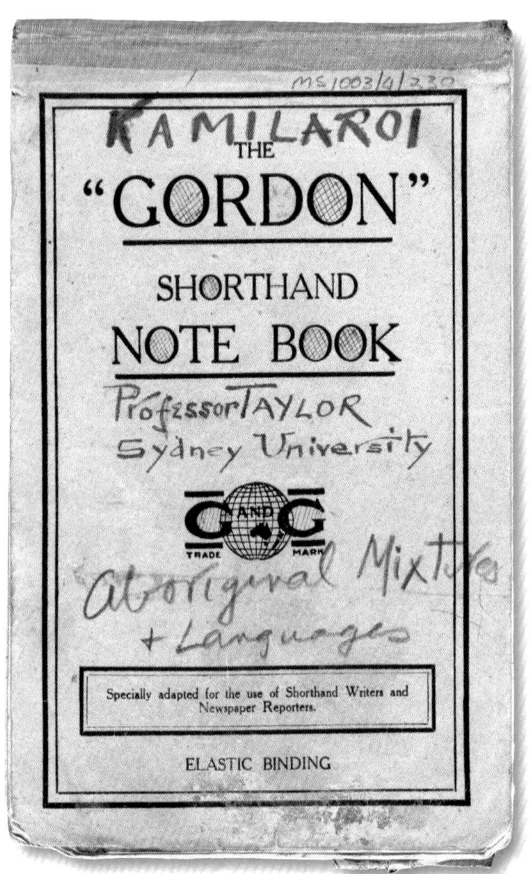

Taylor's notebook on the Kamilaroi, 1924. Pursuing his new-found identity as a race theorist, Taylor studied the Kamilaroi people of northern and western New South Wales in 1924. This notebook from his field trip detailed his observations of people—language, culture, physical data, family lines—as well as the landscape through which he journeyed.

> Nothing is so dangerous to a people as complete isolation. The natural barrier which preserved the Australian aboriginals from invasion also resulted in their remaining in the same low state of civilization for 100 000 years.[84]

In becoming a student of 'civilisation', Taylor entered the world not only of physical but also of cultural anthropology, associated with scholars such as Cambridge professor Alfred Court Haddon. Taylor had met Haddon's daughter when he was a Cambridge student, and escorted her on several occasions. (Had the two married, Taylor would have acquired a social-scientific pedigree for his children, rather than the Priestley lineage of scientist-explorers). In 1909, Taylor wrote to his sister that he had met Miss Haddon of Newnham, 'whose dad "did" Torres Straits'. He had also accompanied Miss Sollas, daughter of anthropologist and geologist William Sollas, on numerous occasions: 'I had a merry talk with Miss Sollas about Aborigines, in which I gave my views (and today have seen a long article by her father totally opposing them!).'[85] In 'doing' the Torres Straits, Haddon was the more innovative of the professors, as he helped introduce studies of culture alongside anthropometric studies of biology. Haddon still took stock in the value of physical measurement in anthropology but he combined anthropometry with extensive studies of everyday culture and folklore—children's games and toys in England, for example. A decade on from his Cambridge days, Taylor began to follow this trend, though he treated culture much more casually even than he did anthropometry. On his Australian trips, he collected linguistic 'evidence' (basic bits of vocabulary) as well as whatever tools, songs, stories and family histories he could extract. In a string of scholarly articles,[86] he drew conclusions based on material which he had recorded rapidly, as little more than amateur dabbling. In one sketchbook, labelled 'Kamilaroi, Aboriginal Mixtures and Languages', he took notes on individuals' names (first and last), physical characteristics, 'intelligence', ages, family lineages, caste quotients, skin tone, eye colour, plus translations of terms, descriptions of songs and dances, and sketches of a few of their locations. This was Taylor at his bower-bird best, or worst, raiding every scrap of cultural evidence that appeared to corroborate his theories of racial migration.

In contrast to his comfort with anthropometry, Taylor was often befuddled or bemused by cultural anthropology.[87] When he met Haddon again in 1923 on a field trip to Broken Hill (arranged as an extension of the Sydney meetings of the Pan-Pacific Science Congress), he recognised that he had much to learn from the master.[88] Acting on Haddon's advice, he decided to minimise his use of cultural data in his publications on racial evolution but he continued to plot linguistic evidence as 'the most important single aspect of culture'.[89] While Taylor was prepared to accept a public dressing-down from the Cambridge professor, who criticised Taylor's zones-and-strata theory at the congress,[90] he glibly dismissed US cultural anthropologists, led by Franz Boas. Social scientists, who emphasised culture and adaptation over physical and environmental determinism, seemed unscientific to Taylor. Thus, when he heard Margaret Mead, a Boas student, deliver a lecture on New Guinean customs and beliefs, he wrote it off: 'too much psychology for me—I always want to say "Prove it"'.[91]

Margaret Mead might have asked the same of him, since Taylor plucked the cultural evidence he mounted to support his migration-zone theory from sources of dubious authority. According to Taylor's model, people from comparable zones—that is, people 'pushed out' from the cradleland along peninsulas at similar times in the past—shared cephalic readings as well as languages and cultural practices. The evidence he presented to substantiate this correlation was colourful and bizarre: a zone of peoples with a head index of 76 (Hottentots, Portuguese, Punjabis, Micronesians, Hurons) share the custom of couvade, where fathers abstain from certain food and practices after their wives give birth; groups with a head index of 78 (Japanese, Marquesan and Maori) all practise tattooing; Scottish Highlanders and the Dusans of Borneo, along the same 'isocephalic line', not surprisingly both wear tartan kilts. In the same way, he drew correlative links between the languages of Southern India and of Australian Aboriginals, with the barest smattering of philological data: 'agglutinative with many suffixes'. Of course the two had similar speech elements, he aimed to convince his readers, since they shared the same cephalic index and had migrated in the same early thrust from Central Asia.

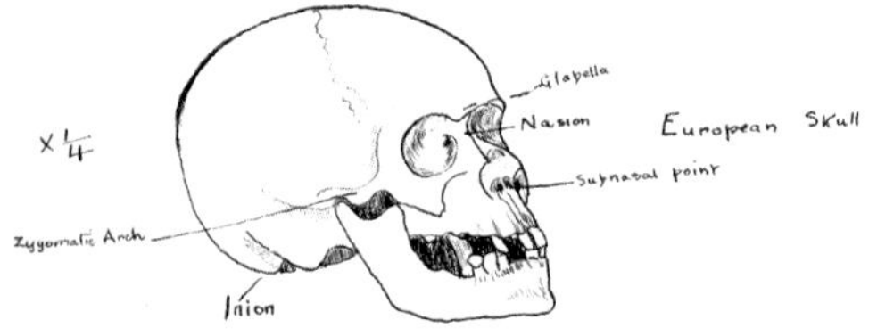

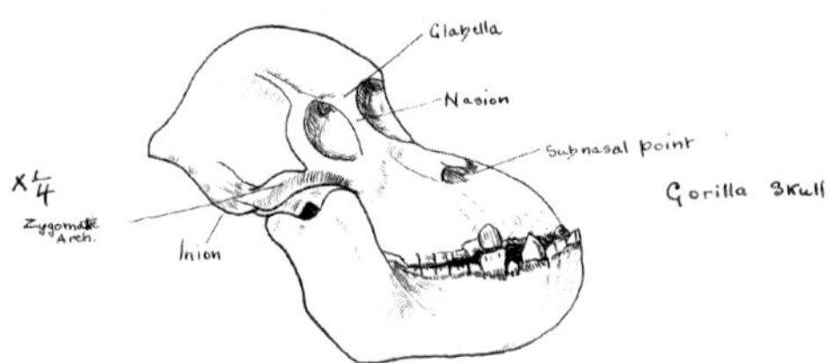

Dorothy Taylor's notes from her brother's lectures on anthropometry, 1926. Under Taylor, the third year of geography at the University of Sydney was largely devoted to the study of racial difference. Dorothy ('Pal') was a top student and succeeded him as acting lecturer in geography on his departure for Chicago in 1928.

This conjunction of physical and impressionistic cultural anthropology formed a central plank in Taylor's geography program at the University of Sydney. Since he believed so firmly in the physical environment's controlling role in the evolution and distribution of race, he ensured that anthropology be given as significant a place in the curriculum as geology. He claimed, rightly, that he was the first professor at the University of Sydney to offer anthropology, since he taught anthropometric and ethnographic theory to his geography students five years before Radcliffe Brown founded the anthropology department, Australia's first. The syllabus Taylor set for Sydney's geography students took them on the same intellectual journey that he had travelled as a student, public servant and academic. It began with geology, the literal groundwork, followed in the second year by meteorology, and then ethnography in the final year of study. By 1925, the examinations he set his students had a decidedly Tayloresque hue. He required them to write essays on three separate fields of inquiry: 'Ethnology', 'Australian Settlement &c' and 'Pacific Problems &c'. Typically, the ethnology questions concerned the 'races of man'. 'How do you account for the preservation of Tasmanian and Australian Aborigines to modern times?' was one question. Another was: 'Discuss the past and present distribution of the Nordic and Alpine peoples in Europe and Western Asia. What are the chief ethnological characteristics of each race?'[92]

The prominence of Taylor's 'new ethnology' in his geography teaching is evident in the surviving lecture notes and exercise sheets written by one of his top students—his sister, Dorothy. Familiar with her brother's ideas on race, as expressed and elaborated in endless family letters, she became the geography department's map drawer in 1921, then a demonstrator and diligent student in 1924.[93] Dorothy had first enrolled at the university in 1904, but suspended her study a year later, possibly to take up responsibilities at home, after their father James struggled to find contract work and Mater was left alone for long stretches. When she re-enrolled at the University of Sydney 20 years later, credited for her earlier studies in arts and science, Dorothy worked under an instructor who spared her no criticism. If anything, Taylor's expectations for his sister were likely higher than for his other students: 'good, but try ink', he wrote in red pencil across the intricate drawings and maps she drew in her Geology 1 Practical notebook. Along with her classmates, Dorothy completed worksheets on Antarctic winds, on the geomorphology of the Illawarra coast, as well as on 'The Races of Man and their Dispersion' and 'Ethnology–Anthropometry'. For the latter, she worked out calliper measurements for 'Europeans', 'Egyptians' and 'Aboriginals', drew a European skull and a gorilla skull, practised measuring noses and ears on models, and calculated the height of fellow students according to her brother's instructions.[94] She followed his directions well, and completed her Bachelor of Science degree (with high distinction in geography) at the end of 1927, only days before their father died.[95]

James Taylor lived long enough to see his only daughter become a scientist but not quite long enough to see her become acting lecturer in geography for a year in 1929, on the departure of her brother for Chicago. His first-born son also had a chance to make an impression when he proudly presented his father with a copy of *Environment and Race*, which Oxford University Press published a month before James succumbed to bladder cancer. An associate of Taylor's, David Stead, reviewed the book favourably in the *Sydney Mail* in a major two-page spread. In pain, but refusing all medication, James might have found comfort in the flattering commentary Stead offered his son's work:

> This book will be eagerly sought by students of man's evolution, of present and future migration, of world settlement, and of the social order ... Taylor's work holds a very special interest [in Australia] and it is quite fitting that a large part of [the book] has been devoted to one or other aspects of past, present and future diffusion of man in our great and unique island continent.[96]

After years of public opposition to Taylor's pronouncements on Australian settlement ambitions in Australia's desert and tropical regions, and after his battles with the university over his salary and status, this glowing review would have made a welcome change for everyone in the family.

Taylor looked forward to further positive responses to *Environment and Race*, hoping for a promotion at the University of Sydney or, if that failed, the chance to graft himself onto the impressive line of Harvard and Yale-based scholars, whose mentorship and friendship he had cultivated for 10 years. He shared his dream with Huntington. 'With all humility,' he commented disingenuously of his book, 'it seems a fair companion for Dixon's "History" and your "Character".'[97] (The 'Dixon' he mentioned was Harvard anthropologist Roland B. Dixon, a former student of Franz Boas, while 'History' was Dixon's *The Racial History of Man*, 1923.) The US reception was far harsher than he had hoped, however. Dixon, like many anthropologists, rejected much of Taylor's racial theory. For a start he 'dissent[ed] seriously' from Taylor's disinterest in variability: '[No] study of racial questions today can expect to get favourable reception among anthropologists which fails to take into account the range and character of the variations within each human group.' Dixon also criticised Taylor's links between mammalian and human migration; he objected to Taylor's use of the term 'most primitive' and advised him to use 'earliest'; he completely rejected the concept of one centre of evolution, since Taylor's own evidence seemed 'to quite disprove the whole hypothesis as to an Inner Asiatic Center since it is a region which on the whole is extremely barren of any evidence of "buried strata"'.[98] While Dixon was notoriously fractious, many sociologists responded similarly. Columbia's Bernard J. Stern essentially advised Taylor to stick to geology and geography, since he judged him:

> unaware of the existence of anthropological material that completely upsets his basic classifications. As a geographer he has attempted to deal with a subject which at first is charmingly refreshing but becomes distressing when one realizes the author's insufficient orientation in the literature in the field.

Geographic possibilists dismissed his work as well. Berkeley geographer Carl Sauer judged that Taylor had pushed determinism to limits 'which Ratzel in his most exuberantly speculative moments could scarcely have attained'.[99]

James had fortunately passed away before he had to see his son so handily dismissed. *Environment and Race* did attract some other, more positive scholarly reviews, however. The curator of prehistoric archaeology at the American Museum of Natural History, N.C. Nelson, wrote to Taylor after reading a mixed but lengthy review of the book in *American Anthropologist*, telling him that he and Louis Sullivan (whose anthropometry manual Taylor had used) had been thinking along the same lines as Taylor for several years. American Stephen Visher, who had worked on Australian meteorological data and long admired Taylor's talent for data presentation, gave *Environment and Race* a positive review in the journal *Ecology*, starting a decades-long friendship. Visher recommended *Environment and Race* to all ecologists because of 'its leadership in graphic presentation, its suggestive speculations, and its striking examples of influences of the environment'.[100] And crucially, geographers Huntington and Bowman stuck by Taylor, still admiring his imaginative reach, while questioning its factual foundation. Only one scholar endorsed it wholeheartedly: Ratzel's former pupil German geographer Karl Haushofer, who reviewed it in *Volk und Rasse*. Although Taylor later dissociated himself from Haushofer, whose theories were adopted by Nazi policymakers, his comments impressed Taylor sufficiently for him to translate the review into English to distribute to his colleagues.

Even though anthropologists reacted to Taylor's racial theories with puzzlement and sometimes even contempt, for Taylor himself, the die was cast: somewhere between his Bureau work on settlement and his publication of *Environment and Race* in 1927, he morphed from a natural scientist into a human scientist—from identifying as a geologist to identifying as a geographer. His curious agglomerations of disparate data collected by others, his disarming metaphors and innovative images, and the sheer sweep of his ideas made *Environment and Race* difficult to ignore. Like Huntington's *Character of*

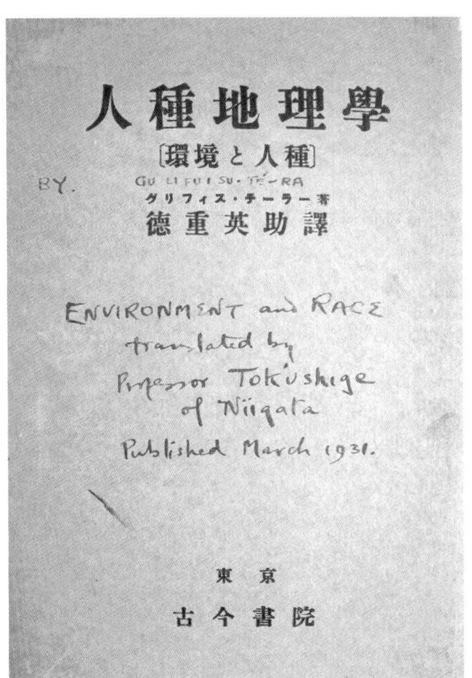
人種地理學
〔環境と人種〕
BY.
GU LI FU I SU・TE–RA
グリフィス・テーラー著
徳重英助譯
ENVIRONMENT and RACE
translated by
Professor Tokushige
of Niigata
Published March 1931.
東京
古今書院

Taylor's theories about Asian superiority garnered him an interested audience in that region. This Japanese translation of *Environment and Race* appeared in 1931.

Races, it attracted enough criticism and praise to convince Taylor that it amounted to something very impressive indeed. Although it was never a best seller, Oxford reprinted it five times; over the 1930s and 1940s it was translated into Chinese, Japanese, French and Spanish. This international recognition convinced Taylor to republish it with new material as *Environment, Race and Migration* in 1937, after he moved to Canada, revising it yet again (with new Canadian material) in 1945.[101]

By the time he had reached his forties, Taylor had moved well beyond his six-year-old observations on the London 'China man', to elaborate a grand theory about racial hybridity and hierarchy. Yet his evolution as a racial theorist rarely registers in present-day assessments of the man, in which scientists herald his work on Australian land and resources, and polar enthusiasts celebrate his historic place on the most famous of Antarctic expeditions. Taylor's idiosyncratic ideas on the origins of man, on climate and white settlement, and on racial characteristics and race-mixing, were integral to this scientific work, always literally grounded in his assessment of the environment. Taylor himself acknowledged that his racial theories launched his international career, and even after publishing scores of books he always regarded *Environment and Race* as his greatest intellectual work.

The Daily Telegraph
SYDNEY, MONDAY, JUNE 25, 1923.
WILL SOMEBODY TELL HIM?
Professor Griffith Taylor (Sydney University) asks: Why are we so horror-stricken at any suggestion of marriage with Mongolians?
Aklavik
Caribou Pastures
Limit of Root
Churchill
Limit of GRAIN where soils favourable
LIMIT OF DENSE WHEAT
Clay Belt
Agriculture
Vancouver
ARID
U.S.A.
COAL

Prophet and Pariah

4

As Taylor warned his fiancée, she had engaged herself to a scientist, not a religious man. 'After 15 years [of] fairly close scientific training,' he explained, 'I must see some why or wherefore or analogy to something I know to be true before I can ascertain a theory ... Meditation on unselfish things is about as far as I ever get in a church.'[1] There was nothing meditative about Taylor's character, though. He was a born communicator, who made it his business, once he ascertained the truth, to spread it, not just within an elite circle of specialists but to the wider public as well. Professor David taught that scientists, in particular, had a duty to educate the citizens of a country like Australia—newly federated, vast and still largely unexplored by Europeans. In the 1910s, Taylor followed David's creed by writing his bulletins for the Bureau of Meteorology. Once his wish for an academic post finally came true in 1920, he approached his duty with increased zeal through his teaching, his professional publications and addresses, and, most controversially, his contributions to the popular press. Far from marrying a cool-headed agnostic, Doris formed a partnership with a pugnacious prophet of scientific nation-planning.

Working in Sydney, and later in Chicago and Toronto, Taylor promoted geography as a vital tool for the development of nations and the moulding of good citizens. He believed that modern geography, over every other discipline, offered governments a rational basis for national development through comprehensive understanding of environmental possibilities and limits. 'What more exalted study can there be than the science which directly makes for the well-being of the nation? What subject better deserves study by our statesmen?'[2] While his students, many of them future teachers of geography, were prepared to accept such lofty claims, the governments and public Taylor addressed were not so readily convinced. His predictions, based on 'Nature's plan', earned him both praise and condemnation—far more of the latter in the 1920s, when his critical stance towards national population and settlement policies turned him into a pariah.

Spurned in his own country, he decamped to the US in 1929, where he cultivated his deterministic approach to geography, well aware that this involved stroking against the dominant current of 'possibilism'. By the time he made his move to Toronto in 1935, his determinist credo remained unaltered: '[T]he best economic program for a country to follow has in large part been decided by Nature.'[3] What *did* change, though, was the reception his predictions of Canada's future development received. In Australia's 'sister dominion' he became a harmless optimist, able to point out Canada's untapped environmental assets without causing a stir. The impact he made as a geography teacher and author of best-selling geography school texts was far greater. In Canada, Taylor fulfilled his mission to educate youth and train the country's future nation-planners. By the time he retired in 1951 and moved back to Australia, there were few young Canadians who had not read a Taylor textbook.

Taylor, the secularist, took seriously his duty to spread the gospel of modern geography. Casting himself as a nation planner performed a number of functions. It allowed him to endure the 1920s, over which he kept the faith, in spite of the criticism he faced, much of it personal and hurtful. 'The geographer has, and will, come under much abuse in this connection. He is accustomed to such terms as "Doctor Dismal" and "Modern Jeremiah", to mention no worse!'[4] While the Australian popular press named him 'Jeremiah', the bearer of lamentable tidings about the nation's future, Taylor considered himself more like another Old Testament prophet—Elijah, who called upon the people and their leaders to reject their misguided faith and to embrace the truth of his message. Understanding himself as a prophet had other benefits for Taylor: it fed his faith that his ignorant critics would ultimately accept the validity of his predictions, and it affirmed his sense of himself as exceptional, a man who craved respectable credentials while clinging, simultaneously, to his professional marginality. His participation in volatile public debates in Australia—and his more tempered work as an educator in the US and Canada—involved more than just conjuring the 'right numbers' and appropriate 'racial composition' of a country, or determining its best environments for future settlement; it was about the role of science and 'truth' in public affairs. This was all very personal for

Taylor, who never doubted he was right, but felt keenly the forecaster's frustration when his wise predictions were ignored, dismissed or declared heretical.

'Useless': Australian Nation-building

Taylor's first contribution to nation-building involved precisely that: direct involvement, as the Bureau of Meteorology's physiographer, in the location planning and naming of the new capital for a federated Australia. Accepting this assignment as a public servant in the 1910s gave him good reason to consider himself a patriot, and provided him solace once he began to face charges of disloyalty only a decade later. Federal planners relied on Taylor for detailed studies of the Canberra region to supplement the preliminary topographical survey he had prepared with Professor David's help. In 1912, he was assigned to conduct a geological survey of the Federal Capital Territory with a view to assessing its environmental resources: an undertaking he found 'more congenial than weather forecasting in the Melbourne office,' he recalled, although it involved considerably more exertion.[5] His fieldwork style was impressive, if eccentric, according to the men he worked with: 'One morning, a delicate-looking young man was early astir in the camp, his pockets ... bulging with newspaper packets, bread and cheese.' With a push bicycle he proceeded across the mountains in a manner almost as absurd as his approach had been to Glacial Tongue in Antarctica, though at lesser risk. 'A few days later he returned, bike and all,' a fellow surveyor noted. 'I have since been over that country, and to this day I do not know how he did it. It was Dr Griffith Taylor—and that explains it all.'[6] This shows Taylor at his most gifted: indefatigable and capable of swiftly preparing accurate, detailed maps that formed the basis for the capital's planning.

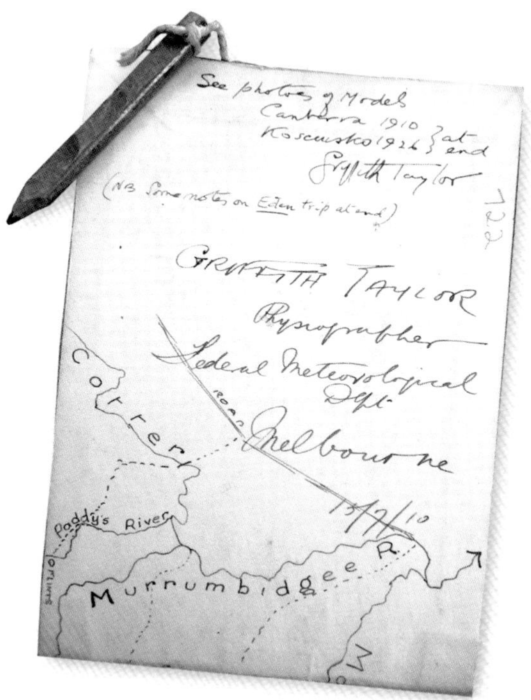

Taylor's sketchbook with pencil attached, 1910. Taylor was assigned to survey the new Federal Capital Territory, which he traversed on foot and by bicycle.

'Laying the Foundation Stones ... Programme', 1913. Taylor attended the windswept ceremony which founded Canberra, 12 March 1913. He claimed credit for naming the Australian capital-to-be.

Taylor was an official invitee for the ceremony that commemorated the founding of Canberra in March 1913. After earlier receiving his King's Polar Medal at Buckingham Palace, the Canberra event was something of a colonial letdown; a windswept affair conducted against a backdrop of sheep paddocks. Nevertheless, the Prime Minister, the Governor General and Lady Denman attended, and the capital which Taylor had helped plan finally received its official name. (Considerable debate had preceded the choice but Taylor congratulated himself for having recommended the eventual winner.)[7] After this ceremony, his connection to Canberra moved from practical planning to professional reflection. In a talk given to the (British) Royal Geographical Society, later published as 'Evolution of a Capital', he conceded that the establishment of a purpose-built, inland capital had been politically expedient, a necessary federal compromise between rivals Sydney and Melbourne. Yet he assured his fellow geographers that no compromise had been made on environmental grounds, thanks to his surveys. The location of Canberra conformed to the country's overall 'south-seeking' population pattern. 'Hence we see that on the basis of future economic development, the capital should be situated south of the tropic [of Capricorn].' More specifically, the site included a large river, and low but reliable rainfall sufficient to sustain future population growth. Four months of the year were cool, but he thought this would provide the stimulation politicians needed ('conducive to earnest work, at any rate in winter') and a climate 'suitable for British-born residents'. Taylor approved of Chicago-based architect Walter Burley Griffin's modernist design for the future city, since it made the most of the environment. Inspired by the City Beautiful movement, Burley Griffin designed its streets along a cobweb pattern and proposed that its major civic buildings be set against the 'beautiful panoramas' of surrounding mountains. With such plans in place, Taylor predicted, Canberra would become 'the official and social centre of Australia'.[8] For Taylor, creating a capital was nation-planning in microcosm, a rational process through which modern environmental and urban-design expertise informed political decisionmaking, producing the optimum outcome in the public interest. If Canberra was 'a city built to plan',[9] there was no reason why the whole nation would not likewise benefit from rational, environmentally informed planning.

In contrast to Taylor's involvement in capital planning, government-commissioned and government-approved, his vision of the nation's development was unsolicited and unpalatable to Australians intoxicated with dreams of national greatness. Although his Bureau work on future white settlement in the tropics was considered controversial, his assessment of arid Australia was far more notorious and touched off a torrent of public criticism. Australians accepted without question that the continent included tropical zones, yet many refused to believe that it also included desert regions that set limits on grand hopes for agricultural development and population expansion.[10] Taylor argued consistently that much of Australia was 'uninhabited' (meaning uninhabited by Europeans) precisely because it was 'useless'—unsuitable for stock or for crops. Not even improvements to transport and communication routes—which had expanded over the 1910s and 1920s into South Australia, Western Australia and the Northern Territory—had produced appreciable population increases in what Taylor called the 'sparselands'. Large areas of the continent had 'no white population at all'—the Arunta region in the Northern Territory, the eastern part of Western Australia and the Western Desert. In a paper, 'Uninhabited Australia and the Reasons Therefore', which he delivered at the 1923 Pan Pacific Science Congress, Taylor showed that almost half of Australia contained fewer than 10 000 settlers. The reason? '[T]his kind of desert does not support a population anywhere else in the world, [so] why would it here?' His expert contribution to this critical national issue was too important to confine to a circle of experts:

> I conceive it a duty to educate the Australian public in this very important problem, when we see almost every day prominent politicians, and even cabinet ministers, making the most unwarranted statements as to our arid and tropical lands.[11]

'Is it a Sahara?', *The Sun*, 13 May 1924. When Taylor referred to much of Australia's centre and west as a 'desert', many Australians, harbouring grand dreams of national greatness, objected. In the 1920s, his assessment of Australia's limited growth potential was considered unpatriotic.

Taylor took to the popular press to fulfil this self-appointed duty. In the metropolitan dailies he wrote feature articles on 'arid Australia', including maps to illustrate which areas of the country were best and least suited to different forms of economic exploitation, based on his expert assessment of 'physical controls', particularly temperature, rainfall and geology. Based on that knowledge, he mapped areas that suited close settlement: the eastern seaboard and its western slopes, as well as the temperate south-west coast and south-west tip of the continent. Much of the remainder of the country, moving inland, was appropriate for pastoral or sparse pastoral development. But then he drew large circles around sections of central-west Australia and scored them 'ALMOST USELESS' and 'USELESS'.[12] Patriotic Australians who saw Taylor's maps in newspapers were enraged, especially those who had personal, financial and nationalistic investments in the young country's promise. To them this land was *useful*, filled with resources waiting to be tapped by 'White' Australia. Expectations of the country's potential had been high from the moment of Federation but they expanded greatly after the sacrifices the country made during World War I. In an anxious era, when nationalism took on greater stridency, Taylor's cautionary message appeared insidious and disloyal.

Billy Hughes (Labor Prime Minister between 1915 and 1923) was one of the 'well-meaning propagandists' Taylor tried to set straight on the matter of settlement and environment. When Hughes claimed the new nation-continent could attract and sustain 100 million people, Taylor considered the politician's estimate absurd. Set against numbers so huge, Taylor's environmentally determined maximum of 20 million looked pessimistic; worse still, his insistence on proclaiming it from every Australian daily generated negative publicity for a nation eager to present itself to the world as brimming with potential for (white) population growth. For Taylor, though, projecting future population and settlement was not a guessing game for amateurs: it was the business of experts assessing where the environment was suitable for growth and where 'Nature' dictated no increase, no matter how shrill the cries of patriots and investors. There was no reason for public money to be squandered on portions of the continent with poor soil and meagre rainfall, when rich land in temperate climates remained available for development.

Taylor's criticisms of grandiose plans to populate arid and desert Australia were based on the sound data and physiographic analysis he had gathered and analysed in his years at the Bureau of Meteorology. Unlike the loose and inexpert ethnological work he was then undertaking, his analysis of the Australian desert—affected by its poor position relative to the Antarctic rain belt on the one hand, and the Equatorial rain belt on the other—was thoroughly documented.[13] Next to the Poles, the Antarcticker claimed, 'Australia as a whole is situated along ... economically, the least attractive latitudes in the world'.[14] To Australians who fully anticipated that their country's future would be as bright and profitable as the comparably sized United States, Taylor's scientific statements were fighting words, even traitorous. If Australia's first settlers had heeded his cautionary pronouncements about 'useless' land, one of Taylor's Western Australian critics protested, '50% of the wheat belt of W.A., to say nothing of the pastoral area, would still be in the possession of the blackfellow'.[15]

The more misguided and unrealistically optimistic the opposition became, the harder Taylor hammered his 'dismal' forecasts, gaining increasing notoriety and attracting opprobrium along the way. Yet he just couldn't stifle himself: 'Unfortunately for me I was seized with an impelling desire to find out precisely why the "Empty Space" remained empty!'[16] The content of Taylor's environmental assessments was objectionable on its own without the addition of his provocative delivery style, inflaming nationalist nerves and embarrassing his more circumspect colleagues. His 'homoclime' method, for instance, effectively illustrated the environmental links between regions of the same latitude. When he used this method to compare Australia to the US, it was uncontroversial, since Australians considered it a model for development; in contrast, his homoclime maps, which he used to illustrate Australia's climatic similarity to Northern Africa, provoked condemnation.[17] Taylor used every major newspaper in Australia, every public talk, every course of lectures, to challenge his opponents to think geographically rather than patriotically when they considered future settlement. Taylor asked whether they would contemplate sending their own families to the:

> mouth of the Congo, or the coast lands of Mexico, or on the east and south coasts of India? Yet these are the homoclimes of Broome (Western Australia), Nullagine (Western Australia), Darwin, and Wyndham.[18]

The Professor and the Public

When Taylor was just a public servant, printing his environmental assessments in bulletins for the Bureau of Meteorology, he had a relatively modest footing from which to argue his expertise; once he became the country's foundation chair in geography at one of its top universities, he felt that his authority to pronounce on nation-planning issues ought to be incontestable.

A separate department of geography at the University of Sydney had been Edgeworth David's dream since his own appointment in 1893. Who better than his former demonstrator to make it a reality? David successfully lobbied the professorial board and university senate to establish a geography department and to make Taylor a formal offer to head it. However, it was unclear for several months whether Taylor would accept the job. In a replay of his earlier dance between the Antarctic expedition invitation and the Bureau offer, Taylor contemplated an alternative offer in 1920: Isaiah Bowman had contacted him about the prospect of moving to New York to work for the American Geographical Society. Taylor was tempted by the position, and excited at the thought of leaving Australia for the US, where his research had won acclaim. The prospect of moving to a city and a nation that he thought could keep up with him clearly attracted Taylor, but he didn't jump before pressing for the highest salary and position that the

University of Sydney might offer. While David struggled to maintain professorial support for his former student's appointment, Taylor played Sydney's proposal off against Bowman's. When Sydney offered a lectureship at £600 per annum he turned it down, since it merely matched his current salary. He responded by demanding more money and higher academic status. He also laid out two further conditions: he expected that geography would become a science department, and he wanted the university to hire his sister, Dorothy, to be his assistant. Late in June, he put further pressure on the university, informing the senate that the American Geographical Society had just offered to pay him $4000 per year, along with a $2000 allowance for a half-year's fieldwork. Professor David wasn't dazzled by the American offer, and soberly advised Taylor that he would be 'more comfortable working here with our own British people than in New York as a citizen of the USA'. Committed to filling the geography position, David managed to broker a sweeter deal for Taylor once again.[19] In July 1920, the senate raised Taylor's salary offer by 50 per cent, offering him £900, and it agreed to appoint him as an associate professor. This tipped the balance, and Taylor respectfully turned down Bowman's offer, explaining he preferred a university position, and revealing that Doris was unhappy at the thought of living in New York: she 'rather dreads the high cost of living in New York and the totally new environment of life in America'.[20] Dorothy seconded Doris's concerns but focused on her nephew and brother: 'I don't want Bill to be a lil' Yankee ... and as for a rapid nerve temperament like yours the Yankee rush is most unhealthy.'[21] For the time being, at least, Taylor's English 'lass' could remain in the Empire, and he and his family could return to a city filled with Taylors, Bill's grandparents, his uncles, aunts and cousins.

The brief to head his own university department was challenging without being daunting; besides, Taylor believed he offered the university unique qualities: 'my not inconsiderable practical experience in the fields of Geology and Climate, not to mention ten years' scientific travel'.[22] He also brought a philosophical approach to geography, which he considered superior to the old 'names and places' and 'know your capitals' version of the subject most Australian students learned. His confidence and optimism were undermined from the outset, however. He wrongly assumed when he accepted the post in November 1920 that the founder of Australia's first geography department would quickly receive the promotion and pay rise that such a position warranted but in fact the university's professoriate failed to grant the department of geography academic respect, and regarded its brash public intellectual an irritant. It was acceptable to engage fellow scholars in professional discussion but to publish inflammatory articles in the popular press as Taylor did was indiscreet. Feeling unsupported and unappreciated, Taylor put his head down and stormed ahead, refusing to retreat into quiescence. He poured his energy into establishing a demanding degree program in the 'new geography', the approach Oxford's Halford Mackinder had pioneered and Taylor had long admired.[23] It certainly worked: geography attracted a large number of students drawn to Taylor's argument that the discipline was best suited to assess man's relation to his environment. Teaching this message—in the lecture hall, the lab, the field and the public press—

became Taylor's personal mission, in spite of the dismissive responses from colleagues and the insults suffered in the press.

Controversy shadowed Taylor's entire career at the University of Sydney. In 1921, just as he settled into his new position and shortly before the birth of his daughter, Natalie, the University of Western Australia's (UWA's) governing body notified him that it had removed his 1911 book, *Australia*, from the 'Manual of Public Examinations'. The textbook was consequently 'banned from the University' and the acting director of education further threatened to ban it as a teacher's reference book, since it 'grossly misrepresented' Western Australia and contained inaccuracies about the state's environmental shortcomings.[24] Although the book had been used for a decade, Taylor's more recent newspaper writings and 'USELESS'-zoned maps focused unwanted attention on Western Australia in particular, and state authorities resented that his use of the term 'desert' compromised the state's concerted efforts to attract settlers.[25] William Sommerville, a vocal nationalist and member of the UWA senate thought that Taylor was misusing his position: 'It is a source of astonishment to me that a University Professor should be so dense as to fail to grasp the reason for the resentment shown at his use of the word "desert".'[26] Taylor knew that his maps were 'distinctly unpopular' in Western Australia but he held to Professor David's creed: '[I]t is the geographer's duty to try to explain "absence of settlement".'[27] Duty aside, he might have anticipated that comparing Western Australia to the Kalahari and the Sahara would provoke outrage in 'White' Australia[28]—but choosing a more palatable word, such as 'wilderness', would never have elevated Taylor into a national figure. The 'banning' of his textbook in Western Australian schools and the university confirmed that he was misunderstood *because* he was right and *because* his opponents did not approach the subject as scientists. As a result he saw himself as a persecuted bearer of the truth, and this perception stuck with him long after his environmental analyses gained support.[29]

opposite left

'Professor's Plain English', *Sunday News*, 1 May 1927. The debate about Australia's population and environment was a press staple over the 1920s. Taylor capitalised on this, regularly writing up his own research for popular audiences in newspapers.

opposite right

Poster: 'What Does the Future Hold for Australia?', c.1923. As an important public intellectual, Taylor juggled lecturing at the University of Sydney with a constant round of talks given to local groups on key national questions.

University of Sydney Extension Lectures

KILLARA CENTRE

What does the Future Hold for Australia ?

The Populating of Australia is a Matter of VITAL IMPORTANCE.

How many people can we accommodate here and where can we put them ?

IS A MILLION FARMS FOR A MILLION PEOPLE A SOUND ECONOMIC PROJECT ?

PROFESSOR GRIFFITH TAYLOR will give the Scientific Facts of the Problem TO-MORROW NIGHT,

TUESDAY, JUNE 23rd

at 8.15 in the

Killara Hall

Lecture will be illustrated by Lantern Slides, and is of absorb- interest.

ures EVERY TUESDAY NIGHT until July 28th, when the Rt. W. M. Hughes, P.C., K.C., L.L.D., etc., will give us first hand nation about the Peace Conference.

n't - Miss - These

Advocate Print, Hornsby. Tel. Wah. 113.

SUNDAY, THE SUNDAY NEWS MAY 1, 1927

PROFESSOR'S PLAIN ENGLISH

Vital Problems — About Which Australians Know Little and Care Less — Knowing Ourselves — Proposed Geographical Society

Professor Griffith Taylor

By Professor Griffith Taylor, Professor of Geography at Sydney University

FROM the point of view of human biology the most characteristic feature of the Australian nation is that it is an experiment in adjusting man to his environment.

Australians are, very largely, of British stock. This means that, for several thousand years, our race has been subjected to the conditions of north-western Europe. These may be expressed in terms of a cool, damp climate with an average annual temperature of some 50 degrees. The whole method of English life was founded on this environment.

Now occurred a transfer of many thousands of British stock to the Australian continent, where the average temperature is 70 degrees, where there is nothing resembling the conditions in the British Isles, and, indeed, very little resembling those of any part of Europe.

Southern Australia has the environment of Algeria and southern Spain. Northern Australia is akin to Nigeria.

We have, in effect, moved to a hot, dry continent, the direct antithesis of western Europe.

Australians' Apathy

It is unnecessary to point out how this change must affect every aspect of Australian life.

But it is amazing that the vast majority of Australians know little and care less about all those environmental problems which are the special study of the modern geographer. Possibly this is largely due to the fact that our school system does not encourage students to engage in this branch of education. The old geography, with its lists of capes and bays, and its total lack of any relation between cause and effect, was, indeed, a dreary business.

Elementary geography is compulsory, I believe, for young children, but for various reasons, partly from lack of adequate teachers, the study of their own environment is dropped just when they are at an age to begin to appreciate its importance and interest.

Indeed, the study is often replaced by other subjects totally unconnected with Australian surroundings, but sanctioned by a tradition based on the needs of several centuries ago far away in Western Europe.

Many definitions of a good education have been given.

But surely a good education should fit a man to take an intelligent interest in the great problems of his own nation. I will instance only two or three of these. How are we to settle our vast continent? This is emphatically a geographical problem, and it has been the geographer's unpleasant duty, in face of fierce opposition, to point out that a large part of the area of the Commonwealth is entirely unsuited for any noteworthy settlement at the present.

How do we stand with regard to the foreigners pressing upon us on our northern shores? Every man in Australia has views on this matter, which are largely not supported by science. The question is to a very large degree ethnological. Nowhere, except at our University, is there any serious attempt to study these problems scientifically.

Dispelling Ignorance

A group of citizens feels that this ignorance would be in part dispelled if a flourishing Geographical Society could be established.

Sir Edgeworth David has pointed out that modern geography may be described as the best guide to nation-planning. What better aim could be set before the proposed Geographical Society of Sydney?

There is a further reason why a society is desirable, and should flourish in New South Wales. Many young teachers and students have passed through the Department of Geography at the University of Sydney in the last six years. They have, it is believed, acquired a real knowledge of modern scientific geography, in which principles and causes, rather than places and statistics, are chiefly studied. We may hope for valuable research from this group of potential members.

Big Field Open

In a relatively new land like Australia there is, however, a very large amount of purely descriptive work to be done before the more scientific correlations can be deduced, and here is an enormous field for valuable work.

We may reasonably hope that our membership will soon reach several hundreds. The Historical Society in this State has a membership of over 800. A quarterly journal could then be published, which might be so edited as to appeal to the intelligent public, to the teacher, and to the research student. Such a journal has received the support of the Australasian Association for the Advancement of Science.

I propose to take steps so that a public meeting may be convened. It is hoped that those interested in the proposal will send their names to me, so that a powerful sering committee may be formed.

There was a certain naivety to Taylor's commitment to present the facts, no matter what, and in this respect he was much more a prophet than a politician. Scientific forecasting needed no apology: it simply stood for itself, as far as he was concerned.[30] Over the 1920s, he learned the hard way that the terms in which facts were presented could override the meaning of the facts themselves. He nonetheless refused to bend to popular protest over his use of the term 'desert' by coming up with a more palatable synonym. To the layman, he explained over and over, desert connotes 'a sandy waste, an abomination of desolation, wherein there is little or no life'—but to a geographer (meaning a detached, rational expert) a desert is 'simply a region in which the average rainfall is below a certain figure'.[31] The great Australian public ought to appreciate that he was merely applying Vladimir Köppen's classification of climate systems—authoritative in the 1920s (and still in use)—to Australia. In an aptly titled article, 'Nature Versus the Australian', Taylor proclaimed that there had been 'too optimistic a trust in Nature's endowment of the continent'.[32] The tempest his advice generated was not unlike the stir J.W. Gregory had caused with his provocatively titled book *The Dead Heart of Australia* (1906). Even though Gregory ultimately became a critic of Taylor's population and settlement forecasts by the 1920s, both geographers were declared unpatriotic by a public unprepared to acknowledge Australia's environmental limits. When Prime Minister Stanley Bruce chastised Taylor in 1924, he invoked the memory of Gregory's title: '[T]he heart of Australia is not such a desert as those who desire to malign our country would have us believe.'[33]

Underlying such patriotic claims about Australia's potential was the question of public money. Members of Parliament from Western Australia, and state and territory politicians, made it their business to push the Commonwealth to invest heavily in the infrastructure considered necessary to develop these vast regions and Taylor's arguments jeopardised their dreams. He claimed, quite reasonably, that public money should not be wasted on arid areas or regions with sandy soil and he rejected expensive irrigation schemes and railroad plans as 'beneath contempt'.[34] In this respect, he followed directly in his father's footsteps. James Taylor's humble beginnings and his commitment to scientific truth had allowed him to resist the temptation to tell profit-mad mineral prospectors what they hoped to hear, even though he struggled to secure private consultancies after his government mining contract expired. His son was more fortunate, better able to defend scientific freedom from a secure salaried position at the university, but more exposed to public scorn and designation as a political persona non grata.

Taylor complained to Isaiah Bowman that as the sole professional voice against the 'propagandists', he had a public duty to expose such 'wild-cat schemes'.[35] Private investors also had a stake in these schemes and they insisted on the viability of infrastructural development, citing the example of transcontinental railways in North America. Australia, the boosters insisted, ought to follow suit and enhance its rail links as well. Although the country's East–West railway had been completed in 1917 (Taylor himself had travelled on it on his trips to Ooldea and Western Australia), the new route under consideration in the 1920s was a North–South railway from Darwin to Adelaide. The idea had first been suggested in the 1870s and, according to Taylor, it remained a 'perfectly idiotic proposition for a debt-ridden country'.[36]

Far from maligning his country, Taylor insisted, he was labouring in its best interests; his opponents, who claimed to be faithful Australians, were the false patriots.[37] One such man was Labor member for the Northern Territory, Harold Nelson, a passionate advocate of settlement and development in the north.[38] Although Taylor had many critics, he referred to Nelson as his 'bête noire' and publicly asked why Nelson and other 'numerous optimists' refused to read the readily available science on the matter.[39] In 1925, Nelson experienced his environmental comeuppance when he nearly died of dehydration in the Northern Territory desert after wandering three days without water. Reports of the event noted that he had resorted to drinking engine oil. He was rescued, but he didn't escape some cruel jokes Taylor and Bowman exchanged about the incident, as Nelson's fate brought the men closer as friends and fellow scientists. As Bowman replied to the news:

> Your picture of a politician, who is supposed to need no lubricant in order to speak recklessly on any subject, with his mouth full of lubricating oil, perishing in a desert that he says does not exist, is one of the funniest things in the history of science.[40]

In the mid 1920s, barely a month went by without a sheaf of columns and letters in the dailies disputing Taylor's views on Australia's land and population. Well-known anthropologist and journalist Daisy Bates took Taylor on, keeping the issue alive. Living in her tent alongside Aboriginal people at Ooldea in South Australia for 16 years from September 1919, Bates had just missed Taylor's fleeting visit, but the two met often enough in the popular press. For Bates, Taylor's cautionary remarks about future population growth were unpatriotic and unmanly compared to the pioneer spirit that had built Australia: 'The early British pioneer knew nothing of "physical controls", and geology ... But when he saw his few sheep, cattle and horses thrive, he knew the land was good.' New generations of Australian men, she wrote pointedly, needed to 'find [their] manhood and ... Australian citizenship'.[41] For Taylor such comments made little sense, since he considered his scientific expertise his major, if under-appreciated, contribution to Australian civic life: he was proud to be a different kind of pioneer who made his own manly contribution to the nation's development—at great personal cost and considerable self-sacrifice at that.

Taylor's friends urged him to adopt a less combative approach in order to attract more converts and to soften resistance. Isaiah Bowman was not only a prominent geographer but also, in contrast to Taylor, an astute and experienced politician. Rather than dwell on deserts, he suggested:

> [W]hy not begin yourself to talk about the advantages of a particular section that is well favored? Tell what settlers in the sparse pastoral area can do, not what they can't do ... You are so dead right in the whole matter that I want to see you receive the recognition that is your due.

Bowman thought that Taylor would do better to argue from the front foot, and embark on 'an entirely new campaign of a constructive character and aim not at scientists but at the public'.[42] He should present himself clearly as a nation-builder. A more statesmanlike manner, such as the 'admirable temper' of Edgeworth David, ought to be his model.[43] Taylor thanked Bowman for his 'kind letter about "Statecraft & the Deserts"', but, as the next few years would reveal, he found it easier to read such advice than to heed it.[44]

Taylor could appreciate Bowman's point on an intellectual level but he found the pull of public sparring in his field of expertise irresistible. Living on the edge appealed to the Australian geographer, even as it frustrated and distressed him. And it had its compensations: it allowed him to be not just right, but self-righteous, and it provided the opening passage in his tale of vindication. Over the 1920s, Taylor confidently predicted that he would eventually be proven correct but resigned himself to a present in which he had to shout into deaf ears. He also despaired: 'How can our political administrators deal efficiently with the vital national problems of the day if they remain ignorant of the scientific principles involved therein?'[45]

In fact, more people were listening to Taylor and voicing their support than he let on. His was a slightly disingenuous martyrdom, a manufactured marginality. Some politicians railed against him but various Commonwealth departments solicited his expertise on settlement. The Defence Department commissioned him to write a topographic and economic handbook for the use of the Imperial General Staff, which involved a six-week trip to north-west Australia in December 1924. Likewise, the Commonwealth Development and Migration Commission—charged with advising on settlement and population policy—took him very seriously. In 1927, his methods were praised in a report to the commission for offering a 'straightforward scientific and economic basis' for planning. 'A clear cut plan of this nature is naturally not a reliable prophecy of the course of future events, but it supplies the criterion essential for the co-ordination and judgment of practical measures.'[46] That Taylor's work found official favour in bureaucratic and political quarters spoke louder than his petulant and irritable protests that no-one listened.

Since issues of population and settlement far exceeded the question of Australian land specifically, Taylor also attracted international recognition. In the aftermath of World War I, the globe's so-called empty lands were closely scrutinised as population pressure became a matter of growing political and strategic concern. Journalist David G. Stead's review titled 'The Crowded Earth and Australia's Empty Spaces: A Study of Professor Griffith Taylor's Great Book, *Environment and Race*' flagged this larger context.[47] At international meetings on land and population, Taylor's name came up as *the* Australian authority, sometimes alongside Gregory's. He was recommended by fellow Australian geographer Marcel Aurousseau (who in the 1960s tried hard to secure him a knighthood) as 'the best equipped' to address Australian issues at the World Population Conference in Geneva in 1927.[48] And the Institute of Pacific Relations—a Rockefeller-funded think tank, concerned to increase US knowledge of the Far East and the Pacific Rim nations in the spirit of Wilsonian internationalism—was particularly interested in Taylor's opus. The institute had local branches and Taylor was appointed chair of the NSW Branch of the Executive Committee. The institute's general secretary heralded him as 'Australia's first authority on climate and population'. While it was not Taylor but one of his most

'The Crowded Earth', *Sydney Mail*, 16 November 1927. The viability of Australian 'emptiness' was part of a much larger debate about world overpopulation. David G. Stead's positive review of Taylor's book, shortly after it was published in 1927, placed the author squarely in this international context.

THE SYDNEY MAIL, WEDNESDAY, NOVEMBER 16, 1927.—Page 8

The CROWDED EARTH

And Australia's Empty Spaces

A Study of Professor Griffith Taylor's Great Book, "Environment and Race,"

— By —

David G. Stead

of living is immeasurably below that of people with less valuable natural resources, and a much lower average of human industry." These latter peoples are considered "inferior" by the former. And therein lies a basic difference, and a difficulty so vast as to shake the structure of the human family to its very foundation.

successful students, economist Persia Campbell, who ended up attending the Institute of Pacific Relations meeting in Honolulu in July 1926,[49] his involvement in this Pacific network gave his work a new US orientation. For Taylor, facing eastwards across the Pacific towards North America began to become as familiar as facing westwards, the traditional route back towards Cambridge and the Home Country.

'Half-frozen Scientific Gentlemen': Taylor, Huntington and Stefansson

Ironically Taylor's growing international associations provided further ammunition for his Australian critics, who speculated that his disparaging comments about the Australian environment must be foreign imports from the US. One journalist with the populist paper *Smith's Weekly* lumped Taylor together with American Ellsworth Huntington, who also dismissed grandiose Australian development schemes: 'Taylor swells the chorus of half-baked youthful Americans ... there is little to be said for this ephemeral cry of half-frozen scientific gentlemen with mental chilblains.' Like Taylor, Huntington made his views known through newspaper articles; writing to the *New York Times* in 1925, he described the Australian Government's plans to increase the population of the continent by massive amounts as 'criminal'. Huntington's articles provoked swift and strongly worded opposition from the Australian Commission in the US. The *Times* published an official response and the letter gives a clear sense of the political forces Taylor and Huntington faced:

> I desire to state that efforts of the Commonwealth and State Governments in Australia are centered in a policy designed to exploit vast areas awaiting only the advent of settlers to turn virgin country into highly productive land. The present population of the Commonwealth totals no more than that of the City of New York ... There is no immediate intention, and no expectation to increase the population to 100,000,000 but it is the Commonwealth's serious objective to exploit through legitimate channels, persons available in the more congested countries of the Northern Hemisphere, and particularly citizens of the United Kingdom ... Australia enjoys a generous rainfall, and it is only a question of locking the water for discreet distribution to our rich lands.[50]

Since Huntington's and Taylor's professional association was well known, public censure of the former could easily be used to damn the latter. *Smith's Weekly* took the opportunity to accuse Taylor of succumbing to the US 'fad' for climatology, and of following the nonsensical American practice of misnaming North America's 'semi-arctic climates' as 'temperate'. If Taylor and his American compatriot had a problem with sunny Australia, they must both be suffering 'the degrading effect of cold climate'. Surely an Antarctic explorer should know better.

Another North American found a balmier reception in Australia. As the desert settlement controversy raged, the Commonwealth Government commissioned Canadian explorer and Arctic anthropologist Vilhjalmur Stefansson (1879–1962) to resolve it, hoping that he would see vast potential for Australia's development. Stefansson's mission was to demonstrate the possibilities of settlement in unpeopled lands and, in this respect, his Australian commission made some sense. In other respects, however, the Canadian was a curious choice, to say the least, as a man to evaluate arid regions in the Southern Hemisphere. His Icelandic parents had migrated and settled in 'New Iceland' in Manitoba's north. After studying anthropology at Harvard, he had joined the Anglo-American Arctic Expedition, living in Mackenzie Delta communities in Canada's north-west, a region Taylor later surveyed. In 1914, Stefansson had led a disastrous expedition that left many men dead. Nevertheless, he proceeded with a further expedition in 1921 to 'colonise' Wrangel Island, north of Siberia; this time all the men died. The irony of the titles of Stefansson's subsequent books, *The Friendly Arctic* and *Northward Course of Empire*, was lost on few, and definitely not on Bowman, who wrote to Taylor about Stefansson's dubious reputation in the North: '[H]e will not return for further exploration in the Arctic because if he lost his life it would tend to diminish the force of his theories.'[51]

Despite Stefansson's spectacular failures as a coloniser, he arrived in Australia in 1924 heralded as an intrepid explorer, not a frozen-headed foreigner, like Huntington. Taylor, along with Professor David and polar aviator Hubert Wilkins (who had seconded Stefansson in the Arctic) turned up to greet him in Sydney, swayed, perhaps, by polar loyalties. Stefansson was honoured by the Royal Society of New South Wales as 'an explorer who had added 100,000 square miles of territory to our knowledge of the Polar regions'.[52] The Taylors also invited him for dinner, a friendly and hospitable gesture that came with a caveat: 'You know my views,' Taylor wrote: '"Settle the homelands first". They will always be the most important.'[53] Stefansson accepted and replied with a statement that supported possibilism over Taylor's defeatist determinism:

> I am thinking of making a life study of those parts of the earth that are supposed to be worthless either because they are too cold or too hot (humid and disease-ridden) or too dry ... [I have] a large general faith in the ingenuity of man ... I consider it a valid general proposition that the pessimists about any country are more likely to be wrong than the optimists because the pessimists consider permanently insoluble those problems which we are at present unable to solve, while the optimists expect to conquer not only the difficulties which they know how to deal with but also others the solution of which the future will bring forth.[54]

With Stefansson's arrival, the Australian daily papers had just what they wanted: two colourful characters, on opposite sides of a divisive national issue equally forceful, equally credible, at least in the public eye.

Predictably, Stefansson argued for the considerable possibilities of Australian settlement, based on visits he made to Oodnadatta and Alice Springs in the central region of the continent in July and August of 1924. He concluded that a fourfold increase in population was possible in the region and he suggested that a north–south railway be built, and that better telecommunications were needed in order to spur settlement. This was music to the ears of Taylor's bête noir Harold Nelson, who used Stefansson's report in the House of Representatives to paint Taylor as a misguided meddler:

> Has the Prime Minister's attention been drawn to the glowing press reports in which Dr Stefansson states that he has found oases in the centre of Australia, but that so far he has been unable to locate the alleged desert? In the interests of Australia, will the Prime Minister see that Professor Griffith Taylor, of Sydney, is supplied with a copy of Mr Stefansson's report on Central Australia, accompanied by a word of advice to that gentleman to desist from his perpetual slander of Central Australia?[55]

Taylor, undeterred, stuck to his guns, publicly supported by Edgeworth David, who wrote to *The Sydney Morning Herald* pointing out that Stefansson had not travelled within 50 miles of the main desert that Taylor referred to; in fact, he had merely observed the zone that Taylor labelled 'sparse pastoral', not 'useless'.[56] As far as David and Taylor were concerned, Stefansson had neither the credentials nor the fieldwork expertise to assess the region or its potential. He was an 'adventurer' rather than a 'scientist'. So why, Taylor puzzled, did Australians embrace the Canadian and reject him? As he complained to Huntington: 'It is not all beer and skittles being a minor (or minimus) Latter-day Prophet!'[57]

'Taylor-made Australia'

By 1925, Taylor found himself more a pariah than a respected academic in Australia. This was not just by virtue of the desert debates but also because he began to apply his race-mixing theories to the politics of 'White' Australia. Because he had long found the concept of racial hybridity intriguing on a theoretical and academic basis, he felt compelled to contribute to public debate over the policy at the heart of Australian nation-planning. Just as arid zones were a scientifically verifiable fact, so was racial hybridity, Taylor argued, and it was a fact that intelligent people ought to accept. 'Our British race is a mixture of many strains of Nordic-Mediterranean and Alpine blood ... Race mixture is inevitable.'[58]

> [T]he whole teaching of ethnology shows that peoples of mixed race are the rule and not the exception; that they have founded and developed powerful states in the past; and that what was true in the past will hold good in the future.

This was always going to be an uphill battle, since race-mixing was strongly associated with 'mongrelism' and degeneration. While some Australian states implemented policies meant to promote the 'mixing' of so-called half-caste Aboriginal people and Europeans, the object was to 'elevate' Indigenous people and to breed out indigineity. But projecting racial hybridity's benefits to British people through Asian–white mixing, and proclaiming the racial superiority of 'Alpine-Mongolian' peoples, was a different proposition altogether. Taylor based his argument on his studies of racially specific cephalic readings, which proved 'our Mongolian neighbours have the advantage of a somewhat higher ethnical status than that of the British stock'.[59] If the Anglo-Saxon hybrid was universally extolled, he explained, even greater advantage could result from blending British stock with the Chinese 'round-headed' people, with even higher cephalic index readings.

Taylor understood that it was natural to wish to keep 'our own country entirely to ourselves', a statement he made as a proud 'Britisher'. Nonetheless, his readings on racial evolution impelled him to campaign against that wish. 'Even in Britain, the most virile nation on earth,' he reported to an audience at the Royal Colonial Institute, 'there is more than one racial stock.'[60] Far from insulating the nation through its anti-Asian immigration policy, politicians bent on excluding Asians were short-changing the nation. Taylor, again, was the *true* patriot, since he believed that 'the ultimate mingling of the European and Sino-Japanese types' would evolve into 'a dominant race'.[61] As Nordic racial chauvinism and the search for racial purity gained momentum during the 1920s, not only in populist politics but also in academia, Taylor's attack on racial exclusion was a timely truth, both for Australia and the world. No-one listening to his calls could mistake them for anything but broadsides fired against the White Australia policy.[62]

In an arrogantly British young nation facing far more populous Asian nations to its north, Taylor's high estimation of Chinese and Japanese racial qualities were so contentious as to be outrageous, almost comical. Unlike his environmental assessments, which many in government took seriously, his ideas on racial mixing were more the stuff of satire than debate. When geologist and colleague Keith Ward read Taylor's work on cephalic indices, he replied that he'd need some good quantitative proof of this supposed superiority of Asians: '[T]he mere yellow colour is not going to impress me a bit. Fat-headedness may count a little, but I want more proof than that.'[63] In the popular press Taylor became an object of verbal and visual caricature, his ideas exaggerated into calls for all-out interbreeding, and his face distorted with a protruding forehead and ludicrously proportioned skull. One cartoon placed Taylor as an exotically robed priest presiding over the marriage of a 'Chinaman' to pure, white 'Miss Australia'.[64] Another

The Daily Telegraph

SYDNEY, MONDAY, JUNE 25, 1923.

WILL SOMEBODY TELL HIM?

Professor Griffith Taylor (Sydney University) asks: Why are we so horror-stricken at any suggestion of marriage with Mongolians?

had a narrow-eyed Taylor cradling a freakish mixed-race baby in his arms: 'Counsel for the Yellow Streak' was the caption, followed by 'T. Griffith Taylor, A.B.C.D., Etc.' (a stab at his insistent credentialising). Yet another portrayed Taylor as a 'Chinaman', complete with queue.

Taylor learned quickly that he had driven a collision course into the heart of the new Australian national identity. What concerned him was the nation's future in its wider geographical and geopolitical region: 'The writer has always advocated such a modification of the White Australia Policy as would diminish the friction between Asia and Australia.'[65] He may have been vindicated as Australia's restrictive immigration measures attracted growing criticism over the twentieth century; in the 1920s, however, his calls and claims undermined the nation as it then imagined itself. In his own mind, his criticism of 'White' Australia, which he offered as a racial theorist and educator, was nation-correction. Even if Australians could not quite see it yet, the nation needed him and his viewpoint.

opposite

'Will Somebody Tell Him?', *Daily Telegraph*, 25 June 1923. Taylor opposed the White Australia policy, and argued the benefits of marriage between Europeans and Chinese: 'Our Mongolian neighbours have the advantage of a somewhat higher ethnical status than that of the British stock.'

left

'T. Griffith Taylor, A.B.C.D., Etc.', *Smith's Weekly*, 14 July 1923. This cartoon accompanied a damning article which maligned Taylor as 'Counsel for the Yellow Streak', while the caption poked fun at his insistent credentialising.

Chicago's 'Marginal Man'

Waiting for Australians to catch up with his forward thinking ideas grew more tedious for Taylor over the 1920s. One solution, which his American friends suggested, was to move to the US. His Australian opponents were less friendly and a lot less tactful in advising something similar: 'My critics asked why, if I did not like Australia, I did not leave it for some more felicitous environment.' Taylor was not the only Australian public intellectual to face political heat in the 1920s and to look to North America for less hostile posts. The socialist economist Herbert Heaton abandoned the country for Queen's University in Canada, and wrote sympathetically to Taylor in 1925 over the 'hot water' he was in: '[Y]our sin has been to criticise the ignorant boasting of national boomsters; mine has been to probe the profiteering of inefficient and selfish moneybags.' When Heaton heard that the University of Toronto might establish a geography department, he wrote to its president, strongly hinting that Taylor was 'the most "live" geographer' he knew.[66]

The time for Toronto was not quite ripe, though. An alternative temptation for Taylor was presented to him in 1928, when the University of Chicago set out to hire a professor to complement their well-established geography department. Harlan Barrows, Chicago's department head, asked Bowman and Huntington to suggest suitable candidates, and both replied that Taylor might well be the man. No need to apply in his case, since the vice-president had already approved the hiring and was prepared to offer Taylor a salary of $6000. Even more tempting was the title of 'professor' that came with the offer.[67] At that point, the University of Sydney senate still refused to elevate Taylor's position from the rank of associate professor, a point of contention from the start of his tenure. After serving the university for seven years, he considered the snub a deliberate insult, considering that recent chair appointees, such as Leo Cotton in geology and Radcliffe Brown in anthropology, had been hired as professors even before they had proved they could establish a program as vibrant as the geography department's. Chicago offered Taylor a graceful exit from Sydney and a step-up to a position he believed his standing warranted. He managed to induce Doris to make the US move, buffered by a long holiday, and accepted the position.

Taylor's closest Sydney colleagues and his loyal students gave him an affectionate farewell: a lunch in the university's natural history museum, the Macleay, where he was surrounded appropriately by rock specimens, skeletal remains and ethnographic artefacts. The family left Sydney in October 1928, bound first for England and Christmas with the Priestleys at Tewkesbury. Doris, Bill and David (born in 1925) remained in England for the winter while Taylor continued on alone to New York in January 1929. Clearing customs at Ellis Island at 11.30 am, he was visiting Bowman at the American Geographical Society offices by 2.00 that afternoon. Just as swiftly, he boarded a train and travelled west to Chicago where he began teaching two days later.[68] Over Taylor's

top

Brave smiles covered ambivalent feelings as the Taylor family prepared to leave Sydney for Chicago, via London, in 1928.

right

Taylor's passport photo for entry into the United States, 1928.

time in Chicago from 1929 to 1935, his sons Bill and David grew up, while he himself also grew in different ways.

Giving up his Sydney job had meant leaving a small community of academics in a geographically remote nation and trading it for one of the largest and most dynamic universities in the US. The chilliness Taylor had often experienced from senior colleagues and politicians back home was replaced in Chicago with a highly sociable community of professors, most of whom lived in the Hyde Park area. The Taylors took up flat life on 58th Street, in an apartment block west of Jackson Park, south-east of 'Little Africa' and right in the midst of Al Capone's gangster territory. Despite the unsavoury environs, it was the custom for Chicago professors to live close to campus and as a result, the Taylors found themselves amidst a series of interesting neighbours in and around their apartment building. Physical chemist Thorfin Hogness, who later directed plutonium research for the Manhattan Project, lived directly below them and the families socialised easily. Margaret Mead moved in for a spell, and Taylor noted that he learned about New Guinean sorcery from the famous anthropologist downstairs.[69] Professors and their spouses regularly dined together and entertained each other with tales of research and travel. When new appointees of interest arrived (such as Radcliffe Brown, who followed Taylor from Sydney), Doris could always be counted on to host a dinner or throw a party, assisted by their maid, Ethel. The Taylors played bridge with other academics and their spouses at the Quadrangle Club, the same place where the Innominate Club of 30 University of Chicago scientists (including Nobel Prize-winning physicist Arthur Compten) met for monthly dinners.[70]

As Taylor claimed in the preface to *Environment and Nation*, his major work of the period, Chicago boasted 900 faculty members, allowing him access to 'experts in most of the branches of human knowledge'. Bowman and Huntington both predicted that his career would flourish once he joined a livelier circle of geographers but they had also predicted he might find it difficult to work in a department headed by another man. Both knew about his earlier rivalry with Hunt in the Bureau of Meteorology, which stemmed from his urge to lead, rather than follow. Taylor's problems with his Chicago geography departmental chair turned out to be a variation on this theme. The chairman, Harlan Barrows, was Taylor's opposite in intellect and academic style. Initially, relations between the men were cordial. When Taylor underwent an operation in August 1929 to remove a benign tumour and a lymph node near his appendix, Barrows visited him in hospital and brought flowers. He also supported Taylor's bid in 1930 for a rise in salary to $7000, making him the highest paid professor in the department next to himself. But Barrows was a cautious thinker noted for his patient attention to detail, which meant that he had 'published practically nothing', as Huntington had warned Taylor before he began. No tentative writer himself, he thought Taylor had a lot to learn from his new chairman: '[L]et yourself be criticized by a man such as Barrows in smelling out errors in detail.' Bowman's advice was similarly insightful, urging Taylor to capitalise on the 'spirit of friendly criticism' that Barrows and the Chicago department offered—'strong enough to incite you to do your best, friendly enough to give you all the intellectual and spiritual encouragement that any man could wish to have'.[71] Huntington and Bowman might as well have saved their letterhead and typewriter ribbon.

As Barrows learned, and as these two friends undoubtedly soon realised, Taylor was loath to alter his ways, whether that meant refining his environmental determinist convictions or reducing his prodigious pace of publishing, his conference presentations or his public lecture appearances (a sideline that boosted his salary by 30 per cent in 1930). Taylor found it impossible to heed his American colleagues' advice to 'go rather quietly at first' and ease himself into the department. Chauncy Harris, a Chicago student during the 1930s and later a faculty member, recalled that Taylor 'wrote more than all other members of the Department put together'.[72] He hadn't changed a bit since his Sydney days.

Nor did Taylor's move to the University of Chicago reorient his research towards US geography. Barrows hired Taylor to teach several of his research specialties—Australasia, meteorology and climatology—as well as a course on 'Environment and Race'. The department was well stocked with faculty members specialising in US geography, including Barrows himself, and many of the department's men acted as government consultants (including Barrows, who provided advice to the Federal Government on the Tennessee Valley Authority). This meant that Taylor's comments on nation-planning remained oriented towards Australia, informed by regular updates from the family clippings service—news items on settlement and climate matters mailed to him by his sister Dorothy ('Pal') and Mater. From his satellite base in Chicago, his criticism of plans to build rail lines in Australia's arid regions and his objections to its immigration policy ruffled no local feathers, and he gave up his constant appearances in the Australian press. In these respects, taking on the Chicago position offered relief but it also produced a different quality of alienation, less intense than it was in Australia but evident all the same.

Taylor found himself in a peripheral position in US geographical circles, largely due to the dominance of possibilism in academic geography. Associated with French geographer Vidal de la Blache (1845–1918) and historian Lucien Febvre (1878–1956) of the Annales School of history, this approach stressed the capacity of human ingenuity and effort to maximise nature's potential. In short, the land and its resources provided possibilities that societies developed, some more successfully or profitably than others. As a counterweight to the deterministic orientation of Ratzelian anthropo-geography, possibilism gained adherents by the early twentieth century, notably in the US, where it fitted comfortably with American Progressivism. Increasingly, environmental determinism, or 'environmentalism' as it was often labelled, seemed too rigid, too simplistic to most geographers, who moved towards detailed regional studies rather than large-scale models in the natural history tradition. By the 1920s, only a handful of prominent determinists remained—among them Ellen Churchill Semple and Taylor's intellectual mate Huntington, whose 1924 book *The Character of Races* was the definitive determinist tract of the day. Otherwise, as Berkeley geographer Carl Sauer observed, the 'great retreat' from determinism was well under way by the time Taylor arrived at Chicago.[73] Ironically it was here where Semple had taught anthropo-geography from 1906 to 1924 (afterwards moving to Clark University) and where environmental determinism had enjoyed its last firm foothold. Although Taylor had not been hired as Semple's replacement, he found to his annoyance that critics of determinism placed his work in her mould.

Coming across to his colleagues as old-fashioned was the last thing that Taylor, an exponent of 'modern geography', savoured, especially if it meant fitting uncomfortably into the shoes of 'Miss' Semple, whom he had met briefly in 1929 when he delivered several lectures at Clark University. In the tiny world of Australian geography, Taylor had never had to define himself as either a determinist or possibilist in their technical geographic senses; once he began to teach and publish at Chicago, however, he felt it necessary to take sides as he searched for ways to stand out in a new crowd. Being an Antarctic expert certainly helped, especially as the Byrd and Wilkins expeditions drew Americans' attention to aviation-based polar exploration in the late 1920s and 1930s. And he was the only expert on Australian geography in the country. His problem was that his pride and joy, *Environment and Race* (1927), identified him, unmistakably, as a determinist.

Unwilling to revise his notion of environmental controls, Taylor came up with his own modified brand, distinct from Semple's, which he described as 'stop-and-go determinism'. Essentially a variation on the Matthew-inspired theory he applied in his analysis of racial evolution, it could be summed up in a phrase: 'Man's material progress is <u>predominantly</u> the product of his environment.' 'Predominantly' highlighted the limited role of man's contribution, which he likened to the work of a traffic officer who could 'accelerate, slow or halt progress' but not alter the path or direction that Nature had set.[74] In the opinion of one of his departmental colleagues, Taylor 'used freely the term "geographic controls" even though other members of the Department regarded this term and concept as unfortunate.'[75] By charting this contrary course and holding fast to it, fully aware that determinism had fallen out of favour among US geographers, Taylor tended his academic persona and affirmed his sense of himself as an intellectual outlier.

Being a determinist—stop, go, or otherwise—made it difficult for Taylor to feel a sense of intellectual or administrative belonging in his own department. Throughout his tenure at Chicago, his relationships with colleagues from other departments and institutes at Chicago were far closer. Although he had finally been appointed a professor, he was no longer a founder or a leader as he had been at the University of Sydney and more widely on the Australian political stage. During his Chicago years, he bounced in all sorts of intellectual directions, partly because there was a lot to bounce off. The 1920s and 1930s were the peak years of the famous Chicago School of Sociology, where the concept of ecology was receiving close attention. The leading figure in the field was human ecologist Robert Park, who cited Taylor's theories of racial hybridity in his influential 1928 article 'Human Migration and the Marginal Man'. Park's title unwittingly described Taylor's career trajectory, as he moved from being notoriously marginal in Australia to being a bit too marginal for his taste in the US.

Taylor's longstanding inclination towards interdisciplinarity, his tendency to see links and dynamics between natural and social objects, between environmental and human agents, meant that there was latent potential for him to rethink his work as 'ecological'. Enormously excited by the concept, Taylor grafted his pre-existing ideas onto this intellectual development. Like other human and social scientists, he was eager to apply natural scientists' understanding of organisms in relation to each other and as part of an interacting system. Harlan Barrows, for example, wrote a 1923 piece under the title 'Geography as Human Ecology'. The new field had the potential to give Taylor's ideas an up-to-date gloss, and he began to reframe his work in this way. In 1932, he described his ever-favoured 1919 article, 'Climatic Cycles and Evolution', as a 'fairly detailed ecological study of the differentiation and migration of man', and when he republished sections of it in the Chicago journal *Ecology* he retitled it 'The Ecological Basis of Anthropology'. Suddenly he declared that 'human ecology' was shorthand for the discipline of geography itself, a seemingly bold statement but one he took directly from Barrows.[76] Embracing urban ecology as well, Taylor developed an interest in the emergence of towns and cities, which had originated with his physiographic role in Canberra's founding. Numerous publications on urban geography appeared in quick succession, a sure sign of Taylor's intellectual excitement. His titles alone offer a sense of the miscellany of ideas he crammed into his writing. Consider for instance: 'Environment, Village and City: A Genetic Approach to Urban Geography, with Some Reference to Possibilism'.

For the first time in his academic career Taylor had the opportunity to immerse himself amongst geographers—yet he gravitated more towards scholars in sociology, linguistics, political science and history. His engagement with historians at Chicago, as well as his concern over mounting national and ethnic conflicts, turned his interest towards the history and geography of European nations. He volunteered to teach the geography department's 'Problems of Europe' course, since he had earlier begun to teach a similar course at Sydney.[77] The lectures he prepared for this course became first-draft material for his follow-up to *Environment and Race*, which he called *Environment and Nation: Geographical Factors in the Cultural and Political History of Europe*. Although weightier than its predecessor (571 pages as opposed to 354) it analysed a mere 1000 years, from 900 AD to the end of World War I, rather than the millennia that *Environment and Race* covered. The book was Taylor's attempt to compensate for two disciplinary problems he identified—the tendency for US geographers to study the environment's economic potential while neglecting its influence on culture and politics; and the overemphasis

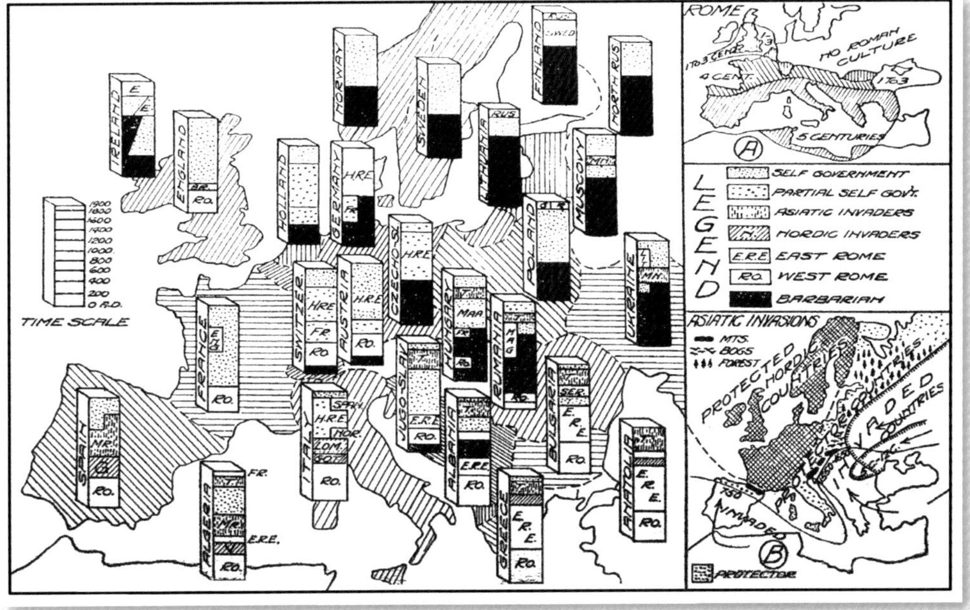

Time–space chart from *Environment and Nation: Geographical Factors in the Cultural and Political History of Europe* (1936), Taylor's major project during his time in Chicago. His dimensional mapping of time and space was equally applicable to European history. This book confirmed his reputation as an environmental determinist.

historians placed on the personality of powerful leaders in charting the course of history. As he explained in the preface:

> This present book is an attempt to show how much history has been influenced by these non-personal environmental factors. It is in a sense a liaison-study of a field lying between geography and history, but belonging to both.

Although he correctly predicted that historians would disparage the book's reliance upon generalisations concerning regimes, language, religion and race—his usual expansive array of categorisable criteria—his move to history provided a new way for Taylor to satisfy his penchant for prophecy. Historians, he argued, were unable to predict the future course of history because they refused to acknowledge that topography and climate have determined history; accordingly, geographers were better able to predict the future, based on their expert knowledge of each nation's land-build, its climate and its people.

Amidst all of his writing about nations in the early 1930s, Taylor conspicuously avoided writing about the US, with the exception of one article in which he compared Australian and American deserts. This reticence would contrast starkly with the ease and swiftness with which he would position himself as a Canadian expert, once he moved to Toronto. Sidestepping US geography was partly a product of his continued work on Australia, which remained in demand. Bowman sought him out in that capacity to provide research and analysis for his international projects on the 'Limits of Settlement' and his related work on 'Pioneer Belts'. Various government departments and research authorities approached Taylor, largely at Bowman's direction, to become involved. The US Department of Agriculture, for example, informed him of its $120 000 investment in the Canadian arm of the project, and indicated that similar funds might be secured for an Australian study.[78] (The prediction proved correct, and the Pioneer Belt project eventually linked Australia, Canada and the US, the three nations of settlement which Taylor came to know best from an international, not restrictively national, point of view.) Even though he continued to seek British academic appointments (his brother-in-law, Ray, thought a position might open at Birkbeck), contributing to comparative projects on settlement created a bridge to his earlier Australian work. Questions about frontiers, pioneers and settlement were not the top geographic questions of Old World Oxford and Cambridge, but they were live issues in the New World, the vast continents where issues of colonisation and settlement remained to be sorted.

In all, Chicago's vibrant varsity life, the growing reception of his work on Australia beyond the country's borders, and the constant flow of ideas he encountered in the US buoyed Taylor after the public ridicule he'd met in the 1920s. Surrounded by luminaries, however, his ability to stand above the crowd diminished. Even his son Bill grew taller than him, brimming with intellectual arrogance. So when the University of Toronto came calling in 1934, in search of a professor to found and head the country's first geography department, Taylor sensed an opportunity to trade marginality for centrality: a prestigious post and a new pioneering position.

Canada, the Sister Dominion: 'And Griff Said, "Let There be Light"'

Taylor might easily have landed in Toronto a decade earlier, since University of Toronto political economist and ardent nationalist Harold Adams Innis had begun lobbying for a separate geography program in the mid 1920s.[79] Innis, who had taught Canadian geography through the department of political economy, felt strongly the need for a separate department at Toronto to develop a thorough understanding of Canada's geography. A Canadian candidate, trained in Canada, would have been ideal—but the next best prospect, he judged, was a geographer who had expertise in a comparable 'new land'.[80] Innis may have become familiar with Taylor's research through Huntington's work, since he used Huntington's *World Power and Evolution* in his economic history courses. When he had approached Taylor several weeks after the Australian arrived in North America, he'd extended an invitation to visit Toronto to deliver a lecture and provide advice as someone 'thoroughly cognizant of the problems of the subject in a new country'. While not exactly a job offer, it contained a hint of one: '[W]e are anxious to get a good man who will build it up.'

Determinism may have been unfashionable in the US, but Innis's staple thesis, which he developed over the 1920s, was perfectly compatible with Taylor's environmentalist orientation. In *The Fur Trade in Canada* (1930), Innis authored one of his most quoted lines: '[T]he present Dominion emerged not in spite of geography but because of it.'[81] Innis was keen to see the university hire Taylor as the foundation professor of geography, partly out of his frustration over the dearth of good up-to-date maps, necessary to illustrate the connection between the country's geography and its economic development; more significantly, he believed that geographical research conducted in Canada was critical to national development. Innis spoke Taylor's language but Robert Falconer, the University of Toronto president in 1929, held to the notion that what was British was best. Why not hire a promising young Oxbridge man to teach geography courses, at much less expense? Taylor seemed too old and too Australian to the president.[82] It took another six years, and the appointment of a new president, Canon Cody, for Innis's persistence to pay off. In the spring of 1935, the university offered Taylor a position that would cast him in a familiar starring role: founder and head of a department in a British dominion. Sliding back into comfortable academic territory, Taylor resumed his campaign to enhance citizenship through the teaching of geography and the skills necessary to predict the nation's settlement prospects. While he had pursued this mission at great personal cost in Australia, he would pay no such price in Canada over the 15 years he headed Toronto's geography department, largely because he acquired a reputation as a national optimist.

Taylor's arrival and subsequent success at creating a department out of a void was an act of divine intervention, according to his Toronto students, who wrote a skit, 'Oro-Genesis', to extol his foundational work: 'And Griff said, "Let there be light", and there was light.'[83] Taylor's introduction to the University of Toronto certainly put him in the limelight. Compared to his arrival in Chicago in the winter of 1929, when he succumbed to a digestive ailment that turned out to be peritonitis, he settled in Toronto late in the summer of 1935, healthy and happy to be greeted cordially by the academic fraternity, the local populace and leading politicians. The official welcome from the Lieutenant-Governor of Ontario was a reminder that he had left a republic and returned to a dominion governed by British law and custom. 'Nice to see the Union Jack and the helmeted bobbies!', he wrote home to Doris when he first arrived. Although Canada was even colder than the US, and far colder than Australia, it seemed more familiar, both to Taylor and to his English wife, who fitted more easily into Toronto's

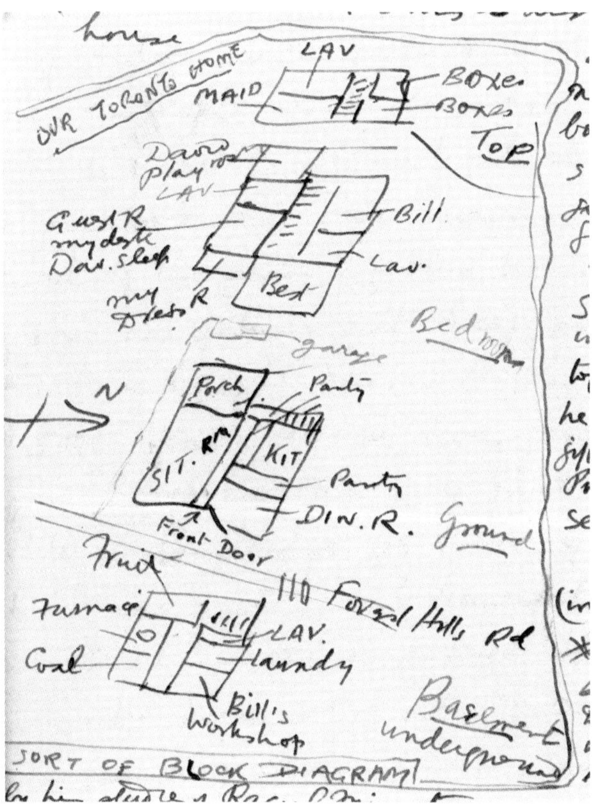

The Taylors swapped a series of small flats in Chicago for an expansive house and garden in one of Toronto's wealthiest suburbs, Forest Hill. Taylor sketched the house in September 1935 for the benefit of his relatives.

anglophile, Protestant-dominated milieu. Chicago's convivial academic life had never fully eased their discomfort with the skyscrapered polyglot city, with its 'smoke and gun men'.[84] But Toronto, Taylor reassured Doris, seemed 'fresh and free from factories and foreigners'.[85]

Settling in Toronto also led the Taylors back to the comfortable upper-middle-class lifestyle they had enjoyed in the suburbs of Sydney's stylish North Shore. Innis helped Taylor to find a substantial house close to his own home in Forest Hill, one of Toronto's stateliest neighbourhoods. The eight-room brick house, including maid's quarters, stood opposite the elite Upper Canada College for boys, where they enrolled David. Bill stayed on in Chicago, in residence at International House, while he finished the final year of his science degree. That whittled down the household to three family members (plus Mildred, the live-in maid, and Tigga, the chestnut setter). They rented at first, but thanks to deflated Depression prices, purchased the house in October 1935 for $15 000. Like many, they had lost money in the bank failures of the early 1930s but they had $9000 available to invest from the sale of their Mosman home and their share of

1003/9/164 1935

University of Toronto

Professor Griffith Taylor, B.A., B.E., D.Sc., F.R.G.S.,
recently appointed to the Chair of Geography,
will deliver his inaugural lecture on

"Illustrations of the New Geography"

in

Convocation Hall, Thursday, November 7th
at 8.30 p.m.

This lecture will be under the distinguished patronage of
His Honour, the Lieutenant-Governor of Ontario.

Chairman - President H. J. Cody

Admission free — The public cordially invited

TO MEMBERS OF THE CANADIAN GEOGRAPHICAL SOCIETY A SPECIAL INVITATION IS EXTENDED.

Taylor's inaugural lecture at the University of Toronto in 1935 was a major affair, attended by dignitaries and an audience of a thousand.

family property south of Sydney.[86] Doris was relieved to settle in her own home again, after the nomadic Chicago years: 'I'm fed up to the hilt with moving.'[87] For Taylor, who had called himself a 'pauper professor' in Chicago, Forest Hill suited him nicely, since it hosted some of the richest Torontonians. Close by was university benefactor Sir Sigmund Samuel, the 'Jew Millionaire', who Taylor joked might leave him a quarter of his fortune after reading his article, 'Aryan, Nordic, German, Jew'.[88] Although Doris missed the friends she'd left in Chicago (no fewer than three going-away parties had been held in the Taylors' honour), she recognised immediately that moving to Toronto was the right decision: 'Grif is his old keen enthusiastic self once again,' she assured Mater. 'Chicago received his ideas coolly and quietly dropped his suggestions, so he was losing his enthusiasm for his work. Now he is his old whistling self.'[89]

Launching Toronto's geography department took months of planning in the fall of 1935 but, with help from his young assistants, Taylor was teaching a series of geography courses by spring term of 1936. Having never studied Canadian geography didn't trouble him, since he considered his 20 years of teaching experience of more value. Nevertheless, he felt the country's first geographer ought to have some fieldwork experience in order to 'lecture authoritatively on the great Dominion in which I was now domiciled'.[90] Two tours were enough. Prior to his arrival in Toronto, he took 18-year-old Bill on a long car trip across eastern Canada. More accurately, Bill took him, commanding the wheel while his father made rapid-fire notes and sketches. These weren't the most peaceful of expeditions, with the father irritated by the son's speeding, and the son annoyed by the

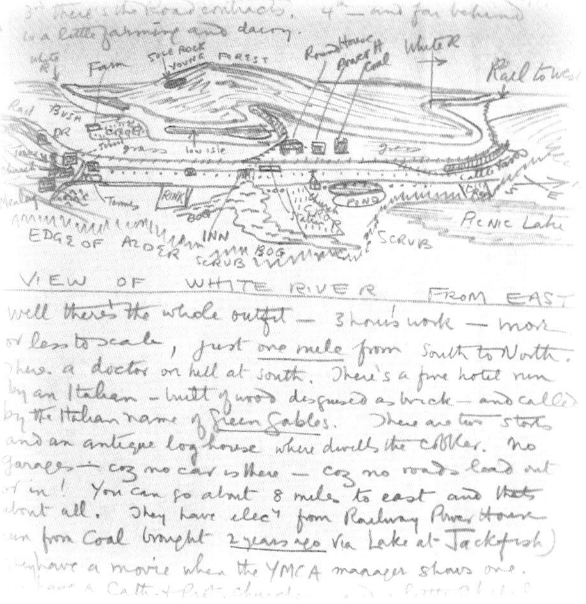

Sketch of White River, Ontario, 19 June 1936. Taylor journeyed extensively through Canada. Whenever Taylor travelled, his letters home always doubled as field notebooks, which formed the basis for subsequent articles and books.

father's stingy food budget and ban on political talk. The following year, Taylor headed west, on his own, by rail on the Canadian Pacific's tab, which allowed him to make one of his classic whistlestop tours of towns and cities. From Fort William, he wrote to 'Dear Folks' (Doris and David): 'Why do you get long letters—Partly because I have to write the stuff ... Very little because you love reading them, coz you don't!!'[91] The letters Taylor 'had' to write home were, as usual, drafts of future lectures and publications, in this case providing the text for 'Fundamental Factors of Canadian Geography' (1936), and supplying him with enough material to fill 16 hours of lectures per week.

Taylor began teaching in the fall term but his first official duty, to mark the establishment of geography as a university discipline in Canada, was to deliver a public lecture at Convocation Hall, a domed building in the style of the Sorbonne's Great Amphitheatre. Close to a thousand Torontonians attended the event. Reporters from the *Toronto Globe and Mail*, *Telegram* and *Mail and Empire* attended, and *Saturday Night* magazine covered it; Dr Charles Camsell, founding president of the Canadian Geographical Society, and H.A. Bruce, the Lieutenant-Governor, extended the official welcome; and Doris and the boys watched on as Dr Cody introduced Taylor to the podium. His topic was 'Illustrations of the New Geography'. For anyone conversant with the pedagogical reforms to geography teaching that Mackinder had called for at the turn of the twentieth century, the topic was old news, but it was novel talk for most Canadians. With typical Taylor confidence, he stitched his well-worn settlement ideas to the fabric of Canada. As the *Globe* reported, the professor gave an illustrated talk in which he claimed that

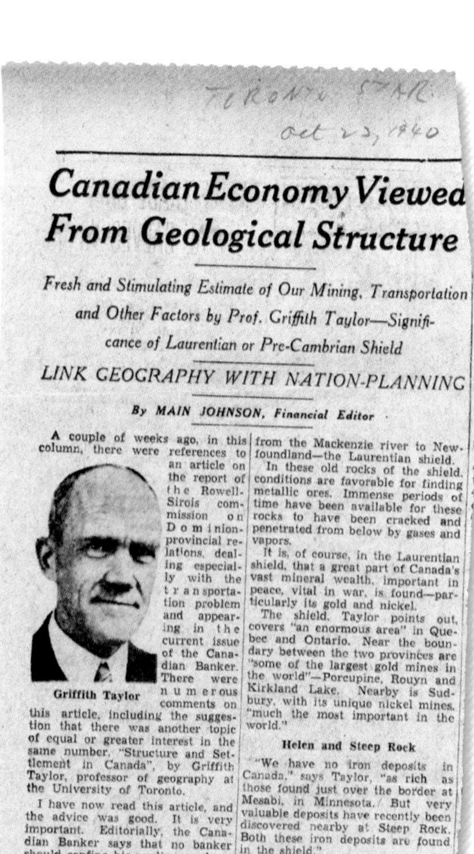

Toronto Star
Oct 23, 1940

Canadian Economy Viewed From Geological Structure

Fresh and Stimulating Estimate of Our Mining, Transportation and Other Factors by Prof. Griffith Taylor—Significance of Laurentian or Pre-Cambrian Shield

LINK GEOGRAPHY WITH NATION-PLANNING

By MAIN JOHNSON, Financial Editor

A couple of weeks ago, in this column, there were references to an article on the report of the Rowell-Sirois commission on Dominion-provincial relations, dealing especially with the transportation problem and appearing in the current issue of the Canadian Banker. There were numerous comments on this article, including the suggestion that there was another topic of equal or greater interest in the same number, "Structure and Settlement in Canada", by Griffith Taylor, professor of geography at the University of Toronto.

Griffith Taylor

I have now read this article, and the advice was good. It is very important. Editorially, the Canadian Banker says that no banker should confine his reading so closely to banking matters as to be ill-informed about the country "whose production and trade it is his business to finance." This is true of business men generally.

"In the conduct of our war effort," the Canadian Banker goes on, "and in the reconstruction of the Canadian economy which will come after the war, it is imperative that Canadians should appreciate not only the technical facts and problems of their own business or area, but also that they should be able to see these in the light of the situation of the country as a whole and of its role in world affairs. To this understanding the study of geography can make a fundamental contribution." This becomes obviously correct when men of the calibre of Griffith Tay-

from the Mackenzie river to Newfoundland—the Laurentian shield.

In these old rocks of the shield, conditions are favorable for finding metallic ores. Immense periods of time have been available for these rocks to have been cracked and penetrated from below by gases and vapors.

It is, of course, in the Laurentian shield, that a great part of Canada's vast mineral wealth, important in peace, vital in war, is found—particularly its gold and nickel.

The shield, Taylor points out, covers "an enormous area" in Quebec and Ontario. Near the boundary between the two provinces are "some of the largest gold mines in the world"—Porcupine, Rouyn and Kirkland Lake. Nearby is Sudbury, with its unique nickel mines, "much the most important in the world."

Helen and Steep Rock

"We have no iron deposits in Canada," says Taylor, "as rich as those found just over the border at Mesabi, in Minnesota. But very valuable deposits have recently been discovered nearby at Steep Rock. Both these iron deposits are found in the shield."

Strangely enough, Prof. Taylor does not mention the Helen mine of Algoma Steel Corp. at Micnipicoten, which is actually producing a substantial tonnage, whereas Steep Rock is in the earlier development stage.

Steep Rock, by the way, is attracting market attention again, with rumors that there may be aid for the project in some form or other from the Ontario government.

Granites of Selkirks

On the boundary of Manitoba and Saskatchewan, Prof. Taylor recounts, are the copper-zinc deposits of Flin-Flon. "From here to the Selkirks we have a broad expanse of young rocks which are not likely to contain metals. It is not till the granites of the Selkirks are reached that valuable

'Canadian Economy Viewed from Geological Structure', *Toronto Star*, 23 October 1940. Although Taylor found his way into the Canadian press on a regular basis pronouncing on Canada's natural resources and growth potential, he never touched the national nerve as he had done in Australia.

'geographers were able in some measure to predict the future of crops and population'. His population prediction for Canada was stunning: 179 million, almost nine times the population he projected for Australia. If anyone doubted the credibility of his claims he backed them up with his long experience in predicting 'the future white population of the world and how it would be distributed'. Over the next few weeks he repeated his message, lecturing in multiple venues from the Women's Canadian Club to the university's faculty of applied science and engineering.

Taylor's instant proclamations about a sustainable population of hundreds of millions for Canada might have been a little too rosy to be taken seriously, however. Writing of the White River region, for example, he could see:

> hopeful prospects for expansion in much of the Shield. The soil was good. Water was plentiful. Climate seemed suitable; and timber was abundant, either for fuel or for hydro-electric purposes. I wish I could say the same of 'Empty' Australia.'[92]

Indeed, when the Canadian public reviewed Taylor's predictions of the nation's future economic development and population growth they seemed inordinately positive, not unpatriotic. 'It's funny how exactly opposite folk are here from Australia,' he wrote to Doris. 'They don't think the Empty Canada so good as I do—and doubt its population growing to 100 millions!! I shall be the Canadian optimist yet.'[93] The joke was that Taylor had used the term 'optimist' for 20 years to insult sentimental proponents of

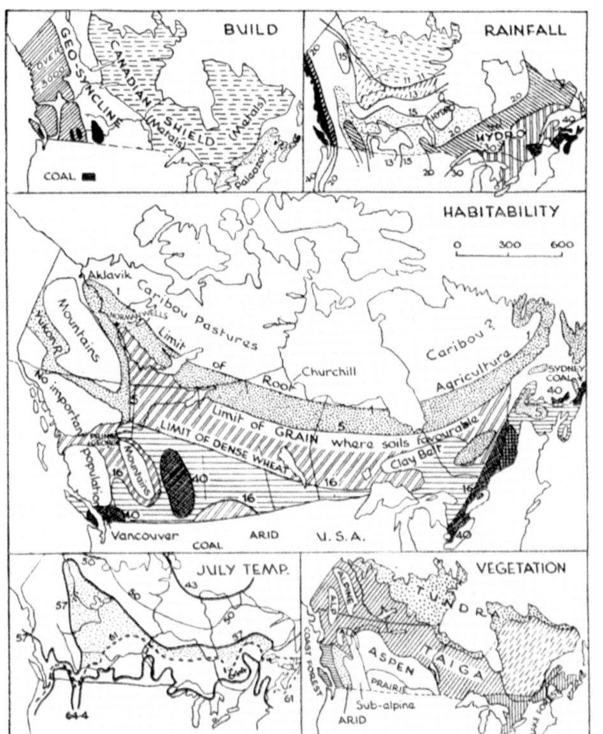

Frontispiece to Taylor's 1947 book, *Canada: A Study of Cool Continental Environments and Their Effect on British and French Settlement.* This book twinned his earlier work on Australia, hot climates, and white settlement.

settlement in Australia's arid lands. Even though his sanguine predictions for Canada's development were based in the same science he had drawn upon in Australia, the once-pilloried pessimist now looked wide-eyed and naive to those who questioned Canada's capacity to support a vastly expanded settlement, particularly beyond its most temperate regions. For Canadians in the 1930s and 1940s, claims about the nature and composition of settlement carried few geopolitical anxieties. The issue of settlement and population might be interesting, and even important, but it was never as controversial as it had been in Australia.

Even though he consistently argued for vast Canadian development, Taylor also acknowledged the lines beyond which settlement would be inadvisable in the far north. If in Australia the problematic line was the Tropic of Capricorn, in Canada it was the 'Root-Crop line across Northern Canada'. In contrast to Stefansson and his colonisation of the 'friendly Arctic', determinist Taylor always applied his knowledge to ascertain Nature's limits. Canada and Australia proved useful comparative extremes, and handy opportunities for Taylor to ground his theory of 'stop-and-go determinism' against possibilism. He clucked that 'hot arid Australia' and 'cold sterile Canada' proved how wise it was for geographers to be 'a little more doubtful if man really has much control over Nature'. Taylor compared the two dominions far more readily than he

UNIVERSITY OF TORONTO

DEPARTMENT OF GEOGRAPHY

U. S. S. R.-LAND AND CULTURE

SIX ILLUSTRATED LECTURES ON

THURSDAYS AT 8 P.M.

IN THE

AUDITORIUM OF THE ECONOMICS BUILDING

273 BLOOR STREET WEST

January 23rd —U.S.S.R. and Canada: Similarities of Build and Climate.

January 30th —Racial History and Cultural Development.

Professor Griffith Taylor

February 6th—Soils and the Basis of Agriculture.

February 13th—Agricultural Policy and Recent Experiments.

Professor D. F. Putnam

February 20th—Political Geography of Pre-Revolutionary Russia.

February 27th—Political Geography of the U.S.S.R.

Professor George Tatham

The place of meeting for lectures 4, 5, and 6 will be announced later.

ADMISSION FREE

Taylor's son Bill travelled in the Soviet Union in 1935, while Taylor himself grew interested in Soviet geography and nation-planning after the war (beginning his study of the Russian language in 1945). Taylor referred to Siberia as Canada's 'homoclime'. Along with his fellow Toronto geography department lecturers, he delivered some of the university's earliest lectures in Soviet studies in 1946.

did the US and Canada. From a geographical point of view, his Canadian–Australian comparisons were bizarre, but they made perfect sense in relation to his commitment to nation-planning: '[T]he geographer is the interpreter who links the factors that must be combined to produce a vigorous nation.'[94] Taylor's kinder possibilist critics saw his point. His Chicago friend Quincy Wright observed: 'Perhaps the fact that you have studied and dealt more with pioneer countries like Australia and Canada has been one circumstance to lead to your emphasis upon the deterministic hypothesis.'[95] In Chicago, Taylor's environmentalism had marginalised his work; once he moved to Canada, an enormous country sparsely populated, he eagerly returned to his earlier mission—that of the expert advisor in a land subject to climatic extremes.

After the bitter battles of the 1920s, Taylor lost his taste for controversy but he never lost his hunger for recognition. And so he found it odd that Canadian policymakers neither condemned his pronouncements nor enlisted him for advice. He was surprised that Canadian authorities turned him down when he offered his expertise. For example, his prediction that the Mackenzie Valley and northern Alberta were capable of supporting major population growth failed to impress the Canadian Reconstruction Commission, which invited submissions in 1942 on Canada's future development. The commissioners thanked Taylor for his advice but nothing further came of the exchange.[96] This confirmed Taylor's belief that Canadian policymakers regarded him as 'a dangerous optimist'. The adjective was a touch dramatic, especially since mainstream agencies, such as the Alberta Department of Trade and Industry, Canadian Pacific Railways and *Canadian Banker Magazine* supported his research in the 1930s and 1940s. In Canada, it was Taylor who labelled himself 'dangerous', in an attempt to recreate something of his earlier notoriety, spared of its painful effects.

Motivated by a need to develop syllabi for Canadian geography courses, Taylor began to explore Canada's corresponding environments in countries that shared similar climates. If the Australian deserts corresponded to the Sahara, then Canada's homoclime, he decided, was Siberia. Taylor's interest in Siberia was likely extended by Bill's involvement in communist and socialist organisations and his travels through the Soviet Union as a 21-year-old in 1937. He and Bill agreed to 'differ on Stalin', but father and son came to share a deep interest in Russia and the Soviet Union.[97] Taylor studied Russian, a language which both infuriated and fascinated him, from 1944,[98] and after the war was a keen supporter of the establishment of a department of Slavonic studies at the University of Toronto, giving public lectures and courses on 'the Soviet peoples'.[99] In the interests of sound Canadian nation-planning, he wrote, the country would do well to maintain 'the most friendly relations with the USSR, since we have so much to learn from them ... Canada has more interest in Arctic lands and in Northern Pacific affairs than any other nation save her friendly soviet rival.'[100] This was the Northern Hemispheric version of advice Taylor had offered earlier with respect to Australia's need to study 'Our Foreign Neighbours', as he titled one article. But Canada was in a very different global and geopolitical neighbourhood. If the Australian region had prompted his ethnological work and his long interest in racial difference, Canada's region across the Northern Pacific prompted different scholarly observations. The link between Taylor's pronouncements in the two countries was his commitment to geography's critical role in nation-planning, and the related idea that geography was crucial to the formation of citizenship.[101]

Back in the 1920s, Taylor had criticised Stefansson for his superficial fieldwork in outback Australia. Now Taylor was doing more or less the same thing, proceeding through the vast provinces of Canada, gaining a car-seat and train-carriage impression of people and place. Taylor was neither carefully collecting rock samples as a geologist, nor seriously amassing physical or cultural data as an anthropologist. Nor, indeed, was he analysing anything like the meteorological data he had meticulously gathered during his times in Antarctica or in Melbourne. Instead, he 'surveyed' the country, while rolling along at great pace. He barely stopped in one place for more than a morning, an afternoon, or overnight. Nonetheless the letters and notebooks he produced during the trip are filled to overflowing with geographic and, occasionally, ethnographic observations, and they later appeared, barely edited, in his 1947 book *Canada*.

Both because of Taylor and in spite of him the geography department at the University of Toronto flourished. Between 1935 and 1951 (when he retired), he built up geography enrolments within the department and within the teacher training program at the Ontario College of Education (located near his offices on Bloor Street). His promotional efforts solidified the discipline's status within the university and the Canadian educational scene, although, as usual, he ruffled feathers along the way. In university politics he swung his broadsword at the old and enduring target of compulsory Latin studies—like the University of Sydney, Toronto maintained Latin at the core of its liberal education mission. For years he wrote cranky letters to Professor Walter Brown, head of the university's Victoria College, to complain about the university's requirement that high school students graduate with Latin qualifications. It was pointless for him to devote so much of his time (Monday nights during term, plus summer sessions) instructing high school teachers how to teach modern scientific geography if those teachers found it impossible to teach the subject because Latin courses crowded the curriculum. If any subject should be compulsory, it was geography. Surely the outbreak of a second world war proved that students ought to learn the 'material and cultural affairs of other nations of the world', in order to establish 'a harmonious peace'?[102]

Espousing the cause of geography within Canadian secondary schools and universities allowed Taylor to frame himself as the educator of future nation-planners. In a 1941 article, he recapped his achievement. In the beginning, all was dark, since Canada was the 'last of the literate countries of the world to establish a Department of Geography at a university'. The only light was Innis, who passed the flickering flame to Taylor. Lab work began in 1936, consisting primarily of training students in mapping and modelling techniques. By 1938, he provided them with a training manual, a new edition of *The Geographical Laboratory*, originally co-written with his sister Dorothy in 1925 and now reissued with Taylor as the sole author.[103] His students' principal object of study was the local environment of Toronto and Southern Ontario. In their second year, they were trained in cultural geography—by which Taylor meant 'the problems of human distribution', based on his studies of environment, race and migration. By 1940, the flame burned brightly as the department finally established an honours and PhD program. Though Canada lagged far behind comparable nations, Taylor urged: 'I do not need to stress the necessity for young Canadians to learn something of the relation between the resources and present and future settlement in the Dominion.'[104]

Striding up and down the aisles of his lecture halls in his dusty black gown, in darkness sliced by the glow of his lantern-slide projections, Taylor continued his longstanding practice of teaching from his own research. By setting assignments and exams on this basis, he aimed to instil his particular approach to geography as a scientific method of prediction. Teaching the nation-planners of Canada's future, his methodology was simple: 'I find it well to remind my students that the geographer carries out such research in four stages; the Plan, the Pattern, the Principles and then the Prophesy!'[105] It was entirely appropriate that Taylor's geography department was located in the University of Toronto's McMaster building, originally occupied by a Baptist college, and that he lectured in its former chapel; as he approached his sixties, Taylor channelled his energy into cultivating disciples rather than risk the prospect of roaming the wilderness of the maligned or unheeded visionary.

Through his students, Taylor made a significant, albeit indirect, impact on Canadian public policy. In a 1941 article on 'Geography at the University of Toronto', he reported on the positions the department's students had earned, not only in newly established geography departments at McGill University, the University of Western Ontario, McMaster University and the University of British Columbia, but also in Federal Government agencies, including the Resources, Mines, Statistics and Development Department. Several Toronto geography graduates found wartime employment in the Intelligence Staff and its Geographic Bureau, one student as bureau head. Others took up jobs with the Provincial Department of Land Development, and with local councils that hired town planners. Taylor had also turned his south polar expertise to Northern Hemispheric use by training students for Canada's Arctic Institute, which focused on a region of increasing resource and strategic significance.[106]

The classroom had never confined Taylor's commitment to teaching, ranging from his Workers Education Association talks in rural New South Wales, to his radio lectures on race in Chicago, and his Antarctic talks for Toronto's ladies' clubs. As a speaker, he was always in demand but he also wrote extensively for the education market, no more so than during the Toronto phase of his career. Taylor's most significant impact during his Toronto years was as a trainer of geography teachers and a prolific and successful textbook writer. From Toronto, he wrote *Australia: A Study of Warm Environments and Their Effects on British Settlement* (1941), which he described as 'an attempt to produce a text for use in high schools and universities along modern lines'. Methuen of London, the book's publisher, approached Taylor in 1941 to produce a similar book on Canada. It appeared six years later (delayed by wartime austerity measures) as *Canada, A Study of Cool Continental Environments and Their Effects on British and French Settlement.*

This companion to his Australian text had an air of authority but was inappropriate for pupils younger than high school age—the burgeoning market that Ginn and Company, a Canadian textbook specialist, attempted to tap in the late 1930s but failed to reach until restrictions on paper production began to relax after 1945. Ginn proposed that Taylor, along with two Montreal-based co-authors, produce a series on Canadian geography geared towards students in grades four to eight. In 1947, two texts rolled out: *Canada and Her Neighbours,* and *Friends in Faraway Lands.*[107] Far from being banned like his earlier student texts in Western Australia, these volumes became educational bestsellers, thanks in part to the baby boom and the adoption by most provinces of Ontario-led curriculum standards. By the 1950s, an entire generation of children across the country toted copies of Taylor's books in their schoolbags. He netted himself handsome royalty cheques in the process: in 1952, the first year of his retirement, he earned $1880.37, a figure that allowed him to double his pension of $1800. Sales remained firm, with Ginn selling over 400 000 copies of his texts annually into the late 1950s. This was education for responsible citizenship writ large, and it gave Taylor a wider platform than he had ever commanded in Australia or the US. These royalties from the late 1940s through the 1950s allowed him to live in comfortable retirement, content that his message had been widely broadcast.

The Geographer's Lament

The mainstream textbook writer of the 1940s and 1950s was a different man from the earlier firebrand scourge of 'ignorant optimists' in the 1920s, even if Taylor found it difficult to forget the contempt and derision his views had then provoked. By the time he'd reached Toronto, he had begun to sense that his earlier battles against misguided Australian patriots had paid off:

> The forecast made by the writer over twenty years ago is now generally accepted by Australians. It was to the effect that the future millions of Australia are going to find their dwelling places and occupations in the lands already known by 1865. The 'Empty Lands' of Australia are a burden to the Commonwealth rather than an asset, and their 'vast potentialities' exist only in the mind of the ignorant booster.[108]

By the time of his first return trip to Australia in 1948, he discovered to his delight that the country appeared eager to welcome him back. The trip was prompted by an invitation from one of his old Sydney supporters, economist R.C. Mills, who requested his advice on introducing geography as a field of study in the country's established universities and its new research-oriented institution, The Australian National University in Canberra. Taylor accepted the brief, and used his acceptance letter to inform Mills of the success he had enjoyed as the founder of university-based geography in Canada as well as Australia. Of course he would be happy to take up the cause of geography again after 20 years of exile. Now, belatedly, the naysayers might heed his word.

One of the first places Taylor visited on his 1948 return trip was the University of Sydney, scene of his academic career's start and erstwhile end in Australia. Although his move to the US and Canada led to higher positions and greater honours, his mind remained focused on the difficulties he had faced in the 1920s. Speaking to the University of Sydney's Engineering Club, he reflected on the price he had paid for holding his line on Australia's environmental limits: 'Indeed I believe I am considered the arch

Taylor's devoted Toronto students dedicated 'The Geographers' Lament' to him, when he left for a tour of Australia in 1948.

heretic, owing to my advocacy of the study of Environmental Control—which is, in a sense, a form of Determinism.'[109] Using the past tense would have been more accurate, however, and the term 'arch heretic' gives a false impression of utter friendlessness. Controversy no longer followed Taylor's environmental pronouncements. Delivering the presidential address to the Australasian Association for the Advancement of Science in 1954, his speech barely raised a ripple, let alone released a torrent of criticism, as his speech to the same body had done back in 1923: '[N]obody turned a hair as I discussed Australia's relatively small areas of cool, fertile lowlands, not much bigger, in toto, than tiny Britain!'[110] As a man more accustomed to calling himself unorthodox, Taylor found acceptability perplexing, even disappointing. Other successful men might have decided to forget past impediments in their senior years but Taylor preferred to display his scars, his only version of war wounds, while trumpeting his achievements at the same time. This contradictory impulse—the ageing prize fighter who steps back into the ring to shadow-box in a respectable suit—was partly a function of age. In Taylor's case it also signalled something deeper: his lifelong urge to lead the pack from a marginal position.

Before Taylor had left Canada for his Australian university consultation tour he had been serenaded with 'The Geographers' Lament', a song written by three students in the University of Toronto's geography department. The tune was plodding, but the gesture was affectionate.

> From the dungeons in the south lab, to the grad rooms way up high
> In the dear department that we love so well,
> See the students all assembled, to sing a fond farewell
>
> To our Chief who is a going far away—
> From Canada's humid forest to Australia's arid shore
> Call her migratory prophet to return.
> We will serenade our Chief when he is far away
> And we will shed a sorry tear at his farewell.
> [Chorus]
> We are poor little geographers who have lost our Chief, boo, hoo, hoo
> We are lost mappers who are filled with grief, boo, hoo, hoo
> Gone are block diagrams over the sea
> Gone from Arctic red to Murrumbidgee
> Lord have mercy on such as we,
> Boo, hoo, hoo.

The lyricists and 35 fellow students signed the sheet music, and decorated it à la Canadian with pencil-coloured images of maple leaves. It was a homage after Taylor's own heart: mischievous, yet respectful, touching on references to his life and teaching. And confirmation that in some measure the prophet had fulfilled his own prophecies.

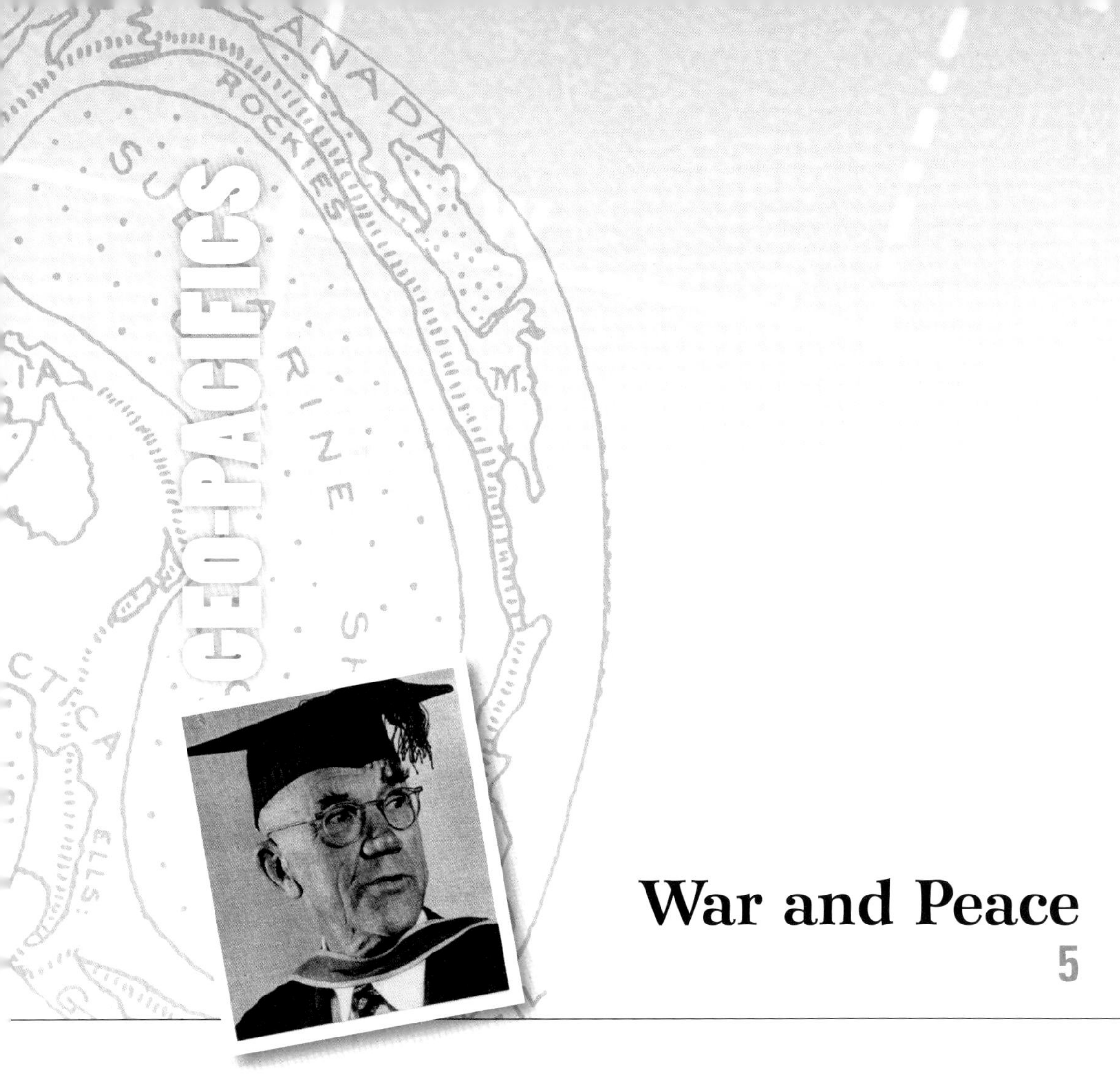

War and Peace

5

In August 1939, Taylor took a rare two-week holiday with his family and several Chicago friends in Muskoka, Toronto's cottage country. As the families swam, played cards and fished, he stationed himself on the porch, putting the finishing touches on his latest manuscript, a high school text on Australia.[1] Enjoying the last days of summer, the couples also kept abreast of escalating events in Germany and Poland. The Taylors had a tiny radio at the lakeside ('we could just hear if we had our ears glued to the opening') and on 31 August they heard the alarming report of Hitler's plan to reunify German territory by seizing the Danzig Corridor, which the Treaty of Versailles had assigned to Poland at the end of World War I. The news set Taylor to thinking: what if Poland could be convinced to cede the land, appeasing Hitler and thus averting war? He rushed to the post office and cabled his proposal to the British Admiralty in London:

> Suggest to Foreign Office that Poland exchanges corridor and Dantzig for equivalent strip of East Prussia near Memel, thus unifying German territory STOP Exchange peoples and compensate for railways and canals STOP[2]

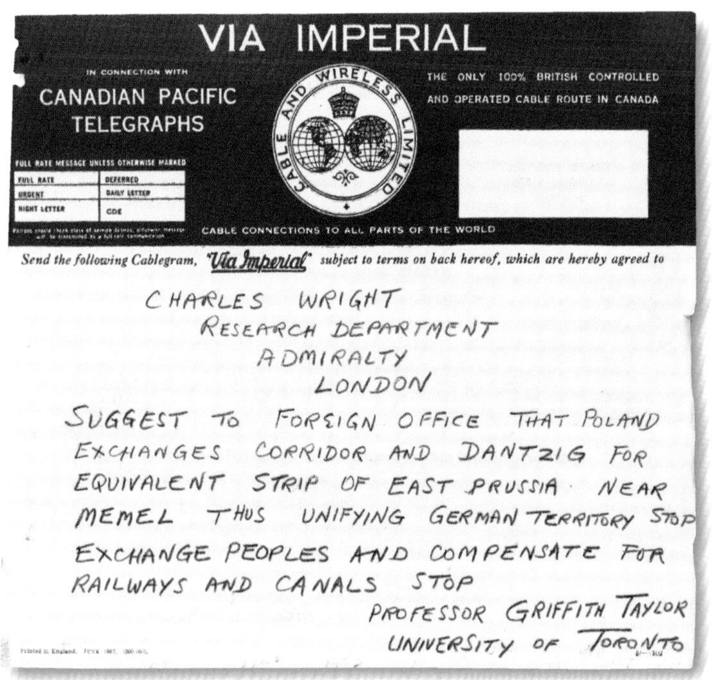
VIA IMPERIAL

IN CONNECTION WITH CANADIAN PACIFIC TELEGRAPHS

THE ONLY 100% BRITISH CONTROLLED AND OPERATED CABLE ROUTE IN CANADA

CABLE AND WIRELESS LIMITED

FULL RATE	DEFERRED
URGENT	DAILY LETTER
NIGHT LETTER	CDE

CABLE CONNECTIONS TO ALL PARTS OF THE WORLD

Send the following Cablegram, 'Via Imperial' subject to terms on back hereof, which are hereby agreed to

CHARLES WRIGHT
RESEARCH DEPARTMENT
ADMIRALTY
LONDON

SUGGEST TO FOREIGN OFFICE THAT POLAND EXCHANGES CORRIDOR AND DANZIG FOR EQUIVALENT STRIP OF EAST PRUSSIA NEAR MEMEL THUS UNIFYING GERMAN TERRITORY STOP EXCHANGE PEOPLES AND COMPENSATE FOR RAILWAYS AND CANALS STOP

PROFESSOR GRIFFITH TAYLOR
UNIVERSITY OF TORONTO

Taylor telegrammed his solution to the Danzig crisis to the British Admiralty on the eve of World War II, 31 August 1939. 'It reached London the very hour when Hitler fired the first gun on Poland—which was a bit late!' (Taylor, *Journeyman Taylor*, 1958).

Having recently published *Environment and Nation*, a geopolitical study of European states and their geomorphology, Taylor assumed his geographical expertise would assist international diplomacy. Besides, he had a personal contact in the Admiralty, his Cambridge comrade and brother-in-law, Charles Wright. 'I was so moved by the brilliance of this idea,' he wrote of his epiphany to a Chicago friend. But unfortunately the telegram 'reached London the very hour when Hitler fired the first gun on Poland—which was a bit late!'.[3]

While Taylor had established his academic career by preaching scientific nation-planning, he had begun to peddle another message by the time he was an established professor: geography was fundamental to understanding war and peace. As noted by a journalist who interviewed him on his return to Australia, Taylor was touting a 'new gospel of "Geopacifics"'.[4] Taylor came up with this term during the war in an effort to describe how his understanding of geography differed from German 'geopolitics'. As he explained to the reporter:

> [Geopacifics] shows where the leading nations must arise. It emphasises leadership, not conquests. It shows how absurd are conflicts based on racial differences. It explains the realities of climatology, preaches the improvement and development of the better portions of the earth, instead of the worse, and so tries to economise human effort. In short, it is geography for peace.[5]

More an aspiration than a theory or ideology, geopacifics was a big space and big time idea which he promoted for the rest of his life. Yet it sprang directly from his earlier theories of environment, race and migration. Indeed, its central plank was his insistence on racial hybridity as a scientific fact and his corresponding dismissal of national bids for racial purity. Adopting such a position in the 1930s and 1940s marked Taylor as a progressive thinker, even though it incorporated his unaltered belief in racial hierarchies.

The older Taylor grew, the more anti-nationalist and internationalist his analytical perspective became. The globe, over the nation, captured his imagination, and it became the unit through which he pondered the relation between 'man' and environment. In part, his increasingly global and internationalist approach expressed the extraordinary times in which he lived. His was an unmistakably twentieth-century life, in which race-based and ultra-militaristic nationalism caused wars, in which the phenomenon of total war was a reality, transforming into a constant threat in the Cold War of the 1950s. Towards the end of his life, Taylor's commitment to internationalism would be tested in a personal way, as national rivalries played out on the Cold War's coldest front—Antarctica.

'Let's Mix Good Stocks 'til the World's One Nation': Geopolitics in the 1920s and 1930s

After World War I, the boundaries of European nations as well as those of European colonies across the globe were redrawn as people and places were redistributed amongst the allied powers. Geographers were critical contributors to this process, and key among them was Isaiah Bowman, who American President Woodrow Wilson appointed as his top advisor at the Versailles Peace Conference in 1919. Bowman anticipated that the Treaty of Versailles would establish the geographical conditions necessary for a 'new world' of international cooperation. His 1922 book, *The New World*, summed up the hopes of a postwar generation, whose cause was internationalism. In this new order, Bowman contended, world leaders would see:

> the great practical value of an international court of justice and of experiments in the field of international labor, international postal regulations and patent agreements, the international exchange of data ... and other modes of promoting international exchange of ideas.[6]

Imperialism, nationalism and militarism had dragged the world into war in the 1910s; for liberal thinkers like Bowman, internationalism appeared to offer the only path towards securing peace.

Bowman's *The New World* had inspired Taylor's first major work on Europe, *Environment and Nation*. But the stronger intellectual link was suggested by Bowman's subtitle—'Problems in Political Geography'. Building on his nation-planning credentials from the 1920s, Taylor was well placed to join the burgeoning field of political geography, which addressed the entwined global issues of war and peace, nationalism and internationalism. In the postwar world of the 1920s and 1930s, geography and politics were all.[7] English writers likes Bowman and Taylor were closely connected to the work of German *geopolitiker*, led by Karl Haushofer. They all spoke the same geographical language, since they had a shared intellectual line of descent. Their most distant common ancestor was the Prussian Alexander von Humboldt, whose major work was the five-volume *Kosmos* (from 1845). On the German-speaking side, they shared an intellectual grandfather in Friedrich Ratzel (author of *Politische Geographie*, 1897, and *Lebensraum*, 1901), while Halford Mackinder (author of *Britain and the British Seas*, 1902) was their English forebear. This was the political geography family tree, in which Taylor and Haushofer were cousins, initially in distant contact, later to become estranged.

Haushofer was lecturer in geography at the University of Munich from 1919, and publisher of the monthly *Zeitschrift für Geopolitik*. His early studies focused on Japan, and his resulting book, *Geopolitics of the Pacific Ocean* (1925), gave him a special interest in the region in which Taylor also claimed expertise. In Munich, Haushofer befriended and influenced Rudolf Hess, the conduit to Adolf Hitler, whose *Mein Kampf* (1925) contained many of Haushofer's particular geopolitical interventions: the idea of land power, of *lebensraum* ('living space') for an organic nation-state, and of 'pan-regions'—the continent-level conception of the globe which also characterised Taylor's thinking.

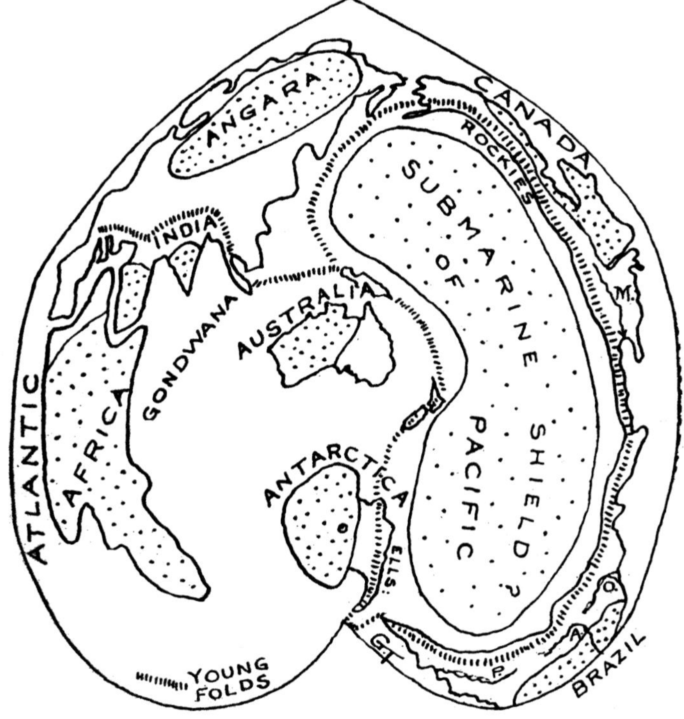

Taylor continued to produce idiosyncratic maps throughout his career. This one appeared in the *Canadian Geographical Journal* in May 1937.

In 1928, before geopolitics had been tainted by Nazism (though the connection with German foreign policy and *lebensraum* was already evident), Haushofer offered a complimentary review of Taylor and *Environment and Race*. Observers based in the Pacific like Taylor, Haushofer wrote, were far more conscious than Europeans of the significance of environment and race and their connection to politics. If these social questions were being avoided by the League of Nations in Geneva, he said, they:

> are being sought and discussed freely by the peoples of the Pacific spaces: In Honolulu, Sydney and Pacific America ... In the Pacific recognition of racial problems is growing and is not denied.

Haushofer praised Taylor and his book wholeheartedly:

> If ever an investigator on the relationship between environment and race and the expansion of power of a state and building up of a nation, has understood the art of translating into practical effect his discoveries ... it is the Australian Griffith Taylor.[8]

Moreover, Haushofer was unreservedly impressed with Taylor for daring to oppose the White Australia policy. Deeply knowledgeable about Japan, Haushofer himself was an advocate of 'Panpacific justice to races' (as he put it in the review). Taylor and Haushofer stood together in opposing this particular racial policy as unjust, albeit for different reasons.[9] The review was published in the monthly semi-popular magazine *Volk und Rasse*, which included a fair sprinkling of anti-Semitic and pro-Aryan articles. Certainly it was the most positive of all the reviews of *Environment and Race*, and an item which brought Taylor great pride: he translated it into English, typed it up and kept a copy in his papers.

In 1933, when the National Socialists came to power in Germany, Taylor was in Chicago delivering another iteration of his zones-and-strata theory in a series of broadcasts transmitted through the university's radio station, WMAQ. 'I get no fee and it's a lot of bother, but it makes one feel alive still,' he wrote to Mater on his radio debut.[10] Based on his *Environment and Race* lectures, these talks were accompanied by a new 'Atlas of Environment and Race'—110 maps and diagrams especially published to explain his lessons (his audience was expected to purchase the atlas and look along while listening). His invisible audience received two clear messages. First, conflict between races has no biological basis. 'Most of the so-called racial problems which trouble the world are national (i.e. cultural and man-made) rather than racial. They could conceivably be altered in a generation.' Second, Taylor announced, once the world realised that humans are more alike than different, it 'should help us to arrive at a World at Peace'.[11]

While geopolitics and race theories were driving the German state towards war, Taylor tried to steer his students and those hearing his public talks towards peace. Chicago University played a significant role in driving his campaign, since social sciences at the university had a decidedly internationalist bent. The Norman Wait Harris Memorial Foundation ran a yearly think tank known as the Harris Institute, for which the university had received a trust fund, charged with the 'promotion of a better understanding on the part of American citizens of the other peoples of the world, thus establishing a basis for improved international relations and a more enlightened world order'. It was led by international lawyer Quincy Wright, who attracted a cross-section of professors from sociology, economics, history, Soviet studies and, latterly, Griffith Taylor from geography. The institute's interdisciplinarity suited Taylor down to the ground, and he benefited significantly from it by circulating drafts of *Environment and Nation* and other works in progress. Exposure to this field of international relations and internationalism, as well as the quickly changing political context of the 1930s, encouraged new twists to Taylor's pre-existing work on racial evolution, settlement and geography's role in politics, war and peace.

With this base in the US, Taylor developed his intellectual network across the country as well as in Europe, making contact with geographers, anthropologists and linguists. He established particularly close links to German biological anthropology in the 1930s. Thus when Baron von Eickstedt, impressed with *Environment and Race*, invited Taylor to become associate editor of *Zeitschrift für Rassenkunde*, he was happy to oblige. 'I guess I'll kindly agree,' he wrote offhandedly to Mater, but this seemingly casual response was disingenuous. Taylor was delighted that his ideas were finally receiving the attention they deserved: 'My anthropology ideas are arousing great interest at last—after 15 years.'[12] Like Taylor, von Eickstedt was a racial typologist, largely of Europeans, and was similarly inspired by W.Z. Ripley's *Races of Europe* (1899). However, the two differed markedly on racial theory.[13] While Taylor insisted on the nonsense of 'Nordic' as a racial category, von Eickstedt's scientific mission was to refine the category, and to demonstrate the particular purity of the 'Teuto-Nordics'. Despite these differences, Taylor's zones and strata peppered the pages of publications like *Volk und Rasse* and *Zeitschrift für Rassenphysiologie*. If only there were English journals where scholars could discuss such ideas so richly, US anthropologist Earl Wendell Count commiserated with Taylor.[14]

Taylor's association with German racial theory and geopolitics in the 1930s should be carefully assessed, especially since his writings on race both redeemed and damned him in his own lifetime and beyond. Certainly he was one of the more vocal opponents of this period's strident 'Nordicism'. Commentators outside the European and North American mainstream were particularly impressed with his bold stance. Indian anthropologists, for example, appreciated his scholarly criticism of 'the Nordic fashion' and embraced his work enthusiastically. J.N. Bose wrote excitedly to Calcutta anthropologist Panchanan Mitra about Taylor's 'The Ecological Basis of Anthropology' (1934): it was 'totally at variance with the fashion of the day, bold, refreshing and authoritative'. So many scholars had fallen for the 'Nordic craze', he wrote. 'I, therefore rejoice to find that the researches of Dr Taylor are directed towards setting this science to perform its legitimate function.'[15]

Taylor also spoke out strongly against anti-Semitism and the Nazi fabrication of an Aryan race. Although he based his arguments on what he considered to be science, he was happy to use no-nonsense titles, like 'Aryan Absurdity', to describe his talks and papers. Indeed, Nazi racial theory became one of the chief topics of his public lectures, radio classes and publications by the mid 1930s. In 1935, the *University of Chicago Magazine* published one of his addresses titled 'Aryan, German, Nordic, Jew', in which he vented less at Nazi politics than at Nazi claims that Jews and Aryans were alien races. This was a nonsense, he explained, because 'Aryan' was properly a linguistic category, 'German' a political category, 'Jew' a religious category, and 'Nordic' a biological category.[16] Hitler was not so much evil as a faulty ethnologist, and the problem with Nazism was its ideology of racial purity, which was so much scientific rubbish. Any politician who read his zones-and-strata theory, he believed, would see that 'Race Prejudice is but another name for Ethnological Ignorance'.[17] Taylor stuck to his message in Toronto, a city where anti-Semitism was plainly evident after the police failed to press charges against instigators of an ugly pro-Nazi riot in 1933. Toronto's Jewish community welcomed Taylor's arrival and the Jewish Council of Women invited him to address Nazi racial theory. The *Toronto Globe and Mail* reported the event ('Hybrid Origin of Jews Makes them Kin to Germans, says Prof. Griffith Taylor') and summarised his talk as a 'highly scientific address, simplified with slides and spurts of humour'.[18]

Taylor typically turned to humour and his trademark nonsense poetry, even in these sober circumstances. In one attack on Nazi aspirations to racial purity he rewrote a poem by Hilaire Belloc, who had produced anti-German poetry for the British War Propaganda Bureau during World War I. Belloc was, like Doris, a descendant of Sir Joseph Priestley, so it was all in the family for Taylor to borrow his work to prick the Nordic superiority bubble. Taylor's 'Rhyme of Race' rejigged his long-held racial theories into a plea for peace, internationalism and racial harmony, based on biological unity:

> Folk far beyond the 'Middle Sea'
> *Mediterranean* seem to be.
> Short and dark (some call them Dago)
> First from the Caspian Cradle—*they* go!
> In Europe—right from edge to edge—
> Extends the thrusting *Alpine* Wedge,
> Their heads are broad, eyes are dark, straight hair
> No lack of daughters to each pair.
> Lastly arrives the *Nordic* man
> Built on a *most* superior plan,
> Blue eyes and hair that's (sometimes) gold
> (Yet wise men say his tale is told).

This is the meaning of my rhyme,
Let's have goodwill and lots of time
Let's send race-hatred to damnation
Let's mix good *stocks*—till the world's one nation.[19]

It was all progressive sounding (if awkwardly scanned), with ironic jabs against Nazi racial theory. But the Nazis and Taylor would have agreed over the footnote that followed his ditty, which explained Taylor's exception to the rule of race-mixing and unity:

> The rather poor achievements of the negro race in world history make it uncertain if they are to be considered as 'good stocks'. We should suspend judgment until they have had equal opportunities with the other races for several generations.

In this regard, Taylor himself was not one to afford equal opportunities. His was an unequivocal prejudice, a deeply personal as well as an intellectual block. Nothing in Taylor's theoretical or ethnological excursions, or his opposition to 'race prejudice and national jealousy' shook him from his conviction that 'negro peoples' were the least evolved of the races of man. Over and over, the phrase 'apart from the negro' appears in his statements on race: 'On every count they stand on a lower plane than the white or Mongolian.'[20] When he encountered African American Delilah Jones at the Berkeley Institute of International Relations conference in 1930, for example, she challenged his statement that 'the Europeans [are] no higher than any coloured race except the negro'. As he recounted to Mater and Pal in a lengthy description of that exchange, he considered her defence 'pathetic'. 'But for slavery,' Jones had claimed, 'the negro would be ranked equal with any Yankee.' Rather than respond to her historically grounded argument, Taylor tossed back anthropometry: 'So I said I was a narrow-head & lower than Poles and Russians, but folk only laughed at that—whereas it's not funny for negroes. It was quite pathetic.'[21] Although Taylor judged his conference performance a hit, his anecdote reveals an extraordinary confidence that his racial understandings were based in science, as opposed to the 'ethnic ignorance' of which he so readily accused others.

Taylor had been passing judgment on 'the negro race' long before he met Delilah Jones and worked in a part of Chicago that abutted the district known as 'Little Africa'. This assessment was there from his earliest attempts to work out his racial migration theory. 'Apart from the negroes,' he wrote at the end of *Environment and Race*, he could see no reason for claiming 'that one race is in any important respect, better than another'.[22] When White Australia supporters attacked his endorsement of 'British–Mongolian hybrids', he always clarified his position by distinguishing between the salutary effects of European–Asian racial mixtures and the unfortunate results of unions between 'low whites' and 'poorly educated negroes' in the US: 'only a few generations removed from the barbarous cannibals of Dahomey'. As US history showed, he argued, former slaves had 'not progressed rapidly'; furthermore, their hybrid offspring with 'less desirable whites … did not produce outstanding citizens'.[23] Glib statements of this nature repeatedly exposed an unexplained paradox in his theories: an exception which he never substantiated scientifically, not even by his own loose standards.

On the one hand, then, Taylor was an outspoken critic of racial exclusion in Australia and anti-Semitism in Europe. Over the 1920s and 1930s, he began to develop an alternative version of geopolitics based on the argument of the biological unity of humans. He wrote with conviction: 'There is no "yellow race" and no "white race", so that there cannot be biological conflict between them.' Recognition of this, he always argued, was the key to the diminution of conflict and the success of sustained peace. On the other hand, Taylor consistently omitted discussion of a 'black race' in these statements, which gave his calls for world peace through 'one humanity' a hollow ring. Taylor's recipe for peace, based on 'Mixing til the world's one nation', never included all of the world's ingredients.

Taylor in Wartime

Prospects for internationalism and unity of the 'family of man' were tested in World War II. Sitting on the cottage porch on the lake, north of Toronto, Taylor contemplated the choices he would make, as a man, as a scientist and as a citizen of the British Commonwealth. For Taylor, a man who preferred to work for peace, conscientious objection provided one option for action; however, he left no evidence to suggest that he considered it. Age gave him an out in 1939, since he was 58, well past sign-up. Yet he was well aware that senior men *did* serve in war. Edgeworth David had done so in World War I, similarly aged 58, and had returned a decorated hero.

Neither a warrior nor a pacifist, Taylor approached war as he did race: as an opportunity to advance his career. At most, he was a military thinker, never an actor. In World War I his expertise in meteorology and physiography constituted his patriotic contribution, and it was something along those lines that he attempted to reproduce in Toronto in World War II. By this point, as Canada's founder of the discipline of geography, Taylor assumed it was inevitable that the government would require his expertise and counsel. While Doris threw herself into Red Cross war assistance and turned their house over to British billets, and while son Bill worked as a tool designer in a Toronto plant producing airplane parts, Taylor pitched in too—by contacting the Royal Military College in Kingston to offer geography courses for military personnel. The military's polite refusal puzzled him. In a Mother's Day letter ('from your eldest'), he revealed that in spite of support from Colonel Grant Suttie, his offer to teach 'topography for officers' fell flat. 'They didn't do any of this at Sandhurst' was the only explanation the military brass had offered him.[24] To Bill, he attributed the response to the Canadians' backward, colonial mentality: '[T]hey feel that the orthodox military way of looking at topography—as taught in England—must be better than the professional geographer's way—as taught at Toronto.'[25]

Beyond the Royal Military College's snub, Canadian officials closer to the ground actively impeded Taylor's geographical work during wartime. Ever since he had begun wandering about the countryside in Australia measuring Aboriginal people's cephalic indices and taking clippings of their hair, he had attracted a fair degree of interest from local police. In Australia, most officials had been happy to assist him in his ethnographic work but his propensity to sketch and record data could also provoke hostile responses. In 1931, while travelling in north-eastern Croatia, he was arrested and given a crack on the head before he could convince the gendarmes that he was a geographer ('the least attractive of my numerous arrests as a spy!'). Seven years later, one of Mussolini's carabinieri detained Taylor after finding him sketching the town hall.[26] Less violent but more frustrating incidents occurred in Canada. As he complained to London geographer Charles Fawcett, his journey through Quebec in the summer of 1942 had worried the authorities: '[E]verywhere I was bailed up by the police to whom a geographer has all the trademarks of a German Spy.' Work became impossible: 'Every day I was interrogated, and finally at Quebec I was arrested, escorted through the streets in a side car to the head office and there grilled for an hour.'[27]

Even more infuriating was the Canadian Board of Censorship's decision to 'clamp down' on an article Taylor attempted to publish in the *Canadian Geographical Journal*, based on his study of settlement patterns along the St Lawrence River. '[They] thought the maps might conceivably help [enemy] submarines,' he wrote, outraged, to his family.[28] He complained to the censor as well about similar restrictions placed on one of his sketches of Charlottetown. 'You will note that this diagram gives nothing of value to the enemy,' he explained, adding that tourist maps of the Confederation city contained more detailed information. Thus he thought it legitimate to publish his drawing in a forthcoming volume dealing with 'civilisation'. 'Moreover,' he made one final plea, 'it is hardly likely that my book on Civilization will ever reach enemy hands.'[29]

Undeterred by his encounters with Canadian wartime officialdom, Taylor soldiered on in his own way and at his own work place. He offered the University of Toronto's officers-in-training a set of courses in military geography, which he taught through the wartime Department of Military Affairs. Convinced that 'any young officer in modern warfare should understand more than how to "read maps"',[30] he was equally certain that he was the best person to teach them how to interpret the earth's surface, to understand its 'build'. Even before his course began in September 1940, he worked feverishly on his putty model of the Western Front, one more project for Doris to trip over in the house: 'He works at terrific pressure and then gets too tired to eat but I can't teach him better ... My family are all like this—interesting but a joy to have an occasional holiday from!'[31] He would have been happy to receive a boost to his salary for the extra lectures but this was the kind of work Taylor would have done gratis, using his lectern and lantern slides to address modern problems. In the summer of 1941, he sent off a proposal for a book on military geography, based on his syllabus. While wartime restrictions on the publishing industry hamstrung the project, he did push on with numerous articles developed from his course work, including 'The New Western Front: A Geographical Approach' and 'Canada's Role in Geopolitics: A Study in

Situation and Status', both published in 1942. This was Taylor's version of nation-planning under conditions of war: training citizens into soldiers fit with geographical knowledge.

Geopacifics

Promoting himself as an expert in military geography during World War II did not mean that Taylor had abandoned hope in peace. Like many internationalists, he spent the war looking forward to fascism's defeat and the prospect of a just resolution to the geopolitical conflicts that had led to war. Two invitations encouraged him to articulate his particular vision for the postwar world. The first, which came in 1941 from Cornell University, was a request to deliver the 1944 Messenger Lectures on a topic related to 'civilisation'; the second was an invitation to speak in New York in 1943 at a forum on 'pioneering for a civilized world'.[32] As it happened, Taylor had selected the title 'Geography of an Evolving Civilization' for his Messenger lectures, so the two briefs fitted together nicely.[33] It was through his effort to prepare for these engagements, and his revisions to the Messenger lectures (ultimately published in his 1946 book *Our Evolving Civilization*), that Taylor came up with the idea he called 'geopacifics': an 'antidote' to the poison of German geopolitics.[34]

The formal objective of the Messenger fund was to bring leading thinkers to Cornell to deliver 'a course of lectures on the Evolution of Civilization for the special purpose of raising the moral standard of our political, business, and social life'. The first lectures were given by one of Taylor's Harris Institute colleagues, Professor Breasted, and previous lecturers included Bowman (1936–1937) and London anthropologist Branislow Malinowski (1932–1933). The series provided a prestigious venue for intellectuals to present large-view scholarship on natural sciences, earth sciences, social sciences and the humanities—perfect ground for the global vision and interdisciplinary cast of Taylor's work. Writing to inform Bowman, Taylor could barely contain himself as he listed off his big ideas:

> I have in mind a sort of survey of the field linking Environment and Civilization. I have been lecturing on this for 20 years ... I had in mind an attempt to evaluate the deterministic and possibilistic aspects in the whole field of European Civilization. I might start with racial concepts, pass on to national concepts, then to international concepts ... I am going to give them the World Plan—its effect on early migrations, its bearing on the evolution of Race ... The control of national development; the relation of environment to the growth of cities; and perhaps a final lecture on Environment and Post War Problems.[35]

This laundry list of topics, any one of which could easily occupy the most ambitious of scholars for decades, struck Bowman as typical Taylor: 'Is it sixty or eighty volumes that you are planning?' he wrote, as the 'civilisation' project gained momentum.[36]

Since the horrors of two world wars posed a conundrum for belief in the advance of modern civilisation, few big thinkers of the mid twentieth century had nothing to say on the subject. In forming his own ideas Taylor was inspired by the work of Harold Adams Innis, who had examined civilisations in terms of the administration of empires and media of communication. After Innis's death, Taylor told his son, Donald (a former geography student of Taylor's in Toronto), that Innis deserved credit for making him think more philosophically about geography: 'I should not have been able to publish my Evolving Civilization but for his valued assistance.'[37] Other historians, such as Arnold Toynbee, also influenced Taylor, though not in a way that made him feel so beholden. Toynbee worked on the rise and fall of 'civilisations', rather than on nations or ethnic groups, and he authored a well-known multivolume *Study of History*. Taylor had first read him in 1916: 'V. good Internationalist' was his quick review.[38] Taylor assumed that Toynbee would benefit from studying his zones-and-strata theory, and sent him various off-prints and books, prompting an appreciative acknowledgment letter: 'I have found this theory ... extraordinarily illuminating; for I believe it is the key to the distribution not only of race but of all kinds of human ideas and techniques.'[39] Taylor watched anxiously as Toynbee's publishing output began to outstrip his own (three volumes in his series by 1934, six by 1939, on the road to 11 volumes by 1961). In response, Taylor began retrospectively to place his own major books in a series, which he judged rivalled Toynbee's. By 1946, his 'tetralogy on Cultural Geography' comprised *Environment, Race and Migration* (the later edition of the original *Environment and Race*), *Environment and Nation*, *Urban Geography*, and *Our Evolving Civilization*. 'In my very prejudiced opinion,' he wrote to Quincy Wright, '[they] give a much more objective and helpful picture of the way to promote civilization than Toynbee's famous books.'[40] Toynbee might be a 'great writer', he conceded, but he had one major shortcoming: he 'pays little attention to the vast accumulation of geographical data of the last thirty years; which in my opinion alters the whole concept of the growth of nations, and of civilization itself'.[41]

Taylor understood 'civilisation' to mean the environmental processes that led to 'man's ... slow evolution from ape-man to citizen of the world at peace'. His Messenger lectures stuck close to this long-held determinist reasoning: the 'World Plan' set out 'the way in which nature has "controlled" (or as many geographers prefer to say "conditioned") man's activities'. Reaching right back to his 'Antiquity of Man' expertise, Taylor set out seven stages of evolution: homo pre-sapiens, racial differentiation, Dark Ages, the age of nationalism, overseas conquest, industrial revolution, leading up to the modern 'age of Scientific Explanation of man's environment, industries and psychology'. Unfortunately this was also 'an age of world war, based on the overcrowding of the world for the first time'. Nevertheless, Taylor felt there was reason to feel hopeful about the postwar period:

> the age of aviation, the conquest of the tropics by central cooling, of electronics, and atomic power. It is the age of the New Deal, and of widespread attempts to relieve social injustice, with the most striking developments taking place in new lands like NZ, the United States and USSR.[42]

Taylor's own contribution to that more highly evolved stage of civilisation would be his prescription for peace: geopacifics. But he had first to distance his ideas from Haushofer's.[43] In 'Canada's Role in Geopolitics' (1942), Taylor claimed the term had been hijacked for evil purposes:

> Haushofer and his school seem to imply that Geopolitics necessarily includes discussions of world domination and of racial superiority. To the present writer these are arbitrary and unnecessary extensions of the term Geopolitics.[44]

For a time, he thought that 'humanised geopolitics' might better explain his meaning. By the late 1940s, however, further distancing from the irredeemable word seemed advisable. In search of a better term, and one that he could lay personal claim to, he came up with 'geopacifics', which he defined as 'the antithesis of German Geopolitics'.[45] While it retained a connection to earlier traditions of political geography, the term unambiguously differentiated his work from that of the disgraced German *geopolitiker* whose enthusiastic review of *Environment and Race* Taylor had cherished 20 years earlier. In his 1944 Messenger lectures and the follow-up book, *Our Evolving Civilization*, Taylor took pains to remind his readers that his version of determinism was a 'moderate branch', whereas German geopolitics belonged to 'an extreme and unscrupulous "wing" of the Determinist school'.[46]

While he worked on his Cornell lectures and gave his courses in military geography, the editor of the *New York Herald Tribune* invited Taylor to participate in a forum (hosted by the paper), gathering a variety of thinkers from academia, politics and the arts, each of whom was to present her or his vision of the postwar world. Taylor rarely turned down paid invitations, especially ones that brought him into company with the famous—in this case the President and Eleanor Roosevelt, Vice-President Wallace, and 'lots of brass hats, not to mention Greer Garson and Paul Robeson,' he bragged to Mawson (one of his few opportunities to do so). Being put up at the Waldorf-Astoria made the request even more attractive but for Taylor the most important drawcard was the opportunity to sell his ideas, and even, on this occasion, to have them published by the *Herald Tribune* and broadcast live.[47] Although he titled his address 'Geography and Nation Planning', his talk focused on the role of geographers in predicting the future industrial power of nations. He further asserted that geographers' expertise was

NEW YORK HERALD TRIBUNE, WEDNESDAY, NOVEMBER 17, 1943

Forum Hears Dewey Describe New York's E

Drucker-Hilbert

THE TWELFTH FORUM ON CURRENT PROBLEMS—Robert E. Sherwood sounding keynote at afternoon session at the Waldorf-Astoria

which the civilian population could fulfill a part of their obligation to the men who gave their lives in

Sherwood Sees

'The Twelfth Forum on Current Problems', *New York Herald Tribune*, 17 November 1943. Taylor participated in a forum on postwar preparedness held at New York's Waldorf-Astoria hotel. He shared the platform with politicians and celebrities, from President and Eleanor Roosevelt to Greer Garson and Paul Robeson.

a necessary contribution towards a peaceable future, a service that was 'legitimate, as opposed to German geopolitics'.[48]

Taylor's Messenger lectures, delivered at Cornell five months later before less illustrious audiences, allowed him to elaborate his geopacific ideas; however, he found his academic listeners less welcoming than the Waldorf-Astoria ballroom audience. 'It was very disconcerting to receive many criticisms of my mss by folk who have no knowledge of my biological approach to anthropology and history,' he complained to his brother-in-law Bert Priestley.[49] Even though he had predicted that historians would object to his 'heretical ideas'[50] (since historians had given his *Environment and Nation* bad reviews), he was disappointed all the same. And although Cornell University Press normally published the Messenger lectures (indeed, this was a condition in Taylor's original invitation, which offered him $750 for the talks and a further $750 on their publication), he ended up having to flog his weighty manuscript elsewhere. After much promotional effort, it was published in 1946 by Oxford University Press and the University of Toronto Press as *Our Evolving Civilization: An Introduction to Geopacifics, Geographical Aspects of the Path toward World Peace*—complete with his map of Charlottetown.

Cornell might well have refused to publish such a fat book (370 pages in print), given that it was to have been based on six slim lectures. Taylor, though, always wrote as expansively as he thought. In Part IV of the book, 'Geopolitics and Geopacifics', he defined the latter as 'an attempt to base the teachings of freedom and humanity upon real geographical deductions; it is humanized Geopolitics'. His epigram summarised several years of thinking and several decades of work on race-mixing and environmental determinism but it resonated differently now as a message for the postwar world. It took geographical knowledge to demonstrate how diverse cultures can coexist in 'a world at peace', he claimed, and only a geographer like Taylor could accurately predict future patterns of migration and economic development—precisely the sort of work he had been doing ever since he joined the Bureau of Meteorology. While Taylor's geopacifics concept never really gained purchase in academic geography or history, some scholars did appreciate the politics of his intervention. Czech-born American sociologist Joseph S. Roucek called *Our Evolving Civilization* a 'must' book for all social scientists, praising it unequivocally: '[I]t is good to read one Anglo-Saxon original thinker who, with sledge hammer and tongs goes after German geopolitics … he demonstrates that the facts of geography are, and will continue to be, the foundations of history.'[51]

Taylor already had a formula for dealing with rejection: if he was ignored or criticised, the fault lay with his backward-thinking critics, not his forward-looking ideas. And long after his 'desert' battles had subsided, he continued to see himself as a prophet, committed to spreading the truth whether or not anyone listened. In one sense, geopacifics expressed his conviction that geography played a vital role in citizen education; by spreading knowledge of the geographical World Plan, geographers could educate students to understand 'where the leading nations must arise; be it understood to lead not to conquer'.[52] This argument emerged directly from his understanding of the geographer as forecaster. In the aftermath of a war that unleashed the possibility of world annihilation, there was never a time in history when it was more important for the international community to use the power of the natural environment wisely.

The enormous costs of World War II convinced Taylor that small ethnically determined sovereign nations ought to become a thing of the past; instead, he began to advocate the establishment of several large blocs of European peoples, even one bloc (thereby anticipating the European Union). National self-determination was unnecessary and dangerous, since it was clear from the examples of Canada and South Africa that it was possible to combine two 'founding races' (the indigenous populations in these places did not figure into his reckoning). According to Taylor, these two dominions were British success stories in preserving and protecting minorities within bigger national units.[53] Alongside many other internationalists, he upheld the British Commonwealth as a possible model for international cooperation. Something like the Commonwealth, or the League of Nations, in spite of its flaws, was still needed, he wrote, and institutions like world courts should be given powers to rise above nations.[54] When the San Francisco charter for the United Nations emerged in 1945, the initiative and the institution garnered his full and enthusiastic support. As he put it a year later in *Our Evolving Civilization*, '[t]he emphasis on Nationalism is a step backward'.[55] Influenced by the work of Chicago philosopher Mortimer Adler and his 1943 book *How to Think about War and Peace*, Taylor envisaged the postwar era as one that would witness the 'growth of man beyond the petty selfish ideas of a juvenile Nationalism'.[56] This was a set of abstract ideas that called for another Taylor slogan: 'Let Internationalism in-ter Nationalism.'

As the possibility of nuclear war between the postwar superpowers grew in the late 1940s, Taylor joined public debates about the relationship between science, war and peace. While he felt optimistic about science's contribution to the development of atomic energy, he felt that scientists ought not to facilitate the development of nuclear weapons. Albert Einstein, one of the postwar era's leading critics of the arms race, wrote to Taylor on 6 August 1947 (the anniversary of the Hiroshima bombing) on behalf of the Emergency Committee of Atomic Scientists. The form letter urged Taylor (along with hundreds of other scientists who received it) to speak out against nuclear warfare. Taylor was more than ready to support the cause and he was certainly eager to paste the signed letter in his scrapbook. Einstein's advice echoed Taylor's own sense of the scientist's duty: '[K]eep up the good fight for rationality and science against destructive impulses of humanity.'[57] Einstein's encouragement affirmed the worthiness of Taylor's geopacific cause. He flaunted the letter and quoted excerpts in his addresses on geography's relation to world peace, as if it were sacred text:

> In the shadow of the atomic bomb it has become apparent that all men are brothers. If we recognize this as truth and act upon this recognition, mankind

> may go forward to a higher plane of human development. If the angry passions of a nationalistic world engulf us further, we are doomed.[58]

Taylor didn't disappoint Einstein. He kept up the good fight for the rest of his life, increasingly comfortable to exchange his status as nation-planning prophet for the title 'prophet for peace'.

By the late 1940s, there was no podium from which Taylor failed to promote geopacifics. In addition to preparing a chapter on the subject for his edited collection, *Geography in the Twentieth Century*, he began to give public talks in which he explained geopacifics (and taught listeners the correct way to pronounce it, by emphasising the third syllable). When the Australian Government enlisted him to assess the landscape of geography education in the country, he mapped geopacifics onto that landscape. On ABC Radio in Sydney and Melbourne he gave an address titled 'Geo-Pacifics (Geography and World Peace)' (1948), and the local dailies covered the speech as well. The *Daily Telegraph* placed Taylor in its 'Personality' column with the title, 'He Whistles—and Talks Geopacifics'. The article covered Taylor's proclamations about the 'absurdity' of racial conflicts and the need for scientific leadership over military conquest, and it included a forecast—of the reception geographers might give geopacifics and the way Taylor would likely respond:

> The high pontiffs of the world's geographical guilds are now dissecting Professor Taylor's geopacifics. But even if the learned colleagues of Thomas Griffith Taylor disagree the professor will care little. Throughout his life he has gone his own way.

The Antarctic Cold War

After witnessing two world wars, teaching military geography and writing *Environment and Nation*, Taylor tended, like most internationalists, to orient his thinking about war and peace towards Europe and Asia. Soon after the war, though, a different place, closer to home both geographically and personally, became a danger spot in postwar international relations. Antarctica had been entangled in the major developments in world politics since the mid nineteenth century: the shift from the age of empire, to the rise of nationalism to the descent into Cold War. Like Africa in the 1880s, Antarctica had been quickly staked out and carved up as various expeditions walked, sledged, flew and drove over the continent, planting flags along their way. Competition between nations, and the potential to exploit Antarctica's coal resources, eroded respect for international law. Nazi Germany momentarily claimed its own share of the Antarctic continent in 1939, dropping hundreds of swastikas from the air. In the face of these appropriations, a growing number of explorers and scientists, who had once travelled to Antarctica under national flags and for personal glory—men like Taylor's fellow Australian Hubert Wilkins, who had accompanied Stefansson on his Canadian Arctic trips and flown across the poles—warmed to the idea of international scientific cooperation.[59]

In the early phase of Taylor's career, he had participated in a quintessential imperial expedition, which claimed sections of the continent as 'British'. His very inclusion on Scott's team was itself testimony to the way the British Empire worked in these matters: the benefits of a scholarship scheme to draw bright young colonials to Oxbridge; Scott's Royal Navy rank, and the warm reception his fundraising tour received in 'overseas dominions'; Taylor's post-expedition lectures in South Africa 'to tighten the bonds of empire'; and the sorry Union Jack that fluttered beside Scott and his party of four doomed men at the South Pole in 1912. This became one of the most famous images of the British Empire on the cusp of decline, between the end of its own 'rise' and the beginning of its 'fall'. Yet the Scott disaster failed to halt British claims-making or territorial acquisitions by its former colonies in Antarctica. For a while the Americans dominated, particularly with Byrd's highly celebrated South Pole flights. He named a whole sector of the continent after his wife (Marie Byrd land) and named other Antarctic features after famous Americans and men who had supported him, including Rockefeller Mountains and Daryl Zanuck Mountains (after the bank-rolling Hollywood producer).

Australia's turn to assert its national claims came in the interwar period, when it jockeyed for position with other competing claimants. Australian scientists, legislators and politicians regarded the Great Southern Ocean as Australia's backyard and a legitimate sphere of influence. In 1929–1931, Mawson led an explicitly land-grabbing expedition which saw his team chart 480 kilometres of coast and claim vast swathes of land for Britain. Soon after, territory legally passed to Australian administration. Australia claimed Heard Island in 1947, the same year that journalist Walter Lippman coined the term 'Cold War', and 14 men were stationed there for a year in the Commonwealth's bid to establish effective occupation. Another party was left to winter at Macquarie Island, again for the purpose of rendering Australia's claim unambiguous. And it was Australia that built the first permanent observation station in 1954, a move that doubled as territorial occupation and as a means to facilitate the compilation of scientific data, particularly meteorological readings.

Meteorologist Sir George Simpson, 'Sunny Jim' of the *Terra Nova* days, followed these developments with interest and he discussed them with Taylor. Many of the old Antarctickers renewed ties in the postwar period, prompted by the release of the 1949 Ealing Studios film, *Scott of the Antarctic* (starring John Mills and scored by Ralph Vaughan Williams). It was not just the film or developments in meteorology that prompted Simpson to write to Taylor in 1959 but concerns about the Cold War's implications for Antarctica. Simpson was pleased that an Australian science base and an Emperor penguin rookery at the foot of Taylor Glacier had recently been named after Taylor. 'I congratulate you on the honour of having your name on the map of

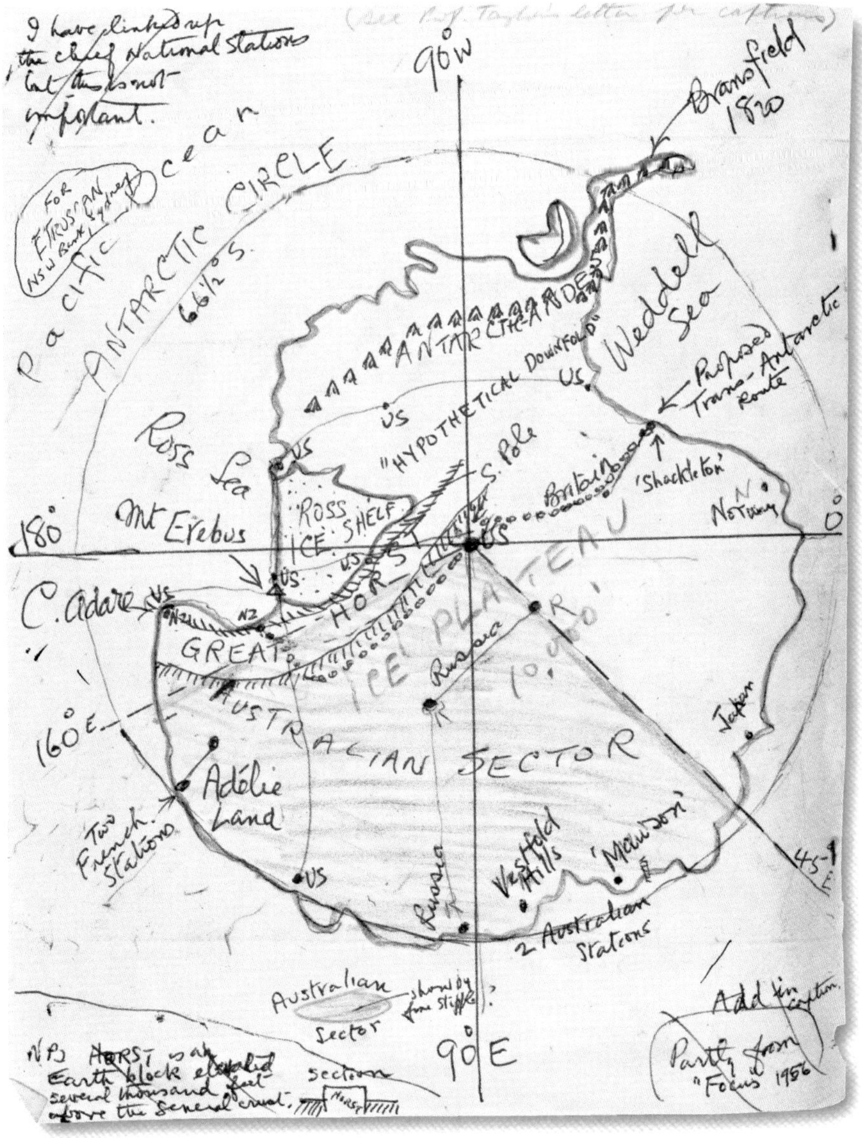

During the Cold War, national claims on the Antarctic continent took on ominous tones. Taylor's 1956 map shows the Russian, Australian and US claims, and the growing number of scientific stations established since his own scientific trip, conducted in an earlier era of imperial rivalries.

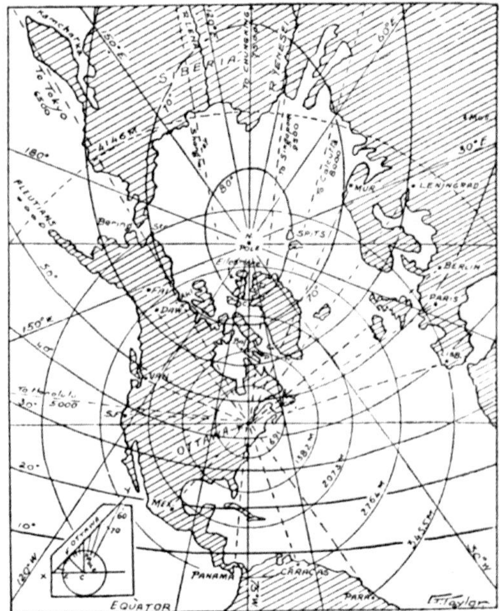

left

'Air-route chart' from Taylor's *Canada: A Study of Cool Continental Environments and Their Effect on British and French Settlement* (1947). Commercial air travel altered global geopolitics. Taylor was interested in transpolar flight and its potential to link Canada and Europe.

opposite

'Professor of the Ologies', *People Magazine*, 17 December 1952. Renewed popular interest in Antarctica in the 1950s, as well as Taylor's public message on geopacifics, made him a regular feature in the press after he retired to Australia in 1951. His links to the 'heroic era' of Antarctic exploration were always foregrounded, despite his persistent effort to highlight the importance of scientific knowledge and world peace.

Antarctica', he opened, then added, 'will it stay there when the Russians take over the whole of the Continent?' Sunny Jim was only half joking. The Russians had arrived in Antarctica in 1955, the same year that the Soviet Union formed the Warsaw Pact (to counter the power of the North Atlantic Treaty Organization) and tested its first thermonuclear device. The atomic arms race was well underway and there was good reason for internationalists the world over to fear a Soviet takeover of Antarctica.

Soviet and rival national threats to Australian Antarctic claims presented Taylor with a tough choice: support national claims over a territory where he and his closest friends had pioneered polar science, or apply his geopacific principles and promote the international governance of Antarctica in the interest of peace. Had Taylor retired in Toronto he might have been able to dodge the question; more likely he would have been pulled towards Arctic politics, particularly the establishment of joint US–Canadian radar warning and control systems, widespread flouting of the Law of the Sea, and the threat of Soviet missile strikes. Taylor's period in Toronto coincided with a new sense of Canadian purpose about the north, its economic and strategic significance. He was part of Harold Innis's Arctic Survey (1943–1944), funded by the Canadian Social Science Research Council and the Rockefeller Foundation. And he was acutely aware of and interested in the changing global positioning of Canada, the more likely transpolar air routes to Europe became.[60] Yet even in Canada, Taylor had remained closely connected to Antarctic science and exploration. In his office at the University of Toronto he reached for his picture of the *Terra Nova*'s officers and scientists whenever students prompted him to reminisce. And giving talks on Antarctica remained Taylor's bread-and-butter

PROFESSOR OF THE OLOGIES

Griffith Taylor, one of the most famous living Australians, not only went with Scott to the Antarctic. He followed this with 40 world-renowned books and a new approach to global peace.

A MIND CEASELESSLY INQUISITIVE

AUSTRALIANS can discourse at length with precision and some authority upon Sir Donald Bradman, Les Darcy and Dalray. The first 10 Australians questioned on the identity, occupation and achievements of Professor Griffith Taylor, however, preserved an embarrassingly stony silence or sought refuge in wild conjecture. These included two girls who respond obligingly to telephone calls at Sydney University and Sydney University's Department of Geography.

One of Professor Griffith Taylor's contributions to the good of mankind and Australians in particular was the foundation of the Chair of Geography at Sydney University in 1920. It is still the only self-contained Department of Geography in Australia. Other contributions by the professor to world welfare include the foundation in 1935 of the first self-contained Department of Geography at any Canadian University (the University of Toronto), the compilation of 120 works on various subjects of scientific research, including 80 on the subject of geography, and the leadership of the Western Party in Captain Scott's ill-fated expedition to the South Pole in 1911 and 1912.

Still more have been the authorship of 40 internationally-honored and respected books on geography, ecology, paleontology, physiography, climatology, meteorology, glaciology, anthropology and ethnology and the discovery of the first and only land animal — the Antarctic springtail — that exists on the great iced-under land mass (twice the size of Australia) that surrounds the South Pole.

The now 72-year-old professor is a genial giant of more than 6ft. His high forehead is lined, his eyes have the piercing qualities of the Ancient Mariner's, and the edges of his strong mouth deepen into glacier-like wrinkles when he laughs heartily.

The professor has never had much time to devote to sport, but has spared plenty for camaraderie. This is how one of his Antarctic expedition mates, Cherry-Garrard, who found the dead body of Scott and his two companions, Wilson and Bowers, described Taylor in his book *The Worst Journey in the World*. "Griff, our chief meteorologist, was a greedy scientist. When his pen was still (rarely), his tongue wagged and the arguments he led were legion. The hut below Mt. Erebus was a merrier place for his presence. When the weather was good he might be seen striding over the rocks with a complete disregard of the effect on his clothes. He wore through a pair of boots quicker than anybody I have known and his socks had to be mended with string.

"He would throw himself into his curtained wooden bunk with a show of ferocity whenever he was bored or emerge from it to take part in some argument which was troubling the mess table. A demon note-taker, he had books protruding from every pocket on sledge journeys. Hung about his body would be sundial, prismatic compass, sheath knife, binoculars, geological hammer, chronometer, pedometer, camera, aneroid (to measure heights) and an ice-axe, which he used as he went along to the possible advancement of science and the certain disorganisation of his companions.

"His giant, untamed appearance was atoned for by a halo of good fellowship."

Professor Taylor is not so gaunt and untamed today. He no longer sports the matted dark brown beard he had in the Antarctic. He lives in retirement with his cheery, sea-blue-eyed, West Country English wife in a small, modern, tidily-kept and gardened buff brick house at Seaforth. His trim and compact home houses the copy of Sir Ernest Shackleton's book, *The Heart of Antarctica*, autographed by all members of the Scott expedition, which Captain Scott used to plan and carry out his valuable but disastrous 1911-12 journey to the South Pole.

On the inside of the front cover of the book Shackleton has written, "Griffith Taylor in asking me to add my name to the list opposite is paying me a great compliment and it is with peculiar pleasure that I note the well-worn appearance of this volume — Ernest Shackleton, May 31st, 1913." Captain Scott used Professor Taylor's copy of *The Heart of Antarctica* because he had lent his own copy to his expedition's Northern Party.

The walls of Professor Taylor's home are hung with huge scale photographs of the gallant men, including the immortal Titus Oates, who bunked next to Taylor in the hut, and with equally large and clear photographs of the famous glaciers, cliffs, mountains, ice caverns, plateaus and other landmarks of Antarctica. The bookshelves are crammed with works of science by the most famous scientists of the past 100 years and 40 books of Taylor's own compilation. The professor's still exceptionally active and inquiring brain — and his wife's equally active feather duster — keep them from becoming dusty.

One paper between the leaves of a voluminous tome of science contains the original geological survey made by Professor Taylor for Australia's national capital, Canberra. Another paper he also wrote contains suggestions for the naming of the capital which may have wielded a decisive influence on Canberra becoming Canberra instead of Cooktown or Bankstown.

Professor Taylor's scientific report on how the naming of the national capital should be gone about was made to the relevant committee on January 14th, 1913. The capital's name was announced less than two months later. The report traced how and why the American and Canadian cities of Washington, Philadelphia and Ottawa were so named. It suggested that, as Australia had no character of the magnitude of George Washington, the use of a personal name would not be ideal.

It pointed out that Philadelphia had been named from the Greek Philos which means "loving" and Delphos which means "a brother" and thus became known, for a time anyway, as the City of Brotherly Love. It revealed that the name of the Canadian capital, Ottawa, was a native name and proposed that the Australian capital be named after the name of the parish in which it was built — Canberra.

In addition to all these contributions to the general cause Professor Taylor has compiled monumental and invaluable surveys or road traverses of such geographically remote and varied parts of the world as Queensland's Barrier Reef, the New Zealand Hot Lakes, Newfoundland, the Canadian Rockies, the southern edge of the South Australian Desert, the northern edge of the Sahara Desert, the Swiss Alps, the Yukon Trail and the Sturt Highway. At 50 he became probably the first scientist to have compiled traverses of the seven continents of the world.

Professor Taylor has advanced three major theories in his long life, two of which were recognised, after a wait in each case of 20 years. The third was flung to the world 10 years ago and the Professor doubts whether he will live to see it generally accepted. His first objective was "to get Australians to realise what a big problem our desert and semi-desert areas offered to the development and even population of their continent."

The deserts are still dry

Taylor wrote a book on that subject in 1910. The West Australian Government of the time promptly banned it as a school book, though its State was the one most vitally concerned. West Australian parliamentarians and their advisers claimed that the areas the professor described as unreclaimable deserts were not really deserts at all, but potentially productive and inhabitable areas. By 1940 Professor Taylor's views on this subject were accepted with resignation. The deserts are still deserts.

The professor's second life's aim was to get the world to realise that the broadheaded Chinese and their biological allies in Asia, Eastern and Central Europe were in no respect inferior biologically, indeed probably superior, to the narrower-headed Western peoples which include the British, Americans and, of course, ourselves. This pet brainchild of the professor's was naturally not popular because it concluded that the peoples of the Soviet Republics and those of the countries behind the Iron Curtain in the West and the Chinese curtain in the East today are biologically superior to the Western nations. It is least of all popular now.

But Professor Taylor, who detests everything Kremlin despotism stands for, is just as strongly opposed to the rejection of logical scientific deductions purely on the ground of their unpopularity. He agrees with the late Ben Chifley and the living R. G. Casey that Australians should do all they can to make friends with the Chinese people, whom he believes will eventually break with Russia.

Continued next page

The wardroom of the famous Terra Nova, the Antarctic research ship. The bearded Griffith Taylor is front left. Standing second from right is the heroic Captain Oates. At the head of the table is expedition leader Scott.

Page 24 PEOPLE December 17, 1952 December 17, 1952

topic (although he found it hard to impress Canadian audiences with tales of extreme cold). The Taylors' decision to return to Australia after his retirement brought him geographically closer to Antarctic politics and to his old Antarctic friends. He and Mawson had seen each other for the first time in decades on Taylor's 1948 tour and they began to correspond frequently after he moved back to Sydney in 1951. Shifting events in Antarctica also brought Frank Debenham, Charles 'Silas' Wright and Raymond Priestley back. By the 1950s it was impossible for Taylor to avoid Antarctica.

Like it or not (and he did), Taylor fell under the Antarctic spotlight after returning to Australia. One of the Taylors' neighbours in Seaforth, the northern Sydney suburb where Taylor, Doris and David settled, was Jack Oughton, who edited the Australian edition of *People Magazine*. In 1952, his interview with Taylor resulted in a four-page spread, titled 'Professor of the Ologies'. It described Taylor as 'one of the most famous living Australians [who] not only went with Scott to the Antarctic. He followed with forty world-renowned books and a new approach to global peace'. Taylor regularly puffed himself up with such hyperbole but this feature added two inches to his height:

> The now 72-year-old professor is a genial giant of more than six ft. His high forehead is lined, his eyes have the piercing quality of the Ancient Mariner's, and the edges of his strong mouth deepen into glacier-like wrinkles when he laughs heartily.

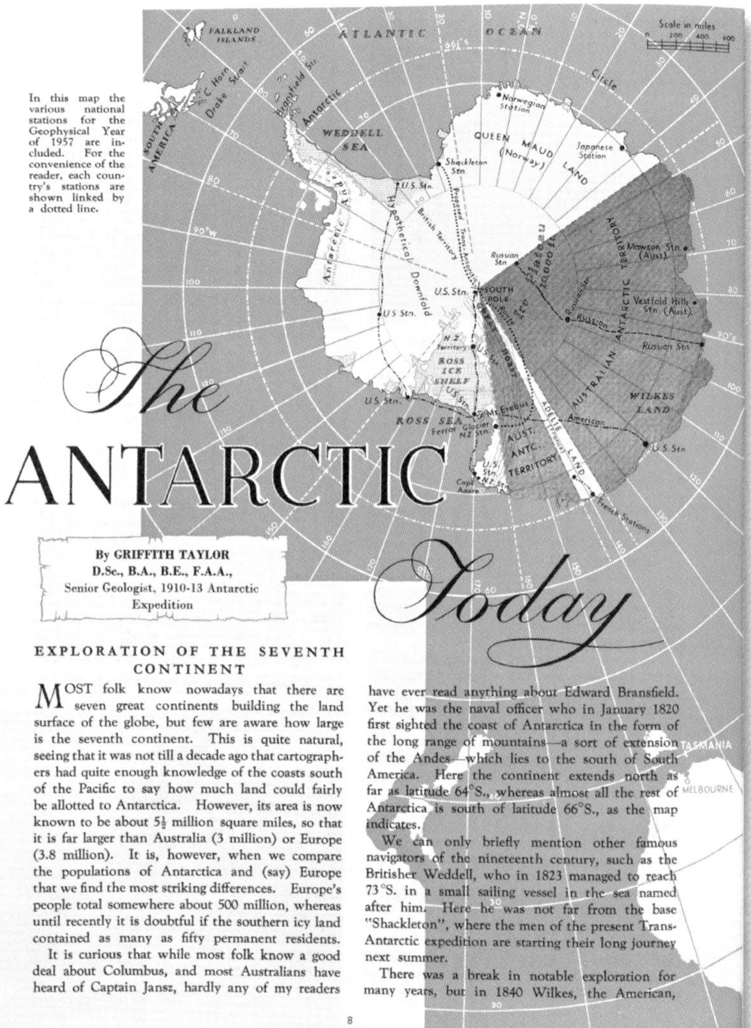

The ANTARCTIC *Today*

In this map the various national stations for the Geophysical Year of 1957 are included. For the convenience of the reader, each country's stations are shown linked by a dotted line.

By GRIFFITH TAYLOR
D.Sc., B.A., B.E., F.A.A.,
Senior Geologist, 1910-13 Antarctic Expedition

EXPLORATION OF THE SEVENTH CONTINENT

MOST folk know nowadays that there are seven great continents building the land surface of the globe, but few are aware how large is the seventh continent. This is quite natural, seeing that it was not till a decade ago that cartographers had quite enough knowledge of the coasts south of the Pacific to say how much land could fairly be allotted to Antarctica. However, its area is now known to be about 5½ million square miles, so that it is far larger than Australia (3 million) or Europe (3.8 million). It is, however, when we compare the populations of Antarctica and (say) Europe that we find the most striking differences. Europe's people total somewhere about 500 million, whereas until recently it is doubtful if the southern icy land contained as many as fifty permanent residents.

It is curious that while most folk know a good deal about Columbus, and most Australians have heard of Captain Jansz, hardly any of my readers have ever read anything about Edward Bransfield. Yet he was the naval officer who in January 1820 first sighted the coast of Antarctica in the form of the long range of mountains—a sort of extension of the Andes—which lies to the south of South America. Here the continent extends north as far as latitude 64°S., whereas almost all the rest of Antarctica is south of latitude 66°S., as the map indicates.

We can only briefly mention other famous navigators of the nineteenth century, such as the Britisher Weddell, who in 1823 managed to reach 73°S. in a small sailing vessel in the sea named after him. Here he was not far from the base "Shackleton", where the men of the present Trans-Antarctic expedition are starting their long journey next summer.

There was a break in notable exploration for many years, but in 1840 Wilkes, the American,

8

'The Antarctic Today', *The Etruscan* (vol. 6, 1956). National claims to the Antarctic continent began to clash with Taylor's growing internationalism. By the late 1950s, he declared that Australia's large sector should be sacrificed to some form of international governance: 'I would give this up tomorrow if it would help.'

Several images of Taylor taken during the course of the Scott expedition, including Ponting's famous teardrop glacier photo, adorned the article, along with a rare image of Taylor and Doris together at their dining room table. Her honorary status merited note: 'She is the sister of one of his Antarctic colleagues.'[61]

Taylor's appearance in *People* renewed Australian awareness of his association with Antarctica. In November 1954, the Royal Society of New South Wales requested that he speak at a special screening of Ponting's 1933 film *Ninety Degrees South*. Taylor had just completed a series of sittings for a portrait by artist Dora Toovey, who had been looking for a '"Famous" subject' to paint for the 1955 Archibald portrait competition. ('We like the result,' Taylor wrote to his brother Evan, 'with a map of the Aus–Ant. region as a background.')[62] A year later, he spoke on 'Australian Antarctica' at the Royal Australian Historical Society meeting, and described how Australia had come 'to possess such an enormous area of the earth's land surface'.[63] Taylor updated his Antarctic credentials in 'The Antarctic Today', an article he published in *The Etruscan* magazine in 1956. While he didn't mention the Soviet expedition underway at the time, he did note the Commonwealth Government's decision to send three Australian expeditions in the previous six years. The title page featured a large map of Antarctica with 'the Australian Antarctic Territory' highlighted to emphasise its scope.

In spite of this relentless attention to Australian interests, Taylor, like other scientists, gradually came to view Antarctica through the lens of internationalism. The forces of cooperation were gathering momentum, perhaps nowhere more clearly than in Antarctica, where scientists participated in International Geophysical Year (IGY). This endeavour, carried out between 1957 and 1958, involved researchers from 66 countries, and the venture excited Taylor enormously. Aside from the prospect that new aerial-mapping techniques might confirm his early hypotheses about the geological structure of Antarctica first published in 1914, the participants' abandonment of international rivalries in the interest of science provided a model for his geopacifics. IGY was based on two previous International Polar Years. Taylor was an infant at the time of the first in 1882–1883, when Arctic explorers still searched for the Northwest Passage and for Franklin's lost parties, and when no human had yet set foot on Antarctica. The second International Polar Year, 1932–1933, occurred when Taylor was living in Chicago, three years after he had published *Antarctic Adventure and Research*. By the time of IGY, his 40-year career of commenting on Antarctic science dovetailed with his mission to explain geography's contribution to world peace. In 1957–1958, geophysics met geopacifics.

That year also saw re-energised Australian and British moves to assert territorial claims which tugged at Taylor's loyalty as a Britisher. Had he been well enough, he might have participated in the British Trans-Antarctic Expedition of 1957–1958; as it turned out, a rather more famous explorer, Sir Edmund Hillary, led the expedition, along with Vivian Fuchs, who later visited Taylor, the elder statesman of polar exploration.[64] But Taylor never regarded this expedition as a great contribution to science. The British, not to be outdone by the Soviets, conducted it more as a propaganda exercise than a scientific expedition.

National and military interests also prompted return visits to Antarctic by several of Taylor's closest associates who were fit enough to travel. Each of these old men was sponsored by the Canadian, US or British governments. Taylor's brother-in-law, Silas Wright, sustained a strategic and scientific interest in Antarctica after leaving the Admiralty and returning to Canada in the 1950s. Wright remained active as a researcher for the Canadian Defence Research Board and, in 1960, he travelled to Antarctica to study electromagnetic fluctuations for the Pacific Naval Laboratory. He sent Taylor photographs of the Taylor Dry Valley and the Wright Dry Valley as they looked, not from a man-hauled sledge but from the vantage point of a state-of-the-art US helicopter. Wright found it amazing (and amusing) that their old huts were being restored as national monuments.[65] Raymond Priestley's visits to Antarctica were also closely linked to strategic matters. He returned twice: in 1956 he travelled with the Royal Cruise and escorted the Duke of Edinburgh on an Antarctic tour attached to a royal visit of the Falkland Islands dependencies; and, in 1958–1959, he participated in 'Operation Deep Freeze', as an official British observer for US Navy manoeuvres in Antarctica.

At no point in his career had Taylor developed such close links with government but he was still willing to bend to nationalistic loyalties for his own purposes. As late as 1958, self-interest and his perpetual scrounging for royalties prompted him to approach publisher Angus & Robertson to reissue an abridged version of *With Scott* for an Australian audience. His proposed angle of approach was telling: 'Australia is becoming very conscious of Antarctica these last years, which is natural since we control more of the White Continent than any other nation.'[66]

In other words, Taylor found it difficult to 'in-ter' his own nationalism when it came to Antarctica. For some time, he managed to have it both ways: an internationalist and card-carrying 'geographer for peace' when it came to Europe and Asia, and a Britisher with nationalist loyalties when it came to Antarctica. His balancing act tipped in favour of internationalism only by the late 1950s, when he began to speak publicly in favour of Antarctica's supranational governance. His participation in the international Special Committee on Antarctic Research (SCAR), which he joined as soon as it formed in 1957, was one factor in his political shift. A spin-off of International Geophyscial Year, the committee allowed elderly researchers unable to travel to Antarctica to collaborate with scientists from several nations. From the late 1940s Taylor had found air travel difficult on his ears and by the mid 1950s he experienced pain and deafness when flying. So he was happy instead to take the train from Sydney to Canberra in 1959 to keep up to date with polar research. Meeting at The Australian National University, where his 1948 tour had helped to establish geography as a field of study, he delivered an invited address titled 'Science in the Antarctic Fifty Years Ago'. 'Lots of foreigners,' he informed Sunny Jim:

> At our hotel was little Picard from Buenos Ayres … two Russians … Leclavier (French President of SCAR) … Japs and dozens of Americans ... I managed to speak French to Picard a little, for I've forgotten my Spanish which I could smatter in 1930. I have never tried to speak Russian before—tho I can read easy geography. However my efforts amused the two Russians.[67]

Although he was the 'sole living teetotaller' among the delegates, he felt at home in this united nations of polar scientists.

The United Nations proper was very much on Taylor's mind in 1959, as he prepared to give his presidential address to the newly formed Institute of Australian Geographers on 'Geographers and World Peace'. His preparations for the paper (he always worked for months on presidential addresses) occurred amidst negotiations in Washington, where delegates prepared an agreement to 'freeze all territorial claims' in Antarctica. While this meant that Australia could retain almost half the continent, Taylor told his old friend Charles Laseron (a biologist on Mawson's Australasian Antarctic expedition of 1911–1914 and a regular bridge partner of the Taylors): 'I would give this up tomorrow if it would help world peace.'[68]

This is exactly the advice he gave to his fellow geographers, who met in Melbourne in January 1960. In an excited letter to his former pupil Marie Sanderson (a 'cross between a lecture on gardening and a sermon on peace'), Taylor recounted the purpose of his address: 'I hope that geographers will realise that they are in a better position in education than most folk—to link science with human problems involved in war and peace.'[69] To his son Bill, he admitted there was 'not much new in my talk'. He was right, in the sense that he had given a talk with the identical title at a Sydney meeting of the World Movement for World Federal Government in 1954. But one thing was new. After rambling through a 9000-word review of his life's work, Taylor reached his internationalist punch line:

> I am convinced that nationalism is outmoded … we geographers … should begin to show that we should be cautious of ultra-nationalism. The spread of U.N. powers is greatly to be encouraged … In view of the remarkable example of I.G.Y. in Antarctica as illustrating practical inter-nationalism, I would even advocate that we consider handing over 2½ million square miles of our territory to [the] U.N. My suggestion, if followed, would remove possible discord, and be a demonstration of Australia's belief in Internationalism as the sole practical way of obtaining world peace.[70]

Taylor's radical prescription upset Australian territorial chauvinism, but never in a way that made him a public pariah again. Indeed, an editorial in *The Sydney Morning*

Herald supported his talk and pointed to the alarming prospect that the Soviets might set up rocket bases in Antarctica. It was a 'brutal fact' that Australia didn't have the power to protect its citizens, let alone its interests. The *Herald* put the case even more convincingly than Taylor: it was in 'Australia's true national interests' that the United Nations govern Antarctica.[71]

Although the Antarctic Treaty of 1959 came into force two years later, it failed to incorporate Taylor's call for supranational governance. National claims, including Australia's, continued to be asserted, and the treaty explicitly provided for this. One of its concessions to the 12 signing nations (including Australia) was that there be no 'renunciation by any Contracting Party of previously asserted rights of or claims to territorial sovereignty in Antarctica'. The treaty sidestepped the question of possible conflicts over competing territorial claims (an issue yet to be resolved) but it did realise some of Taylor's aspirations for the continent. Its first article stipulated that military operations and weapons testing be prohibited: 'Antarctica shall be used for peaceful purposes only.' This represented the first international agreement for arms control in the midst of the nuclear arms race. With explicit reference to the success of IGY, it called for ongoing international scientific cooperation between existing national scientific organisations, the agencies of the United Nations and other interested international scientific organisations. Antarctica failed to become the purely UN-administered continent of Taylor's dreams, yet the treaty did check the very real possibility that it might have become a site of disastrous international conflict.[72]

Taylor was far less sanguine when it came to his own claims-making in Antarctica, however. He never questioned Captain Scott's authority to name a glacier and dry valley after him, and he was thrilled to discover in 1958 that a science base was to receive his name. At the time, he was still reeling from his own Antarctic 'international incident'. In 1946, Norwegian cartographers published an atlas that renamed Taylor Glacier as Bretangen. Taylor knew nothing of this until Mawson discovered the error in 1955, and complained about it on Taylor's behalf to Phillip Law, head of the Antarctic division of the Commonwealth Government's Department of External Affairs. When the Commonwealth reproduced the error in an official Australian map of Antarctica in 1956, Mawson protested again.[73] While the naming dispute was finally resolved in Taylor's favour, he resented the Norwegians' symbolic incursion, as he explained to Mawson: 'There are hundreds of unnamed glaciers, so why couldn't they give the supplanter's name to one of those.'

In November 1958, at a special screening of British Petroleum's ultra-nationalist film about the Hillary–Fuchs expedition, Taylor perked up when he heard the film narrator announce: 'Now we go to the new station, "Taylor", 60 miles west of Mawson.' This was the first he learned of the Australian Government's decision in 1957 to establish a weather station in honour of the former Commonwealth meteorologist. 'So now I have a possible city named after me,' he gushed to his friend Stephen Visher, 'as well as two glaciers and various odds and ends in Australia.' More happy news arrived, after the penguin colony at the foot of Taylor Glacier was given his name as well. He was in a jolly mood when he appeared on ABC television a week later to participate in a forum on Antarctic exploration. One of the participants, an Australian MP, had recently travelled to Antarctica to explore its economic development potential for Australia. While there, he had snatched a biscuit from Scott's Discovery Hut. Possibly disgruntled by Australian bids to exploit Antarctica commercially, Taylor ate the 57-year-old biscuit on camera. 'I think it pleased the audience.'

As the fiftieth anniversary of Scott's Antarctic expedition rolled around in 1960, Taylor was one of the few men from that era of exploration still alive to celebrate it. Douglas Mawson had died in 1958, aptly in IGY, and Taylor began work on a biography of his friend and rival; one of his last books, published in 1962.[74] Apsley Cherry-Garrard had committed suicide in May 1959, suffering seriously from depression ever since his return from Antarctica, and his discovery of Scott's body, what he called 'the worst journey in the world'. But those who were still alive were keen to remember and celebrate the early years at a time when the Antarctic acquired a renewed public interest. To honour the anniversary, Frank Debenham hosted a sherry party for several of Scott's men and their descendants at the Scott Polar Research Institute in Cambridge, which he had directed from its foundation in 1920 to 1946. Because Taylor, now aged 80, was too weak to travel, he sent an audio recording to hail his Antarctic mates. 'Half way through the sherry we were shushed into silence,' 'Deb' recounted the occasion, 'and, a surprise to nearly everyone, your voice rang through the large room, very clear ... Sunny Jim, now nearly stone deaf, sat over the instrument with his hearing aid and enjoyed every minute of it.'[75] Sunny Jim, like Priestley and Wright, had been knighted, and Taylor paid special homage to these three men: 'They didn't get the knighthood because they happened to be explorers, they got the knighthood for scientific work.'[76] Even though Taylor's own scientific work on the Antarctic was still being used, and remained respected to the end of his life, he never doubted that his greater contribution to Antarctica had been made through geopacifics. His professional satisfaction may have gone some way to compensate for his personal disappointment, which his family knew well. As his brother Evan commiserated: 'It was quite a score that Scott's party collected 3 knights. We all think it is a great shame that there was not a 4th—yourself'.[77]

The fate of Antarctica's Taylor Station paralleled the progress of Taylor's geopacific mission. On 5 August 1959, it burnt down. Taylor thanked Phillip Law for relaying the news and hoped that he would '<u>preserve</u> the honour' of the penguin rookery's official name.[78] Once Law reassured him of this, he could look back wryly, calling the station, 'Taylor, that ill-starred metropolis'. Taylor's base might have gone up in flames but geopacifics failed to spark enthusiasm among geographers. After he had given his Institute of Australian Geographers presidential talk, he'd offered it to the organisation's journal but the editor refused to publish it. He presented it to other journals for years until, out of kindness, Oscar Spate agreed to publish a heavily abridged version in

Australian Geographical Studies in 1963. A Cambridge-trained geographer a generation younger than Taylor, Spate captured Taylor's lifelong tendency to magnify his marginality while seeking widespread agreement and support: 'He liked to have it both ways—to proclaim himself a lone battler against fearful odds, and to assert that all informed people were on his side.'[79] And if that didn't work, there was always the response Taylor had perfected over decades: that given time, the world would come to see the light of his ideas. In this case he forecast: 'I do not believe my ideas on Geopacifics will get the attention they deserve much before 1976.'[80]

Taylor was not alone in making improbably grand statements as a scientist on the world peace theme. Finding few followers for geopacifics, Taylor nonetheless remained resolute and upbeat into his eighties. He saw a glimmer of interest from the Universal Knowledge Foundation, which contacted him in 1963 to request his contribution to a book called *Modern Prophets Speak for Man*. ('Sent Geographers and World Peace,' he noted on the letter.) Reaching the end of his life, he wanted more than anything to be remembered as a prophet for peace. As he summed up his mission to a colleague:

> For some forty years I found it wise to 'Tell the truth, and shame the booster' ... My second slogan is even more important, 'In times of peace—make Peace secure'.[81]

Founding Father

6

The title page of Taylor's autobiography, *Journeyman Taylor* (1958), introduces readers to a book about 'the education of a scientist'. Indeed, a rather impressive scientist:

PROFESSOR GRIFFITH TAYLOR
D.SC, B.E., B.A. (RESEARCH, CAMBRIDGE)

Senior Geologist of Captain Scott's Antarctic Expedition
One-time Professor of Geography at Sydney, Chicago, and Toronto
Past President of the Australian, British, American, and Canadian Geographers
Fellow of the Australian Academy of Science

Taylor opens by recounting how he sailed between several disciplines and occupations before he landed on geography at the age of 40. Despite his late start he lived another 43 years, over which time he became a founding father of the discipline, not only in his own eyes but in others'. By the 1960s, his admirers had named numerous scholarships and essay prizes in geography after him; even the University of Sydney, site of his triumphs and trials as a disciplinary pioneer, deigned to honour him by housing the department of geography in its new Griffith Taylor building. Although he managed to insert miniature reviews of his career into almost everything he published, his autobiography allowed him to narrate his story at greater length—260 000 words to be exact. Yet for all those typescript pages he bundled off to his publisher, Robert Hale, there was much to the journey, and many fellow travellers, he edited out.

Taylor was not unlike other men of his era, who recounted their lives in science as if their families mattered little to their careers. While *Journeyman* cast his family and his relatives in cameo and supporting roles, 'family' mattered deeply to Taylor—his family of origin, the family he joined by marrying Doris, the intellectual family he inherited and developed as a student of Edgeworth David, and his 'geography family', composed of former Taylor students who responded warmly to his paternalism. *Journeyman* opens with a homage to ancestors on both sides of his family. By drawing attention to his father's origins in poverty he amplifies James Taylor's remarkable achievements and the example he set for each of his children, his elder son in particular. Taylor also pays his respects to the Priestley line—Raymond, his fellow Antarctic geologist, later knighted, and Doris's famous ancestor Joseph Priestley, another knighted scientist. Lineage through blood and affiliation were critical to Taylor's understanding of his own success; equally, it guided his behaviour towards those whom he fathered, both his own children and his students. He modelled himself expressly on Sir Edgeworth David, and anticipated that his students would hold him in equal esteem. In the University of Toronto's large geography department particularly, many students adopted him, as he had adopted Professor David, as a father figure who took an interest in their personal lives as well as their careers. Family and career went together literally in Taylor's life, and geography was, from the start, a family affair: his parents spotted his mapping skills early on, his wife read and edited everything he wrote, his sister worked beside him as a geographer in her own right. But his sons ultimately followed different paths.

While *Journeyman* only hints at these stories, they emerge fully through his letters, journals, sketchbooks and diaries, all of which Taylor donated to several repositories after he retired. The vast majority of his papers ended up in the National Library of Australia, where he assumed that archivists would 'sort out the useless stuff'. Later generations would find his memoirs dull, he figured, since they contained nothing on 'sport, jazz or sex'.[1] While he did hate organised sport, despised modern art and music, and never mentioned sex, he little realised how useful this 'stuff' might become to others, as evidence of the ways in which a very public man's family and professional life were closely connected.[2]

In the mid 1950s when Taylor was working on *Journeyman*, he stayed more or less put in the suburb of Seaforth, on Sydney's north shore, where he set up his retirement household with Doris and David. Slowed by old age, growing deafness and mounting injuries, his travels became fewer and more modest, while his lifelong tendency towards retrospection became one of his chief preoccupations. What would his legacy be, he wondered, as a geographer and as a family man?

Sydney: Founding Father and the Family Business in the 1920s

Professor Mills's official invitation, requesting that Taylor return in 1948 to assess the state of geography in Australia as a university discipline, came with a personal bonus for Taylor—an opportunity to visit at government expense the family he had left behind in Australia 20 years earlier. After leaving Sydney in 1928, he had travelled to South America, Europe, Africa and the Arctic, but never back to Australia. Both of his brothers, Rhys and Evan, had homes in metropolitan Sydney, and Dorothy continued to live in the family home, Cartref, after Mater passed away in 1943. Taylor had still to meet all of his brothers' children, and his son, Bill, who had moved back to Sydney, had met a woman (another Dorothy) and married her in 1947. When the *Daily Telegraph* interviewed the infamous 'migratory prophet', the reporter noted his local family ties: 'Professor Taylor belongs far more to Sydney than Toronto, anyway.' Taylor agreed. As he informed *Telegraph* readers, 'I have decided myself to come back and settle here as soon as I retire.'[3]

Retiring from Toronto, at the agreed-upon age of 70, was nothing like his earlier resignation from the University of Sydney amidst a storm of controversy and ill feeling. In numerous addresses and publications Taylor had elevated the dramas that prompted him to abandon Australia into his stock legend, which has prevailed ever since. But this prodigal parable overshadows the experiences of another Taylor geographer, whose story resolved rather differently. From March 1921, geography's infancy at Sydney, Dorothy Taylor had been critical to the program's establishment and success. She had started out as Taylor's attendant and map drawer, with her prior prize-winning start in physiography her formal qualification. She helped train the department's students in laboratory work, including map and model-making as well as block diagram drawing, and she also supervised geological and topographical fieldwork. While Doris rarely joined field trips, Dorothy led class excursions to many of the same locations she and Taylor had both visited under Professor David's instruction, including the Illawarra coast, where Mater had invested in a parcel of investment property at Bulli. Dorothy's plain skirts and sturdy shoes never impeded her from walking and climbing as confidently as she had tramped up and down the Hochstetter Glacier with the Antarctickers-in-training back in 1910.

Although she worked for her brother (and studied under him from 1925 to 1928), Dorothy nevertheless established herself as a professional geographer in her own right.

She wrote portions of the text and contributed many of the images that went into the department's instruction manual, *The Geographical Laboratory* (1925). The two Taylors appeared as the authors of the manual which the elder always called 'our own little book' (measuring it against his own bricks, no doubt). The brother and sister team also played leading roles in the establishment of the Geographical Society of New South Wales in 1927. Dorothy was voted its vice-president (the presidency was his) and she was also the first co-editor of the organisation's journal, *The Australian Geographer*. It seemed fitting, then, for Taylor to recommend that Dorothy be appointed acting lecturer on his departure for Chicago, a brotherly bequest of the family business as well as a bid to ensure that geography would continue to be taught Taylor-style. Or so he hoped when he left his department in the hands of 'Pal' and the incoming chair, Glasgow University graduate James Macdonald Holmes.

Tension mounted quickly between Dorothy and the new man, however: 'I cannot report any thrills of rapture on our acquisition,' she confessed, after Holmes arrived in 1930. The new associate professor was 15 years Dorothy's junior and, unlike her brother, held only a Bachelor of Science degree. She complained to Taylor that Holmes intended to put his stamp on the department by wiping out theirs. He removed *The Geographical Laboratory* from the syllabus and 'he discounts most of our efforts as "not accurate" or "of no value"'.[4] Worse still, Holmes had no intention of formally appointing Miss Taylor as a lecturer, she discovered, despite the fact that she had headed the department in 1929 before his arrival. Demonstrator positions would do for Dorothy, as well as for Miss Nell Stanley, the other female demonstrator from the Taylor days. So would limited-term appointments, rather than the longer-term contract Dorothy had anticipated. The final straw was Holmes's accusation, never proven, that she had stolen books from the departmental library. Without her brother to champion her cause before the senate, Holmes won and her services were terminated in 1931.

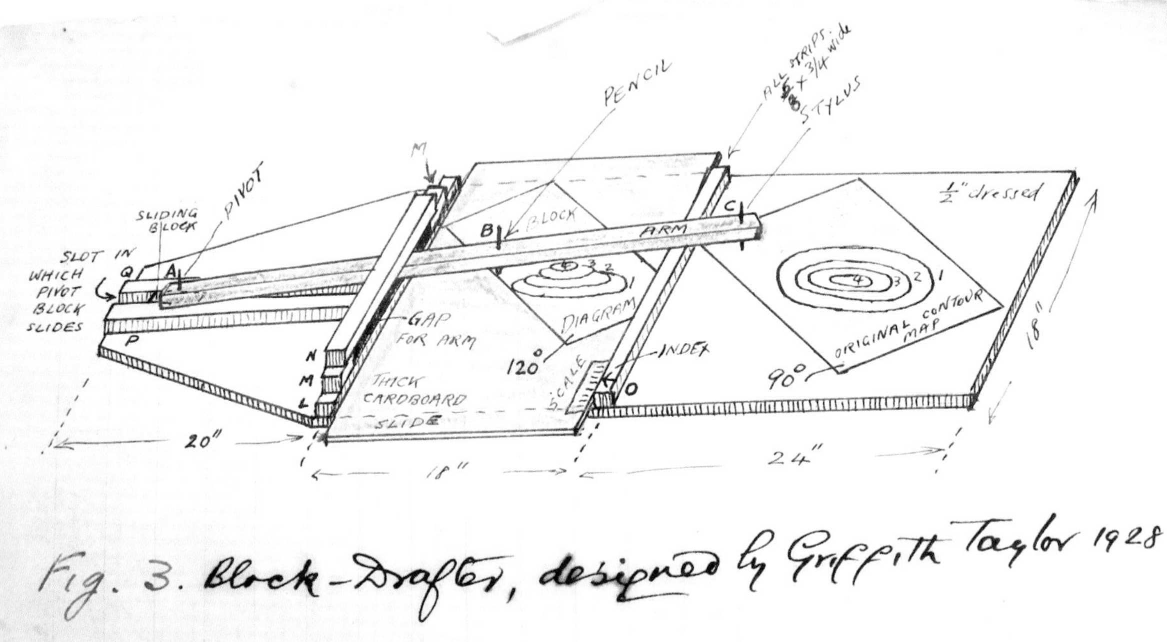

Fig. 3. Block-Drafter, designed by Griffith Taylor 1928

opposite

Block diagram drafter designed by Griffith Taylor, 1928. As professor and demonstrator respectively, Taylor and his sister, Dorothy, instructed the University of Sydney geography students in the science and art of block diagram drawing. Professor William Davis of Harvard University taught Taylor the technique.

above

The University of Sydney's inaugural geography class on a field trip in 1922. Taylor actively encouraged women to study geography, though only a few followed him into academic posts. Taylor is standing at the back to the right, and his demonstrator, Dorothy Taylor, is the second woman to his right, standing in the middle of the group.

left

Dorothy Taylor, c.1927. Despite replacing her brother as lecturer in geography after his departure in 1928, Dorothy Taylor's academic career would prove to be short-lived.

above

Doris and Griffith Taylor, c.1927.

left

Doris Taylor with their first son, Bill, c.1920. On the back of the photo is written: 'Best wishes to Dear Daddy for December 1st [Taylor's birthday] from Bubba and Mumma.'

Receiving this news from his secure position at Chicago troubled Taylor, both as an older brother unable to protect his sister from bullying, and as an academic patriarch. He wrote immediately to the vice-chancellor on Dorothy's behalf: '[I]t is painful to contrast the kindly farewell given to myself with her ignominious dismissal without notice.' In truth, Taylor knew that Dorothy had decided never to return, both defeated and exhausted by the unpleasant affair: "I am sick of being despised,' she admitted in 1930, 'I have no courage or conceit left.'[5] No matter how incensed Taylor felt over the opposition he had faced in his public battles of the 1920s, his indignation over the transfer of power at Sydney ran deeper. It was personal: an inferior had undermined his legacy as Australia's founding father of geography and scuttled his sister's career in the process. For the remainder of his life, Taylor dwelt bitterly on the fact that he had handed over his department to an unworthy stepfather ('my successor' to colleagues, and 'the kilted one' or 'our mutual unfriend' in letters to Pal).

Remembered through his sister's and his own humiliation and through the clouds of public controversy he created, Taylor's version of the period he spent in Sydney at the helm of the department appears unrelievedly gloomy. While he provided a face-saving account of it in *Journeyman* which saw him leave because the University of Chicago offered a better salary, better conditions and a highly ranked department, he painted the 1920s in Sydney as a time of persecution and loneliness. In contrast, the personal letters and diaries he wrote from the same period reveal a far wider range of shades to his life, both dark and light. His opponents' attempts to rubbish his reputation caused him great anxiety (which often physically manifested in painful boils and bouts of eczema) but these frustrations were mixed with professional rewards and a close family life, drawn closer after he returned to the city where his family still resided and his old scholarly connections remained strong.

After moving from Melbourne, Taylor had chosen a substantial brick house in Mosman, only a fifteen-minute walk from his parents' home in Cremorne. This brought him back into the family fold after more than a decade of travels. For Doris, the company of female in-laws compensated for her separation from her sisters and mother in England. Doris had used the transition from Melbourne as an opportunity to make an eight-month trip back home to visit her family with Bill. Shortly after she returned early in 1921, she became pregnant again. Unlike Bill's arrival, the birth of their daughter, Natalie, took place within the Taylor family circle, allowing Doris to turn for support to Mater, Pal and her sisters-in-law—Rhys's wife Linda and Evan's wife 'Doy'. She was closest to her mother-in-law and Pal, with whom she attended Mosman Congregational Church. These female outings were more pleasant than her attempts to drag along her secularist husband, who preferred philosophy to sermons. Indeed, Taylor preferred most anything: 'Took Bill to Church … Left before sermon. Went zoo saw zebras.'[6]

The Taylor family also reliably stepped in whenever Taylor left on extended ethnographic field trips and conference jaunts. His trip to the Pan Pacific Science Congress in Tokyo in 1926 took him away for three months, over which time he packed in plenty of stops in locales later described in his lucrative newspaper travelogues. Before he could attend the Tokyo conference, Japanese Government regulations strangely required that each delegate's wife provide written permission for her husband to travel. The formality 'occasioned a good deal of amusement', as he later recounted in *Journeyman*. 'I don't know whether there was some fear lest the Geisha ladies might have prevented our return, or whether there had been a recent epidemic of wife-desertion.'[7] At the time, though, Doris's permission was a foregone conclusion. In this configuration of family, everyone understood that Taylor's prolonged absences spelled career-building, not desertion, and certainly not geishas.

Although Taylor worked intensely over the 1920s to build his geography department and establish his academic standing, he played hard as well. In spite of being a teetotaller he was no wowser, and the jocularity of his bearing, which his Antarctic mates earlier had grown to appreciate, made him an affable family man as well. He and Doris socialised with the Taylor clan, whose members shuttled between houses, hosting each other in weekly rounds of suppers, teas and card parties, as well as the odd evening out in the city for musical theatre, with Gilbert and Sullivan always a popular choice. When not spending time with the family, he and Doris were visiting and relaxing with his colleagues. Taylor often claimed that the entire Sydney professoriate (with the exception of Professor David) was against him over his environmental and racial claims in the 1920s, yet he and Doris enjoyed close relationships with university men and their families. Leo Cotton, who succeeded David as chair of geology in 1925 and travelled with Taylor to Tokyo, was an old mate with whom Taylor had studied as an

undergraduate. He was also a fellow Antarcticker (from Shackleton's *Nimrod* expedition) and a close friend of Pal's. Senior professors and their wives numbered among Taylor's academic and family friends as well and included mathematician H.S. Carslaw and bachelor English professor E.R. 'Sunny' Holme. Younger men like 'Tas' Lovell, a psychology professor, and his wife Alice, became the Taylors' regular opponents at the Mosman Tennis Club. Latin professor Frederick Todd, who sparred with Taylor over his attacks on compulsory classics training, nevertheless picnicked with the Taylors and their children at Sydney's parks and beaches. His most faithful friend turned out to be R.C. Mills, the university's young economics professor. Over the 1920s, Mills supported Taylor's outspoken opinions and thought well enough of him to invite him back 20 years later, as a patriarch of geography. These ties and affiliations provided emotional ballast for Taylor, while the political and professional storms of the 1920s rocked him and tested his resolve.

Over the same period, Taylor endured two great personal losses, only one of which he discussed publicly. His father's death in 1927 at the age of 77 was to be expected, yet it shocked Taylor, who seemed to have regarded him as indestructible. James met his last illness, cancer of the bladder, calmly, while his eldest son was alarmed at the news. Writing in his diary, he pressed the word 'CANCER' in block letters, tracing it over and over, indelibly. In subsequent entries he jotted notes about his father's pain and his daunting stoicism. On 14 December 1927, James was dead, having refused pain medication in keeping with his lifelong distrust of medicine and commitment to hydropathy.

Taylor attended the Pan Pacific Science Congress in Japan in 1926. Here he appears (sitting at the front of the group, in the middle and wearing a hat) with delegates on a field excursion.

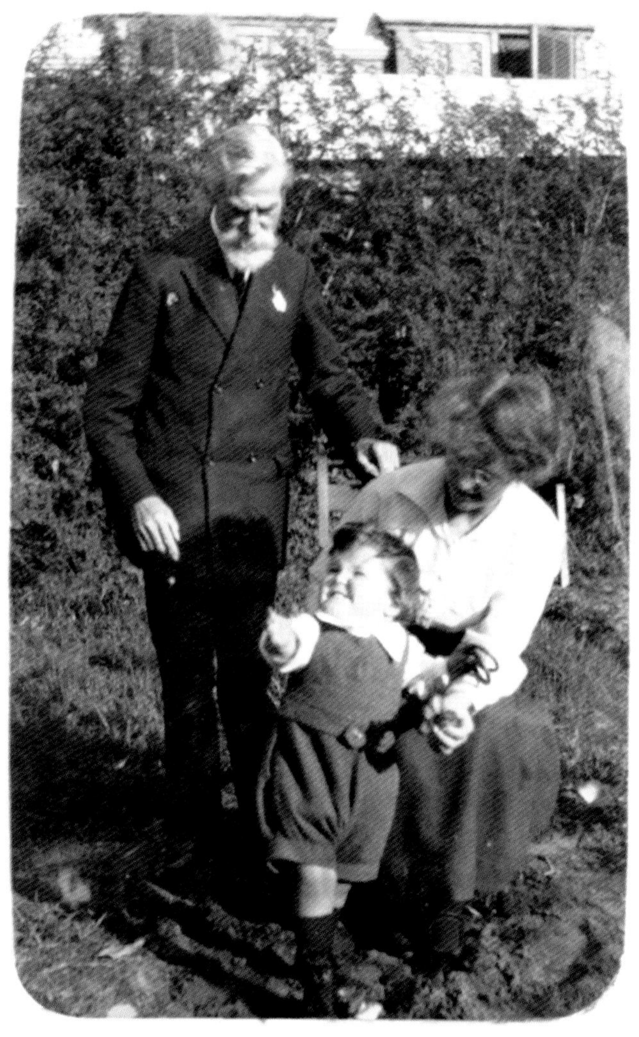

James Taylor with daughter-in-law Doris
and grandson Bill in Sydney, c.1917.

Pal, who seems to have been her father's favourite, felt the loss keenly, and her grief may have left her with little energy to fight the university administration. She adored their father and wrote a biography of him decades later, while Taylor was working on *Journeyman*. She painted James as a 'dear sweet man', even though he was 'never anything but an infrequent visitor in his own home', especially after he left his government mining assessment position and took up contracts. There is no resentment in her tone, nor any sense of abandonment. Mater felt differently from her children, since her husband's peripatetic nature had required her to run the large household with little assistance other than the house servant she insisted upon. James's eccentricities were legion. He lived on little besides porridge, eggs and butter, and his drink of choice was milk, which he consumed even if sour. Despite his remarkable class elevation, he dressed shabbily, oblivious to social convention and impervious to his wife's disapproval. More than just an avid walker, he thought nothing of tramping or cycling for hundreds of miles. Penny-pinching Griff was a spendthrift compared to his father, who rode a bicycle from Sydney to Melbourne in 1919 in order to avoid paying shipping and insurance costs for the transportation of a platinum crucible he sold to a Melbourne buyer. Five years later, at the age of 75, he, 'Doulah' (his nickname for Dorothy) and a girlfriend of hers cycled for days along the rough trails and roads in the Snowy Mountains. For Pal, at least, Pater's mineralogical expertise and his merriness made a welcome contrast to Mater's more practical nature.[8] Taylor had presented his parents' differences more diplomatically in a courtship letter to Doris: 'My dad is <u>the</u> scientist in the family and has no belief in money at all—while mater is practical and a better business man.'[9] Like Pal, Taylor not only tolerated James's oddities but admired them. The obituary he wrote in the university's *Hermes* magazine praised his father's old-age bicycle jaunts along with his scientific achievements.

The rewards of grandfatherhood came to James, who lived long enough to know all three of Taylor's children. But he and Mater had also suffered a parent's greatest loss: the death of a child. Jeffrey Owen Taylor does not appear in *Journeyman*. Only in the sketchiest of ways, in his diaries and letters, does Taylor reveal the fond relationship he developed with his youngest brother, the family's late arrival born in 1898. When Taylor left home for Cambridge on his 1851 Scholarship, Jeff was 10, old enough to read the letters Taylor sent him, full of academic counselling, study advice and silly poems and anecdotes about Cambridge goings on. Although Jeff had a weak constitution, he managed to complete his schooling and start work as a chemist in a sugar refinery; another man of science in the making by his teens. On his Easter holidays in April 1916, he travelled with Mater down to Melbourne to visit Doris and his brother, who had just received his Doctor of Science. In July, Jeff contracted pneumonia; two days after falling ill, he died of heart failure. Although everyone had a soft spot for the baby of the family, Mater was crushed at the loss of her 18-year-old son. Taylor, the agnostic, tried to comfort her: 'There is no doubt that if there is any higher state, Jeff has the best right of any young fellow [I've] known—so he will be rewarded'. He believed that education, not sorrows, provided the route to 'spiritual progress'. Thus he counselled his mother to seek answers in science, not faith: 'If one is worried and discontented one can't spare time on improving ones environment, and the latter is the true religion.'[10]

Some residue of Christian faith may have comforted Taylor, nevertheless, when his own child died in 1923. No-one looking at little Natalie could have doubted that the chubby toddler, with her broad high forehead and strong jaw, was his daughter. Her birth on 11 October 1921 tickled him: 'Baby very gigorous clucking Much hair. Good delivery quite natural.' Over the next two years he recorded every infantile accomplishment ('Natalie puts thumb in mouth. One week ago she chuckles') and childhood ailment ('Natalie worried about all teeth'). Then, shortly after Elsworth Huntington's month-long visit with the Taylors, details of symptoms, disturbingly familiar after Jeff's death, appeared in Taylor's diary:

> 27 September: 'Natalie sick.'
> 3 October: 'Natalie temp 102–3.'
> 4 October: 'Natalie temp 105 ... Doris bad night 1 hr sleep I dozed.'
> 10 October: 'Dr Mills at 6.12 Bronchopneumonia.'
> 24 October: 'Natalie bad night Pulse 160 (103).'
> 27 October: 'Natalie died 11.15 am.'

Were it not for the subject matter, the dry detail of these notes differs little in tone from his Antarctic meteorological logs. Yet Taylor was not an unfeeling father. There was no detail of his children's health or personalities that failed to interest him. The extraordinary stoicism that his own father exhibited on his deathbed was a part of his make-up as well. Lack of expression in these Britishers was not absence of emotion.

The Taylor's daughter, Natalie, aged two, in a studio photo taken shortly before her death in 1923.

Taylor pushed on and arranged for the burial, while he dosed Doris with sleeping draughts. Irrespective of his earlier opinions on mourning, Natalie's death drove him, like Mater before, to seek spiritual solace. Publicly, he participated in the rituals of goodbye; privately, he released his anguish in a poem:

> *'Natalie'*
> She is not lost
> She goeth on before
> And to her mother's love and care
> Must a perfect witness in that life shall bear
> And since the aim of this past life below
> Is but preparation for a nobler sphere
> Take comfort who remain, no dearer soul
> E'er entered heaven than our two year's babe.
> Cheerful and earnest happy yet helpful too
> If as some say
> No tithe of good can ever fade away
> So shall our baby's life have helped to pay
> That claim that God doth make on human aims
> Each but a link in the great chain every man to God
> There she shall grow to the most perfect form
> So shall she meet us
> But for a moment's harm
> She goeth on before.[11]

If this verse reveals Taylor's need for religious consolation at this moment of grief, his comfort faded, as did his faith. In family conversations in later years he declared it impossible to believe in a God who could take his child away.[12] In contrast, his faith in science never faltered. After a two-week trip with the family to the south coast of New South Wales, he was back to his 'Environment and Race' manuscript, back to his ethnological fieldwork, back to his 'USELESS' maps, his popular journalism and his public lecturing. And back to his geography department, with Pal at his side.

Once engaged in preparations for his departure to Chicago, Taylor realised that leaving Sydney and giving up his post as Australia's founding father of geography would be wrenching. Even without foreknowledge of the problems his 'successor' would cause, he had to abandon a pioneering academic project which was as much Edgeworth David's as his. The professor was disappointed at the news: 'National calamity to British Empire if lost Taylor.'[13] While other faculty members felt the loss less keenly (some had eagerly encouraged the gadfly to leave), his colleagues had the grace to hold a farewell luncheon. The occasion brought out reporters from the *Evening News* and the *Sun*, the same papers that had helped make him a public figure. The *News* remarked on the 'genuine regret' and 'genuine appreciation' Taylor's fellow academics expressed.

Sketch of Taylor as a block diagram, 1928. When Taylor left Sydney for a new post at the University of Chicago, his students expressed their affection by depicting their professor as a block diagram.

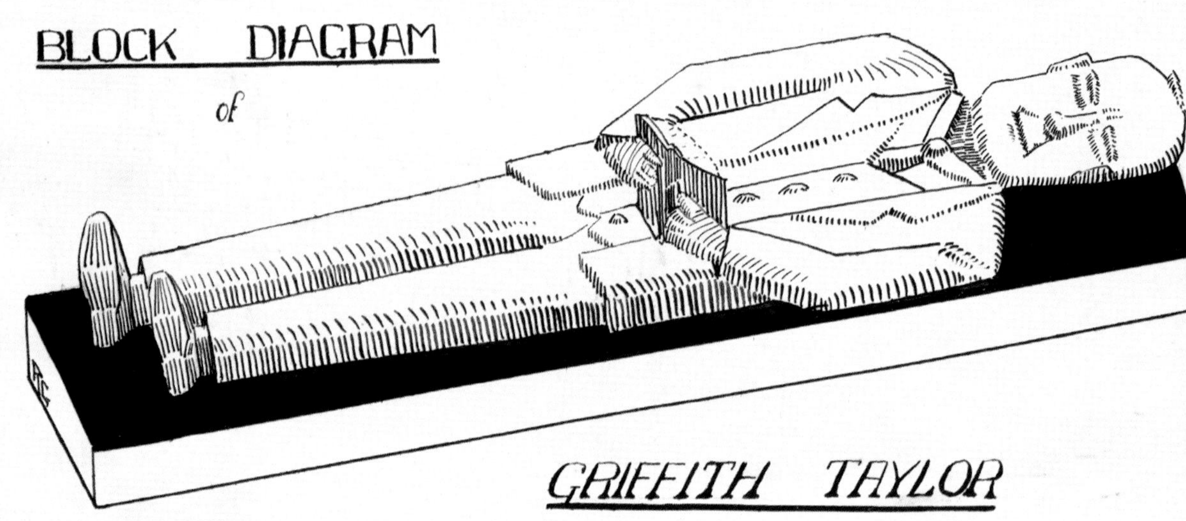

Vice-chancellor Wallace praised his 'down-rightness, honesty of purpose and devotion to his subject' and summarised these qualities as 'fine indiscretions'. Sir Mungo MacCallum, the deputy vice-chancellor, congratulated Taylor for his 'great fearlessness in pricking what he thought to be certain bubbles' on land settlement issues. One of his sternest opponents, law professor and chairman of the university's professorial board, Professor Peden, declared it impossible for him to judge the quality of Taylor's science; 'as a man', though, he regarded him highly. Taylor accepted the gift of a gold watch, and confessed that since making his decision to move to Chicago he found it 'harder and harder to go away'.[14] Leaving his students was even more poignant. Their gift was worthless in pounds but priceless in sentiment, something Taylor recognised by holding onto it: a bound book of images inspired by his lessons and drawn by one of his more artistically talented students. One picture interpreted Taylor as a block diagram (lying down and reading a book) while the final image, which turned an outline map of Australia into a girl tearfully waving good-bye, positioned Taylor off the east coast, standing in silhouette, waiting for an ocean liner to take him away.[15]

Although many Australians were happy for Taylor to leave the country, his students were sad to see him go. One of them, Ruth Godden, created this image for the final page in the student tribute book in 1928. It depicts Australia as a girl, waving goodbye to Taylor as a passenger ship steams toward him.

Chicago: Travels of a Family Man

On the face of things, moving to the United States marked a new phase in Taylor's career, but it also altered his relationship with his family. As a faithful and voluble correspondent, he remained close to his siblings and to Mater but his daily activities began to revolve more tightly around his boys, in whom he invested great expectations. Fifteen months after Bill lost his sister, a new brother came along in January 1925. When they decided to call him David, after Sir Edgeworth, it meant that both boys carried the names of senior men whom Taylor admired. From his infancy, and throughout his life, David proved to be in turn a delight and a worry for his parents, owing to his chronic eating and sleeping difficulties. As the family assembled at the wharf in Sydney on 26 October 1928, with three-year-old David held in Taylor's arms and 12-year-old Bill standing stiffly at his father's side, mixed feelings abounded as Pal took their picture. The Taylor family, now minus Pater, saw them off at the wharf, none of them knowing whether they would ever all be together again. They put on brave faces and hoped for the best. Once again Doris was following her husband and his career but she managed to squeeze in her own wish—a detour to visit her relatives in England and a chance to show off the new toddler while Taylor settled into his new job and new city.

No sooner did Doris and the children arrive in Chicago from England than Taylor prepared for a trip to South America, the only continent he had yet to visit. Over his time at the University of Chicago (1929–1935) he would spend long periods away, on field trips and attending conferences in the US and Europe. The early 1930s were major travelling years for Taylor, spent largely with other male scientists, including his son Bill. 'Why do men think that these "men only" trips are so much easier to arrange?' Doris asked her mother-in-law, possibly after a day of washing, ironing and folding his clothes.[16] Isaiah Bowman always criticised Taylor for jumping from one project to another but was happy enough to facilitate leaps that suited his own purposes, particularly his massively funded project on the environmental possibilities and limits of settlement around the globe. Staff members at the American Geographical Society made the arrangements that allowed Taylor to make his way to Panama, Venezuela and Colombia over November and December 1930. Officially he travelled on American Geographical Society business; however, his trip was rather aimless, comprising visits to this and that village, this and that topographical feature, not unlike his earlier 'wanderings' in the South Pacific. After returning, he admitted to Stefansson: 'I'm now trying to make a paper of my heterogenous and rather disconnected data.' In fact, it took Taylor only a few months before he obliged Bowman with a paper for his *Geographical Review*. His real motive, he admitted, had been to outscore his sometime friend, sometime rival geographically: 'As I boast to everyone I've now been in all seven continents.'[17]

Taylor had inherited his taste for travel from both parents and pointed this out frequently in his publications. The South American trip allowed him to visit the region where his father had worked as a mining consultant before marrying Lily. Taylor considered Mater an intrepid traveller also, even though marriage and motherhood had bound her to home. For her birthday in 1930, he sent her a novel about a pioneer woman: 'what you might have [been] if you'd gone to the backblocks of Queensland'.[18] Pal inherited the urge, too. After she found herself unemployed in 1931, she and Mater decided to travel to England. Since Taylor had already planned to attend the International Geographical Congress in Paris, followed by the British Association for the Advancement of Science meetings in London, he arranged to meet his sister in August. The two then set off on an ambitious trip designed to combine their professional and personal interests:

> we sailed together to Bergen, each of us carrying a rucksack weighing about twenty pounds. We had decided to 'fetch the compass' together about Central Europe, by way of Oslo, Trollhatten, Copenhagen, Berlin, Bucharest, Belgrade, Zagreb, Graz, Hallstadt, Interlaken, Perpignon, Barcelona, Madrid, Avila, San Sebastian, and Paris. A curious itinerary, involving the crossing of ten countries.[19]

Few travelling companions on a summer tour of Europe would have considered it appealing to spend hours examining relics of the Pleistocene ice cap or speculating on the formation of hanging valleys. Even fewer would have been happy to walk 50 kilometres a day, up and down gorges, and to rest only in the cheapest guesthouses available. After several weeks, Pal peeled off in Geneva to attend the Paris Geographical Congress but not before the pair steamed down the Danube to make a personal side trip to Maidanpek, Serbia, the village where they had lived as toddlers. Looking back with adult eyes, they still found it idyllic. A coda to their geography department excursions, the trip was their chance to relive their childhood, on a journey only brother and sister could take.

Doris, meanwhile, held the fort in their Chicago apartment. Aside from her occasional chaperoning contributions on the geography department's field trips, she stayed home while Taylor travelled, or she took the children with her on separate trips over their summer vacations. Even during summers, when the Taylors cottaged with other university families on the shores of Lake Michigan, Taylor spent most weeks in the city, where he lectured over the summer term to pad his salary. Staying close to other families made these short absences easier for Doris, but Taylor's longer periods away from home made her ill at ease. 'The flat felt very dead when Grif left,' she disclosed to Pal and Mater in a letter written while he was away on a two-month tour of the US south-west with two biologists.[20] These practices differed markedly from Taylor's courtship predictions of their united lives. In his agonising separation from his fiancée in South Africa he had written: 'Doris my darling—you'll go along with me, or I won't budge.'[21] Early in their marriage, however, she discovered that his wandering urge was stronger than his desire to rest at home with her; just as significantly, he discovered that he had married a resourceful spirited wife, who capably managed numerous charitable and social organisations in addition to their home.

When Taylor was away, Doris at least had one less person to feed and dress ('men at U are expected to have clean shirts every day, which is hard in a city as dirty as Chicago').[22] She also had more time to enjoy American hospitality, which suited her taste for socialising. And she was popular: barely a week went by without a dinner or party invitation. While Mater had married a man who was rarely at home, and consequently grew 'rather lonesome and miserable',[23] Doris found it easy to make 'millions of friends' in Chicago.[24] 'I'm beginning to think I get even more invitations when a "grass widow".'[25] As the Depression deepened, she devoted herself to university-based charitable work, in organisations such as the University of Chicago Settlement League, where she served as corresponding secretary. She was forever organising and participating in events with other faculty wives who shared her taste for a little learning (book reviews, French conversation classes, current events) and exercise (swimming, tennis), along with socials. Although the Taylors ended up living in a series of cramped flats after deciding it was too expensive and bothersome to heat a house, Doris, assisted by her maid, enjoyed hosting guests and visitors, no matter what the conditions: 'Doris had 22 women over ... we couldn't get the front room over 52°F! So they sat in comforters and coats playing bridge!'[26]

Neither Taylor nor his university colleagues were welcome at these ladies-only events but the University of Chicago social network offered numerous ways to bring couples close together. Aside from spending time in his own university clubs, which were largely male gatherings, Doris and Taylor joined other university types for indoor and outdoor tennis, dance lessons and bridge tournaments. 'You would be amused at some of the recreations of 500 sober Professors,' Taylor wrote to an old Sydney colleague, Professor Carslaw:

> We all live together in about six blocks to the northeast of the Campus … two or three nights ago my wife and I entered for the Bridge Tournament and came second … We also belong to a class in Danish Folk-Dancing which is run by the Dean of Social Science. It is not quite so active as Jiu-Jitsu but nearly as heating and much more fun. Then we have the Helio-toto-gabalus club where we read prose and poetry and travel to each other. The dean of the University Chapel entertained us with Maine Poets last time, only I had to give my 99th lecture on Antarctica to the British Club on that night and missed all but the supper.[27]

In February 1933, Doris and Taylor treated the 'Totoes', as they dubbed the group, to an 'Australian evening'. Doris started with a reading ('Devaney's book on the "Death Bone"') and Taylor followed up with 'rather a nice lot of Aborigines curios', which he described and passed around. 'Well, they liked it very much.'[28]

This Machine has 5 motions:
Travelling
Swivelling
Luffing
Hoisting
Biting
Memory Sketch of the
Great Mechanical Grab
in Jackson Park
Post Script – Remember the Sprocket Chain...

Fifteen-year-old Bill Taylor's letter to his father, 22 August 1931. Like Taylor, Bill was a talented draughtsman. Unlike his father, he pursued a career in engineering, rather than in geography.

The couple made compatible partners on the dance floor but their approach to raising their sons differed, and those differences deepened in the early 1930s. As serious-minded Bill excelled in his studies and became increasingly opinionated, the much cheerier David suffered frequent bouts of illness and began to experience emotional difficulties, which neither parent could quite fathom. Doris tried her best to care for David, while Taylor focused on grooming Bill into a young man worthy of succeeding him (and his father) in the realm of science. Taylor's expectations of his first-born son were just as high as Mater's and Pater's had been of him—even higher, considering Doris's learned relatives. With roots so impressive, he had no doubt that his family tree ought to flourish.

In childhood and into his teens, Bill showed signs of fulfilling his father's dynastic dreams. At the age of five he was drawing maps marked with desert and wheat-growing regions: 'so I guess heredity is working,' Taylor wrote proudly to a family friend.[29] In high school, Bill concentrated on maths and sciences, and he tinkered constantly with contraptions he constructed. When his father and Auntie Pal were on their way to the Norwegian icefields in 1931, 15-year-old Bill wrote to 'dear Daddy' with a request for a Meccano sprocket chain, to replace the one he'd worn out through 'hard usage'. Like his father, he thought it correct to illustrate his letter with scale drawings, in this case of his electric motor, commutator brush protector, and armature spindle.[30] Bill was equally talented academically. In Chicago, he attended the university's feeder school, which put him directly into competition with the children of Taylors' colleagues. 'Several professors tell me how their boys and girls at the High School speak with awe of Bill's erudition!' he bragged to Mater and Pal. Undaunted by the stiff competition, Bill entered the university on a scholarship and earned top marks in biology and chemistry.[31]

Doris understood better than her husband, however, that raising a son as intelligent and hard-working as his father was a recipe for friction as well as parental pride. She freely admitted that she found Bill 'hard to live up to' as he 'bubbl[ed] over with acquired knowledge'. Taylor never felt intimidated by his son's 'erudition' (or anyone else's) but Bill managed, miraculously, to force his father to admit there were things he didn't know:

> Grif is experiencing new sides of life all together! He's had to take a back seat so often that I notice he no longer flatly contradicts Bill's statements but asks for their origin and bows to his superior knowledge quite often!!!

Bill's radical sympathies and his brazenly modern attitudes were another matter altogether. Taylor could not abide listening to Bill declare that communism was the solution to the world's problems and that psychology could unlock the mysteries of the human mind. Their disagreements turned into arguments, as neither father nor son was inclined to give ground. 'Bill says my capitalistic ideas are due to senile dementia,' Taylor wrote half-amused, half-exasperated.[32] By the mid 1930s, they agreed to disagree, mainly because Taylor much preferred to lecture than to be lectured to: 'It gives me the heeby jeebies to hear him, so we're off Politics ... other folk laugh at his youthful certainty, so perhaps he'll get a sense of humour and lecture less in the future.'[33] Doris found Bill's strong opinions and humorlessness equally challenging; however, she approached her son differently: 'I enjoy [Bill] in my own way and can generally see his point before Grif and so often take the role of peacemaker, but it is wearing and I'll enjoy a holiday with David.' Doris was no psychologist but she had insight: Taylor and Bill clashed because they were overworked and overconfident. '[T]oo much brain stimulation is as unwise as too much anything else in my humble opinion!' she told Dorothy, adding that she was grateful that 'David shows signs of a happy balance and adjustment to the world he lives in'.[34]

The only trouble with David was that life threw him off balance so easily and without warning. In addition to his constant digestion problems, his insomnia and his proneness to colds and flu, he suffered from nervousness and anxiety. In 1934, after looking at newspaper photos of the Spanish Civil War, the nine-year-old 'got a shock—like a motor accident!'. For a week David couldn't manage to eat. In a letter Taylor wrote to Mater, he tried to put the best gloss on the incident: 'He's very sensitive.' Years later, after David's 'nerve storms' grew in intensity and duration, and after numerous consultations with

Taylor and his sons, Bill and David, in March 1935, shortly before moving to Toronto. Doris took this picture on the balcony of their flat located near the campus of the University of Chicago.

doctors and psychiatrists, he would write 'the start of David's troubles' in the margins of the letter (which Mater had saved).[35] If Bill and Taylor were too much alike, there was a chasm of difference between David and Taylor, the son easily overwhelmed and sapped of spirit and the father intensely productive and boundlessly energetic.

Taylor always assumed that his scientific traits and ambitions would be transferred by blood and by example to his children. Reluctantly, he grew to realise that neither biological inheritance nor his express expectations would ensure that his sons would embody his wishes. At Chicago, Bill's professors advised him to complete a graduate degree in plant ecology at Cambridge, and Taylor approved even though it cost him dearly in tuition fees. After completing his Soviet Union tour, Bill arrived in England in 1935 (with Uncle Raymond and Frank Debenham there to keep a close eye on him). Before long, though, he realised that his heart wasn't in botany. Confiding first in his Uncle Bert Priestley at Leeds, he eventually admitted to his parents that engineering was his passion. 'Bill has wanted to be an engineer for sometime,' Doris informed Pal, 'but hates to disappoint his Father.'[36] Indeed, Taylor considered the move foolish: 'Bill has decided to leave Cambridge to do Civil Engineering at Toronto. I was sorry he didn't like England ... [and] he may be sorry in the future. It means 5 more years at University.'[37]

Before long, however, Taylor shifted back to boasting about Bill's grades ('16 A's out of 21!'), especially in mathematics. Since this was one of Taylor's weakest subjects, he wrote to Pal, he figured that Bill must have inherited his talent from their father, James: '[E]vidently Grandpa's gold medals ... are doing good work on him.'[38] On schedule and at the top of his class, Bill graduated in June 1942 with a second bachelor's degree in engineering and a wartime job supervising tool production in an aeroplane factory on Toronto's outskirts.

Over the same period, David's illness had worsened, despite the various strategies and treatments his parents tried. After the Taylors moved to Toronto they referred David to physicians for his insomnia and digestion problems but none of them proved able to treat or prevent their son's mental breakdowns. In letters Taylor and Doris wrote to family members, they shared their worries, giving a clear impression of buffeting constantly between hope and despair. In the early 1940s, Taylor commiserated with his brother Evan, who was helping Pal deal with Mater's mental decline and her proneness to delusions: 'It must be very wearing not to know how to cope with her imagination. We have had a taste of it when D. gets a bad turn.' Happily, David was still young, so his parents managed a measure of optimism: '[I]t is possible that his neurotic tendencies will be much less as he gets older.'[39] Evidence to the contrary piled up over the 1940s, however. In December 1941, as Taylor was about to catch the train from Toronto to New York to attend the annual meeting of the Association of American Geographers, David experienced 'quite a turn of delusions again', after a three-year period of stability. To go or to stay? He and Doris made the decision in a trice, and Taylor proceeded to New York to deliver his presidential address at the Barbizon-Plaza Hotel. 'So that took some of the gilt off the gingerbread.' Taylor raced back the moment he finished his address:

> I dashed up to get my slides ... handed my address to Huntington and asked him to give it to the Editor ... dashed out to get my bag ... dashed into a taxi ... dashed through New York ... dashed to get a Pullman, and finally landed in the train about 5 minutes before it was due to leave for Toronto. I reached here at 1:30 [a.m.]; and find that David is a little better.[40]

When David had spells like this they called in a nurse but Doris always supervised his care. 'I still have the bad habit of waiting on all my family,' she confessed to Dorothy and Mater, who knew something about the sacrifices of domestic life. 'I know it's bad for David and Bill but it seems to be a confirmed habit—I enjoy waiting on them.'[41] Had tender home care been the solution, David could have been cured. By the mid 1940s, however, they resorted to professional care and hospital treatment, and psychiatrists eventually convinced them that his illness was something to be medically managed, not wished or nursed away. Breakdowns in 1948 and 1953 led to extended hospital stays, and ultimately a diagnosis of manic-depressive illness.

Toronto: The Geography Family

In many ways, creating a geography family was infinitely less complicated and almost as rewarding. Taylor was 54 when he stepped into his new job in Toronto in 1935, his status as the 'father' of a discipline and a department restored. His earlier wish that his sons might follow in his footsteps remained unfulfilled but the excitement he felt as he set off to train a new generation of geographers was intense. And although he established the new department with strangers, rather than his sister as in Sydney, it took only a short while before a geography 'family' formed under Taylor's headship. Although he was a one-man show for the first two years (junior lecturer Donald Putnam was hired in 1938, followed by George Tatham in 1939), he headed a team that included demonstrators, laboratory assistants, graduate students and a secretary, Mildred Brookstone, all of whom met daily at 4 pm for tea and biscuits. Two of his first demonstrators, Australian Ann Nichols and Manitoban Andrew Clark, worked closely with Taylor and socialised with the family. His approach to the talented pair resembled the care and interest that Professor and Lady David had earlier bestowed on him. Nichols and Clark, along with a growing coterie of senior students, became frequent guests at the Taylors', where 'the Chief' talked geography and Doris fed them dinners, threw them parties and inquired into their personal lives—their engagements, their wedding plans, their children. These ties endured for decades, long after his students graduated and moved away. Nichols corresponded regularly with Doris and Taylor years after she went to Berkeley, married (becoming Ann Marshall), had children, and was appointed Australia's first female geography lecturer since Dorothy Taylor, at the University of Adelaide. Fittingly, in 1989 she became the first recipient of the Institute of Australian Geographers' Griffith Taylor Medal 'for distinguished contributions to geography in Australia'.

Taylor's ties to Andrew Clark were even stronger while he was a Toronto student, although they would be tested by an incident that Taylor interpreted as insubordination. In 1935, Clark enrolled for his Master's degree and became Taylor's first assistant at Toronto. When they met, the professor treated his student like a latter-day Harry Brearley, calling him his 'lab boy', despite the fact that he held a Bachelor of Science degree and had worked in the insurance industry for four years. After Clark completed his degree in 1938, Taylor appointed him his assistant for the summer trip he planned to England (where he was to deliver the presidential address to the geography section of the British Association for the Advancement of Science) and to central Europe, the Mediterranean and Algeria. Their subsequent traversing produced a clutch of academic articles—'Sea to Sahara: Settlement Zones in Eastern Algeria' (1939), 'Cultural Aspects of Romania, Yugoslavia and Hungary' (1940), 'Trento to the Reschen Pass: A Cultural Traverse of the Adige Corridor' (1940), 'Mediterranean Pilgrimage: A Study of Ancient Sites' (1940), 'Cultural Geography along the Rome–Berlin Axis' (1940)—all of which bore Taylor's name as 'the' author. Clark understood his place: benefiting from the professor's paternal support depended on his observing hierarchical relations. He went on to complete his PhD with Carl Sauer at Berkeley—a decisive move away from Taylor's determinism towards 'possibilism' and a different vein of cultural geography altogether. Thereafter he became founding chair of geography at Rutgers University and later moved to a professorship at the University of Wisconsin.

Taylor's own career had been greatly aided by his talent for ingratiation, which he displayed by seeking the approval of senior scholars whom he praised both privately and publicly. By the mid twentieth century, however, this tradition of masculine patron–client bonding clashed with an increasingly meritocratic academic culture. In 1951, a difficult exchange between Taylor and Clark, sparked by the former pupil's mixed review of his master's work, exposed the mismatch of cultures and soured their relationship. Stephen Visher of Indiana University, Taylor's old geography mate, tipped him off. Visher had admired Taylor's work since he first encountered it in the 1920s and he was also familiar with the cardinal rule of patronage: insult not thy master. When *The Geographical Review* published Clark's review of Taylor's *Canada: A Study of Cool Continental Environments and Their Effects on British and French Settlement* (1947), the older men agreed that Taylor's junior had violated the unwritten law. Clark did praise his professor ('Through his energy and promotional ability he has developed at Toronto in 15 years one of the largest departments of geography on the North American continent') but mixed his admiration with criticism ('Yet Taylor's unceasing spate of writings and pronouncements has perhaps only served to drive other Canadian geographers farther into their encyclopedic foxholes'). More galling was Clark's admiration for McGill professor George Kimble, to whom he gave credit for 'breaking new intellectual ground and winning wider scholarly and scientific respect for geography in Canada'.[42]

Unless it came from a respected senior colleague, Taylor rarely took criticism well: he ignored it, dismissed it or lashed out to discredit critics. When Macdonald Holmes wrote an unfavourable review of his 1941 book *Australia: A Study of Warm Environments and Their Effect on British Settlement*, Taylor wrote to the editor of the *Australian Journal of Science*, accusing the journal of having solicited a biased reviewer.[43] Clark's review upset him far more. It was disloyal. And it hurt. 'I am prepared for geographers to disagree with me,' Taylor wrote crisply, 'but I feel that the trouble I took to help you on your entrance into geography merited a better return than you have shown so far.' Taylor's accusation came with a gratuitous reminder that he outpublished Clark:

> I have written 20 books, and collaborated [on] 30 more as well as publishing about 130 other papers. Does your output entitle you to criticise the work of far older and more experienced writers?[44]

To his credit, Clark stood his ground. He defended his right to dismiss Taylor's 'esoteric terminology and [his] deterministic approach'. More significantly he defended his obligation, as a fellow scientist, to criticise: 'I am astonished that you, who have so often stressed the importance of unfettered objective criticism, should imply that personal feelings should ever enter into scholarly or scientific judgements.'[45]

But, of course, they did. And in the end it was Clark who backed down. In 1959, he published a fawning review of *Journeyman Taylor* in which he described the author as 'one of the most honored, most widely known, most controversial ... and most beloved geographers of the century'. Taylor saved this second review and tucked it into his personal copy of the book. The family ties had been restored—on his terms.

Taylor's students were not the only ones from whom he expected unstinting loyalty. The department at Toronto would never have expanded so rapidly had Taylor been unable to rely on able assistants and colleagues. As he racked up professional titles during his Toronto tenure (including the presidency of the British and American geography associations and an appointment to the Royal Society of Canada), his junior colleagues ran day-to-day operations. Colleagues never questioned Taylor's command of teaching nor his gifts as a lecturer but people close to him were painfully aware of the professor's administrative shortcomings. He freely admitted that he had neither the brain nor the stomach for administration: 'If there were one thing I, as a teacher, disliked more than another, it was attendance at Faculty Committees.'[46] He was a team leader who lobbied hard for his department and his students but he wasn't a team player, according to former colleague Donald Kerr, who worked under Taylor in the late 1940s. The department operated without staff meetings and Taylor preferred to make the big decisions himself and to leave the details to others. 'Grif depended very much on [staff members] Putnam and Tatham, so that he could get back to his typewriter.'[47]

While Taylor carped constantly to the university president about his department's staff shortages, his own frequent absences put considerable strain on his colleagues. He was on friendly terms with Canon Cody, thanks largely to Doris's charity network (Cody's wife, Barbara, and Doris were both office holders in the university Settlement administration, the Visiting Homemakers, and the Faculty Wives Association). Taylor also knew how to work every funding angle to facilitate his research trips. After he returned from the New York meeting of the Association of American Geographers in 1941, he dropped a line to Cody: 'I seem to remember that you spoke of a fund for paying some travelling expenses.' Six months later, he travelled on university funds to British Columbia, where he conducted further topographical studies. In 1944, shortly after he returned from Cornell, where he spent a month delivering the Messenger Lectures, he travelled on Harold Innis's Arctic research budget to conduct a two-month survey of the

Postcard of McMaster University. Constructed originally as a Baptist college, the McMaster building was converted into the University of Toronto's new geography department's lecture rooms, laboratories and offices in 1935. 'In fact, most of my lectures on Cultural Geography [later to be re-orientated toward geopacifics] were delivered in what had been the Baptist Chapel,' (Taylor, *Journeyman Taylor*, 1958).

Mackenzie and Yukon river deltas. The following year, he was away over August and September, surveying the Maritimes and Newfoundland, funded again by the Canadian Social Research Council. Then there was the government-funded five-month Australian university geography tour, to which he attached side-trips to Hawaii and Fiji, as well as field trips to Tasmania, Western Australia and Queensland. After that, there was another European trip in the spring of 1950 when he presented a paper on geopacifics at the Inter-University Geographical Conference in Birmingham, followed by field excursions in England and Scotland. The 'poor little geographers' he left behind to run the shop had good reason to lament.

On one occasion at least, a faculty member revealed his irritation with Taylor—the department's absent father. As a geographical possibilist, George Tatham differed with Taylor philosophically but he may have harboured differences of a more personal variety. A former honours student wrote to Taylor and claimed that Tatham had disparaged the department head:

> [He said you were] not too bright, while Dr. Tatham was the brains of the department, organizing the graduate school and doing the administrative work of the department while you were writing your many books ... which meant you collected the publicity and he did all the work.[48]

Whether or not Tatham actually uttered these words, his essay on geographical possibilism in Taylor's *Geography in the Twentieth Century* was respectful and his correspondence with Taylor after he retired was invariably cordial. Nevertheless, his alleged remarks have a ring of truth. As one who could not abide working for someone he considered his equal or inferior, Taylor never worried that bright ambitious men working under him might feel the same way, particularly after he had well and truly had his innings as departmental chair.

In some respects Tatham was right: Taylor was past his scholarly prime by the 1940s. Harold Innis had reached the same conclusion shortly after Taylor arrived in Toronto. As a once enthusiastic suitor, he cooled considerably towards Taylor, observing his slap-dash traversing and his mad rush to publish. Isaiah Bowman, who had recommended that the University of Toronto hire Taylor, had given Innis fair warning about Taylor's 'outer fringe of lunacy'.[49] Although Innis was prepared to exploit Taylor's undisputed surveying and mapping skills, which he required for his Canadian Arctic project, and in spite of their families' closeness, he never treated Taylor as his intellectual equal. Remarkably, Taylor was prepared to accept his place: 14 years Innis's senior, he publicly acknowledged him as an intellectual inspiration.

Taylor never required external stimulation to bring energy to his work. Scholars in a variety of disciplines, particularly history and anthropology, had always questioned Taylor's theories but no-one criticised his commitment. As an ageing professor he maintained his full roster of lectures in his final year at the University of Toronto while keeping up his staggering publishing pace. Soon after *Our Evolving Civilization* appeared in 1946, and quick on the heels of Professor Mills's 1947 invitation to visit Australia, Taylor began to compile a major compendium, which he hoped would supersede Richard Hartshorne's authoritative *The Nature of Geography* (1939). Taylor's new collection, *Geography in the Twentieth Century*, would focus on modern geography. He solicited essays from 23 scholars (in addition to his own contributions which comprised the introduction, four chapters and a glossary of geographical terms). The names of his oldest friends (Huntington, Bowman, Visher, Stamp, Fawcett, Wooldridge) appeared in the table of contents, and he also invited essays from two of his Toronto colleagues, Tatham and Putnam. Intellectually, the essays covered the development and topical range of geography; on a personal level, they represented the bookends of Taylor's career as a geographer, from his first publications in the *Geographical Review* to the essays written by his students, whom he had trained to become well-respected geographers themselves. If Bowman represented one of the men who had shaped his career, two of his outstanding students, John K. Rose and Wreford Watson, showed how Taylor's teaching career had shaped the discipline.

Geography in the Twentieth Century, published by Methuen in 1950, Taylor's final year in Toronto, reached its third edition by 1957 and was reprinted four times in the 1960s, despite receiving only lukewarm and negative reviews. 'Its effect on the attentive reader is at once exhilarating and disheartening,' an anonymous reviewer, W.G.E., commented, 'for while the book lacks intellectual and artistic unity, leaves so much unsaid and yet says so much, it is a symposium from which the reader can select at will chapters which enlighten, stimulate, irritate, or offend.'[50] W.G.E. might have been thinking of Taylor's entire opus, his career, or indeed his personality. But criticism of this sort rattled Taylor less as he approached retirement; strong sales figures, numerous reprints, a British publisher and the pleasure of seeing his name appear atop the title, 'Geography in the Twentieth Century', meant far more to him.

In December 1950, Taylor celebrated his seventieth birthday, which occasioned the usual departmental party. This time, it also marked the end of his career at the University of Toronto. Rather than leave part way through the year, he stayed on to complete his teaching in the spring term (nature artist Robert Bateman fondly recalls attending his lantern-slide lectures in his final year). There was much to arrange as Taylor prepared his move—selling and donating books, selling the house (which had doubled in value), sorting out his pension and taxes. Aside from these tasks, the more pleasurable aspects of winding up awaited him. Official recognition of his contribution to the university and to his discipline accompanied his appointment as emeritus professor of geography in 1951. He knew from experience that his farewell, held at the Faculty Club, would occasion a roasting from his colleagues. Tatham's likening of Taylor to a cyclone amused him, but Innis's comments struck a little close to the bone, as he wrote to Bill:

> Innis talked for half an hour, ragging all the time—about my grabbing rooms, and writing too many books, and how Cody chose me because I'd managed to get so much in 'Who's Who' and how I hated evil reviews, and how geography was only capitals of Counties, but I included everything.[51]

Sipping his grape juice while the other men smoked and drank, he might well have felt like he was back in his Antarctic winter quarters, listening to his mates' jibes and japes. In good spirit, he took it all in his stride. More sentimental was the smaller departmental party, hosted by the people he called 'the geography family'. The highlight was the unveiling of a studio photograph which the department had commissioned, 'a sort of [Karsch] portrait, chosen from 30 poses of my humble self. I think it is very like my scowling self—but the ladies say that at a close-up you can see a glean of humour.'[52] Addressing his Toronto staff, lab assistants and graduate students for the last time, he paid special heed to Innis and Cody, whom he called the department's 'fosterfather[s]'.[53] No need to name its father.

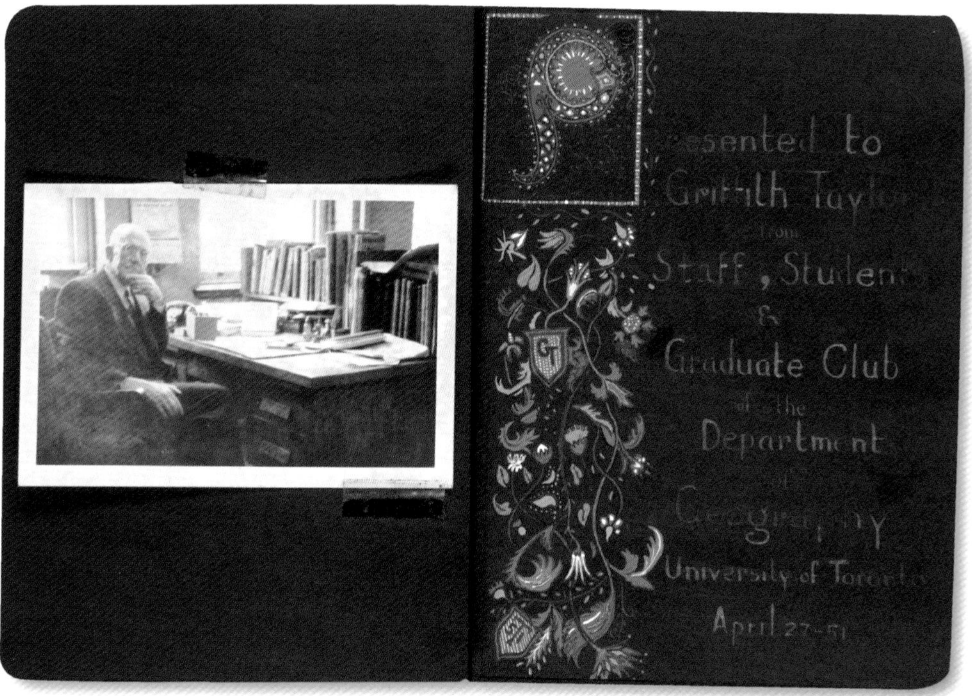

When Taylor retired from the University of Toronto in 1951 his geography students presented him with an album of memories. The photo shows 'the Prof' in his office.

Many of Taylor's students shared his drawing talent and sense of humour. William Wonders sent this image (confirming that he had reached 82° 38′ 20″ north latitude) to Taylor in 1952 as a 'salute to "The Chief"'.

Retiring to Sydneyside Scenery

In the mid twentieth century, long before the marketing of 'lifestyle' retirement, most men regarded the close of their paid working life as an ending. Taylor's retirement was no different: it marked the end of his career as a professor and the end of his association with the University of Toronto and with Canada. The closing of these doors opened new ones back in Australia, however. His 1948 trip had come at the right time, reassuring him that the nation was prepared, at last, to accept his ideas and to recognise his authority. Privately he had other reasons to feel optimistic. He and Doris had dreamed of returning to England to retire and live in a house with a garden on London's outskirts, but the extended Taylor family pulled them towards Sydney instead, not just the older generation, but their recently married son. The Taylors traded their three-storey house with its established garden in central Toronto for a six-room brick bungalow (which they named 'Talinga') in Seaforth, a picturesque, undeveloped suburb perched on a bluff above Middle Harbour.

Taylor and Doris at home, Seaforth, Sydney, December 1952. The Australian edition of *People Magazine* published a large, four-page spread on Taylor in which this candid shot of the couple appeared.

Bill had moved to Sydney shortly after the war ended and took a position in engineering at the University of Technology. Although he bore the full burden of Taylor's paternal expectations after his brother David's illness became undeniable, he resisted them as he worked towards independent adulthood. Like his father, he was a late bloomer in romantic relations. Throughout his twenties and thirties, his parents and assorted relatives had needled him to stop working like a fiend and to make an effort to mix with people. 'Why not Chess or bridge, or some such frivolity?' Taylor had urged Bill in 1941 when he was working 10 hours a day in a factory.[54] In 1942, Bill's escort of one of Taylor's departmental assistants to the movies was significant enough to merit a diary entry. His social skills evidently improved when he returned from Canada to Australia, where he met Dorothy Clarke, the woman he wished to marry. Announcing his engagement in 1947, Bill anticipated congratulations; instead, he got a blast of fatherly anger and disappointment. In the most insulting and elitist terms, Taylor accused Bill of compromising the Taylor–Priestley pedigree:

> on both sides of the family our people belong in the professional classes. Your only disability has been very heavy work in the war plants—from which you have reaped a great deal of nervous strain—as is but natural ... I don't understand eugenics in our family. One of my sons is physically much below par. He can't prevent that ... But I cannot understand why a man with your advantages should make so little attempt to join the most worthwhile social circles ... I must admit that my forethought for the best type of marriage has not resulted in the normal amount of happiness for my two boys.[55]

Taylor failed to consider that Bill's fiancée might have made his son happy. All he saw was that the woman soon to be Mrs Bill Taylor was divorced with a young son, worlds apart from Doris Priestley, honorary Antarcticker and descendant of Sir Joseph. Nor did she remotely resemble the Misses Haddon and Sollas, learned daughters of learned men. Neither Taylor nor Doris bestowed their full blessing until their son's marriage produced a grandchild they considered their own.

After his marriage Bill's communication with his father remained business-like and respectful, although the rift cooled their relationship. Bill moved his wife and child to Melbourne in 1955, after disputes over his pay and workload at the University of Technology prompted him to resign from his position and opt for a similar post at the Royal Melbourne Institute of Technology. Along the way, he had encountered financial problems, which prompted Taylor to step in, not with financial aid but with professional advice. He offered to write to Clunies-Ross, the director of the Commonwealth Science and Industry Research Office, and to mention Bill's 'wonderful list of A's'. Or better yet, why didn't Bill write a book on production engineering and turn himself into an authority? Any professional man in his mid forties might have read such fatherly involvement as interference—after all, Taylor had felt the same way when James advised him to accept the Commonwealth Bureau position in 1910. But Bill had a far more valid reason to resist his father's help.[56]

David, in contrast, could not survive without it. There was no question that he would continue to live with his ageing parents on their return to Sydney, since his illness made it impossible for him to support himself. He continued to suffer debilitating periods of depression and was hospitalised and taken to rest homes regularly. When David was well enough, Taylor found him jobs close to home in Seaforth, and his uncle Evan employed him from time to time as a machinist in his engineering works. Taylor overembellished things now and then, telling his associates that both of his sons were 'engineers',[57] yet he knew deep down that there would be no independent life, no career, no marriage, no children for his second son.

While he and Doris cared for David, Taylor encountered health concerns of his own. He had experienced minor illnesses his whole life, including eczema, lumbago, nephritis and severe hay fever, but he described these as bothersome, rather than debilitating. None of these afflictions was life threatening until July 1950. Shortly after returning to Toronto from a conference trip in Binghampton, New York, Taylor was diagnosed with cancer. A lifetime of abjuring alcohol and tobacco had failed to protect him, like his father, from the identical condition: a tumour in the bladder. Taylor's first operation in 1929, two years after his father's death, had rattled him: 'Hope if things go wrong they give Doris a pension,' he wrote in his diary.[58] In the second operation, the prospect of Doris becoming a widow was much greater. The procedure put him on his back for 12 weeks, the longest period of physical inactivity in his life. Although the procedure was successful, he admitted to close friends that he could never be sure he was 'out of the woods'. Rather than dwelling on the possibility though, he managed to resume his publishing commitments and teaching duties by the time his seventieth birthday rolled around. Unlike many of his less fortunate colleagues, such as Innis, who died of cancer in 1952, Taylor would live for more than his allotted three score and 10 years.

Taylor's brush with mortality and his retirement gave him a legitimate excuse to slow down or simply to enjoy himself, though enjoyment meant work and activity in Taylor's mind. Eight months after his operation, he resumed his routine of walking every day between Forest Hill and the university campus, a distance of three miles. In spite of his starchy, meat-filled diet (more like Stefansson's famous meat-only diet than his father's vegetarian staple of porridge), he remained a trim 165 pounds (75 kilograms) and he quickly regained his extraordinary stamina, which he then put to use at his new home in Sydney. The yard at 28 Allan Avenue, which measured almost 75 square metres, was 'four feet deep in weeds' when they arrived in October 1951. Taylor tore a leg muscle dragging out the old growth but stuck to his task and planted beds of flowers and vegetables: 'So I think I'll turn Possibilist!'[59] His gardening ordeals and occasional conquests featured in the letters he wrote to his former Toronto associates. As he joked to

Innis when he first heard his old colleague was ill, 'I have deteriorated from a loquacious Professor of Geography to a very indifferent imitator of a Chinese gardener.'[60]

The academic side of Taylor's life lulled in the first two years of his retirement in Sydney, while he tried to fill its place with domestic activities. As the corresponding secretary for the Seaforth Progress Association, he lobbied local councils for improvements to footpaths and bus routes. He and Doris enjoyed weekly bridge games with Pal at Cartref, the old family home. He consumed hundreds of Penguin mysteries, English detective stories and science fiction novels, and when he wasn't reading he gardened and went to the cinema. Still, he confessed early in 1953, 'Doris has too much to do and I have too little.' The loquacious professor couldn't keep his mouth shut or his typewriter quiet for long, however. Soon he began a series of new projects. The location of their new home inspired *Sydneyside Scenery* (1958), a popular book he prepared with his family's assistance. Indeed much of the initial work for that book had been a joint brother–sister effort back in the 1920s. But the most famous of the Taylors acknowledged neither his sister's geographical input nor, for that matter, his brother Evan's photographs. The person he did make sure to acknowledge was Sir Edgeworth David, to whose 'grateful memory' he dedicated it, on the centenary of David's birth: yet another contribution to his professor's legacy. *Sydneyside Scenery* was part popular geography, part guidebook, part memoir of his life in and around Sydney as a child and young man. Taylor bounced between childhood reminiscences ('when I was a youngster'), his recycled block diagrams and quotes from Darwin. In his description of the historical geography of the seaside suburb of Manly, he recalled the Taylor family's land and the holiday shack he had built in 1907 with his brothers, just a stone's throw from his Seaforth home.[61] The geographical and the personal were barely distinguishable by now.

Reflecting on his earlier life, Taylor cherished fond memories of family. In contrast, when he recalled his earlier professional career as the founder of the University of Sydney's geography department, his bitterness lingered and intensified. Taylor's ill feeling towards Holmes, his successor, was so profound that he was loath to set foot in the department. The 'kilted one' held on to the geography chair for 33 years and retired, finally, in 1961. Before that red-letter day, Taylor boycotted the department. Whether it was a case of Holmes intentionally denying his predecessor his due or, far more likely, the latter's festering resentment over the events subsequent to his departure, the men engaged in a mini cold war over the 1950s. Holmes tried several times to bury the hatchet but Taylor stood pat, in spite of Doris's and even Dorothy's counsel to move on. After all, the whole incident had been much more about her, than him. 'We are all getting too old for hard feelings,' Dorothy wrote to him. 'I have no wish to see him humiliated and you have other things to think about.'[62] Not until Holmes retired and his replacement, George Dury, took the geography chair did the ice melt. 'It is nothing to my credit,'[63] Taylor admitted to Bill.

Taylor did begin to teach geography again at the University of Sydney, through courses commissioned by the Workers Education Association, not the geography department. His general-interest students were affable, he thought (and liked him so well that they urged him to teach a follow-up course on contract bridge); however, he felt wasted 'scientifically', his ideas so many 'pearls before tyroes'.[64] Without an academic posting, Taylor forged connections by joining professional organisations. Members of the Geographical Society, which he had established with Pal's assistance in 1927, greeted him warmly, and in 1952 they made him an office-holder (vice-president) again. And through the Australian and New Zealand Association for the Advancement of Science (ANZAAS), which met in Sydney shortly after his return in 1951, he became acquainted with a new crop of geographers. 'They are good enough to say that this is in some measure due to my propaganda journey through Australia in 1948,' he reported to one of his Canadian textbook co-authors, 'for nearly all these young geographers have been appointed since.'[65] On Taylor's seventy-second birthday, a representative of ANZAAS wrote to request that he accept the presidency of the geography section. A polite 'yes' was his answer ('Big change since 1923!' was the comment he penned on the letter).[66] Through these professional networks, as well as Bill's academic position, Taylor began to explore the prospect of teaching proper university courses again. This boosted his post-retirement, as well as paternal, pride: 'I have been approached to give a course of lectures on Australian Resources at the new University of Technology,' he informed his Toronto colleagues, who had sent him a telegram on his birthday and a Christmas card. 'Bill—whom many of you know—is now in charge of Production Engineering there.' Although he recycled his old lectures and the maps he had used for decades, returning to the classroom gave him a new sense of mission: 'If Churchill can run an Empire at 78 why can't I still teach young folk something sensible about Australia's resources—and debunk some of the rubbish still poured out by journalists and politicians.'[67]

Taylor in his study, Seaforth, Sydney, c.1958. Taylor learned to type in his first paid job in the New South Wales Treasury Department. He typed all of his own correspondence and manuscripts.

After his first course in climatology proved successful, he offered a course on his very first lecture topic: 'The economic geography of Australia'. Now, almost 40 years later, he listed a few more credentials on his syllabus: 'First Professor of Geography in Australia (1920–1928), President of British Geographers 1938, and of American Geographers 1941, Emeritus Professor of the University of Toronto 1951, Fellow of the Australian Academy 1954, etc.'[68] He also responded to publishers' requests for updates to old editions of his lucrative textbooks, and supplied material for new editions of *Geography in the Twentieth Century*. With his academic activities picking up speed and his royalties healthier than ever, by the mid 1950s he began to feel his old self again.

Taylor's appointment to the Australian Academy of Science, like his elevation to the Royal Society of Canada in 1942, was not nearly as prestigious a marker as a knighthood or a nomination to the Royal Society in England would have been but, as usual, he was eager to add to his sack of status markers. Writing to Hale, *Journeyman*'s prospective publisher in London, Taylor mentioned that young Queen Elizabeth's first visit to Australia had included a trip to Canberra, where she bestowed a charter on the newly established Australian Academy of Science. 'This is the first Royal Charter of this kind, since the London Royal Society was founded by Charles II.'[69] Hale's history lesson was meant to confirm Taylor's rising status among scientists and to convince him, accordingly, that he would be wise to publish *Journeyman*. But Taylor had reason to boast. Although he had had to ask his more heralded friend, *Sir* Douglas Mawson *FRS*, to nominate him, the newly formed Academy of Science named only 30 new members, and he was the sole geographer among them. At every opportunity he pointed this out—atop syllabi, in personal letters, at any occasion where he could crow.

Over the 1950s, the accolades stacked up—honorary presidencies, awards and prizes in his name at several universities—and these alone might have induced the University of Sydney to celebrate Taylor's academic career with an honorary doctorate. But the upturn of political and popular interest in Antarctica in the late 1950s also worked in his favour. Mawson's death in 1958, and his Commonwealth state funeral, drew national attention to the imminent end of an era. Soon all of the men who had 'manhauled' their sleds across Antarctica would be dead. With Mawson no longer casting his long shadow,[70] Debenham and Taylor took centre stage at the degree ceremony together: the only remaining Sydney alumni who had voyaged to Antarctica prior to the age of flight and mechanisation. The *Daily Telegraph* announced the degree ceremony accordingly: 'EXPLORERS HONORED. Antarctic veterans receive degrees.' Debenham already had two honorary doctorates under his belt but had never undertaken a PhD; consequently, his alma mater awarded him an Honorary Doctorate in Science. Since Taylor had earned his Doctor of Science degree in 1916, his would be a DLitt—Doctor of Letters, *honoris causa*—deeply ironic in view of his career-long crusade against the classics. Nevertheless, he happily bowed his head to receive a new hood. Standing before convocation, shoulder to shoulder with his lifelong friend Deb, he beamed for the assembled Taylors and the *Daily Telegraph* photographer. 'I am three bachelors, two doctors and four Fellows now,' he informed Visher. Then the disingenuous jest: 'You know the old joke, "It takes nine tailors to make a man?" ... I hope soon to be an average man.'[71]

Taylor was the last person to consider himself an average man and many others, particularly his students, agreed. Two of his early and most loyal students, John Andrews and Ann Marshall, informed him that they were preparing to honour him with a festschrift (eventually published in 1966), while Marie Sanderson, his 'leading lady of Honour Geography',[72] wrote her PhD seminar paper on him, placing Taylor in the company of great geographical thinkers, including von Humboldt, Karl Ritter, W.M. Davis and Carl Sauer.[73] Twenty-seven years later she would publish a biography of her beloved professor (described in the *Geographical Review* as a 'sympathetic tribute').[74] Just as Taylor had become one of Edgeworth David's adoptees, these students became prominent members of the extended Taylor family. Aside from their admiration for Taylor, they valued the connections they formed with his family. 'I remember how Mrs Taylor used to ask us up to your home, for dinner—and bridge, and ping pong in the basement—and how we enjoyed ourselves,' Sanderson recalled fondly.[75] In the hands of such knowledgeable and affectionate biographers, his professional legacy was assured.

Journeyman's End

Deeply appreciative of these publishing ventures in his honour, Taylor still sought the final word. Although he had completed the first draft of his autobiography by 1952, revisions and publishing delays consumed the better part of the decade. Never a fan of the genre himself, Taylor believed that his would be superior to most: 'It has one merit over many Reminiscences in that it consists largely of extracts from my journals ... They are not the mouldy recollections of a slippered pantaloon who has forgotten the brighter moments of 70 years.'[76]

The manuscript of Journeyman was certainly fatter than most. In the midst of writing it, he provided his old staff members at Toronto with a progress report: 'I am now at page 773 quarto typescript, and propose to keep on till I see 1100 at the top of the page.'[77] Taylor ultimately submitted a 5 kilogram manuscript to his publisher: 'Surely such a weighty tome should meet with a rapturous welcome,' he joked to his brother Evan.[78] If its length and weight were meant to impress, they very nearly led to its rejection—had Alasdair Alpin MacGregor, a writer, broadcaster and freelance literary agent, not intervened, it might have remained in manuscript and become very mouldy indeed. MacGregor took more than a year to plough through it, after which he agreed to edit it only if Taylor agreed to reduce it—by 160 000 words:

> The author might well consider the space to be saved by the omission of lengthy and boring correspondence between himself and various persons

> ... The work lacks plan and continuity, due to its author's having followed a diary chronology ... Much evidence of hurried and careless writing. The work abounds in needless circumlocutions, the ironing out of which would reduce the length considerably.[79]

Taylor wasn't used to such hard-nosed editing, although most of his publications could have benefited from it. He grudgingly agreed to reduce the volume by 350 pages, a process that delayed the book's publication by five years. If his autobiography was not the place for his diaries, journals and letters, he would find another way to preserve the exhaustively detailed record of his life and work.

An unstoppable chronicler of his own output, in retirement Taylor ensured that future generations would be well placed to continue to document his stature in the geographical and historical record. The question of where to place his papers mattered deeply. His visit with Doris to Canberra for the 1954 ANZAAS meeting tipped Taylor towards donating his material to the National Library of Australia. The important point was the word 'national': only such an institution was suitable. Not only did he consider himself a national figure but he valued the role he had played in the siting and establishment of the capital. Despite his turn to internationalism, he never abandoned his commitment as a geographer to nation-planning, for which his capital contributions made a fitting symbol. The Library's chief, Harold White, entertained Taylor and Doris at his home, and knew how to charm the old man. Taylor's papers would:

> form a valued and significant addition to the already great collection we possess on Australia and Antarctica. More than that, they will bring to us material of continuing interest about the work and achievements of a great Australian and of the many fields of knowledge which have been enriched by his researches.[80]

Taylor agreed without hesitation, although he took his time handing the material over.

Flattery of White's sort almost always worked on Taylor, yet he remained open to others eager to receive the record of his life. Because he felt McGregor's abridgement of *Journeyman Taylor* had been too drastic, he began work on a second autobiography, 'Journeyman at Cambridge', and this delayed the deposit of his papers, in spite of White's entreaties. In the interim, geologist Gilbert Butland appeared with a rival bid for Taylor's documents. Butland was only keen on Taylor's Antarctic material, which he promised to display prominently at the University of New England in Armidale, in northern New South Wales. To demonstrate the seriousness of his request, he invited Taylor and Doris to the official opening of the university's geography department in 1960: 'I think it entirely fitting that the doyen of Australian geographers should open the continent's newest Geography building in its youngest University.' The Taylors and Butlands developed an instant friendship; before long both Doris and Taylor were ready to donate their Antarctic-related material, including Taylor's original Antarctic sketch diaries and her original copy of *Aurora Australis*, the first book published in Antarctica during Shackleton's *Nimrod* expedition. As for the remainder of his papers, Taylor informed Butland: 'My family has no desire to keep the piles of stuff I have accumulated.'[81] In the end, his papers ended up in several institutions, but the National Library of Australia became the chief guardian of Taylor's legacy, the bulk of which arrived in 1961, in trunks stuffed with tens of thousands of letters, scores of journals, hundreds of lantern slides, newspaper clippings, photographs and mementos.

Taylor's deeper wish that a record of his life might live on through his own flesh and blood came true in 1958, the same year that *Journeyman* was finally published. Despite the fact that Bill had a step-son, Taylor worried that the Taylor–Priestley line might die out. '[It's] a bit sad to think that there's a complete chain back to Adam and Eve, and yet it stops (so far) at our two boys,' he wrote to a Toronto friend in 1952.[82] For years his relatives, mates and even his students had regaled him with tales of their grandchildren; all he could say was that he and Doris had just about given up hope. Norman Llewellyn Taylor's arrival restored it, though not before the baby's status as a Taylor was settled. Taylor wrote anxiously to Bill in 1959 to seek confirmation: 'adopted or natural?' When the reply was 'natural', Taylor recorded in his diary: 'Norman real grandson.'[83] Doris and David met the baby first: '31st Aug. [1959] Do and Da go to Melbourne to see the grandson ... the baby is a fine kid.'[84] Taylor finally managed to 'introduce [him] self to the sole scion of the Taylors' in January 1960, when the Institute of Australian Geographers met in Melbourne where Taylor was to deliver his presidential address on geographers and world peace.[85] Having met 'the youngest member of the Taylor clan', he was now prepared to make a peace offering towards Bill and his wife: a gift of £1000 and the promise to put Talinga in Bill's name.[86]

Having a grandson raised Taylor's competitive streak again, and he began projecting his ambitions onto the child, well before his nature or preferences were evident. His boast to Donald Putnam, the man who replaced him as the chair of geography at Toronto, was typical:

> My son Bill has a son Norman, a remarkably intelligent boy, 1¼, and takes more notice of his environment than any child I have observed ... if he becomes a geographer, unlike my two sons, I am sure he will believe in environmental control.[87]

In November 1960, Doris and Taylor received more happy news: they now had a granddaughter, Denise ('the best baby on record'). Having decided that Norman was destined to become a geographer, Taylor predicted different professions for Denise. Acting? Politics? Placing his faith in the future, he was confident that the necessary ingredients were now in place. 'You have a fine family,' he congratulated his son and daughter-in-law. Bill's children ensured that father and son would live on in name: 'and so the Griffith Taylor line seems to show continuity—mine as well as yours.'[88]

A few last symbols of generational continuity and legacy awaited Taylor in his final years. George Dury, head of the geography department, graciously invited Taylor to visit the department, and asked if he might display the professor's portrait, the gilt-framed Toovey oil painting in the library. The geography department held a small but symbolic ceremony on 21 October 1962 to unveil Taylor's painting, which they granted a place of honour next to a portrait of Sir Edgeworth David—the original patriarch of the discipline. When Oscar Spate heard the news, he sent a telegram: 'Please convey Griff following stop All in Canberra department rejoice that at last the prophet is not without honour in his own country and send warmest felicitations.'[89] Finally the time had arrived for Taylor to be hailed as the grand old man of geography.

In January 1963, the kindly Dury relayed even more gratifying news: 'the Building and Grounds Committee has resolved to name the so-called Services, or Geography Building the Griffith Taylor Building: I trust that you too will be pleased.'[90] For years Taylor had dreamed that the name of 'Taylor' and geography and the University of Sydney would be synonymous. His former students' plans for a festschrift had touched him and the honorary degree had validated him but assigning his name to the geography building was like bestowing his name on his own child. As his health had declined, though, he knew he would unlikely live to see the building completed. By May 1963, he was effectively housebound, too frail and too prone to falling. People came to Taylor—everyone from bridge partners to passing Antarctickers—until October, when the circle of visitors narrowed to the family. On 24 May, he entered hospital in Manly. In his last days, his family showed him a new snapshot taken by his son David: an image of Bill, Doris and Pal standing outside the Griffith Taylor Building.[91] 'I was able to show him a photo, during his last week, of his name on the outside of [the] new Geography Building at the University of Sydney,' Doris informed Marie Sanderson. 'It gave him great pleasure and satisfaction.'[92]

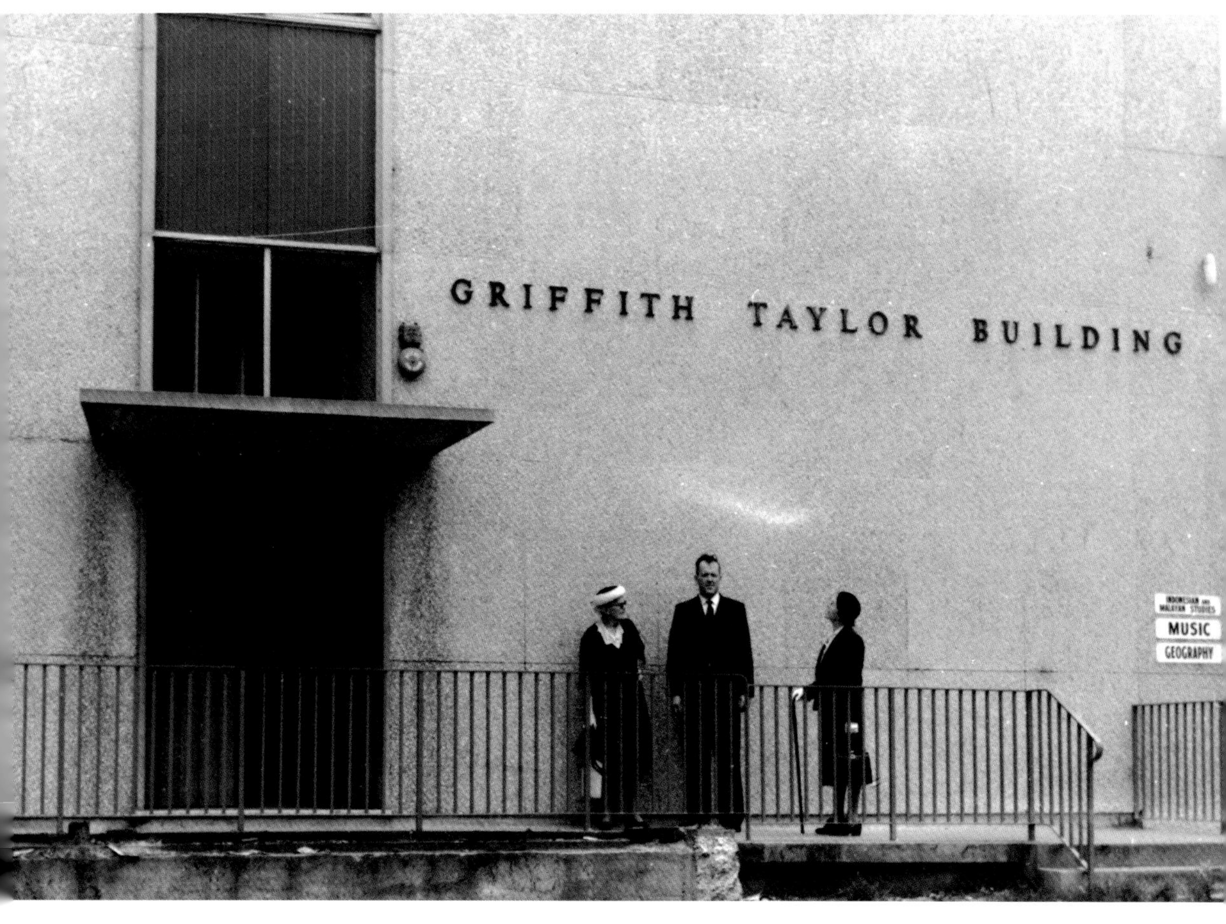

The Griffith Taylor Building, University of Sydney. Taylor's son David took this image of Dorothy, Bill and Doris Taylor admiring the sign in November 1963. Taylor never saw the fully constructed building but he was pleased to see this photo, only days before his death.

Epilogue

Alongside thoughts of his own successes, Taylor's memories of his father's accomplishments preoccupied him in his final years. While Pal honoured James Taylor by writing his biography, her brother, for once, chose action over words. Taylor's achievements far outstripped his father's: more degrees, higher salaries, greater titles, further travels, wider fame and a truckload of publications. Nevertheless, in an effort to measure up, he reflected on James's extraordinary 1919 bicycle trip and turned it into a personal challenge: he would attempt to walk the same route on the eve of his 80th birthday.

Everyone close to Taylor tried to talk him out of the stunt. His father had ridden from Sydney to Melbourne at the age of 70, not 80, and he had travelled on wheels, not by foot. Bill tactfully suggested a car and caravan trip instead but Taylor demurred. His one concession was his promise to stay in guest houses, rather than camp by roadsides. He set himself a training regime of extended daily walks until they produced painful attacks of lumbago.[1] Doris bought him a new pair of boots and convinced him to shorten his trip. The revised destination, Mt Kosciuszko, entailed a walk of 560 kilometres and a climb of over 2100 metres, since he aimed, as always, for the top. It was also

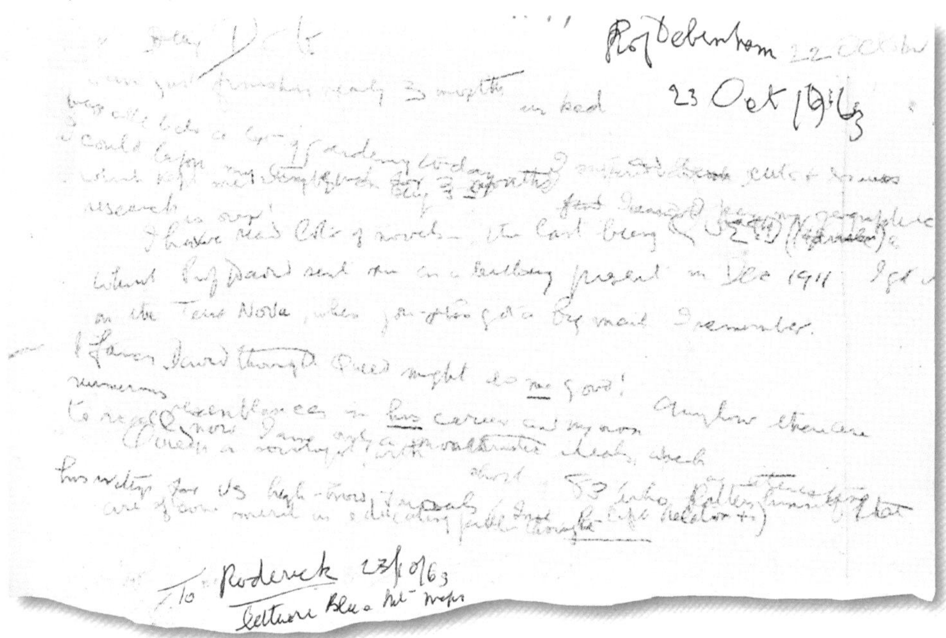

the location he had chosen for the burial of his ashes—a cirque he and Mawson had surveyed in 1907. Days short of his birthday he set off with a rucksack, a bed roll and a small wallet. The strange old swagman walked along the highway with traffic thundering by and memories swirling around his head, not only of his father's ride but of his own memorable journeys—his Cambridge-to-London walk, his sledge trips over Antarctic crevasses and his mad cycle to the Glacial Tongue. He propelled himself along, determined that neither age nor infirmity would defeat him. But it did. At Narellen, a mere 58 kilometres from Sydney, he sprained his achilles tendon and had to return by train. His 'trial tramp' failed. 'It was too much for me', he admitted to Bill, 'and so I ingloriously returned'.[2]

Taylor's walking trip doubled as an effort to prove he could outdo his fellow Antarctic patriarchs with his legendary endurance, even if he could no longer travel to the continent. 'I tried to copy our 1910 walk', he informed 'Silas' Wright, who had just made a trip to Antarctica at the age of 73, 'but two days of this was all I could manage'.[3] His account to a former student was a little more revealing: 'I was proud of my energy; and I tried to keep up a long walk from ten to twenty miles a day so as to keep ahead of my three mates Wright, Debenham and Priestley'.[4] It was as if he was 30 years old again, trying to outhaul Campbell's party as the crew unloaded the *Terra Nova*'s stores. But those days were long over. After his injury left him unable to walk for seven weeks, the octogenarian realised his journeying had come to an end.

Fortunately Taylor could return to a close family and solid circle of friends who retained their faith in him, no matter how much he tested it with his incessant work and his self-righteousness. His trying qualities were always leavened by his more charming features—his self-deprecating absurdist humour and his irrepressibility. Taylor spent his last months laid up in the day bed installed in the study, surrounded by his books and Antarctic photos. Although weakened by falls and almost totally deaf, he maintained his correspondence as best he could. The very last entry in his scrapbook, his copy of a letter to Frank Debenham, conveyed the good news that the University of Sydney had named a building in his honour. In an unsteady hand, he added that he had just re-read the satirical novel *Queed*, which Professor David had sent him for his 30th birthday. The title character names his magnum opus, 'The Science of Sciences' (an attempt to unify all knowledge into a single theory).[5] Queed is a bookish but heroic man, whose life and career reminded Taylor of his own: 'Queed also ends happily'.[6]

For Taylor the end came peacefully two weeks later, on 5 November 1963, and his body was cremated after a small funeral. When Doris passed away in 1965, Bill assumed responsibility for David's care, as well as his father's papers and remains. Taylor had instructed his solicitor that he wished to be laid to rest 'without special ceremony, when times are convenient'.[7] Bill judged that the time had come once his son Norman reached his teens. Together, father and son travelled to Mt Kosciuszko where they buried Taylor's ashes.[8]

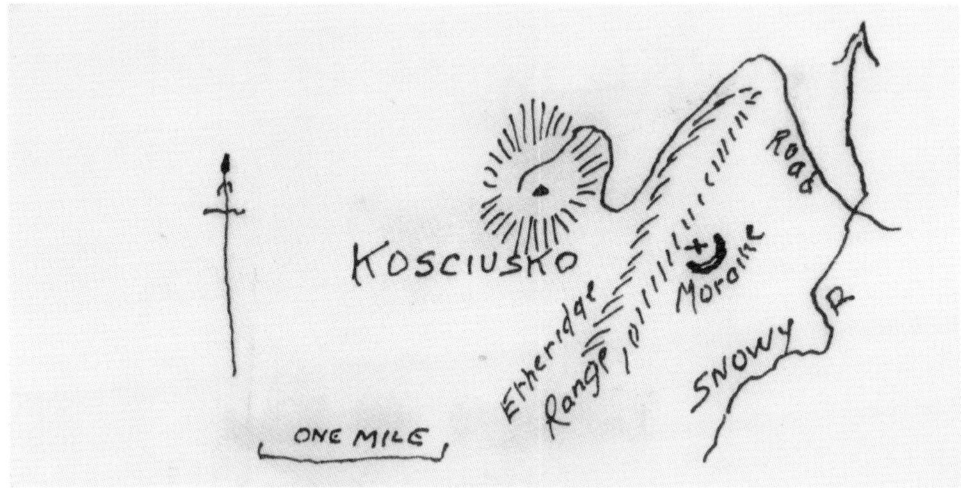

opposite

The final letter Taylor pasted into his correspondence scrapbook, 23 October 1963. Bedridden by this point and unable to type, he wrote to his old Antarctic sledge mate, Frank Debenham: 'I have read lots of novels—the last being QUEED which Prof David sent me ... I got it on the Terra Nova.'

above

In 1958, as he prepared his will, Taylor provided his solicitor with this map of a cirque on Mt Kosciuszko, indicating where he wished his ashes to be buried. Of the many places he mapped over five decades, he selected 'the moraines of Kosciusko, which I had helped to discover in 1922' (Taylor, *Journeyman Taylor*, 1958).

Acknowledgments

While this book is the product of authorial collaboration, we would like to thank many others who have made our collaboration enjoyable and fruitful.

First, without the generous cooperation of Taylor's descendants we could never have produced a book that offers insight into Taylor's personal as well as professional life. His grandson, Norman L. Taylor, granted us permission to read and publish excerpts from Taylor's papers, and his niece, Miss Pattie Taylor, graciously shared her family photographs, allowing them to appear in the book. Both Norman and Pattie shared memories of Taylor and their recollections have greatly enriched our biography.

We are also grateful to Professor Marie Sanderson, Taylor's former student and the author of her own biography of the man, for agreeing to be interviewed, as did Professor Donald Kerr, a former colleague of Taylor in the University of Toronto's Department of Geography. David Branagan, geologist and author of Taylor's mentor's biography, provided further insight on T.W. Edgeworth David. Anne Michaels, who wrote Taylor as a character in *Fugitive Pieces*, also granted an interview and offered interest and encouragement as well.

Taylor donated the majority of his papers and mementos to the National Library of Australia. Graeme Powell, Marie-Louise Ayres and the Manuscripts Collection staff have been unfailingly helpful, as have the Library's Pictures Collection staff. As a recipient of the Library's Harold White Fellowship in 2005, Carolyn Strange was fortunate to receive dedicated office space and financial support. Margy Burn and Chris Merton made her tenure of the Fellowship both profitable and pleasurable.

Staff at the University of Cambridge's Scott Polar Research Institute facilitated our research. In particular, we would like to thank Heather Lane, Lucy Martin and Naomi Boneham. Taylor donated much of his Antarctic material to the University of New England, and the New England Heritage Centre and Regional Archives staff, particularly Nicole McLennan and Philip Ward, were most welcoming and helpful.

In North America, our research was facilitated by staff at the University of Toronto Archives and the Thomas Fisher Rare Book Library; archivists at Yale University, Dartmouth University and Johns Hopkins University, which hold the papers of Elsworth Huntington, Vilhjalmur Stefansson and Isaiah Bowman respectively, helped trace Taylor's correspondence with key figures in his career.

A large team of research assistants in Australia, Canada and England facilitated our research: Stephanie Antsis, Jeannine Baker, Nancy De Castro, Ann Jones, Emily O'Gorman, Samia Hossain, Eva Kater, Peder Roberts, and Harry Wise. At The Australian National University, we received data management support from Chris Blackall, Katie Hayne and Gurol Baba. Without Chris's advice early in the project our research could not have proceeded nearly so efficiently.

We are grateful for the Australian Research Council's Discovery Grant program which provided major support for our research. The University of Sydney assisted financially through the Chancellors Committee Fund, which facilitated research on the university's geology lantern-slide collection, to which Taylor had contributed. We also gratefully acknowledge support from The Australian National University in the form of a Publication Committee Subsidy.

Numerous academic colleagues and friends have provided criticism and encouragement, from the earliest stages of the project. Tina Loo conducted a significant portion of the research, involving intensive (and pleasurable) archival work in Canberra. Many of her insights, particularly on the history of geography, modernity and environmental determinism, have found their way into the book. Stephanie Green took an early and inspirational interest in the project, as did 'The Modernistas': Desley Deacon, Ann Curthoys, Rosanne Kennedy, Jill Julius Matthews and Ann McGrath. Through the research and writing process, Robert Aldrich, Robert Cribb, Tom Griffiths, Julia Horne, Li Narangoa, Jude Philp, Libby Robin and Penny Russell have been wonderful colleagues, responding to ideas and questions and critically reviewing drafts. Desley Deacon offered an accomplished biographer's insight into the craft of writing and provided friendly advice on the project from its outset. We are particularly grateful to Tom Griffiths, who offered not only his expertise on Antarctic and environmental history but also a crucial piece of Taylor's correspondence with Edgeworth David. A critical article on Taylor's Toronto career that we couldn't track down appeared thanks to Trevor Barnes.

From their initial encouragement to present a book proposal to the final stages of production, the National Library of Australia Publications staff have been great partners—professional and convivial. We are especially grateful to Paul Cliff and Susan Hall, both of whom made this a better book through their editorial advice; Joanna Karmel kept a close eye on detail. Paul Hetherington, Director of Publications and Events, provided the perfect balance of forthright criticism, insight and inspiration. We also acknowledge the reviewers of the draft manuscript whose questions and comments improved the final draft.

Our families have, as always, provided interest, support and welcome distraction. In Australia, we thank Oscar and Tessa Brunton and Marjorie and Keith Bashford; in Canada, we warmly acknowledge Mary and Arthur Strange.

Notes

Abbreviations

NAA	National Archives of Australia
NLA	National Library of Australia
SPRI	Scott Polar Research Institute (University of Cambridge, England)

Editorial note
Minor typographical errors in original quotations have been corrected. Otherwise quotations have been left as written with incorrect grammar, punctuation and spelling.

Introduction

1 Robert Scott to T.W. Edgeworth David, 20 October 1911, quoted in David Branagan, *T.W. Edgeworth David: A Life: Geologist, Adventurer, Soldier and 'Knight in the Old Brown Hat'*. Canberra: National Library of Australia, 2005, p. 228.

2 Taylor to Bill Taylor, 14 May 1951, Taylor Papers, NLA MS 1003, Box 21.

3 By tending this personal archive, Taylor led what Thomas Söderqvist names a 'biographical life'. See his *Science as Autobiography: The Troubled Life of Niels Jerne*, trans. David Mel Paul. New Haven: Yale University Press, 2003. For a range of historiographical approaches to scientists as biographical subjects, see Michael Shortland and Richard Yeo (eds), *Telling Lives in Science: Essays on Scientific Biography*. Cambridge: Cambridge University Press, 1996. Mary Jo Nye comments: 'While historians of science often use biography as a vehicle to analyse scientific processes and scientific culture, the most compelling scientific biographies are ones that portray the ambitions, passions, disappointments, and moral choices that characterise a scientist's life.' Taylor generated ample evidence for the historian to do both. See her 'Scientific Biography: History of Science by Another Means?', *Isis*, vol. 97, no. 2, 2006: 329.

4 Flannery names Taylor as 'one of the greatest and most courageous scientists Australia has ever produced' and praises him for daring to 'tell the truth about the future of the nation'. See Timothy Fridtjof Flannery, *The Future Eaters: An Ecological History of the Australasian Lands and People*. Sydney: Reed New Holland, 2005, pp. 363–364. For other flattering appraisals, see Jonathan Stone, 'Empty or Full? The Population Debate in Australia', in *Population 2040: Australia's Choice: Proceedings of the Symposium of the 1994 Annual General Meeting of the Australian Academy of Science*. Canberra: Australian Academy of Science, 1994; Ruth Fincher, 'Geography and the Population–Environment Debate', in *Proceedings of the 2004 Fenner Conference on the Environment*, Australian Academy of Science, viewed 4 January 2008 at www.science.org.au/events/fenner/fincher.htm; B.G. Thom, 'The Man/Land Theme in Geography: A Sydney University Perspective', *Australian Geographer*, vol. 18, no. 1, 1987: 8–19.

5 Anne Michaels, *Fugitive Pieces*. Toronto: McClelland and Stewart, 1996. Michaels also acted as a script consultant for the film version of the novel. See *Fugitive Pieces*, dir. Jeremy Podeswa, Serendipity Point Films, 2007.

6 O.H.K. Spate, 'Journeyman Taylor: Some Aspects of His Work', *Australian Geographer*, vol. 12, no. 2, 1972: 120.

7 Griffith Taylor, *Journeyman Taylor: The Education of a Scientist*. London: Hale, 1958, p. 30.

8 Taylor, *Journeyman Taylor*, p. 18; Family tree provided by Uncle Alfred Griffiths (Taylor's maternal uncle), 11 June 1916, inserted in the back cover of a copy of *Journeyman Taylor*, Taylor Papers, NLA MS 1003, Box 41.

9 T.W. Edgeworth David to Taylor, 24 October 1928, Taylor Papers, NLA MS 1003, Box 8, Item 285, p. 3.

10 Isaiah Bowman to Harold Adams Innis, quoted in G.S. Dunbar, 'Harold Innis and Canadian Geography,' *Canadian Geographer*, vol. 29, no. 2, 1985: 161.

11 Taylor to Doris Priestley, 26 February 1914, Taylor Papers, NLA MS 1003, Box 19, Item 1054, p. 5.

12 Sir Raymond Priestley, 'Griffith Taylor', in John Andrews (ed.), *Frontiers and Men: A Volume in Memory of Griffith Taylor (1880–1963)*. Melbourne: F.W. Cheshire, 1966, p. 4.

Chapter 1 Favoured Son

1 O.H.K. Spate, 'Journeyman Taylor: Some Aspects of His Work', *Australian Geographer*, vol. 12, no. 2, 1972: 116.

2 Sir Raymond Priestley, 'Griffith Taylor', in John Andrews (ed.), *Frontiers and Men: A Volume in Memory of Griffith Taylor (1880–1963)*. Melbourne: F.W. Cheshire, 1966, p. 3.

3 Dorothy Rhodes Taylor, 'Biography of James Taylor', unpublished manuscript, p. 17, Pattie Taylor private collection.

4 'Instructions left by John Owens for the establishment of Owens College (signed 31st May 1845)', viewed 4 January 2008 on Spartacus Educational at www.spartacus.schoolnet.co.uk/EDowens.htm.

5 On industrialisation, religion and philanthropy in nineteenth-century England, see Alan J. Kidd, *State, Society and the Poor in Nineteenth-century England*. New York: St Martin's Press, 1999; Ann B. Rodrick, *Self-help and Civic Culture: Citizenship in Victorian Birmingham*. Aldershot: Ashgate, 2004; F. David Roberts, *The Social Conscience of the Early Victorians*. Stanford: Stanford University Press, 2002; Mark A. Smith, *Religion in Industrial Society: Oldham and Saddleworth, 1740–1865*. Oxford: Clarendon Press, 1994; Ruth Watts, *Gender, Power and the Unitarians in England, 1760–1860*. New York: Longman, 1988; Susan Thorne, *Congregational Missions and the Making of an Imperial Culture in Nineteenth-century England*. Stanford: Stanford University Press, 1999.

6 First Unitarian Church Speakers Program, 10 October 1943, Taylor Papers, NLA MS 1003, Box 16, Item 801.

7 Quoted in Taylor, *Journeyman Taylor: The Education of a Scientist*. London: Hale, 1958, pp. 20–21.

8 Dorothy Rhodes Taylor, 'Biography of James Taylor', p. 32.

9 Taylor Papers, NLA MS 1003, Box 2A, Item 133.

10 Taylor Papers, NLA MS 1003, Box 42, Folder 5.

11 Taylor, *Journeyman Taylor*, p. 24.

12 Taylor, *Journeyman Taylor*, p. 27.

13 Taylor, 'Journeyman at Cambridge: The Lighter Side of Science', unpublished typescript, SPRI MS 351, p. 7.

14 For the most comprehensive source about David's varied career, as well as his impact on his top students, see David Branagan, *T.W. Edgeworth David: A Life: Geologist, Adventurer, Soldier and 'Knight in the Old Brown Hat'*. Canberra: National Library of Australia, 2005. The first biography of David was written by his daughter. See Mary Edgeworth David, *Professor David: The Life of Sir Edgeworth David*. Sydney: E. Arnold and Co., 1938. See also David S. Macmillan, *Edgeworth David*. Melbourne: Oxford University Press, 1965.

15 Taylor, 'Sir T.W. Edgeworth David', *The Journal of Geology*, vol. 42, no. 8, 1934: 849.

16 David Branagan, *T.W. Edgeworth David: A Life: Geologist, Adventurer, Soldier and 'Knight in the Old Brown Hat'*. Canberra: National Library of Australia, 2005, p. 72.

17 Taylor, *Journeyman Taylor*, p. 29.

18 Griffith Taylor and Douglas Mawson, 'The Geology of Mittagong', *Proceedings of the Royal Society of New South Wales*, 1903: 306–350.

19 Taylor, 'The First Recorded Occurrence of *Blastoidea* in New South Wales', *Proceedings of the Linnean Society of New South Wales*, vol. 31, no. 121, 1906: 53–59.

20 Taylor, 'The Geographer's Aid in Nation-planning', *The Scottish Geographical Magazine*, vol. 48, no. 1, 1932: 2.

21 Branagan, *T.W. Edgeworth David: A Life*, p. 42.

22 Taylor, 'A Correlation of Contour, Climate and Coal: A Contribution to the Physiography of NSW', *Proceedings of the Linnean Society of New South Wales*, vol. 31, no. 123, 1906: 527.

23 Raymond Priestley to Bert Priestley, August 1910, quoted in Branagan, *T.W. Edgeworth David: A Life*, pp. 220–221.

24 Taylor, 'Journeyman at Cambridge', pp. 7–10.

25 Taylor, 'Journeyman at Cambridge', pp. 1–2.

26 Taylor, *Preliminary Note on Archaeocyathinae from the Cambrian 'Coral Reefs' of South Australia*, presented to the Australasian Association for the Advancement of Science, January 1907, p. 1, Taylor Papers, NLA MS 1003, Box 45.

27 Douglas Mawson to Taylor, 6 July 1907, Taylor Papers, NLA MS 1003, Box 2, Folder 1, Item 116.

28 Taylor, 'Journeyman at Cambridge', p. 29.

29 Taylor, *Journeyman Taylor*, p. 48.

30 Taylor to Dorothy Taylor, 3 July 1909, Taylor Papers, NLA MS 1003, Box 1, Item 4.

31 Taylor Papers, NLA MS 1003, Box 17, Item 563.

32 Taylor to James Taylor, 12 February 1907, Taylor Papers, NLA MS 1003, Box 1, Item 69.

33 Paul R. Deslandes, '"The Foreign Element": Newcomers and the Rhetoric of Race, Nation, and Empire in "Oxbridge" Undergraduate Culture, 1850–1920', *Journal of British Studies*, vol. 37, no. 1, 1998: 54–90.

34 The literature on Darwinism, its historical development and its multiple interpretations and applications is vast. For a recent biography, see Tim Lewens, *Darwin*. London: Routledge, 2007.

For a survey of Darwinistic thought in the late nineteenth and early twentieth centuries, see Ronald L. Numbers (ed.), *Disseminating Darwinism: The Role of Place, Race, Religion and Gender*. Cambridge: Cambridge University Press, 1999; Timothy Shanahan, *The Evolution of Darwinism: Selection, Adaptation and Progress in Evolutionary Biology*. Cambridge: Cambridge University Press, 2004.

On the impact of Darwinistic thought on studies of the Pacific, see Roy L. MacLeod (ed.), *Darwin's Laboratory: Evolutionary Theory and Natural History in the Pacific*. Honolulu: University of Hawaii Press, 1994.

A.C. Seward, Professor of Botany at Cambridge University and a fellow of Emmanuel College edited a collection of essays for the Cambridge Philosophical Society to commemorate the 1909 centenary. See Seward, *Darwin and Modern Science: Essays in Commemoration of the Centenary of the Birth of Charles Darwin and of the Fiftieth Anniversary of the Publication of the Origin of Species*. Cambridge: Cambridge University Press, 1909.

For an analysis of 1909 as a critical juncture in the history of evolutionary theory, see Marsha L. Richmond, 'The 1909 Darwin Celebration', *Isis*, vol. 97, no. 3, 2006: 447–484.

35 *Cambridge Daily News*, 24 June 1909.

36 On Oxbridge culture and the history of Cambridge, see Paul R. Deslandes, *Oxbridge Men: British Masculinity and the Undergraduate Experience, 1850–1920*. Bloomington, Indiana: Indiana University Press, 2005; Christopher Nugent et al., *A History of the University of Cambridge*. Cambridge: Cambridge University Press, 2004; Jonathan Smith and Christopher Stray (eds), *Teaching and Learning in Nineteenth-century Cambridge*. Woodbridge: Boydell Press, 2001.

37 Taylor, *Journeyman Taylor*, p. 59.

38 Taylor, 'Journeyman at Cambridge', pp. 42, 69.

39 Taylor, *Journeyman Taylor*, p. 60.

40 Taylor, *Journeyman Taylor*, p. 70.

41 Taylor, *Journeyman Taylor*, p. 42.

42 Taylor, *Journeyman Taylor*, p. 65.

43 Taylor, 'Journeyman at Cambridge', p. 77.

44 Professor T.G. Bonney, 15 March 1910, Taylor Papers, NLA MS 1003, Box 1, Items 40–45.

45 Taylor, 'The Archaeocyathinae from the Cambrian "Coral Reefs" of South Australia, with an Account of the Morphology and Affinities of the Whole Class', *Memoires of the Royal Society of South Australia*, vol. 2, 1910: 55–188.

46 Taylor to Mater, 22 April 1909, Taylor Papers, NLA MS 1003, Box 1, Items 1–4, Item 1.

47 Taylor, *Journeyman Taylor*, p. 81; Cambridge Philosophical Society menu, 11 December 1909, Fisher Rare Book Library, University of Toronto, MS 20, Box 25/1.

48 H. Hunt to Taylor, 2 December 1910, Taylor Papers, NLA MS 1003, Box 2, Item 48.

49 Taylor Papers, NLA MS 1003, Box 1, Items 42, 43, 44.

50 Dorothy Rhodes Taylor, 'Biography of James Taylor'.

Chapter 2 The Furthest Frontier

1 For works that highlight Taylor's contribution to Antarctic geology, see Marie Sanderson, *Griffith Taylor: Antarctic Scientist and Pioneer Geographer*. Ottawa: Carleton University Press, 1988; Charles A. Cotton, 'Taylor's Hypothesis of Headward Glacial Erosion', *Journal of Geomorphology*, vol. 3, no. 4, 1940: 346–352; Wayne S. Hanley, 'Griffith Taylor's Antarctic Achievements: A Geographical Foundation', *Australian Geographical Studies*, vol. 18, no. 1, 1980: 22–36; John Pickard, 'Griffith Taylor's Palimpsest Theory of the Dry Valleys of Victoria Land, Antarctica', *Australian Geographer*, vol. 28, no. 1, 1997: 53–67.

2 On Australian scientific exploration and explorers, see Robert A. Swan, *Australia in the Antarctic: Interest, Activity and Endeavour*. Melbourne: Melbourne University Press, 1961; Tom Griffiths, *Slicing the Silence: Voyaging to Antarctica*. Sydney: University of New South Wales Press, 2007; Philip Ayres, *Mawson: A Life*. Melbourne: Melbourne University Press, 1999; Brigid Hains, *The Ice and the Inland: Mawson, Flynn, and the Myth of the Frontier*. Carlton: Melbourne University Press, 2002.

On Edwardian Antarctic exploration and the Scott legend, see David Crane, *Scott of the Antarctic: A Life of Courage and Tragedy in the Extreme South*. London: Harper Collins, 2005; Roland Huntford, *Scott and Amundsen*. London: Hodder and Stoughton, 1979; Diana Preston, *A First Rate Tragedy*. London: Houghton Mifflin, 1998; Susan Solomon, *The Coldest March*. New Haven: Yale University Press, 2002; Max Jones, *The Last Great Quest: Captain Scott's Sacrifice*. Oxford: Oxford University Press, 2003; Ranulph Fiennes, *Race to the Pole: Heroism and Scott's Antarctic Quest*. London: Hyperion Books, 2004; Claire Barwell, 'Frozen Memories: Unthawing Scott of the Antarctic in Cultural Memory', *Visual Communication*, vol. 6, no. 3, 2007: 345–357.

3 David and students to Scott, 1901, SPRI MS 366/15, cited in David Branagan, *T.W. Edgeworth David: A Life: Geologist, Adventurer, Soldier and 'Knight in the Old Brown Hat'*. Canberra: National Library of Australia, 2005, pp. 141 and 557, endnote 8.

4 Edward Wilson, quoted in David Crane, *Scott of the Antarctic: A Life of Courage and Tragedy in the Extreme South*. London: Harper Collins, 2005, p. 398 [1909].

5 *The Times*, 13 September 1909.

6 Robert E. Peary, 'Peary Arctic Club Expedition to the North Pole, 1908–9', *The Geographical Journal*, vol. 36, no. 2, 1910: 129.

7 Edgeworth David to Douglas Mawson, 8 February 1910, Mitchell Library, Sydney, MS 3022/2.

8 Mawson and David were credited for having discovered the location of the South Magnetic Pole. David admitted in 1912 that he and Mawson had likely reached only the 'area' of the Magnetic Pole. This fact was not revealed publicly until 1930. See Branagan, *T.W. Edgeworth David: A Life*, pp. 224 and 570, endnote 24.

9 Douglas Mawson, Abbreviated Log, c.10 February 1910, Mawson Antarctic Collection, quoted in Ayers, *Mawson*, pp. 33–34.

10 Taylor, *With Scott: The Silver Lining*. London: Smith Elder and Company, 1916, pp. 4–5.

11 Taylor to James Taylor, 12 February 1907, Taylor Papers, NLA MS 1003, Box 1, Item 69.

12 Dorothy Rhodes Taylor, 'Biography of James Taylor', unpublished manuscript, p. 36.

13 Taylor, 'Journeyman at Cambridge: The Lighter Side of Science', unpublished typescript, SPRI MS 351, p. 42.

14 Taylor, *With Scott*, pp. 7–8.

15 Taylor, *Journeyman Taylor: The Education of a Scientist*. London: Hale, 1958, p. 82.

16 Taylor, 'Evolution of a Capital, A Physiographic Study of the Foundation of Canberra, Australia', *The Geographical Journal*, vol. 48, no. 4, 1914: 378.

17 J.A. Steers, 'Debenham, Frank (1883–1965)', rev. Elizabeth Baigent, 2004, *Oxford Dictionary of National Biography*, viewed 8 January 2008 at dx.doi.org/10.1093/ref:odnb/32764; G.P. Walsh, 'Debenham, Frank (1883–1965)', *Australian Dictionary of Biography Online Edition*, viewed 8 January 2008 at www.adb.online.anu.edu.au/biogs/A130672b.htm.

18 Taylor, *Journeyman Taylor*, p. 67.

19 *Sun Herald*, 29 November 1959, Taylor Papers, NLA MS 1003, Box 11, Item 158.

20 S. Murray-Smith, 'Priestley, Sir Raymond Edward (1886–1974)', *Australian Dictionary of Biography Online Edition*, viewed 8 January 2008 at www.adb.online.anu.edu.au/biogs/A110303b.htm; G. de Q. Robin, 'Priestley, Sir Raymond Edward (1886–1974)', *Oxford Dictionary of National Biography*, viewed 8 January 2008 at dx.doi.org/10.1093/ref:odnb/31566.

21 Taylor to James Taylor, 11 October 1910, Taylor Papers, NLA MS 1003, Box 2B, Item 46.

22 Taylor, 'Journeyman at Cambridge', p. 7.

23 Taylor, *With Scott*, p. 231.

24 Frank Debenham, Journal, 1 December 1910, SPRI 279, vol. 1.

25 Taylor, 'The Race for the Pole', *Argus*, 19 April 1911: 6.

26 Taylor, 'A Journal of the 1910 Expedition in Dec, 1910 to Jan 1911', 4 December 1910, transcribed in Wayne S. Hanley, *The Griffith Taylor Collection: Diaries and Letters of a Geographer in Antarctica*. Armidale: University of New England, 1978, p. 18.

27 Taylor, Antarctic Diary, 22 December 1910, in Hanley, *The Griffith Taylor Collection*, p. 43

28 Taylor, 'The Race for the Pole', *Argus*, 22 April 1911: 6.

29 Taylor, Antarctic Diary, 6 January 1911, in Hanley, *The Griffith Taylor Collection*, p. 60.

30 Taylor, Antarctic Diary, 15 January 1911, in Hanley, *The Griffith Taylor Collection*, p. 70.

31 On masculinity, heroism and imperialism, see Lisa Bloom, *Gender on Ice: American Ideologies of Polar Expeditions*. Minneapolis: University of Minnesota Press, 1997. Analysis of Taylor is informed by broader historical studies of masculinity. See Michael Roper and John Tosh (eds), *Manful Assertions: Masculinities in Britain since 1800*. London: Routledge, 1991; J.A. Mangan and James Walvin (eds), *Manliness and Morality: Middle-class Masculinity in Britain and America, 1800–1940*. Manchester: Manchester University Press, 1987; Geoffrey Cubitt and Allen Warren (eds), *Heroic Reputations and Exemplary Lives*. Manchester: Manchester University Press, 2000; Martin Francis, 'The Domestication of the Male? Recent Research on Nineteenth- and Twentieth-century British Masculinity', *The Historical Journal*, vol. 45, no. 3, 2002: 637–652.

32 Scott to Taylor, October 1911, quoted in Taylor, *With Scott*, pp. 122–123.

33 Taylor, Antarctic Diary, 7 December 1910, in Hanley, *The Griffith Taylor Collection*, p. 22.

34 Taylor, *With Scott*, p. 120.

35 Herbert Ponting, *The Great White South*. London: Duckworth & Co., 1921, p. 90.

36 Taylor, 'The Physiography and Glacial Geology of East Antarctica', *The Geographical Journal*, vol. 44, no. 10, 1914: 367.

37 Taylor, Antarctic Diary, 7 January 1911, in Hanley, *The Griffith Taylor Collection*, p. 63.

38 Taylor, *With Scott*, p. 132.

39 Taylor, *Antarctic Adventure and Research*. New York: D. Appleton and Co., 1930, p. 112.

40 Taylor, *With Scott*, p. 280.

41 Taylor, 'The Physiography and Glacial Geology of East Antarctica'. On Taylor's geological expertise and its impact on his representations of human geography, see David Oldroyd, 'Griffith Taylor and His Views on Race, Environment, and Settlement, and the Peopling of Australia', in David Branagan and G.H. McNally (eds), *Useful and Curious Geological Enquiries beyond the World: Pacific-Asia Historical Themes: The 19th International INHIGEO Symposium*. Sydney: International Commission on the History of Geological Sciences, 1994: 251–274.

42 Taylor, *With Scott*, pp. 305–306.

43 Taylor, 'Climatic Relations between Antarctica and Australia', *Problems of Polar Research*, special publication no. 7, 1928, p. 287.

44 Taylor, 'Narrative of the Western Geological Parties, 1911–1912', in Hanley, *The Griffith Taylor Collection*, p. 105.

45 Taylor, *With Scott*, p. 194.

46 Scott to Taylor, quoted in Taylor, *With Scott*, p. 240.

47 Taylor, *With Scott*, pp. 230 and 228.

48 Taylor to Taylor family, 13 November 1911, Taylor Papers, NLA MS 1003, Box 17, Item 590.

49 Apsley Cherry-Garrard (foreword George Seaver), *The Worst Journey in the World*. London: Chatto and Windus, 1965 (1922), pp. 307–308.

50 Taylor, *Journeyman Taylor*, p. 81.

51 Quoted in 'The Last Word (Antarctic Heritage Trust in Possession of Bicycle Taken on First Antarctic Expedition)', *New Scientist*, vol. 175, 10 August 2002: 65. Joseph Powell treats Taylor's ride as a metaphor for his academic risk-taking. See Powell, 'The Cyclist on the Ice: Griffith Taylor as Explorer', *Royal Geographical Society of Australasia, South Australian Branch (Incorporated), Proceedings*, vol. 80, no. 1, 1981: 1–28.

52 Taylor to Bill Wonders, 26 August 1961, Taylor Papers, NLA MS 1003, Box 24.

53 Taylor, *With Scott*, p. 340.

54 Taylor, *With Scott*, p. 400.

55 Taylor, 'A Résumé of the Physiography and Glacial Geology of Victoria Land, Antarctica' in Leonard Huxley (ed.), *Scott's Last Expedition, Vol. II*. New York: Smith Elder, 1913: 416–429

56 Review, *Times Literary Supplement*, 6 November 1913: 502, in Taylor Papers, NLA MS 1003, Box 2B, Item 50.

57 Taylor to Lady Scott, 27 May 1914, Taylor Papers, NLA MS 1003, Box 19, Item 1068.

58 Taylor, *With Scott*, pp. 214, 424, 225.

59 Taylor, *Journeyman Taylor*, p. 129.

60 Taylor to Carlyle Smythe, 14 February 1914, Taylor Papers, NLA MS 1003, Box 19, Item 1056.

61 Edward Evans, 16 January 1914, Taylor Papers, NLA MS 1003, Box 19, Item 1056.

62 SPRI, P99/65/12.

63 Taylor to Doris Priestley, 26 February 1914, Taylor Papers, NLA MS 1003, Box 19, Item 1054; Taylor to Doris Taylor, 18 February 1914, Taylor Papers, NLA MS 1003, Box 19, Item 1049; Taylor to Doris Priestley, 26 February 1914, Taylor Papers, NLA MS 1003, Box 19, Item 1054, p. 9.

64 Taylor to Doris Priestley, 20 February 1914, Taylor Papers, NLA MS 1003, Box 19, Item 1050; 22 February 1914, Taylor Papers, NLA MS 1003, Box 19, Item 1052.

65 Taylor to Doris Priestley, 20 February 1914, Taylor Papers, NLA MS 1003, Box 19, Item 1050.

66 Taylor to Doris Priestley, 18 February 1914, Taylor Papers, NLA MS 1003, Box 19, Item 1049.

67 Taylor to Doris Priestley, 20 February 1914, Taylor Papers, NLA MS 1003, Box 19, Item 1050.

68 Taylor to Edward Evans, 27 May 1914, Taylor Papers, NLA MS 1003, Box 19, Item 1066.

69 Leonard Huxley to Taylor, 7 April 1914, Taylor Papers, NLA MS 1003, Box 4, Item 196, p. 2.

70 Taylor to Doris Priestley, 26 February 1914, Taylor Papers, NLA MS 1003, Box 19, Item 1054, p. 4.

71 Scott to Edgeworth David, 20 October 1911, quoted in Branagan, *T.W. Edgeworth David: A Life*, p. 228.

72 Taylor, *Journeyman Taylor*, p. 135.

73 Taylor to Mater, 25 October 1917, Mitchell Library, Sydney, MLMSS Set 460, Box 2.

74 Dorothy Rhodes Taylor, 'Biography of James Taylor', p. 12.

75 Taylor to Dorothy Priestley, 27 July 1914, Taylor Papers, NLA MS 1003, Box 19, Item 1074.

76 Taylor to Mater, 30 August 1916, Taylor Papers, NLA MS 1003, Box 19, Item 1191.

Chapter 3 From Rocks to Race

1 Taylor to Herbert John Fleure, 11 March 1949, NLA MS 1003, Box 21; Taylor to Herbert John Fleure, 2 June 1949, Taylor Papers, NLA MS 1003, Box 21.

2 On nationalist debates about climate and settlement, see Roy MacLeod and Donald Denoon (eds), *Health and Healing in Tropical Australia and New Guinea*. Townsville: James Cook University Press, 1991; Warwick Anderson, *The Cultivation of Whiteness: Science, Health and Racial Destiny in Australia*. Melbourne: Melbourne University Press, 2002.

3 J.W. Gregory, *The Climate of Australasia: In Reference to Its Control by the Southern Ocean*. Melbourne: Whitcombe and Tombs, 1904. Gregory advised Scott on the *Discovery* expedition but did not accompany it.

4 Edgeworth David to Taylor, 27 May 1914, in Wayne S. Hanley, *The Griffith Taylor Collection: Diaries and Letters of a Geographer in Antarctica*. Armidale: University of New England, 1978, p. 195.

5 Taylor, *Journeyman Taylor: The Education of a Scientist*. London: Hale, 1958, p. 156.

6 J. Hogan, 'Notes Prepared by John Hogan (1896–1970)', *Metarch Papers*, no. 2, March 1986, and in *Federation and Meteorology*. Melbourne: Australian Science and Technology Heritage Centre, 2001 (online edition), viewed 10 January 2008 at www.austehc.unimelb.edu.au/fam/0098.html.

7 H.A. Hunt to Taylor, 2 December 1910, Taylor Papers, NLA MS 1003, Box 2, Item 48.

8 Taylor, 'Salient Features of the Climate of Western Australia', *Australian Monthly Weather Report*, vol. 2, 1911: 176–184.

9 Taylor, *The Physiography of the Proposed Federal Territory at Canberra*, Bulletin 6. Melbourne: Commonwealth Bureau of Meteorology, 1910.

10 H.A. Hunt, Griffith Taylor and E.T. Quayle, *The Climate and Weather of Australia*. Melbourne: A.J. Mulett, 1913, inscribed copy in Taylor Papers, NLA MS 1003, Box 41. Hunt and Taylor also co-authored chapters in the section 'Climate and Weather' for volume 5 of the *Oxford Survey of the British Empire*. Oxford: Clarendon, 1914: 91–139.

11 The Bureau's early history is traced in David Day, *The Weather Watchers: History of the Bureau of Meteorology*. Melbourne: Melbourne University Press, 2007; Tim Sherratt, 'A Climate for a Nation' and 'The Weather Prophets', in *Federation and Meteorology*. Melbourne: Australian Science and Technology Heritage Centre, 2001 (online edition), viewed 10 January 2008 at www.austehc.unimelb.edu.au/fam/contents.html.

12 See Alison Bashford, '"Is White Australia Possible?" Race, Colonialism and Tropical Medicine', *Ethnic and Racial Studies*, vol. 23, 2000: 112–135; David Walker, *Anxious Nation: Australia and the Rise of Asia, 1850–1939*. St Lucia: University of Queensland Press, 1999. Scientific discussion on climate and white settlement had a centuries old history. See Mark Harrison, *Climates and Constitutions: Health, Race, Environment and British Imperialism in India, 1600–1850*. Delhi and Oxford: Oxford University Press, 1999; David N. Livingstone, *The Geographical Tradition: Episodes in the History of a Contested Enterprise*. Oxford: Blackwell, 1993; David Arnold, *The Problem of Nature: Environment, Culture and European Expansion*. Oxford: Blackwell, 1996.

13 'Report of the Discussion of the Australasian Medical Congress at Brisbane, 1920', in *Tropical Australia*. Melbourne: Government Printer, 1921, p. 5.

14 Taylor, *Australia in Its Physiographic and Economic Aspects*. Oxford: Clarendon, 1911, p. 242.

15 Taylor, *The Control of Settlement by Humidity and Temperature (with Special Reference to Australia and the Empire)*, Bulletin 14. Melbourne: Commonwealth Bureau of Meteorology, 1916.

16 A. Brienl and W.J. Young, 'Tropical Australia and Its Settlement', *Australian Institute of Tropical Medicine Papers*, no. 3. Townsville: Australian Institute for Tropical Medicine, 1922 [1919], p. 3.

17 Huntington lectured in climatology, economics, and geology at Yale. By the time he and Taylor began corresponding, Huntington had undertaken major field trips through Central Asia. See Geoffrey J. Martin, *Ellsworth Huntington: His Life and Thought*. Hamden, Conn.: Archon Books, 1973.

18 Ellsworth Huntington to Taylor, 19 January 1917, Taylor Papers, NLA MS 1003, Box 19, Item 1202.

19 Bulletin 11 was sent to George Knibbs, L.K. Ward and Professor Masson. Taylor, Field Notebooks, 12 February 1916, SPRI MS 1558.

20 Atlee Hunt to H.A. Hunt, 12 June 1918, NAA NT 1918/1915.

21 Taylor, *Australia in Its Physiographic and Economic Aspects*, p. 253.

22 'J.A.G.', Department of External Affairs, to H.A. Hunt, 9 March 1917, NAA NT 1918/1915.

23 H.A. Hunt to Secretary, Home and Territories Department (Atlee Hunt), 16 August 1918, NAA NT 1918/1915.

24 See W.A. Osborne, 'Contributions to Physiological Climatology: Part II', *Journal of Physiology*, vol. 49: 133–138; 'Wet Bulb Thermometers', *Proceedings of the Royal Society of Victoria*, vol. 29, 1916: 119–122.

25 H.A. Hunt to Secretary, Home and Territories Department (Atlee Hunt), 29 May 1918, NAA NT 1918/1915.

26 H.A. Hunt to Secretary, Home and Territories Department (Atlee Hunt), 16 August 1918, NAA NT 1918/1915.

27 Isaiah Bowman was one of the United States' most influential geographers in the early to mid twentieth century. He was educated at Harvard and Yale, and taught at the latter before taking up his presidency of the American Geographical Society and editorship of the journal. At the Versailles Peace Conference in 1919, Bowman was President Wilson's chief territorial advisor. From 1935 to 1948 he was president of Johns Hopkins University. See Neil Smith, *American Empire: Roosevelt's Geographer and the Prelude to Globalization*. Berkeley: University of California Press, 2003. For the network between Taylor, Huntington and Bowman see Joseph Powell, 'The Bowman, Huntington, and Taylor Correspondence', *Australian Geographer*, vol. 14, no. 2, 1978: 123–125.

28 Isaiah Bowman to Ellsworth Huntington, 19 January 1916, Huntington Papers, Yale University Library, Box 35, Folder 799.

29 Taylor to Harlan Barrows, August 1928, Taylor Papers, NLA MS 1003, Box 18, Item 973.

30 Taylor, Field Notebooks, 16 November 1916, SPRI MS 1553.

31 Masson letter of recommendation, 30 October 1916, Taylor Papers, NLA MS 1003, Box 19, Item 1194. Orme Masson wrote him a fulsome letter of recommendation, praising his 'exceptional' lecturing skills and adding: 'There are few men of his age who have so distinguished and varied a record of work in all of the allied branches of his subject'.

32 Taylor, *Journeyman Taylor*, p. 176; Taylor, 'The Antiquity of Man', c.1906, Griffith Taylor Papers, University of Sydney Archives: P163, Series 2, Item 1.

33 Taylor, 'The Antiquity of Man'.

34 Taylor, 'Racial Zones and Head Indices', 16 May 1928, Taylor Papers, NLA MS 1003, Box 18, Item 932.

35 This was a branch of natural history which geologist Charles Lyell had developed. See, for example, Charles Lyell, *The Geological Evidence of the Antiquity of Man: With Remarks on Theories of the Origin of the Species by Variation*. London: Murray, 1863. See also David R. Oldroyd, *Thinking about the Earth: A History of Ideas in Geology*. London: Athlone, 1996; Peter J. Bowler, *Evolution: The History of an Idea*. Berkeley: University of California Press, 1984.

36 Quoted in Branagan, *T.W. Edgeworth David: A Life: Geologist, Adventurer, Soldier and 'Knight in the Old Brown Hat'*. Canberra: National Library of Australia, 2005, p. 251.

37 Taylor, Field Notebooks, 21 June 1919, SPRI MS 1553.

38 W.D. Matthew, 'Climate and Evolution', *Annals of the New York Academy of Science*, vol. 24, 1915: 171–318.

39 Taylor, Field Notebook, 28 April 1916, SPRI MS 1553.

40 Taylor to Mater, 28 July 1916, Taylor Papers, NLA MS 1003, Box 19, Item 1185.

41 This note was later written in pen on the original letter to Mater.

42 'Asiatic Settlement in Tropical Countries', James Legge to Secretary Atlee Hunt, 19 February 1919, Taylor Papers, NLA MS 1003, Box 6, Item 112. See also diary entry where Taylor notes Hunt's response to Legge's directive as: 'Start of my Ethnol. Work', Field Notebooks, 16 April 1919, SPRI MS 1553.

43 Taylor, Field Notebooks, 16 April 1919, SPRI MS 1553.

44 Taylor to Edgeworth David, 31 July 1919, Edgeworth David Papers, University of Sydney Archives, P11, Series 32, Item 3.

45 Taylor, Field Notebooks, 31 July 1919 and 1 August 1919, SPRI MS 1553.

46 Taylor to Edgeworth David, 4 November 1919, Edgeworth David Papers, University of Sydney Archives, P11, Series 32, Item 3.

47 Taylor, 'Climatic Cycles and Evolution', *The Geographical Review*, vol. 8, no. 6, 1919: 311, 290.

48 Taylor, 'Climatic Cycles and Evolution', p. 300.

49 Taylor to Editor of *Nature*, Melbourne, 27 February 1920, Taylor Papers, NLA MS 1003, Box 6, Item 127, Letter 41C. For further discussion of Taylor and evolutionary theory, see Nancy Christie, 'Pioneering for a Civilised World: Griffith Taylor and the Ecology of Geography', in Roy MacLeod and Richard Jarrell (eds), *Dominions Apart: Reflections on the Culture of Science and Technology in Canada and Australia, 1850–1945*. Toronto: Canadian Science and Technology

Historical Association, 1994; Nancy Christie, 'Environment and Race: Geography's Search for a Darwinian Synthesis', in Roy MacLeod and Philip F. Rehbock (eds), *Darwin's Laboratory: Evolutionary Theory and Natural History in the Pacific*. Honolulu: University of Hawaii Press, 1994, pp. 426–473.

50 Taylor, 'Climatic Cycles and Evolution', pp. 300–301.

51 Taylor, Field Notebooks, 28 July 1921, SPRI MS 1558.

52 Taylor, 'The Evolution and Distribution of Race, Culture and Language', *The Geographical Review*, vol. 11, no. 1, 1921: 105.

53 Taylor, 'Geography and Australian National Problems', *Report of the Congress* (Australasian Association for the Advancement of Science), vol. 16, 1924: 479.

54 For further discussion of Taylor and evolutionary theory, see Christie, 'Pioneering for a Civilised World' and Christie, 'Environment and Race'.

55 Ellen Churchill Semple, *Influences of Geographic Environment: On the Basis of Ratzel's System of Anthropo-geography*. New York: Henry Holt, 1911.

56 Ellsworth Huntington, *Civilization and Climate*. New Haven: Yale University Press, 1915.

57 Taylor, Field Notebooks, 19 January 1925, SPRI MS 1558.

58 Ellsworth Huntington to Taylor, 11 March 1920, Huntington Papers, Yale University Library, Box 41, Folder 1109.

59 Taylor to Ellsworth Huntington, 23 June 1920, Huntington Papers, Yale University Library, Box 41, Folder 1109.

60 Ellsworth Huntington to Taylor, 27 June 1921, Taylor Papers, NLA MS 1003, Box 18, Item 673.

61 Ellsworth Huntington to Taylor, 23 February 1925, Taylor Papers, NLA MS 1003, Box 18, Item 800.

62 Ellsworth Huntington to Taylor, 11 March 1920, Huntington Papers, Yale University Library, Box 41, Folder 1109.

63 Ellsworth Huntington to Taylor, 23 February 1925, Taylor Papers, NLA MS 1003, Box 18, Item 800.

64 Ellsworth Huntington to Taylor, 27 June 1921, Taylor Papers, NLA MS 1003, Box 18, Item 673.

65 Isaiah Bowman to Taylor, 4 June 1928, Taylor Papers, NLA MS 1003, Box 18, Item 964. The gold medal to which Bowman referred was the Livingstone Medal awarded to Taylor in 1925 in recognition of contributions to geography of the Southern Hemisphere.

66 Ellsworth Huntington to Taylor, 27 June 1921, Taylor Papers, NLA MS 1003, Box 18, Item 673.

67 Taylor to Mater, April 1887, Taylor Papers, NLA MS 1003, Box 17, Item 497.

68 Taylor, 'Nullarbor Plain and the Ooldea Soak', *The Sydney Mail*, 17 August 1921, p. 17.

69 Taylor to Doris Taylor, Taylor Papers, NLA MS 1003, Box 7, Item 242.

70 Taylor, 'The Antiquity of Man'. For the broader context of Taylor's practice in this period, see Han F. Vermeulen and Arturo Alvarez Roldán (eds), *Fieldwork and Footnotes: Studies in the History of European Anthropology*. London: Routledge, 1995.

71 Taylor, draft manuscript of 'Environment and Race', c.1924, p. 15, Taylor Papers, NLA MS 1003, Box 51.

72 Louis Sullivan, *Essentials of Anthropology: A Handbook for Explorers and Museum Collectors*. New York: American Museum of Natural History, 1923.

73 Taylor to Doris Taylor, 5 February 1924, Taylor Papers, NLA MS 1003, Box 18, Item 740.

74 Taylor to Doris Taylor, August 1924, Ballina, Taylor Papers, NLA MS 1003, Box 18, Item 781.

75 Taylor, news clippings, *The Sydney Morning Herald*, 1924, 'Anthropology of the Minyung Tribe, Richmond River N.S.W.', 'The Richmond River, Kyogle, Part I', 'The Richmond River, Lismore and Casino, Part 2', Griffith Taylor Collection, Fisher Rare Book Library, University of Toronto, MS 20, Box 21 (03) File: 'Anthropology of Minyung Tribe'.

76 For the tradition of taxonomy and race theory, see Ivan Hannaford, *Race: The History of an Idea in the West*. Washington, D.C.: Woodrow Wilson Center Press, 1996; Vernon J. Williams, *The Social Sciences and Theories of Race*. Urbana: University of Illinois Press, 2006; Lee D. Baker, *From Savage to Negro: Anthropology and the Construction of Race, 1896–1954*. Berkeley: University of California Press, 1998.

77 Taylor, 'The Evolution and Distribution of Race, Culture and Language', *The Geographical Review*, vol. 11, 1921: 55.

78 Typescript 'Racial Zones and Head Indices', response to A.C. Haddon, 'Review: Environment and Race', *Nature*, 7 April 1928.

79 H.G. Wells to Taylor, 7 July 1927, Taylor Papers, NLA MS 1003, Box 39.

80 He read Stoddard in August 1920. Taylor, Field Notebooks, 8 August 1920, SPRI MS 1553.

81 Typescript draft of 'Environment and Race', 1924, Taylor Papers, NLA MS 1003, Box 51.

82 Taylor, 'The Evolution and Distribution of Race, Culture and Language', p. 55.

83 Taylor, 'Geography and Australian National Problems', p. 477.

84 Taylor, 'The Evolution and Distribution of Race, Culture and Language', p. 76.

85 Taylor to Dorothy Taylor, 11 February 1909, Taylor Papers, NLA MS 1003, Box 1, Folder 1, Items 1–4.

86 Griffith Taylor and Fitzroy Jardine, 'Kamilaroi and White, A Study of Racial Mixture in New South Wales', *Journal and Proceedings of the Royal Society of New South Wales*, vol. 58, March 1925: 268–294; Taylor, 'Variation among the Australian Aborigines, with Special Reference to Tawny Hair', *Proceedings of the Third Pan Pacific Science Congress*, 1926, vol. 2, pp. 2386–2389; Taylor, 'White and Black Races in Australia', *Pacific Affairs*, vol. 1, no. 3, 1928: 1–3.

87 For the history of cultural anthropology, see George W. Stocking, *The Ethnographer's Magic and Other Essays in the History of Anthropology*. Madison: University of Wisconsin Press, 1992; Henrika Kuklick, *The Savage Within: The Social History of British Anthropology, 1885–1945*. Cambridge: Cambridge University Press, 1991.

88 Taylor, 'Racial Zones and Head Indices', 16 May 1928, Taylor Papers, NLA MS 1003, Box 18, Item 932; Notebooks of Broken Hill, Griffith Taylor Collection, Fisher Rare Book Library, University of Toronto, MS 20, Box 20 (01).

89 Taylor, 'The Evolution and Distribution of Race, Culture and Language', p. 55.

90 A.C. Haddon, 'Anthropology at the Second Pan Pacific Science Congress in Australia 1923', *Man*, vol. 24, January 1924: especially p. 14.

91 Taylor to Mater and Dorothy Taylor, 25 February 1935, Taylor Papers, NLA MS 1003, Box 20, Item 1631.

92 University of Sydney, Third Year Geography Examination Paper, 1925, Bowman Papers, Johns Hopkins University Library, MS 58.

93 Dorothy Rhodes Taylor, Personnel File, University of Sydney Archives. Although the university records show Dorothy enrolled from 1924, her lecture notebooks commence in 1922.

94 Geography III notebook, c.1924–1927, Dorothy Rhodes Taylor Papers, University of Sydney Archives, P177, Series 1, Item 27.

95 Practical Geography II notebook, Dorothy Rhodes Taylor Papers, University of Sydney Archives, P177, Series 1, Item 27, c.1926; Dorothy Rhodes Taylor, 'Biography of James Taylor', unpublished manuscript p. 47.

96 David G. Stead, 'The Crowded Earth and Australia's Empty Spaces: A Study of Professor Griffith Taylor's Great Book, "Environment and Race"', *The Sydney Mail*, 16 November 1927, p. 8.

97 Taylor to Ellsworth Huntington, 24 April 1925, Huntington Papers, Yale University Library, Box 41, Folder 1109.

98 Roland B. Dixon to Taylor, 28 January 1928, Taylor Papers, NLA MS 1003, Box 18, Item 926.

99 Bernard J. Stern, review of Griffith Taylor, *Environment and Race*, *American Journal of Sociology*, vol. 33, no. 5, 1928: 871–872; Sauer quoted in Stern, review.

100 Stephen S. Visher, review of *Environment and Race*, *Ecology*, vol. 9, no. 4, 1928: 527–529.

101 Taylor, *Environment, Race and Migration. Fundamentals of Human Distribution: With Special Sections on Racial Classification, and Settlement in Canada and Australia*. Toronto: University of Toronto Press, 1937.

Chapter 4 Prophet and Pariah

1 Taylor to Doris Taylor, 26 February 1914, Taylor Papers, NLA MS 1003, Box 19, Item 1054, p. 9.

2 Taylor, 'Geography and Australian National Problems', *Report of Congress* (Australasian Association for the Advancement of Science), vol. 16, 1924: 433–487.

3 Taylor, *Canada: A Study of Cool Continental Environments and Their Effect on British and French Settlement*. London: Methuen, 1950, p. 517.

4 Taylor, 'Geography and Australian National Planning', report of the Australasian Association for the Advancement of Science, vol. 16, 1924, p. 484.

5 Taylor, *Journeyman Taylor: The Education of a Scientist*. London: Hale, 1958, p. 124.

6 Colonel Percy Owen, 'Stories of Fieldwork', *The Sydney Morning Herald*, 9 May 1927.

7 Taylor, *Journeyman Taylor*, p. 125.

8 Taylor, 'The Evolution of a Capital, A Physiographic Study of the Foundation of Canberra, Australia', *The Geographical Journal*, vol. 48, nos 3–4, 1914: 382, 544, 546–547, 549.

9 Taylor, *Our Evolving Civilization: An Introduction to Geopacifics, Geographical Aspects of the Path toward Peace*. Toronto: University of Toronto Press, 1946, p. 243.

10 For discussion of development and Australian land use policy, see Libby Robin, *How a Continent Created a Nation*. Sydney: University of New South Wales Press, 2007; Richard Waterhouse, *The Vision Splendid: A Social and Cultural History of Rural Australia*. Fremantle: Curtin University Books, 2005; Tim Flannery, *The Future Eaters: An Ecological History of the Australasian Lands and People*. Chatswood: Reed Books, 1994. For an unrivalled account of the progressive scientists and economists of Taylor's generation, see Michael Roe, *Nine Australian Progressives: Vitalism in Bourgeois Social Thought, 1890–1960*. St Lucia: University of Queensland Press, 1984.

11 Taylor, 'Uninhabited Australia; and the Reasons Therefore', *Proceedings of the Pan Pacific Science Congress*, vol. 1, 1923: 662.

12 'Is it a Sahara?', *The Sun*, 13 May 1924, news cutting in Bowman Papers, Johns Hopkins University Library, MS 58.

13 Taylor, 'Nature Versus the Australian', *Science and Industry*, vol. 2, no. 8, 1920: 3.

14 Taylor to Editor, *The Sydney Morning Herald*, 6 May 1924.

15 William Sommerville to Taylor, 27 September 1927, Taylor Papers, NLA MS 1003, Box 18, Item 786.

16 Taylor, 'The Geographers' Aid in Nation Planning', *The Scottish Geographical Magazine*, vol. 48, 1932: 5.

17 Taylor, 'The Frontiers of Settlement in Australia', *Geographical Review*, vol. 16, no. 1, 1926: 9.

18 Taylor, 'The Frontiers of Settlement in Australia', p. 11.

19 Edgeworth David to Taylor, 4 June 1920, Taylor Papers, NLA MS 1003, Box 6, Series 4, Item 133.

20 Taylor to Isaiah Bowman, 20 July 1920, quoted in Sanderson, *Griffith Taylor: Antarctic Scientist and Pioneer Geographer.* Ottawa: Carleton University Press, p. 102.

21 Dorothy Taylor to Taylor, 3 July 1920, Taylor Papers, NLA MS 1003, Box 6, Item 127.

22 Taylor, *Journeyman Taylor*, p. 167.

23 Taylor, *Australia in Its Physiographic and Economic Aspects*. Clarendon: Oxford, 1911: Preface. Halford Mackinder (1861–1947) was an influential geographer, first at Oxford and later at the London School of Economics which he helped establish. His work on 'The Geographical Pivot of History' was central to the development of political geography, and his 'new geography' emphasised education. See Paul Coones, *Mackinder's 'Scope and Methods of Geography' after a Hundred Years.* Oxford: University of Oxford, 1987; Pascal Venier, 'The Geographical Pivot of History and Early Twentieth Century Geopolitical Culture', *The Geographical Journal*, vol. 170, no. 4, 2004: 330–336; Gerry Kearns, 'The Political Pivot of Geography', *The Geographical Journal*, vol. 170, no. 4, 2004: 337–346.

24 *West Australian*, 20 September 1921; R. Hope Robertson to Taylor, 20 September 1921, Taylor Papers, NLA MS 1003, Box 18, Item 685.

25 *West Australian*, 20 September 1921.

26 William Sommerville to Taylor, 27 September 1927, Taylor Papers, NLA MS 1003, Box 18, Item 786.

27 Taylor, 'Arid Australia', *The Sydney Morning Herald*, 24 June 1924, Taylor Papers, NLA MS 1003, Box 18, Item 735.

28 Taylor, 'Salient Features of the Climate of Western Australia', *Australian Monthly Weather Report*, May 1911, p. 180.

29 Taylor's image as a persecuted firebrand persists in studies of his Australian environmental pronouncements. Joseph Powell notes that other scientists issued similar warnings in the 1910s and 1920s. He has treated Taylor's self-image critically in '1928: Griffith Taylor Emigrates from Australia', *Geography Bulletin*, vol. 10, no. 1, 1978: 5–13; *Griffith Taylor and 'Australia Unlimited'*. St Lucia: University of Queensland Press, 1992; 'National Identity and the Gifted Immigrant: A Note on T. Griffith Taylor, 1880–1963', *Journal of Intercultural Studies*, vol. 2, 1981: 43–54; *Disputing Dominion: Environmental Sensibilities, Historical Consciousness and Academic Discourse in Australia, 1900–1950*, Monash University Department of Geography and Environmental Science, working paper no. 36. Clayton: Monash University, 1995, pp. 1–29.

30 Taylor, 'Across Australia: Settlement Problems', *The Sydney Morning Herald*, n.d., Bowman Papers, Johns Hopkins University Library, MS 58.

31 Editor, *The Sydney Morning Herald*, 14 August 1924, p. 8.

32 Taylor, 'Nature Versus the Australian' p. 1.

33 Stanley Bruce, House of Representatives, 30 July 1924, *Hansard's Parliamentary Debates*, vol. 107, 1924: 2593.

34 Taylor to Isaiah Bowman, 14 May 1924, Bowman Papers, Johns Hopkins University Library, MS 58.

35 Taylor to Isaiah Bowman, 14 May 1924, Bowman Papers, Johns Hopkins University Library, MS 58.

36 Taylor to Isaiah Bowman, 14 May 1924, Bowman Papers, Johns Hopkins University Library, MS 58.

37 Taylor, 'Geography and Australian National Problems', p. 485.

38 'Central Australia', *The Sydney Morning Herald*, 5 May 1924, news clipping in Bowman Papers, Johns Hopkins University Library, MS 58.

39 Taylor to Isaiah Bowman, May 1924, Bowman Papers, Johns Hopkins University Library, MS 58.

40 Isaiah Bowman to Taylor, 15 January 1926, Bowman Papers, Johns Hopkins University Library, MS 58; Taylor to Isaiah Bowman, 16 December 1925, Bowman Papers, Johns Hopkins University Library, MS 58.

41 Daisy M. Bates, 'A Protest: British Pioneers and Australia', *The Sydney Morning Herald*, 1924 (n.d.), Taylor Papers, NLA MS 1003, Box 18, Item 735.

42 Isaiah Bowman to Taylor, 24 September 1924, Taylor Papers, NLA MS 1003, Box 18, Item 767.

43 Isaiah Bowman to Taylor, 24 September 1924, Bowman Papers, Johns Hopkins University Library, MS 58.

44 Taylor to Isaiah Bowman, 12 November 1924, Bowman Papers, Johns Hopkins University Library, MS 58.

45 Taylor, 'New Lands, Old Education', *Pacific Affairs*, vol. 2, no. 2, 1929: 55.

46 'Report to the Development and Migration Commission', 2 December 1927, NAA CP 211/2/1.

47 For a discussion of Australian land policies in an international context, see Alison Bashford 'World Population and Australian Land: Demography and Sovereignty in the Twentieth Century', *Australian Historical Studies*, vol. 130, 2007: 211–227.

48 M. Aurousseau to The High Commissioner, Commonwealth of Australia, 17 May 1927, Sanger Papers, Library of Congress, Box 191, Reel 122, MSS 16, 700; Marcel Aurousseau Papers, NLA MS 7070, Box 23, Series 11.

49 O.E. Baker, US Department of Agriculture to Taylor, 31 October 1927, Taylor Papers, NLA MS 1003, Box 18, Item 914.

50 D.M. Dow to Ellsworth Huntington, 5 August 1925, Huntington Papers, Yale University Library, Box 43, Folder 1208.

51 Isaiah Bowman to Taylor, 23 June 1924, Bowman Papers, Johns Hopkins University LIbrary, MS 58. See William R. Hunt, *Stef: A Biography of Vilhjalmur Stefansson, Canadian Arctic Explorer*. Vancouver: University of British Columbia Press, 1986; Joseph Powell, 'Taylor, Stefansson and the Arid Centre: An Historic Encounter of "Environmentalism" and "Possibilism"', *Journal of the Royal Australian Historical Society*, vol. 66, no. 3, 1980: 163–183.

52 'Famous Explorer Arrives', *Argus*, 25 May 1924.

53 Taylor to Vilhjalmur Stefansson, 1 June 1924, Stefansson Papers, Dartmouth College Library, Folder 12.

54 Vilhjalmur Stefansson to Taylor, 20 May 1924, Stefansson Papers, Dartmouth College Library, Folder 12.

55 Harold Nelson, House of Representatives, 30 July 1924, *Hansard's Parliamentary Debates*, vol. 107, 1924: 2592.

56 Edgeworth David, 'A Wilderness: Australia's Arid Centre', news clipping, Taylor Papers, NLA MS 1003, Box 18, Item 735.

57 Taylor to Ellsworth Huntington, 27 May 1925, Huntington Papers, Yale University Library, Box 50, Folder 1590.

58 Taylor, 'Our Foreign Neighbours', *The Australian Teacher*, vol. 1, no. 3, 1923: 18.

59 Taylor, 'Our Foreign Neighbours'.

60 'Mixed Races Not Bad, Professor Griffith Taylor's Views', *The Sydney Morning Herald*, 17 March 1926, p. 15.

61 Taylor, *Environment and Race: A Study of the Evolution, Migration, Settlement and Status of the Races of Man*. London: Oxford University Press, 1927, pp. 336, 340.

62 For further discussion of Taylor and the White Australia policy, see David R. Oldroyd, 'Griffith Taylor and His Views on Race, Environment, and Settlement, and the Peopling of Australia', in David Branagan and G.H. McNally (eds), *Useful and Curious Geological Enquiries beyond the World: Pacific-Asia Historical Themes: The 19th International INHIGEO Symposium*. Sydney: International Commission on the History of Geological Sciences, 1994: 251–274; Joseph Powell, *Griffith Taylor and 'Australia Unlimited'*. St Lucia: University of Queensland Press, 1993.

63 Keith Ward to Taylor, 15 November 1924, Taylor Papers, NLA MS 1003, Box 18, Item 768.

64 *Smith's Weekly*, 14 July 1923.

65 Taylor, 'The Possibilities of Settlement in Australia Limits of Land Settlement', in Isaiah Bowman (ed.), *The Limits of Land Settlement*. New York: Council on Foreign Relations, 1937, p. 206.

66 Herbert Heaton to Taylor, 14 September 1925, Taylor Papers, NLA MS 1003, Box 18, Item 822.

67 Harlan Barrows to Taylor, 4 June 1928, Taylor Papers, NLA MS 1003, Box 18, Item 959.

68 Taylor, Field Notebooks, 9 January 1929, SPRI MS 1553.

69 Taylor, *Journeyman Taylor*, p. 248.

70 Taylor to Mater, 22 October 1930, Taylor Papers, NLA MS 1003, Box 19, Item 1286.

71 Ellsworth Huntington to Taylor, 4 June 1928; Taylor Papers, NLA MS 1003, Box 18, Item 962; Isaiah Bowman to Taylor, 4 June 1928, Taylor Papers, NLA MS 1003, Box 18, Item 964.

72 Chauncy Harris, 'Geography at Chicago in the 1930s and 1940s', *Annals of the Association of American Geographers*, Special issue: *Seventy Five Years of American Geography*. vol. 69, no. 1, 1979: 27.

73 Susan Shulten, *The Geographical Imagination in America, 1880–1950*. Chicago: University of Chicago Press, 2001, p. 91. Although she does not consider Taylor's work, Shulten thoroughly contextualises the rise and fall of determinism in US geographical thought and teaching. For the rise of human geography (and a depiction of Taylor as a determinist throwback), see Derek Gregory, *Geographical Imaginations*. Cambridge, Mass.: Cambridge University Press, 1994. On Sauer's role in the repudiation of determinism, see David Livingstone, *The Geographical Tradition: Episodes in the History of a Contested Enterprise*. Oxford: Blackwell, 1992.

74 Taylor, *Environment, Race and Migration: Fundamentals of Human Distribution, with Special Sections on Racial Classification and Settlement in Canada and Australia.* Toronto: University of Toronto Press, 1937: 459.

75 Chauncy Harris, 'Geography at Chicago in the 1930s and 1940s', p. 27.

76 Taylor, 'The Margins of Geography', reprinted from *Schoolmaster,* 1932: 1. Taylor Papers, NLA MS 1003, Box 44.

77 Taylor to Harlan Barrows, 1 August 1928, Taylor Papers, NLA MS 1003, Box 18, Item 973.

78 O.E. Baker to Taylor, 31 October 1927, Taylor Papers, NLA MS 1003, Box 18, Item 914.

79 Harold Adams Innis (1894–1952) pioneered the field of economic history in Canada and became an early theorist of communication. By the time Taylor finally arrived in Toronto, Innis had begun to embark upon sophisticated studies of time and space, which made a significant impact on the thinking of Marshall McLuhan and subsequent generations of communications scholars. For an excellent intellectual biography of Innis, see Alexander John Watson, *Marginal Man: The Dark Vision of Harold Innis.* Toronto: University of Toronto Press, 2006. On Innis's seminal role in establishing the discipline of geography, see Gary S. Dunbar, 'Harold Innis and Canadian Geography', *The Canadian Geographer*, vol. 29, no. 2, 1985: 169–154. On the ambivalence of Innis and other leading Canadian intellectuals to American-style possibilism, see Phillip Massolin, *Canadian Intellectuals, the Tory Tradition, and the Challenge of Modernity, 1939–1970.* Toronto: University of Toronto Press, 2001.

80 Watson, *Marginal Man*, p. 120.

81 Harold Innis, *The Fur Trade in Canada: An Introduction to Canadian Economic History.* New Haven: Yale University Press, 1930, p. 393.

82 Sir Robert Falconer to Harold Adams Innis, 14 November 1929, quoted in Watson, *Marginal Man*, p. 136.

83 'Oro-Genesis', in Mrs Richards to Taylor, n.d. December 1954, Taylor Papers, NLA MS 1003, Box 22.

84 Vilhjalmur Stefansson to Taylor, 5 March 1930, Stefansson Papers, Dartmouth College Library, Box 26.

85 Taylor to Doris Taylor, n.d. spring 1935, Taylor Papers, NLA MS 1003, Box 10, Item 146, p. 2.

86 Taylor to Mick (Evan) Taylor, 26 September 1936, Taylor Papers, MS 1003, Box 20, Series 9, Item 1742.

87 Doris Taylor to Mater, 28 September 1935, Taylor Papers, NLA MS 1003, Box 20, Series 9, Item 1685.

88 Taylor to Mater, 26 September 1935, Taylor Papers, NLA MS 1003, Box 20, Item 1686.

89 Doris to Mater, 28 September 1935, Taylor Papers, NLA MS 1003, Box 20, Item 1685.

90 Taylor, *Journeyman Taylor*, p. 258.

91 Taylor to Doris and David Taylor, 19 June 1936, Taylor Papers, NLA MS 1003, Box 20, Item 1717.

92 Taylor, *Journeyman Taylor*, p. 252.

93 Taylor to Doris Taylor, 23 June 1936, Taylor Papers, NLA MS 1003, Box 20, Item 1718.

94 Taylor, 'Fundamental Factors in Canadian Geography', *Canadian Geographical Journal*, vol. 12, March 1936: 161.

95 Quincy Wright to Taylor, 27 September 1938, Taylor Papers, NLA MS 1003, Box 20.

96 Taylor to Evan Taylor, 28 July 1942, Taylor Papers, NLA MS 1003, Box 20.

97 Taylor to Mater, 6 November 1939, Taylor Papers, NLA MS 1003, Box 20.

98 Taylor to Evan Taylor, 11 January 1947, Taylor Papers, NLA MS 1003, Box 21.

99 Taylor, Preface to memoir on Russia, Taylor Papers, NLA MS 1003, Box 10, Item 59, p. 2.

100 Taylor, 'Parallels in Soviet and Canadian Settlement', *International Journal*, vol. 1, no. 2, 1946: 158.

101 Geography's role in modern citizenship cultivation is explored broadly in a special issue of the *Journal of Historical Geography*. See Felix Driver and Avril M.C. Maddrell, 'Geographical Education and Citizenship, Introduction', *Journal of Historical Geography*, vol. 22, no. 4, 1996: 371–372. Although Powell has written extensively about Taylor's contribution to this field in Australia it has not been studied closely in Canada.

102 Taylor to Walter Brown, 16 April 1942, Taylor Papers, NLA MS 1003, Box 20.

103 Taylor, *The Geographical Laboratory, A Practical Handbook for a Three Years' Course in North American Universities*. Toronto: Toronto University Press, 1938.

104 Taylor, 'Geography at the University of Toronto', *Canadian Geographical Journal*, vol. 23, no. 3, 1941: 152–154.

105 Taylor, 'Future Population in Canada: A Study in Technique', *Economic Geography*, vol. 22, no. 1, 1946: 67.

106 Taylor, 'Geography at the University of Toronto', pp. 152–154.

107 Taylor et al., *Canada and Her Neighbours*. Toronto: Ginn and Co., 1947; Taylor et al., *Friends in Faraway Lands*. Toronto: Ginn and Co., 1947.

108 Taylor, 'Possibilities of Settlement in Australia', in Isaiah Bowman (ed.), *Limits of Land Settlement*, New York: Council of Foreign Relations, 1937, p. 225.

109 Taylor, 'Canada and Australia: A Study in Geographic Contrasts', Annual War Memorial Lecture, University Engineering Club, University of Sydney, April 1948.

110 Taylor, *Journeyman Taylor*, p. 345.

Chapter 5 War and Peace

1 Taylor to Mater, 12 August 1939, Taylor Papers, MS 1003, Box 20.

2 Telegram, Taylor to Sir Charles Wright, British Admiralty Research Department, 31 August, 10.40 am, Taylor Papers, NLA MS 1003, Box 20.

3 Taylor to Mrs Tibbets, 3 October 1939, Taylor Papers, NLA MS 1003, Box 20.

4 Norman Bartlett, 'Geopacifics: Considered as High Road to Peace', *Saturday Night*, 18 September 1948, p. 44.

5 Dr Emery Barcs, 'He Whistles—and Talks of Geopacifics', *Daily Telegraph*, 17 April 1948, p. 9.

6 Isaiah Bowman, *The New World: Problems in Political Geography*. New York: World Book Company, 1922, p. 11. Neil Smith devotes several chapters to Bowman's prominent role in the Paris Peace Conference in *American Empire: Roosevelt's Geographer and the Prelude to Globalization*. Berkeley: University of California Press, 2003.

7 For a contemporary of Taylor's on geopolitics, see Robert Strausz-Hupé, *Geopolitics: The Struggle for Space and Power*. London: GP Putnam & Sons, 1942. Recent examinations of the concept include Gearóid Ó Tuathail, *Critical Geopolitics: The Politics of Writing Global Space*. Minneapolis: University of Minnesota Press, 1996, and Jeremy Black, *Maps and Politics*. Chicago: University of Chicago Press, 1997.

8 Translated typescript, Karl Haushofer, review of *Environment and Race*, *Volk und Rasse*, 3 September 1926, Taylor Papers, NLA MS 1003, Box 18, Item 918.

9 Translated typescript, Karl Haushofer, review of *Environment and Race*, *Volk und Rasse*, 3 September 1926, Taylor Papers, NLA MS 1003, Box 18, Item 918.

10 Taylor to Mater, 16 August 1933, Taylor Papers, NLA MS 1003, Box 19, Item 1569.

11 Taylor, 'Atlas of Environment and Race: 110 Sketch Maps and Diagrams for Use with Lectures Broadcast at the University of Chicago', University of Chicago, Department of Geography, 1933, State Library of New South Wales, MLMSS Set 460, Box 1.

12 Taylor to Mater, 16 November 1934, Taylor Papers, NLA MS 1003, Box 20, Item 1629.

13 Von Eickstedt to Taylor, 4 March 1935, Fisher Rare Book Library, University of Toronto, MS 20, Box 24, Folder 'Von Eickstedt'.

14 Earl Count to Taylor, 13 May 1937, Taylor Papers, NLA MS 1003, Box 20, Item 1764.

15 Bose to Mitra, 7 February 1936, Taylor Papers, NLA MS 1003, Box 20, Item 1706.

16 Taylor, 'Aryan, German, Nordic, Jew', *University of Chicago Magazine*, November 1935: 1.

17 Taylor, 'The Geographer's Aid in Nation-planning', *Scottish Geographical Magazine*, vol. 48, no. 1, 1932: 17.

18 'Hybrid Origin of Jews Makes Them Kin to Germans', *Toronto Globe and Mail*, 20 January 1939.

19 Taylor, 'Aryan, German, Nordic, Jew', p. 2.

20 Taylor, *Environment and Race: A Study of the Evolution, Migration, Settlement and Status of the Races of Man.* London: Oxford University Press, 1927, p. 340. Joseph Powell observes this exception in Taylor's thought when he states: 'with the exception of his early views about the American negro he took a strong stand against ignorant racism'. See Powell, 'Thomas Griffith Taylor, 1888–1963', *Geographers: Biobibliographical Studies*, vol. 3, 1979: 141–153, 145.

21 Taylor to Mater and Pal, 16 August 1930, Taylor Papers, NLA MS 1003, Box 19, Item 1283, p. 8.

22 Taylor, *Environment and Race*, p. 341.

23 Taylor, *European Migrations: Past, Present, Future.* Sydney: Robert Dey, 1928, p. 38.

24 Taylor to Mater, 11 May 1941, Taylor Papers, NLA MS 1003, Box 20.

25 Taylor to Bill Taylor, 6 July 1941, Taylor Papers, NLA MS 1003, Box 20.

26 Taylor, *Journeyman Taylor: The Education of a Scientist.* London: Hale, 1958, pp. 229, 274.

27 Taylor to Charles Fawcett, 23 January 1943, Taylor Papers, NLA MS 1003, Box 20.

28 Taylor to Family, 4 July 1943, Taylor Papers, NLA MS 1003, Box 20.

29 Taylor to Dear Sir, 3 July 1943, Fisher Rare Book Library, University of Toronto, MS 20, Box 4(22).

30 Taylor, *Our Evolving Civilization: An Introduction to Geopacifics, Geographical Aspects of the Path towards Peace.* Toronto: University of Toronto Press, 1946, p. 251.

31 Doris Taylor to Mater, 21 April 1940, Taylor Papers, NLA MS 1003, Box 20.

32 Rogers Reid to Taylor, 12 October 1943, Taylor Papers, NLA MS 1003, Box 20; Edmund Day to Taylor, 22 October 1941, Taylor Papers, NLA MS 1003, Box 20.

33 Taylor to President Day, 2 November 1941, Taylor Papers, NLA MS 1003, Box 20.

34 In Anne Michaels's *Fugitive Pieces*, a mutual interest in the concept of geopacifics connects Taylor, the geography professor character in the novel, to the main character, Athos, a Greek geologist, who saves a Jewish orphan from the Nazis and moves to Toronto to work with Taylor.

35 Taylor to Isaiah Bowman, 28 March 1943, Taylor Papers, NLA MS 1003, Box 20.

36 Isaiah Bowman to Taylor, 16 May 1947, Bowman Papers, Johns Hopkins University Library, MS 58.

37 Taylor to Donald Innis, 7 December 1952, Taylor Papers, NLA MS 1003, Box 22.

38 Taylor, Field Notebooks, 1 March 1916, SPRI MS 1553.

39 Arnold J. Toynbee to Taylor, 4 November 1936, Taylor Papers, NLA MS 1003, Box 20, Item 1749.

40 Taylor to Quincy Wright, 15 November 1947, Taylor Papers, NLA MS 1003, Box 16, Item 849.

41 Taylor, 'Geographers and World Peace: A Plea for Geopacifics', Institute of Australian Geographers Presidential Address, 1960, Taylor Papers, NLA MS 1003, Box 17, Item 396, p. 5.

42 Taylor, *Our Evolving Civilzation*, pp. 359–360.

43 For Haushofer's links to Hitler and Nazism, see Holger H. Herwig, 'Geopolitik: Haushofer, Hitler and Lebensraum', *Journal of Strategic Studies*, vol. 22, 1999: 218–241; Henning Heske, 'Karl Haushofer: His Role in German Geopolitics and Nazi Politics', *Political Geography Quarterly*, vol. 6, no. 2, 1987: 135–144.

44 Taylor, 'Canada's Role in Geopolitics, A Study in Situation and Status', in *Canadian Institute of International Affairs*. Toronto: Ryerson Press, 1942, p. 1.

45 Taylor, 'Geographers and World Peace', Taylor Papers, NLA MS 1003, Box 17, Item 396, p. 5.

46 Taylor, *Our Evolving Civilization*, p. 270.

47 Taylor to Mawson, 12 January 1944, Taylor Papers, NLA MS 1003, Box 12, Folder 6, Item 196.

48 Taylor, 'Geography and Nation Planning', transcript of address, 17 November 1943, Taylor Papers, NLA MS 1003, Box 20.

49 Taylor to Bert Priestley, 24 April 1944, Taylor Papers, NLA MS 1003, Box 21.

50 Taylor to Mawson, 12 January 1944, Taylor Papers, NLA MS 1003, Box 12, Item 196.

51 Joseph S. Roucek, review of *Our Evolving Civilization*, *Social Science*, October 1947: 315, Taylor Papers, NLA MS 1003, Box 39, in the back cover of Taylor, *Our Evolving Civilization*.

52 Taylor, 'Geo-Pacifics (Geography and World Peace), A Plea for Cultural Geography at the Universities in Addition to Mathematics, Physical and Economic Geography', typescript of radio address, April 1948, Taylor Papers, NLA MS 1003, Box 16, Item 855, p. 2.

53 Taylor, *Our Evolving Civilization*, p. 320.

54 Taylor, *Our Evolving Civilization*, p. 325.

55 Taylor, *Our Evolving Civilization*, p. 321.

56 Taylor, 'Geographers and World Peace', Taylor Papers, NLA MS 1003, Box 17, Item 396, pp. 6–7; Taylor, *Our Evolving Civilization*, pp. 359–360.

57 Albert Einstein to Taylor, 6 August 1947, Taylor Papers, NLA MS 1003, Box 16, Item 851.

58 Einstein to Taylor, quoted in Taylor, 'Geographers and World Peace', Taylor Papers, NLA MS 1003, Box 17, Item 396, p. 15.

59 Hubert Wilkins (1888–1958) was a South Australian who led a high profile international life as a newspaper reporter, photographer and explorer. He was knighted after he made the first trans-Arctic crossing by plane. He subsequently received funds from William Randolf Hearst to conduct reconnaissance flights over Antarctica. See Simon Nash, *The Last Explorer: Hubert Wilkins Australia's Unknown Hero*. Sydney: Hodder, 2005.

60 Interest in transpolar routes grew in the context of World War II. See William Carlson, *Lifelines through the Arctic*. New York: Duell, Sloan and Pearce, 1962. On geography's role in military strategy in this period, see Trevor Barnes and M. Farish, 'Between Regions: Science, Militarism, and American Geography from World War to Cold War', *Annals of the Association of American Geographers*, vol. 96, 2006: 807–826. On the impact of polar flight on the reimagination of the earth, see Dennis Cosgrove, *Apollo's Eye: A Cartographic Genealogy of the Earth in the Western Imagination*. Baltimore: Johns Hopkins University Press, 2001.

61 'Professor of the Ologies', *People Magazine*, 17 December 1952, p. 24.

62 Taylor to Evan Taylor, 15 November 1954, Taylor Papers, NLA MS 1003, Box 22.

63 Taylor, 'Australian Antarctica', *Proceedings of the Royal Australian Historical Society*, vol. 41, no. 4, 1955: 158.

64 Taylor to Frank Debenham, 15 August 1959, Taylor Papers, NLA MS 1003, Box 23.

65 Silas Wright to Taylor, 3 November 1962, Taylor Papers, NLA MS 1003, Box 15, Item 427.

66 Taylor to Hughes, 27 September 1958, Taylor Papers, NLA MS 1003, Box 23.

67 Taylor to George Simpson, (n.d.) March 1959, Taylor Papers, NLA MS 1003, Box 23.

68 Taylor to Charles Laseron, 29 May 1959, Taylor Papers, NLA MS 1003, Box 23.

69 Taylor to Marie Sanderson, 7 January 1960, Taylor Papers, NLA MS 1003, Box 23.

70 Taylor, 'Geographers and World Peace', p. 20, Taylor Papers, NLA MS 1003, Box 17, Item 396.

71 'Australia and the Future of Antarctica', *The Sydney Morning Herald*, 29 January 1960, Taylor Papers, NLA MS 1003, Box 23.

72 For an overview of Antarctic science and politics, see Gordon Elliot Fogg, *A History of Antarctic Science*. Cambridge: Cambridge University Press, 1992. On the endurance of national interests in spite of the International Geophysical Year and scientific cooperation, see Klaus Dodds, 'The Great Game in Antarctica: Britain and the 1959 Antarctic Treaty', *Contemporary British History*, vol. 21, no. 2, 2007; Peter Beck, *The International Politics of Antarctica*. London: Palgrave Macmillan, 1986. On Australia's national assertions and rivalries during Taylor's lifetime, see Christy Collis, 'Mawson and Mirnyy Stations: The Spatiality of the Australian Antarctic Territory, 1954–61', *Australian Geographer*, vol. 38, no. 2, 2007: 215–231. On the governance of Antarctica in the wake of the 1959 Treaty, see Arnfinn Jørgensen-Dahl and Willy Østreng (eds), *The Antarctic Treaty System in World Politics*. New York: St Martin's Press, 1991.

73 Arthur Wilcock to Taylor, 19 June 1956, Taylor Papers, NLA MS 1003, Box 22.

74 Taylor, *Douglas Mawson*, Melbourne: Oxford University Press, 1962.

75 Frank Debenham to Taylor, 4 December 1960, Taylor Papers, NLA MS 1003, Box 23, Item 708.

76 Interview with Professor Griffith Taylor, ABC Radio, Sydney, broadcast 16 June 1961.

77 Evan Taylor to Taylor, 8 September 1959, Taylor Papers, NLA MS 1003, Box 23.

78 Taylor to Phillip Law, 8 August 1959, Taylor Papers, NLA MS 1003, Box 23.

79 O.H.K. Spate, 'Journeyman Taylor: Some Aspects of His Work', *Australian Geographer*, vol. 12, no. 2, 1972: 117.

80 Quoted in Ladis Kristof, 'The Origin and Evolution of Geopolitics', *Journal of Conflict Resolution*, vol. 4, 1960.

81 Taylor to Gilbert Butland, 5 February 1963, Taylor Papers, NLA MS 1003, Box 24, Item 274.

Chapter 6 Founding Father

1 Taylor to Stephen Visher, 27 August 1961, Taylor Papers, NLA MS 1003, Box 24.

2 The field of science and technology studies has converged with biographical studies recently, leading to rich studies of the interconnectedness of scientists' private lives, institutional settings, intellectual networks and the cultural, economic and geographical contexts of knowledge production and dissemination. Among the best are Trevor Barnes, 'Lives Lived and Lives Told: Biographies of Geography's Quantitative Revolution', *Environment and Planning D*, vol. 19, no. 4, 2001: 409–429; Mary Terrell, 'Biography as Cultural History of Science', *Isis*, vol. 97, no. 2, 2006: 306–313; Theodore M. Porter, 'Is the Life of the Scientist a Scientific Unit?', *Isis*, vol. 97, no. 2, 2006: 314–321.

3 Dr Emery Barcs, 'He Whistles—and Talks of Geopacifics', *Daily Telegraph*, 17 April 1948, p. 9.

4 Dorothy Taylor to Taylor, 24 March 1930, Taylor Papers, NLA MS 1003, Box 19, Item 1338.

5 Dorothy Taylor to Taylor, 6 May 1930, Taylor Papers, NLA MS 1003, Box 19, Item 1339.

6 Taylor, Field Notebooks, 8 April 1923, SPRI MS 1553.

7 Taylor, *Journeyman Taylor: The Education of a Scientist*. London: Hale, 1958, p. 188.

8 Dorothy Rhodes Taylor, 'Biography of James Taylor', unpublished manuscript, p. 41.

9 Taylor to Doris Priestley, 26 February 1914, Taylor Papers, NLA MS 1003, Box 19, Item 1054, p. 6.

10 Taylor to Mater, 25 October 1917, State Library of New South Wales, MLMSS Set 460, Box 2.

11 Taylor, Field Notebooks, SPRI MS 1553, entries September to October 1923. 'Natalie' poem inserted on 25 September 1923.

12 Pattie Taylor, personal communication, 22 April 2006.

13 Taylor, Field Notebooks, 9 July 1928, SPRI MS 1553.

14 Newspaper coverage quoted verbatim in *The Union Recorder*. Sydney: University of Sydney, 1 November 1928, pp. 273–275.

15 One of Taylor's students, Ruth Godden, drew the images. Taylor Papers, NLA MS 1003, Box 8, Item 490.

16 Doris to Mater, (n.d.) 1933, Taylor Papers, NLA MS 1003, Box 19, Item 1566.

17 Taylor to Vilhjalmur Stefansson, 22 January 1931, Stefansson Papers, Dartmouth College Library, Folder 29: 1931.

18 Taylor to Mater, 22 October 1930, Taylor Papers, NLA MS 1003, Box 19, Item 1286.

19 Taylor, *Journeyman Taylor*, p. 225.

20 Doris Taylor to Dorothy Taylor and Mater, 23 November 1930, Taylor Papers, NLA MS 1003, Box 10, Item 175. The biologists were Chicago Professor Childs and Japanese visitor, Professor Watanabe.

21 Taylor to Doris Priestley, 18 and 22 February 1914, Taylor Papers, NLA MS 1003, Box 19, Items 1049, 1052.

22 Doris Taylor to Mater, 10 February 1930, Taylor Papers, NLA MS 1003, Box 19, Item 1247.

23 Dorothy Rhodes Taylor, 'Biography of James Taylor', p. 14.

24 Taylor to Evan Taylor, 12 February 1936, Taylor Papers, NLA MS 1003, Box 20, Item 1702.

25 Doris Taylor to Mater, (n.d.) 1933, Taylor Papers, NLA MS 1003, Box 20, Item 1566.

26 Taylor to Mater, 6 February 1934, Taylor Papers, NLA MS 1003, Box 20, Item 1591.

27 Taylor to Horatio Carslaw, 18 March 1934, Taylor Papers, NLA MS 1003, Box 20, Item 1592.

28 Taylor to Robertson, 4 February 1933, Taylor Papers, NLA MS 1003, Box 19, Item 1535.

29 Taylor to Theo Ruthven-Smith, 28 December 1921, Taylor Papers, NLA MS 1003, Box 8, Item 488.

30 Bill Taylor to Taylor, 22 August 1931, Taylor Papers, NLA MS 1003, Box 19, Item 1509.

31 Taylor to Mater and Dorothy Taylor, 1 June 1930, Taylor Papers, NLA MS 1003, Box 19, Item 1281; Taylor to Evan Taylor, 18 July 1933, Taylor Papers, NLA MS 1003, Box 19, Item 1568.

32 Taylor, Field Notebooks, 9 January 1935, SPRI MS 1553.

33 Taylor to Mater, 19 July 1935, Taylor Papers, NLA MS 1003, Box 20, Item 1667.

34 Doris Taylor to Dorothy Taylor, 18 March 1934, Taylor Papers, NLA MS 1003, Box 20, Item 1593.

35 Taylor to Mater, 6 February 1934, Taylor Papers, NLA MS 1003, Box 20, Item 1591.

36 Doris Taylor to Dorothy Taylor, (n.d.) (c. November 1936), Taylor Papers, NLA MS 1003, Box 20, Item 1754.

37 Taylor to Mater and Pal, 31 January 1937, Taylor Papers, NLA MS 1003, Box 20, Item 1755.

38 Taylor to Dorothy Taylor, 31 March 1940, Taylor Papers, NLA MS 1003, Box 20.

39 Taylor to Evan Taylor, 28 July 1942, Taylor Papers, NLA MS 1003, Box 20.

40 Taylor to Dorothy Taylor, 31 December 1941, Taylor Papers, NLA MS 1003, Box 20.

41 Doris Taylor to Mater and Dorothy Taylor, 10 January 1940, Taylor Papers, NLA MS 1003, Box 20.

42 Andrew Clark, 'Contributions to Geographical Knowledge of Canada since 1945', *The Geographical Review*, vol. 40, no. 2, 1950: 286.

43 Taylor to *Journal* editor, 5 November 1941, Taylor Papers, NLA MS 1003, Box 20.

44 Taylor to Andrew Clark, 5 March 1951, Taylor Papers, NLA MS 1003, Box 21.

45 Andrew Clark to Taylor, 8 March 1951, Taylor Papers, NLA MS 1003, Box 21.

46 Taylor, *Journeyman Taylor*, p. 260.

47 Interview with Donald Kerr, Toronto, 22 June 2006; interviewed by Carolyn Strange.

48 James Davy to Taylor, 2 September 1952, Taylor Papers, NLA MS 1003, Box 22.

49 Isaiah Bowman to Harold Adams Innis, quoted in G.S. Dunbar, 'Harold Innis and Canadian Geography', *Canadian Geographer*, vol. 29, 1985: 161.

50 W.E.G., review of *Geography in the Twentieth Century*, edited by Griffith Taylor. London: Methuen, 1950, *The Geographical Journal*, vol. 117, no. 3, 1951: 359.

51 Taylor to Bill Taylor, 14 May 1951, Taylor Papers, NLA MS 1003, Box 21.

52 Taylor to Raymond Priestley, 28 April 1951, Taylor Papers, NLA MS 1003, Box 21.

53 Taylor to Bill Taylor, 28 April 1951, Taylor Papers, NLA MS 1003, Box 21.

54 Taylor to Bill Taylor, 31 May 1941, Taylor Papers, NLA MS 1003, Box 20.

55 Taylor to Bill Taylor, 15 February 1947, Taylor Papers, NLA MS 1003, Box 21.

56 Taylor to Bill Taylor, 7 May and 25 June 1958, Taylor Papers, NLA MS 1003, Box 23.

57 Taylor to Jack Wright, (n.d.) April 1961, Taylor Papers, NLA MS 1003, Box 24.

58 Taylor, Field Notebooks, 12 August 1929, SPRI, MS 1553.

59 Taylor to Frank Debenham, 7 December 1951, Taylor Papers, NLA MS 1003, Box 21.

60 Taylor to Harold Innis, 6 May 1952, Taylor Papers, NLA MS 1003, Box 21.

61 Taylor, *Sydneyside Scenery and How It Came About*. Sydney: Angus & Robertson, 1958, pp. 38–39.

62 Dorothy Taylor to Taylor, 19 March 1963, Taylor Papers, NLA MS 1003, Box 24, Item 307.

63 Taylor to Bill Taylor, 3 June 1962, Taylor Papers, NLA MS 1003, Box 24, Item 78.

64 Taylor to Donald Putnam, 28 October 1954, Taylor Papers, NLA MS 1003, Box 22.

65 Taylor to Trevor Lloyd, 4 March 1954, Taylor Papers, NLA MS 1003, Box 22.

66 C. Barnard to Taylor, 1 December 1952, Taylor Papers, NLA MS 1003, Box 22.

67 Taylor to Ethel Priestley, 5 January 1953, Taylor Papers, NLA MS 1003, Box 22.

68 The NSW University of Technology, School of Humanities and Social Sciences: 'The Economic Geography of Australia', lecture notes 'Minor Elective—1955', Taylor Papers, NLA MS 1003, Box 45.

69 Taylor to Robert Hale, 14 May 1954, Taylor Papers, NLA MS 1003, Box 14, Item 31.

70 Oxford commissioned Taylor to write a biography of Mawson for its 'Great Australians' series. Taylor, *Douglas Mawson*. Melbourne: Oxford University Press, 1961.

71 Taylor to Stephen Visher, 30 April 1959, Taylor Papers, NLA MS 1003, Box 23.

72 Taylor to Marie Sanderson, 7 May 1951, Taylor Papers, NLA MS 1003, Box 21.

73 Marie Sanderson to Taylor, 3 May 1961, Taylor Papers, NLA MS 1003, Box 24.

74 Neil Smith, review of *Griffith Taylor: Antarctic Scientist and Pioneer Geographer* by Marie Sanderson. Ottawa: Carleton University Press, 1988, *The Geographical Review*, vol. 79, no. 3, 1989: 358.

75 Marie Sanderson to Taylor, 8 June 1957, Taylor Papers, NLA MS 1003, Box 23.

76 Taylor to Jack Thomson, 30 August 1952, Taylor Papers, NLA MS 1003, Box 21.

77 Taylor to 'Members of the Staff', 18 December 1952, Taylor Papers, NLA MS 1003, Box 22.

78 Taylor to Evan Taylor, 8 May 1953, Taylor Papers, NLA MS 1003, Box 22.

79 Alasdair Alpin MacGregor, reader's report, to Taylor, (n.d.) (c.2 November 1954), Taylor Papers, NLA MS 1003, Box 14, Item 62.

80 Harold White to Taylor, 4 February 1954, NLA Central Registry File, Manuscripts Section, Acquisitions (Prof.) Thomas Griffith Taylor.

81 Taylor to Gilbert Butland, 5 May 1960, Taylor Papers, NLA MS 1003, Box 23; Taylor to Butland, 22 March 1961, Taylor Papers, NLA MS 1003, Box 24.

82 Taylor to Marion Pratt, 18 December 1952, Taylor Papers, NLA MS 1003, Box 22.

83 Taylor, Field Notebooks, SPRI MS 1553, 5 July 1959, 10 July 1959.

84 Quoted in Taylor to Evan Taylor, 14 September 1959, Taylor Papers, NLA MS 1003, Box 23.

85 Taylor to Bill Taylor, 15 January 1960, Taylor Papers, NLA MS 1003, Box 23.

86 Taylor to Bill and Dorothy Taylor, 9 February 1960, Taylor Papers, NLA MS 1003, Box 23.

87 Taylor to Donald Putnam, 8 February 1960, Taylor Papers, NLA MS 1003, Box 23.

88 Taylor to Bill Taylor, 3 June 1962, Taylor Papers, NLA MS 1003, Box 24, Item 78.

89 Telegram, Oscar Spate to Department of Geography, 21 October 1962, Taylor Papers, NLA MS 1003, Box 24, Item 198.

90 George Dury to Taylor, 3 January 1963, Taylor Papers, NLA MS 1003, Box 24, Item 247.

91 Doris Taylor to Marie Sanderson, 10 March 1964, Fisher Rare Book Library, University of Toronto, MS 20, Box 18.

92 Doris Taylor to Marie Sanderson, 5 March 1964, Fisher Rare Book Library, University of Toronto, MS 20, Box 29.

Epilogue

1 Taylor to Bill Taylor, 20 November 1960, Taylor Papers, NLA MS 1003, Box 23.

2 Taylor to Bill Taylor, 20 November 1960, Taylor Papers, NLA MS 1003, Box 23.

3 Taylor to Charles Wright, 20 February 1961, Taylor Papers, NLA MS 1003, Box 24.

4 Taylor to Howard Richards, (n.d.) 1963, Taylor Papers, NLA MS 1003, Box 24, Item 379.

5 Henry Syndor Harrison, *Queed*. Boston, New York: Houghton Mifflin Company, 1911, p. 65.

6 Taylor to Frank Debenham, 22 October 1963, Taylor Papers, NLA MS 1003, Box 24, Item 394.

7 Taylor to Mr. Paynter, 31 July 1958, Taylor Papers, NLA MS 1003, Box 23.

8 Carolyn Strange, personal conversation with Norman Taylor, 22 April 2006.

List of Illustrations

Abbreviations

NLA = National Library of Australia

SPRI = Scott Polar Research Institute, University of Cambridge, England

UNERA = University of New England and Regional Archives, Armidale, Australia

Note: Taylor donated the vast majority of his papers to the National Library of Australia (NLA MS 1003). Many individual items in this collection are unnumbered.

Introduction

Page 2

Erwin Raisz

'Lampoon by Famous Cartographer', 1938

Manuscripts Collection

NLA MS 1003, Box 20

Courtesy Raisz Landform Maps, Brookline, MA, USA

Page 3

'Two Sketches Cut Out of My First Diary. Left. Stromboli; 9th Jan. 1893. Right. Table Top, Toowoomba; 6th July 1894'

sketches from Taylor's diary

Manuscripts Collection

NLA MS 1003, Box 42, Item 414

Page 4

E.P. from a sketch by Griffith Taylor

Ex Libris Griffith Taylor 1913

bookplate in *With Scott: The Silver Lining* by Taylor

(London: Smith Elder, 1916)

Manuscripts Collection

NLA MS 1003, Box 3, Item 108

Page 6

Leonard Frank Reynolds (1897–1939)

Portrait of Taylor, 1919

pen and ink; 26.0 x 11.9 cm

Pictures Collection

nla.pic-an6077305

Page 7

'Figure 1: Geography Correlates the Specified Branches of the Four "Environmental" Sciences with the Four "Human" Sciences

reproduced from *Geography in the Twentieth Century*, edited by Taylor

(London: Methuen, 1951)

Page 8

Unknown photographer

Portrait of Doris Taylor, 1914

Courtesy SPRI

Image P99/65/2

Chapter 1 Favoured Son

Page 12

Unknown photographer

Portrait of Elizabeth Griffiths, c.1860

Taylor family album

Courtesy Pattie Taylor

Page 13

Kingston Studios, Melbourne

Portrait of James Taylor (undated)

Courtesy SPRI

Image P99/65/12

Page 15

Unknown photographer

The Taylor family and Lily's sister, Harriot, at Adderton, Sydney, c.1897

Taylor family album

Courtesy Pattie Taylor

Chapter 2 The Furthest Frontier

Page 51

Unknown photographer

'A Very "Ordinary Seaman"'

reproduced from *With Scott: The Silver Lining* by Taylor

(London: Smith Elder, 1916)

Page 53

The *Terra Nova* epaulet,1910

Manuscripts Collection

NLA MS 1003, Box 53

Page 54

'MacMurdo Sound', 1911

sketch map from Taylor's 'Sledge-Journal of First Western Geological Expedition'

Manuscripts Collection

NLA MS 1003, Box 3, Item 60

'The Volcano of Erebus, 10 000' Showing the Three Camps 1902–1907–1910 (from 20 Miles West)', 1913

sketch from Taylor's diary

Manuscripts Collection

NLA MS 1003, Box 2B, Item 56

Unknown photographer

Group portrait of the British Antarctic Expedition, 1911

Courtesy UNERA: Griffith Taylor Collection

A714

Page 58

Herbert Ponting

Grotto in an iceberg, *Terra Nova* in the distance, 1911 British Antarctic Expedition

Courtesy SPRI

Image Pont 88

Page 60

Taylor's meteorology log book for the British Antarctic Expedition, 1911

Manuscripts Collection

NLA MS 1003, Box 3, Item 57

Page 61

'Our Beauteous Curtains Secluding the Experts Den'

sketch of Discovery Hut from Taylor's diary, 6 May 1911

Manuscripts Collection

NLA MS 1003, Box 3, Item 79

Page 62

Herbert Ponting

Frank Debenham, Raymond Priestley and Taylor in Discovery Hut, c.1911

Courtesy SPRI

Image P79/27/270

'Plan of the Rejuvenated "Discovery" Hut, March 1911'

Taylor's sketch of floor plan of Discovery Hut

Manuscripts Collection

NLA MS 1003, Box 3, Item 83

Page 63

'The Biological Cycle in the Antarctic'

poem by Taylor, artwork by John Murray

Manuscripts Collection

NLA MS 1003, Box 3, Item 132

Page 64

Clive Jeffery

Taylor's ice axe, British Antarctic Expedition, 1910–1912

Courtesy University of Sydney, Australia: Macleay Collection

Chapter 3 From Rocks to Race

Unknown photographer

Portrait of Lily Taylor, c.1916

Taylor family album

Courtesy Patti Taylor

Page 92

'Migration-Zone Classification of the Races of Man'

reproduced from *Environment and Race* by Taylor

(London: Humphrey Milford/Oxford University Press, 1927)

Page 94

'Fig. 3. Five Stages in Racial Migrations in the Old World, Each Representing a Separate Major Race'

reproduced from 'Geography 1932–1936' by Taylor, *Human Biology*, vol. 8, 1936

'The Lava-Flow Analogy'

reproduced from 'The Evolution and Distribution of Race, Culture and Language' by Taylor, *Geographical Review*, vol. 11, no. 1, 1919

Page 97

'Fig. 9. Block Diagram (Scotland to Turkestan) Illustrating an Analogy of Geological Structure Applied to the Migration of Language'

reproduced from *Environment and Race* by Taylor

(London: Humphrey Milford/Oxford University Press, 1927)

'Figure 2 The Ramifications of Modern Geography'

reproduced from *Geography in the Twentieth Century*, edited by Taylor

(New York: Philosophical Library, 1951)

Page 100

Taylor's letter to Mater, April 1887

Manuscripts Collection

NLA MS 1003, Box 17, Item 497

Page 101

Unknown photographer

'½ Caste Driver & GT, Ooldea', c.1919

Manuscripts Collection

NLA MS 1003, Box 52, Folder 5

Page 102

Theo Ruthven-Smith

'Fig. 25. Child-Study in the Buitenzorg Gardens!', 1920

Manuscripts Collection

NLA MS 1003, Box 7, Item 255

Page 103

'Wanderings in the East Indies', 1920

Taylor's diaries, sketches and articles, bound together

Manuscripts Collection

NLA MS 1003, Box 7, Item 242

Pages 104–105

Taylor's cephalic callipers, 1921–1928

Courtesy UNERA: Griffith Taylor Collection

A714

Page 106

'Fig. 12. Scheme Illustrating Variation in Ethnological Criteria'

reproduced from *Environment and Race* by Taylor

(London: Humphrey Milford/Oxford University Press, 1927)

Page 108

Taylor's notebook on the Kamilaroi, c.1924

Manuscripts Collection

NLA MS 1003, Box 7, Item 230

Chapter 4 Prophet and Pariah

Taylor's passport photo for Chicago, 1928

Manuscripts Collection

NLA MS 1003, Box 8, Item 330

Page 142

'A Time–space Chart Showing Historical Strata for the Chief European Nations'

reproduced from *Environment and Nation: Geographical Factors in the Cultural and Political History of Europe* by Taylor (Toronto: University of Toronto Press, 1936)

Page 145

'Our Toronto Home'

sketch of house in Forest Hill, Toronto, in Taylor's letter to family, 28 September 1935

Manuscripts Collection

NLA MS 1003, Box 20, Item 1686

Page 146

Invitation to Taylor's inaugural lecture on 'Illustrations of the New Geography', University of Toronto, 7 November 1935

Manuscripts Collection

NLA MS 1003, Box 20, Item 1641

Page 147

'View of White River from East'

sketch in Taylor's letter to family, 19 June 1936

Manuscripts Collection

NLA MS 1003, Box 20

Page 148

'Canadian Economy Viewed from Geological Structure'

cutting of article by Main Johnson from *Toronto Star*, 23 October 1940

Manuscripts Collection

NLA MS 1003, Box 46

Page 149

'Future Settlement of Canada as Determined by the Environment'

reproduced from *Canada: A Study of Cool Continental Environments and Their Effect on British and French Settlement* by Taylor

(London: Methuen, 1947)

Page 150

'University of Toronto, Geography Department, U.S.S.R.—Land and Culture', 1946

flyer for lecture series

Manuscripts Collection

NLA MS 1003, Box 16, Item 575

Page 155

Taylor's students, Toronto

'The Geographers' Lament', 1948

sheet music

Manuscripts Collection

NLA MS 1003, Box 12, Item 350

Chapter 5 War and Peace

Page 158

Taylor's telegram to Charles Wright, Research Department, Admiralty, London, 31 August 1939

Manuscripts Collection

NLA MS 1003, Box 20

Page 160

'Fig.1—The Build of the World ...'

reproduced from 'Structural Basis of Canadian Geography' by Taylor, *Canadian Geographical Journal*, 14 May 1937

Page 170

Drucker-Hilbert

'The Twelfth Forum on Current Problems'

cutting from *New York Herald Tribune*, 17 November 1943

Manuscripts Collection

NLA MS 1003, Box 20

Page 175

Taylor's sketch map of the Antarctic, c.1956

Manuscripts Collection

NLA MS 1003, Box 23

Page 176

'Fig. 2. Air-route Chart Showing True Directions ... from Ottawa'

reproduced from *Canada: A Study of Cool Continental Environments and Their Effect on British and French Settlement* by Taylor

(London: Methuen, 1947)

Page 177

'Professor of the Ologics'

cutting of article by unidentified author from *People Magazine*, 17 December 1952

Manuscripts Collection

NLA MS 1003, Box 14, Item 364

Page 178

'The Antarctic Today'

cutting of article by Taylor from *The Etruscan*, vol. 6, no. 2, 1956

Manuscripts Collection

NLA MS 1003, Box 45

Chapter 6 Founding Father

Page 188

'Fig.3. Block-drafter, Designed by Griffith Taylor 1928'

Manuscripts Collection

NLA MS 1003, Box 20, Item 1733

Page 189

Unknown photographer

'Geography Department Students Sydney', 1922

Manuscripts Collection

NLA MS 1003, Box 18, Item 708

Unknown photographer

Dorothy Taylor, c.1927

Taylor family album

Courtesy Pattie Taylor

Page 190

Unknown photographer

Portrait of Bill and Doris Taylor, c.1920

Manuscripts Collection

NLA MS 1003 Box 19, Item 1349

Unknown photographer

Portrait of Doris and Griffith Taylor, c.1927

Courtesy SPRI

Image P99/65/8

Page 192

M. Masaxi, Kunamoto

'5th Crater, Nakadake ASO', 18 November 1926

Manuscripts Collection

NLA MS 1003, Box 53

Page 194

Unknown photographer

James, Bill and Doris Taylor, c.1917

Courtesy SPRI

Image P99/65/11

Page 196

Unknown photographer

Portrait of Natalie Taylor, 1923

Courtesy SPRI

Image P99/65/6

Page 198

Ruth Godden

'Block Diagram of Griffith Taylor', 1928

sketch in student tribute book

Manuscripts Collection

NLA MS 1003, Box 8, Item 490

Page 199

Ruth Godden

'The End', 1928

sketch in student tribute book

Manuscripts Collection

NLA MS1003, Box 8, Item 490

Page 202

Bill Taylor

'Memory Sketch of the Great Mechanical Grab in Jackson Park'

drawing in letter to Griffith Taylor, 22 August 1931

Manuscripts Collection

NLA MS1003, Box 19, Item 1509

Page 204

Doris Taylor

Bill, Taylor and David, March 1935

Manuscripts Collection

NLA MS1003, Box 20, Item 1681

Page 209

'McMaster University, Toronto, Canada'

coloured postcard (undated)

Manuscripts Collection

NLA MS1003, Box 15, Item 487

Page 212

'Presented to Griffith Taylor …', 1951

album from students to Taylor

Manuscripts Collection

NLA MS1003, Box 53

Page 213

William Wonders

'Nanook '52', 1952

sketch for Griffith Taylor

Manuscripts Collection

NLA MS1003, Box 22

Courtesy Professor William Wonders

Page 214

Associated Newspapers, Ltd.

'"Griff" and Doris at Home at Seaforth, New South Wales', 1952

reproduced from *Journeyman Taylor* by Taylor

(London: Hale, 1958)

Page 218

Unknown photographer

'The Author in His Study at Seaforth, New South Wales', c.1958

reproduced from *Journeyman Taylor* by Taylor

(London: Hale, 1958)

Page 225

David Taylor

Dorothy, Bill and Doris Taylor, in front of the Griffith Taylor Building, University of Sydney, 1963

Courtesy Fisher Rare Book Library, University of Toronto

MS 20, Box 18

Epilogue

Page 228

Taylor's last letter, to Frank Debenham, 22 October 1963

Manuscripts Collection

NLA MS1003, Box 24, Item 394

Page 229

Taylor's sketch map of Mt Kosciuszko, 1958

Manuscripts Collection

NLA MS 1003, Box 23

Index

GT is the abbreviation used for Griffith Taylor. DT is the abbreviation used for Doris Taylor.
Page numbers in italics refer to illustrations.

C

U

V

W

Y

Z